THE
PERSONAL SESSIONS
Book 5 of
The Deleted Seth Material
Sessions
8/30/78–12/10/80

THE EARLY SESSIONS

The Early Sessions consist of the first 510 sessions dictated by Seth through Jane Roberts. There are 9 books in *The Early Sessions* series.

THE PERSONAL SESSIONS

The Personal Sessions, often referred to as "the deleted sessions," are Seth sessions that Jane Roberts and Rob Butts considered to be of a highly personal nature and were therefore kept in separate notebooks from the main body of the Seth material. *The Personal Sessions* are expected to be published in 7 volumes.

"The great value I see now in the many deleted or private sessions is that they have the potential to help others, just as they helped Jane and me over the years. I feel that it's very important to have these sessions added to Jane's fine creative body of work for all to see." –Rob Butts

THE SETH AUDIO COLLECTION

Rare recordings of Seth speaking through Jane Roberts are available on audiocassette and CD. For a complete description of The Seth Audio Collection, request our free catalogue.. (Further information is supplied at the back of this book.)

For information on expected publication dates and how to order, write to New Awareness Network at the following address and request the latest catalogue. Also, please visit us on the internet at www.sethcenter.com

New Awareness Network Inc.
P.O. BOX 192
Manhasset, N.Y. 11030

www.sethcenter.com

THE
PERSONAL SESSIONS
Book 5 of
The Deleted Seth Material

Sessions
8/30/78–12/10/80

Published by New Awareness Network Inc.

New Awareness Network Inc.
P.O. Box 192
Manhasset, New York 11030

Opinions and statements on health and medical matters expressed in this book are those of the author and are not necessarily those of or endorsed by the publisher. Those opinions and statements should not be taken as a substitute for consultation with a duly licensed physician.

Cover Design: Michael Goode
Photography: Cover photos by Rich Conz and Robert F. Butts, Sr.
Editorial: Rick Stack
Typography: Raymond Todd, Michael Goode

ISBN 0-9711198-9-9
Printed in U.S.A.

I dedicate The Personal Sessions
to my wife, Jane Roberts,
who lived her 55 years
with the greatest creativity
and the most valiant courage.
-Rob

A NOTE ON THE COVER DESIGN PHOTOGRAPHS

June 2003. A note about the photographs Michael Goode used in his strik-ing cover design for The Personal Sessions *series.*

The central colored photograph of Jane and the lower right-and-left-hand shots of her and myself were taken by my father, Robert F. Butts, Sr., in Sayre, PA a year or so after our marriage in December 1954. The upper right one of Jane in trance for Seth was taken (among many others) by Rich Conz, a photographer for the Elmira, NY Star-Gazette, while he witnessed Session 508 on November 20, 1969. (See Volume 9 of The Early Sessions.*)*

I don't know who photographed the young Jane shown on the upper left, but she saved that picture all of those years for me to inherit upon her death in September 1984, when she was 55.

My inventive and versatile father had always taken photographs, and in his later years turned professional, photographing many weddings and other events in the Sayre area (and also Jane's and my wedding at the home of my younger brother Loren and his wife Betts in Tunkhannock, PA). To help my father, my mother Estelle trained herself to hand-color his black-and-white photographs, for color film was not available then—and so she colored Jane's portrait. Now I won-der: do my long-deceased parents, and Rich and the unknown photographer of the young Jane, all know that their creativity will grace the covers of a series of books that I so lovingly dedicate to them, as well as to Jane and each reader? I believe that they do, each in his or her own way.

—Rob

DELETED SESSION
AUGUST 30, 1978 9:27 PM WEDNESDAY

(Today I looked over a Time-Life *book on the ancient civilizations of the Americas—the Aztecs, Incas, Mixtecs, etc, and once more was impressed by their amazing abilities as far as architecture, carving, weaving, astronomy, etc., went. I described what I'd read to Jane, and later she looked at some of the material. We discussed the amazing facts that the American civilizations had existed for centuries concurrently with the European and Far Eastern ones, but with each totally isolated from the other. They might as well have existed on different planets.*

(This idea reminded me of one I've mentioned rather often to Jane lately about watching the news on TV—a recent habit that it seems we'll soon dispense with. But I found it at least roughly reminiscent of Seth's idea of simultaneous time to watch the color broadcasts from different areas of the world each day, and then to mentally hold all of those actions, especially the backgrounds, in mind at once, visualizing them as simultaneous happenings at different places on the planet.

(Then when we watched the news while eating supper at the coffee table, we soon found the mayhem and related misdeeds recited by the newscasters so depressing that we switched channels to an innocuous Mod Squad show several years old—even though those color backgrounds—Nicaragua, Israel, Russia, etc., were still so fascinating. But I saw similarities of course between those various news events happening in far portions of the earth today, and the thought that the American and European civilizations had existed for so long on the same planet, yet completely unknown one to the other.

(I think that at first Jane decided not to have a session tonight, since she asked me if I'd "rather work for an hour." But she changed her mind, obviously; then at 9:25 she told me she knew what Seth was going to talk about: "The horizontal consciousness.")

Now: Good evening—

("Good evening, Seth.")

—you have been reading about ancient American civilizations. They were highly sophisticated, well-organized, complete unto themselves. Some were quite extensive in terms of land, and yet each was largely isolated from the other. The same kind of situation occurred upon all of the other continents during various historical periods.

For unnumbered centuries, you had largely self-contained, unique "sophisticated" civilizations, intensified centers, situated in prime natural territories, but completely unknown one to the other, with thousands of miles of wild earth between, that was explored only by the most daring. There are many such remains still buried, and as earth changes occurred, many were hidden completely—and yet may "turn up" once more in the great future, as still other earth transformations happen.

Such people were using their consciousness in a certain fashion. Because of their isolation, they were often quite specialistic. Racial traits and characteristics were exaggerated by your standards because of the necessary inbreeding. These groups originated back in their own nearly forgotten past as wandering tribes came together, and joined for their own support and protection.

The creation of your particular variety of cultural reality is quite complex and its own unique achievement. Those people had only to deal with their own enclosed civilization, for the conscious mind, in the terms of this discussion, now, could not extend itself to the extent that is now habitual. It could not bear the brunt of communication beyond its own confines. Its focus was sharp and clear, and contained.

Groups of people learned how to get along together. They developed arts and sciences, religions—yet it was as if no other people existed. They had only themselves to take into consideration. The grandeurs and disasters of such civilizations were contained. No great idea would spread from civilization to civilization; no war would leap from land to land. This does not mean that there were not similarities in religious concepts or art forms or whatever, for each level of consciousness has its own characteristics, which will show in all of its works.

Since then, and accelerating in your time, physical methods of transportation and communication have become the main pedestals upon which civilizations rest. Consciousness has become more horizontal in that respect. It must take in and assimilate the existing data from a far vaster amount of space than before.

You are aware of what is happening across the world, say, this evening. You watched the events on television. You must react, then, to events that your forefathers would never have been aware of in the same fashion. Your living room reaches out horizontally in space as far as your consciousness is concerned. There is no isolation in that old manner. This means that consciousness must, and is, learning new manipulations. People are forced to look beyond their own families, cities, and even countries, to that clearly illuminated arena of the world.

(9:48.) A ruler cannot make his decisions based upon national events only, but he must take international ones into mind, and in a more direct fashion, say, than even 10 years ago. Disasters are no longer localized or contained. The private consciousness is forced to contend with world events in a way that is completely new in historical terms. It is a time of turmoil—but it is a time of turmoil partially because consciousness has been willing to extend itself in that particular fashion.

The learning process is indeed being accelerated, though the barrage of stimuli can be most disconcerting. It is the official line of consciousness that has become horizontal, yet in so doing it has also opened up questions to which it would have been blind otherwise—and because of its focus your news events, of course, show only one side of the picture.

That picture, however, provides a kind of exaggeration, throwing back a mirror to the official line of consciousness that it must find most distasteful. Such communications, however, in the overall have great potential, for even unwillingly they stress the unity of the planet—and consciousness itself strains to solve problems on a different basis than before.

In those ancient times, mentioned earlier, one civilization cared not a whit about any other whose existence was known. One did not depend upon the other. It now becomes apparent that a war, or near-war in one country is a threat to all others, and man's consciousness at the level we are discussing is struggling to attain a planetary concern, a sense of life's balances.

The official line of consciousness does stress its own philosophies. No television picture is showing you the silent afternoons spent by an artist who will be called great tomorrow, or stresses the vitality of life that is responsible for the existence of the television sets to begin with. These things, unfortunately, you must remember for yourself.

In past times treacheries in governments or politics or religion were hidden. There are no more today than there ever were—but treachery in your time can seldom remain private. And because of your communications it seems to be everywhere.

There were wars before, and threats and disasters, but people in countries that were safe were not daily confronted with those other realities, so consciousness has taken upon itself this additional opportunity and burden, in that each person, largely speaking, is far more aware of events in other corners of the world—natives in deepest bush country have transistors.

This barrage is meant to push consciousness in its official stance nearly to desperation, so that it opens other doorways of awareness, and extends itself into the intuitional realms, giving itself greater insight, and providing "an extra band" of communication—the merging of man's innate "psychic" abilities with his normally attuned consciousness. The effort then is meant to release another kind of intelligence for which man is innately equipped.

(10:08.) I hope this at least is a partial answer to some of Ruburt's uncomfortable musings, and your own. End of session unless you have questions.

("This afternoon I was wondering how Jim Poett was making out—not when the

article will be published [in the Village Voice*], but what he thinks of what he's doing.")*

I have one point I forgot to make. In certain terms, Ruburt was in contact with your parents the other afternoon. Their images, however, were creative constructions, but the communication itself was valid. Unfortunately, it was also an example of what happens when the official line of consciousness steps into the dream state, as Ruburt realized your father was dead, and at that level then decided he could not be here.

Poett was quite taken with me *(amused)*—but the story is not earth-shaking, and for a time others have entered in ahead. The affair involved an education for Poett, as he struggled with many concepts, and as he struggled against portions of himself, for he wants to be a journalist even while he has no use for it at the same time.

End of session.

("Thank you.")

(10:14 PM.)

DELETED SESSION
SEPTEMBER 6, 1978 9:25 PM WEDNESDAY

(No session was held Monday evening. Instead we worked on the table of contents for Volume 2 of "Unknown" Reality.

(Last night, Jane spent an exhausting couple of hours trying to get through to a young man, Stuart, who called on us unannounced at about 9 PM. He suffered from the attacks of "magicians" who were stealing his energy: "Plates" of energy were being stripped away from his chest in layers, until he feared his inner self would be exposed. He was also stalked by people in vans with antennae—they wanted to clone him.

(Stuart was 23 years old—half-inarticulate, dirty, downcast—seemingly a pathetic case. Like some others we've seen, he was so locked into his reality that he was really quite unreachable. He lived off a government social-security supplemental program for those who can't fend for themselves—pretty shrewd, I thought. He'd read hardly anything Jane had written, and I wondered why he'd sought her out. I never heard Jane give better advice, though I doubted if an interview was going to do much about changing what seemed to be a lifetime's habits.

(The episode upset Jane considerably—more so than she realized it did, at first. Not only because of the lost time and probably vain effort involved, but because as she talked, she knew she was saying things that applied to her as well. "You've got to turn your world upside down," she told Stuart. "If you don't like the reality you've

created, change your focus. Give yourself a chance to use your own creative energy...."
After Stuart finally left, to stay at the YMCA, she walked in the kitchen, better than
I'd seen her do in some time. She slept fitfully, thinking of him often when she woke
up. She talked about him today. We wondered what he was doing today. He'd talked
about going north, or heading back to San Francisco, where he'd seen helicopters
changing their courses in the sky to fly directly at him.

(At 8:30 this evening we got our answer. Stuart was back at our front door. I
refused to let him in. He'd washed his face and looked fresher. He told me that with-
in the last five hours something had happened that he'd feared all his life: he'd lost the
last of his energy. His inner self was exposed and vulnerable. Yet he'd walked the two
miles and more to our house from the YMCA, I thought ironically. His tale showed
that Jane's efforts of the night before had largely been futile. I told him she couldn't
help him, that we didn't have the time. He accepted docilely, and gave me his address
in San Francisco. He left, and Jane still had the impulse to have me call him back
in another effort to help him. I said no in any event. Stuart didn't know when he'd
leave town, so I said he should return to his friends in California. He said he prob-
ably would.

(Today we received a very disturbing letter from Miss Bowman. She's selling
her home and leaving the valley; she has a painting I gave her years ago that she
wants me to have back, so Jane and I will probably make the trip to Athens, PA this
Sunday. Miss Bowman was my art teacher in high school. She lent me the money to
go to art school in New York City. I paid her back out of my wages in the Air
Transport Command when I was drafted to serve in the military in World War II.

(For the session, we both hoped Seth would at least comment on the Stuart
incidents, and in relation to her own challenges.)

Good evening.

("Good evening, Seth.")

Now: we have a young man who felt himself to be unimportant, lacking
in stature or ability—the kind of a person who would be lost in a crowd.

We now have a young man who is quite important. He is so important
that others pursue him psychically. His abilities and powers are so great that others, seemingly now, try to rob him of them. Far from living a colorless life, he
wanders through the country, in the midst of an exciting psychic chase, pursued
by magicians, evil powers, and the most sophisticated weaponry of giant corporations and the government.

He does not have a nine-to-five job. He is constantly in midst of drama,
fleeing for his life. The system supports him, and it would not do so under other
conditions. He has some financial sustenance, then, some freedom, as he understands it, and he is the hero, the good guy who is, however, seemingly at the

mercy of his enemies.

His problems are cosmic in their proportions, or so it seems to him. He has excitement, again, drama, some freedom. These are his boons. On the one hand he knows that he is involved in a façade, playing a game, pretending to be mad. On the other hand, the game itself is becoming too real, getting out of hand, and it has prevented him from learning ordinary skills, say, which seem to be mundane and too ordinary and beneath him.

I mentioned the Cinderella myth—and there, everything will come out all right in the end, somehow. Its opposite is a feeling that nothing will ever come out all right because the universe itself is meaningless. Life is meaningless. Our young man believes this.

Any purpose is better than none, and any intended personalized threat is better than an existence in which no life is important enough to be individually threatened, so these imagined threats serve to convince our young man that his life must have meaning or purpose—otherwise others would not be so intent on destroying him. He is clothed and fed. He lives with adventure, threat, and must forever be on guard. He sees himself fleeing across the continent—again, a hero in a vast drama, a romantic picture. He does not want allies, for he dramatizes his isolation.

Ruburt is correct: he could be a hero of a short story, and so he appears to himself. It is his way of gaining stature in a world he believes is meaningless. He is afraid that he has few abilities of any kind, so he must of course take steps to see that they are never put to the test in the physical world—hence, some disaster or another always prevents the great creativity that he says he has to offer.

(9:43.) He cannot be happy, however, with the circumstances, for if he were the entire fabric of the drama would appear false. He must make token efforts, therefore, to break away—efforts that must be futile, because if they worked he would be in the "real world."

I am doing my best to explain. I do not want you to think I am without compassion. Novelists create heroes who must overcome obstacles. Some such characters are brave and upright; some of your heroes are scoundrels. Then there are, say, the hunchback of Notre Dame or Frankenstein. In your living you literally bring your ideas to life. You form the story of your life. You are involved in a study of the full dimensions of experience, in the interpretation of events themselves. You are involved in a living process—but one of such multidimensional activity that sometimes you see of course but one chapter in a saga whose full complexion is far different.

Give me a moment.... A novelist, being himself or herself writing a book, will nevertheless imaginatively live the actions of all of its characters—the villain, the hero, the madman, the saint or whatever—and a true creative gestalt is involved. Then in the author's mind the characters will interact. The author may know the book's end, or allow the characters themselves to work out their own solutions. Here we will call the author the whole self, and the characters are real. They are themselves. They follow their own unique intents. They are not coerced, say. The plot is left open, but in the deepest terms the whole self, through its personalities, probes deeply into the meaning of life in all of its manifestations.

The young man is setting himself against society, against its ideas of sanity. He is creating a reality that is in its way highly unique—a creation he feels at least is his own. It is anything but boring. Its very danger keeps him on his toes, and forces him to protect his life. It is saving him from suicide. It is therefore a mental device meant to protect his life.

He must protect himself from threats from without. The threats convince him, again, that he <u>must</u> be important and valuable. Beneath this is the feeling that his life is of no value, that he is in fact worthless, weaker than his peers, and he detests himself enough so that he might take his own life. The threats then convince him of his value. To give them up would be to face his feelings of worthlessness. The situation also allows him to use his creative abilities in terms of fantasy and imagination. He was taught not to express himself, so he only uses those abilities to protect his life, which justifies them. His dilemma makes him important.

(10:02.) He expresses in exaggerated form many quite paranoid tendencies that are considered in a milder version as quite normal. The big corporations are out to rule the world. He sees the oil company people out there with helicopters and sophisticated machinery that destroys people's vital energy—simply a more colorful, exaggerated version of the same idea personally applied.

The latest of course is the fear of cloning, but our young man does better than any fear-mongers, for he has the personal cloning people in their eerie vans with antennae, chasing him through the streets. He becomes a sponge for numberless such attitudes, only to him they become critically immediate. He is, however, still alive after each threat, and this convinces him that he will indeed survive. For look what he has survived so far, even though the threats grow more monstrous.

When the entire affair <u>really</u> frightens him, he will look for another solution, and it is too bad your institutions of therapy do not help. Guided imagery could help him, for example, but he would need supervision. Ruburt was quite right in the method he used in speaking to him, and my presence would not have served. He would only have used it, as Ruburt said he would. The creative challenge is there for him, and it is one he chose himself.

Take your break.

(10:10. During break I asked that Seth say something about why Stuart had "picked on Jane," out of all the people in the country. There are many "psychics" in the San Francisco area, for example. I didn't think he'd read her books but very little. 10:18.)

You two are involved in the asking of questions, and the acquisition of knowledge. You want to know about the nature of reality.

You are concerned with what is <u>wrong</u> with the world. You want to know why it is not better than it is. You want to know how reality is created—how and why people create lives that seem to be less than desirable.

Your young man gave you an excellent instance—a "case" that the most noteworthy psychologists or psychiatrists, if they had time, would find fascinating. You were able to gain insights that you simply would not have if you were not presented with exaggerated realities. Your young psychologist was a case in point, with his "crazies," your Andrija Puharich, your young people with the child, about Christmas time.

Now these are not simply people in distress. You are presented with bigger-than-life situations, provided with raw material from life, given exaggerated versions so that from them you can draw the knowledge to help you answer your own questions, and the knowledge to help others whose plights may be less colorful but equally vital.

The people who come here are concentrated, dramatic examples of the human species at large. Their beliefs appear so drastically that you can use them as blueprints for others in whose characters the beliefs will appear more modified, and perhaps nearly unnoticed. You see the beliefs, the motivations, the feelings, of those whose beliefs are carried to extremes, so that you can follow them as if they were psychological clusters or cultures—isolated, so to speak. Then you can study their behavior in others.

All of that is quite in keeping with your own intents, and with the study of human nature with which you are involved. You are then further motivated to seek other answers than the official ones.

(10:30.) You always help those you see—and they present themselves to you not only for themselves, but for others. You are examining the human condition, but seeking answers from the highest reaches of its capabilities. These are goals you set yourselves. If you set out to discover what was <u>right</u> with the world, you would be on a different path. There is much right with the world.

Give us a moment.... Be sure you do not close your eyes to the miracles of the world. Your point was a good one—the young man walked a good way—

the energy was there to sustain him even over his delusions. Beliefs show themselves, however, far more clearly, and can be examined better, through the type of experience those people bring.

Always remember the vitality that sustains them, and that supports them. It is not withdrawn, even though the constructions they form may seem to be extremely faulty. There is much left unsaid, simply because some information available to me cannot be translated properly in ways that will make sense to you. There are explorations of emotional content, for example, very difficult to explain, in which intensities of emotion are explored for their own sake, as one might experiment with the values of red or black—not caring what the form of the painting was.

You might think of a tragic opera, or a musical composition, and so some lives focus upon intensities whose form is not perceived, and which deals with a kind of power that is itself the experience. I can go no further with that verbally.

Your idea of judging the quality of life, or of a life, is highly limited, however, for it may not lie in events as you usually think of them on many occasions.

(Loudly:) End of session, and a fond and hearty good evening.

("Okay." 10:43 PM.

(I'd say that we can follow Seth's analogy about the emotional intensities, above, okay, and also that we try not to be blind to values in life that might not be readily apparent in ordinary terms. I think I've wondered more than once, for instance, about what purposes a given life may be serving that we're quite unaware of, or blind to.)

DELETED SESSION
SEPTEMBER 13, 1978 9:24 PM WEDNESDAY

(We've been having but one session a week while I've been typing the finished manuscript for Volume 2 of "Unknown" Reality. This is mainly Jane's idea; I imagine that for the most part I'm willing to stick to our regular routine. On the other hand, it's great to see the finished pages for "Unknown" pile up.

(We sat for the session at 9:10, and as the minutes passed Jane grew more and more impatient. We had no idea what the session might be about, since we'd posed no questions for Seth. In view of the subject matter that did develop, rather to our surprise, let me note that since late last week President Carter, President Anwar Sadat of Egypt, and Israel's Prime Minister Begin have been meeting at Camp David in pursuit of peace for the Middle East. The conference has been called cru-

cial to peace in our time, etc. The scanty news from their meeting seems to be that matters are moving in "the right direction."

(Finally, at 9:23 Jane said: "Well. I'm about ready. I don't know — it might be short. I didn't feel anything until a minute ago.")

Good evening.

("Good evening, Seth.")

The Arabs and the Jews and your Baptist Carter—a beautiful instructional picture.

I spoke lately about your communications, and some of their more fortunate ramifications. You have had what amounts to local gods, even though one name may be used, so that Carter can say "We all worship the same God."

Fanatics work best in isolation, where their own beliefs are currently and constantly reinforced, and where they are surrounded by sacred yes-men of one kind or another, whatever their designation. Other beliefs are not allowed to intrude, and even those who are firm believers, but not fanatics, naturally prefer the company of their own kind.

Begin, Sadat, and Carter are each "God-fearing" men, sincere believers in their causes. How can "God" be for the Jews and against their enemies, the Arabs, as the Jews suppose, and how can God be for the Arabs and against the Jews, as the Arabs suppose? "Decent" God-fearing men, then, must indeed question how the same God can have such different views, and at least wonder if their own nationalistic histories and prejudices may not have distorted the interpretation of God's word somewhere along the way.

Your communication system is indeed bringing such issues to light more and more. People are faced with beliefs other than their own, and discover that the "enemy" or the "infidel," or the terrorist or the respected head of state, while having completely different views, are each convinced of their own uprightness and virtue.

That sort of exposure, in your terms, has not happened before, and of itself it forces both mind and heart to question some dictates that have been taken for granted in the past—for in the past almost any kind of destruction or war or violence was justified if it was done in God's name, or if the soldiers were marching "on the side of right."

Since this "one God" of Carter's, however, can obviously have such different ideas, saying one thing to one nation and the opposite to another, then men will begin to check their nationalistic lists of divine instructions, discovering that to one extent or another this God would seem to have told several different groups of people that they were chosen above others, that their enemies would be vanquished, and that they might indeed defend their divine rights through whatever unfortunate but necessary means.

At various times this one God of Carter's seems to have said, on more unearthly subjects, that the Jews would be saved, while our infidels languished in the deepest hell, or that the Mohammedans would be saved—and throughout history as you know it, and as you do not know it, the stories have thrived.

It would do Carter well on one level to question this God more thoroughly. Yet on another level he is doing very well, for he is bringing about a situation in which men must question the nationalistic intent of this "one God."

Men have indeed done more harm in the name of God than they have ever done when pursuing their own greedy or ignorant ways. In the name of God, of course, the artifacts of civilizations have been destroyed, libraries ruined—and when such harm is done, in the name of God, then men are trained to feel no guilt. Indeed, their holy sense of righteousness rises in proportion to the harm they have perpetrated against God's enemy, no matter who or what this might be.

(9:46.) Your ideas of God are put to the test in this meeting (at Camp David), for here men who claim to believe in a merciful God discuss their mortal claims to property and land, and each feels behind him the ancient dictates of an archaic God.

Your gods, and your ideas of a God, have always followed the contours of your consciousness, your civilizations, your prerogatives, and your values. These are projected outward as giant-sized psychic patterns, architects' plans for the cultural cities to follow. Such ideas can and have been used most beneficially by simple men and women throughout the ages, and distorted as they are, they still served to remind man that his source is not the world.

Man possesses an innate biological knowledge, however, of right and wrong, and to a large extent religions, as they are utilized, distort much of that information. Left alone, men are not murderers, though some may murder. Men always form some kind of group, in which respect is given of one kind or another to their own species, and to nature. Your communication system may, in time, make the distortions of your God concepts much more visible, so that honest men can at least question "How can God say this to the Jews, and that to the Arabs? Is it possible that we have read the message wrong?" All That Is is within each living thing. All That Is is within that which is not, also. Man is not set one against the other. The old distortions involved with the various religions must and will come to light.

Another point: the meetings in question alter probabilities, and again in a way that in your terms was hardly possible before, for the world looks on, so to speak. As of now, of course, you live in a survivor's world, for all of the catastrophes of a worldwide nature that could have happened thus far, have not.

Unless you have questions, that is the end of the session.

("No questions. That was very good, though.")

My comment for the evening. I bid you a hearty good evening.

("Good night, Seth.")

(9:59.) One comment: have Ruburt discuss his new suggestions with you. He is onto something, and you can help. That is all.

(10:00 PM. "Good night, Seth."

(Jane has mentioned her idea for new suggestions to me, but I haven't seen them yet. We want to go over them together.)

DELETED SESSION
SEPTEMBER 20, 1978 9:18 PM WEDNESDAY

(Jane and I continue to work like mad, typing the final copy for Oversoul Seven *number two and for Volume 2 of* "Unknown" Reality. *I'm into Section 5 now; this weekend Sue Watkins is to deliver all, or nearly all, of the typed appendix material. Jane had but a few more chapters to go for* Seven.

(Lately Jane has been looking over Fabric of The Universe, *a book by Denis Postle. It was lent to us by Carlos Smith. Seth discusses some material that is an outgrowth of the book.)*

Now: I have been sending you psychic telegrams of energy —both of you — for your present endeavors.

This session will be brief. There are a few points I want to make, and that is all. Each individual is a portion of the universe, of course, apropos of the book on the *Fabric of the Universe*, but the universe is everywhere composed of <u>awareized</u> energy—energy "stamped" with its own unique psychic or psychological "individuality."

The individuality may be of a completely different nature than that with which you are acquainted. It is true that you are each versions of the universe, or even that every person alive is somehow a version of each other person, and it is true that a great unity underlies the basis of life, as you know it, that all things are interrelated.

Each conceivable particle or wave "at any given time" possesses its own unique position in the universe, however, and its own privileged viewpoint. In the most basic terms, there are different kinds of realities, but one is not more real or less real than the others.

(9:26.) Give us a moment.... Your world of physical objects is quite

important, in that because it allows you to deal with differentiations, to pin-point energy where you want it while giving you an observable physical effect, so that this training can carry over in other realities in which the same kind of physical feedback is not available, is subsidiary, or is otherwise not as much a part of the camouflage structure.

Using "real objects" now, you learn to manipulate energy with the models before you, so to speak, gaining confidence so that "later" you can trust your-selves in the use of energy without needing the physical appearance of, say, an object before you. Largely speaking, yet in the terms of this discussion, Christianity and ancient Roman religions dealt mainly with the individual, and particularly Christianity overlooked the large unity of being.

The Eastern religions exaggerated the importance of unity, almost losing the concept of individuality in the process. As popularly understood, Eastern religions can lead to spiritual exhaustion, as the individual tries to level himself out, again, so to speak — and the popular understanding of a religion is far more important than the priests or the gurus understand it, for people directed their lives by following their own versions. Period.

The West has forced the individual to stand besieged and alone, under-mined by evolution, in which the individual's only meaning lay in the survival of his species. Individualism was further undermined by the problems involved with capitalism. The poor man must struggle to get ahead, even if that means doing so at the expense of his neighbors, while saving his soul at the same time —a tricky, difficult venture indeed.

So some Americans have become tired of this badge of individuality, and they are ready to throw it over, either to fundamental Christianity, which is again rising, or to a number of various Eastern religions. Life is everywhere both individual and particular, and at the same time united with all being. All That Is "pulsates" with a truly infinite yearning to particularize all of its attributes, to know itself through individualizing all of its dreams, its slightest thought, its most monumental discovery. All That Is composes the fabric of the universe— which is everywhere unified, since nothing exists outside of it, and every wave or particle, or field or whatever within it, consists of a divine psychological fab-ric that is populated by individuation, sensation, meaning, intent, in which the most innocuous shadow of an electron rises up joyfully and shouts "I am I, and not you."

This still is to say that the divine psychological fabric forms all individu-ality, naturally, spontaneously, and that you cannot have one without the other.

(9:46.) Give us a moment.... A note to Ruburt: to impress that universe on a conscious level, you stress your individuality, while at the same time trying to realize that your uniqueness rises each moment from that divine psychological fabric. When you are most yourself, you have the clearest channels to the fountainhead of your being, for you are acting according to the nature, the unique nature, of yourself—and also stressing the great infinity of being from which your own uniqueness emerges. You hold in your mind the thought of your individuality, <u>and</u> of its deep source, so that both thoughts are beautifully poised, bringing about an interaction between the two, that results in a kind of energy, an attraction, an electromagnetic recognition, that refreshes the entire being.

Writing poetry for Ruburt is excellent in that regard.

Where do your thoughts come from—<u>your</u> thoughts, that is? Confine the question to your own individuality. Asking yourself that kind of question can also help put you in touch with the source of your being — again, because you start with your individuality, but also acknowledge its deeper origin.

If you do not have questions I will end the session.

(*"Do you want to say something about my dream, in which I get shot?"*)

It was, as I believe Ruburt has mentioned, a result of deep contemplation on your part about the bookstore murder, but in a larger context, involving probabilities, murderers, victims, and the beliefs involved.

The men were all united—that is, they agreed to the circumstances. No one was trying to run away, and <u>in a way</u> the murderer was performing a service. Any violence or hatred serves a purpose beyond itself, so that man in a way often performs services of which he is not consciously aware.

I am not saying that man is being manipulated, but that in a larger framework, even his seemingly evil acts have constructive meaning. A man who kills with hatred will have his hatred to contend with, but he is not able to kill anyone who has not decided to die—and to die in a particular manner; that is, someone who wants his death blamed on another, who would not commit suicide, who would not choose a long illness—someone who is ready to die but does not want to deal with the circumstances, and wants indeed to be surprised by death.

Now: <u>in those terms, and in the terms of this discussion</u>, specifically, all assassins are paid assassins hired by the victims. Again, in the terms of this discussion, many murderers are overwhelmed by a sense of guilt, and the murderous act pinpoints the reason for the guilt—so the victim pays the murderer by giving a clear-cut, unassailable reason for a monstrous guilt that was before formless, and even more frightening, since it seemed to have no particular base, but an overwhelming vitality.

Now all of those issues, in one way or another appeared in your dream, where for the sake of understanding you became the victim. You then discovered that you were still "alive"—as of course the murdered victim does.

Many such people feel before death that the body is a shell from which death will free them—and here you have a verbal symbol: the shell of the body, with a gun shell, and the soul being propelled out of the body, though that was not part of the dream. But if there is order to being, then there is order—and even the most chaotic-seeming episodes must and do have a larger meaning, and a constructive purpose.

End of session.

("Thank you very much.")

A fond good evening, and you are doing well.

("Okay." 10:08 PM. See my dream notebook for a newspaper account of the murder in question—last Saturday night—at the Adult Book Store in Elmira.)

DELETED SESSION
SEPTEMBER 27, 1978 9:22 PM WEDNESDAY

(An extra carbon of this session is being made for Jane to attach to her dream notebook. Practically all of the session deals with material stemming from her dream adventures of September 25 and 27. See her dream notebook for details. The September 25 dream concerns reincarnation and her decision to spend each reincarnation in one "room," say. Then on the afternoon of the 25th she had a nap-dream adventure featuring a family reunion, my father, and others. It seemed to involve the Sumari family of consciousness, she wrote.

(On September 27, Jane woke up after her nap with a batch of material in mind on: Private Revelation, and the Voice of God, or Divine Dialogues, which she wrote down. The material filled three pages, and Seth leads off tonight's session with material relative to it. Jane wasn't sure why she came up with the material, since she hadn't been thinking about such things, nor had we discussed anything relative to it recently. It sounded like good material for a chapter in a book—perhaps something new is cooking?)

Now: Good evening.

("Good evening, Seth.")

"Revelation, Obedience, and Objectivity"—that is the heading for this evening's discussion.

In the Old Testament, you did what you were told to by the almighty. If he told you to slay your son upon a mountaintop, then it was up to you to obey, and to your son to acquiesce. God's words were not to be taken lightly.

There was not to be any argument given. Obedience was man's largest responsibility to the Godhead of the Old Testament.

Now Ruburt's paper was largely correct, in that Christianity in general, and the Catholic Church in particular, has not only frowned on revelation, but in the past tried with the utmost effort to strike it down. This <u>was</u> largely out of self-interest, and the many Protestant faiths are a proof of the fragmentation that results when man is given <u>some</u> freedom to interpret his relationship with God himself.

That freedom, however, of course has been highly limited in nature, for the dogma of Christianity still largely held. There were, however, other reasons also—to do the church some small justice *(amused).* If God could tell a man to slay a son, and if private revelation were granted validity, then "divinely inspired crimes" might not only be legion, but might also take man's energies away from accepted Godly pursuits—like fighting the infidels or heretics at home *(all louder).*

You could not have a cohesive society based upon the validity of private revelation, <u>when</u> you believed in a God who was so bloodthirsty, and who demanded such proofs of obedience.

Now God at the last moment might stay your hand—but then he might not. Divinely inspired crimes could only be acceptable against the enemies of organized Christendom, or against its own subservients. Thus of course was a certain amount of prejudiced order maintained *(almost sarcastically).*

The church could not trust revelations, lest new orders might come to contradict the old ones, to upset the spiritual status quo, and hence the social organization that developed about it; or that might revive <u>old</u> tenets once a part of Christianity but later dropped—such as a belief in reincarnation.

(9:35.) Give us a moment.... Christ, as you understand him historically to be, spoke in parables and symbols. Men often took him literally, but his message was that the spirit of God was within each person—in terms of the symbolism, each person being a child of the father who dwelled in heaven. But heaven meant an inner reality for Christ, not an exterior one.

For centuries, priests of one kind or another have been put in charge of "reading God's messages," and interpreting them to the rest of mankind, just as in later times the scientists have been put in the position of interpreting man's own world to him—in terms quite as esoteric as those of any religion. So science and revelation seem far apart indeed, for the revelation usually insists upon obedience to a vision that is privately received, and offers as a rule but poor evidence. No questions are allowed. Science on the other hand, constantly questions, and is so objectively occupied that the subjective world is entirely beyond its realm.

The beginnings of science were apparent before its full blossoming—and in a way it is important because of its strict interpretation of objectivity, exaggerated though it may be.

In the past, because of your God concepts, private revelations were indeed highly unwieldy. No common sense was applied to them. They were untinged by objectivity. They justified any act. This applied not only privately, however, but to the mass-accepted revelations of all religions, that could justify righteous wars for God's sake, or justify murder in the name of peace.

You have had a schism, in which reason and emotion seemed to be opposites. Revelation and reason seemed to be enemies. Yet as the approach of the scientific age appeared, before its blossoming, so new tendencies are now showing that do indeed signal a new era, in which the emotions and intellect are no longer regarded as opposing tendencies in man.

Revelations will be encouraged, and yet they will not be put above the common-sense wisdom that insists upon tolerance and justice. Man has indeed forgotten how to interpret his revelations—but more importantly, he has forgotten how to receive them, and then how to perfect them in reason's light.

(9:50.) Give us a moment.... Ruburt's dream about the reincarnational room told him that he had decided to concentrate in each life rather exclusively upon certain issues. He decided not to be distracted even by the public, or by public issues. He does not need, therefore, to have symptoms to force himself to stay at home. He does not need to fear that he will be distracted. He does not need those extra precautions.

He does have the will power to say no.

The next, psychic family dream represented an actual reunion of some Sumari family members, so that Ruburt would not feel so alone, but realize he did indeed have rich emotional connections with others, at other levels, and that he was part of a family of creative initiators, full of energy and vigor, who could go out into the world or cheerfully forget it if they chose.

The dream meant, also, that he was not alone in a different fashion, for the self that he knows is supported by strong and vigorous other portions of the psyche, and other aspects all ready to help him—inner friends he can count upon.

The dream also represented the coming birth of new material, for the "family members" gave each other new information and bits of knowledge, so that this was also a reunion of portions of the psyche.

Do you have any questions?

("I guess not. I haven't taken the time to think of any. Do you?" This was the *first time I'd ever asked Seth if he had any questions <u>we</u> could answer. My little tac-tic didn't work, though.)*

The questions come from you.

("Well. I guess not, then.")

Then I bid you a fond good evening—and again, my congratulations on *"Unknown"*—the book—and all of them do indeed have a part to play in the new era that is approaching. The "New Aquarian Age" may be an exaggeration, and about it are grouped many distorted ideas—yet it is a popular term that stands for an insight on the part of the people, and is a result of quite valid inner knowledge that an era is ending, and that another has to some extent already begun.

End of session. I bid you a fond good evening—and to a sweet creature.

("Okay. Thank you.")

(10:00 PM. Seth's closing reference to a "sweet creature" was a reference to our sweet cat, Willy, who midway in the session had hopped up on the couch and snug-gled himself tight against my left side as I took notes.)

DELETED SESSION
OCTOBER 11, 1978 9:32 PM WEDNESDAY

(Today I finished typing final copy for Session 733 of "Unknown" Reality—leaving just 11 to go to finish the book. Last Tuesday I mailed to Prentice-Hall Jane's second novel on Seven. Since she seemed to be at loose ends, I suggested we have a ses-sion tonight, to "give her something to do." She was going to pass it up again. As it turned out, I think the session was well worth having.)

Good evening.

("Good evening, Seth.")

Remarks: it has been said that when the imagination and the will are in conflict, that the imagination <u>will</u> *(amused)* always win.

It might be a good idea to examine that statement, for in the truest sense of human motivation, the fact is that despite all <u>appearances</u> to the contrary, the imagination and the will are never in conflict.

However scandalous or unrealistic this proposition sounds, the fact is that people do not "will" a specific outcome of events while their imaginations vivid-ly portray the opposing outcome.

Some of the reasons for such activities are sketched in our new book. But what you have is a learned pattern of face-saving self-deception and nefarious *(with amusement)* techniques, taught by parents to children; so often you pre-tend to want one thing, and you may say that you "will it" to happen—perhaps because what you really want is unacceptable, or so you have been taught: it is demeaning, or evil, or whatever. So in many cases people's true motives "escape" them.

It is very important to know what you want. You may discard or dismiss "what you want" as unworthy, evil, but you must first be aware of your motives. This sounds quite simplistic, and yet it is quite practically true, but you have people professing to desire wealth while obviously doing everything possible to insure the continuance of poverty. They may state their purpose as often as they wish, and yet their imaginations carry vivid pictures of future deprivation, so it seems in such cases that the will and the imagination are in conflict.

Such individuals, however, want poverty. They use both will and imagination to seek their goal. They may think that poverty is demeaning or humiliating or threatening, yet want it despite those conditions for other reasons that may or may not have anything to do with money, per se. So the question in such a case is, of course, "Why do I want to be poor?"

There is nothing "wrong" with poverty, or morally reprehensible. But people who write you, for example, saying "I want to make good money, but all my jobs are innocuous, or I have none," are not facing the fact that for the time being, at least, they want poverty.

The imagination usually gives you a pretty good picture of what you really want. It usually escapes all of your attempts to cow it, to reason away its pictures. It is a mirror of your wants, and it is also the mirror of your will — for in it you see what you want to see, even if afterward you say that its pictures are unbidden, or against your conscious intent.

Imagination and will, working together, are miracle-makers, because self-deception does not stand between them.

(9:53.) All of my comments for Ruburt apply to the specific situation at the time they are given—an important point. Lately Ruburt decided, using his will, to walk to whatever degree possible. That desire was clear-cut. Immediately, without trying, at different times his imagination came up with different pictures to implement the desire—the table, the cupboard.

Today he almost walked three times. Imaginatively, he did walk three times. The body immediately responded, so that he wanted to walk more. Circulation was increased. He wants to walk. Keep that desire clear in a creature fashion. Do not tack onto it issues about television or lectures or whatever.

Give us a moment.... Again, you have a joint reality, in all aspects. Apply what I said about wealth to health. The creative abilities are always released when the will and the imagination are together, in whatever area.

Your willingness to help Ruburt walk, your encouragement—these are all important, but the most important issue is the unity, in practical terms, of imagination and will, and the generation of creative ability in health terms, that can be sparked.

That is enough for now. When we return to our ordinary schedule I will more than keep you busy—but the unknown reality applies in such cases, so that unknown motives can become known and dealt with.

It is in its way perfectly all right to be frightened of the world. *(Almost with a laugh:)* Under certain conditions it may be a mark of sanity—but it is highly self-defeating to put yourself in a position where you cannot go out into the world—or more importantly, where you cannot navigate as a creature.

(10:03.) Ruburt thinks it is beneath him to be frightened of the world, so it is easier to pretend you <u>cannot</u> go out in it than to feel you are a coward— which in your society is the interpretation placed upon such feelings. If Ruburt does not want a public life, that is not cowardice. But as private people, and as creatures, you <u>must</u> value your freedom of motion, and your connections with the natural world of the seasons.

Ruburt does not need to feel that he would naturally, left alone, go out into the world, into the arena, and convince the world of our ideas, or think that with his energy unimpeded that would be part of his natural mission. That is not so. Nor would he be necessarily more fulfilled in that role, <u>and it is that imagined, frightening role against which he pushes, and then retreats.</u>

He is not "meant to be" that kind of person.

He <u>is</u> good with people, and with communication—but very much as a sideline and not as a main endeavor. There is no need for him to feel cowardly, or inferior, for not "living up to" that role.

End of session.

("Do you want to say something about the Voice*?" In a rather funny confrontation, Seth and I stared at each other for a few moments.* <u>My</u> *question of course grew out of the first installment of the story about us and Seth that was published earlier this week in the* Village Voice. *Our feelings about it ranged all the way from ridicule to a grudging understanding that Jim Poett had worked hard on the piece. We think the pictures are especially bad, yet could see why the* Voice *had chosen the ones they did.*

(I suppose the two-part article marks the end of our involvement with the media, though this opinion may change. Not likely, though. We're left feeling that it's largely a waste of time, and fraught with a lack of understanding. It's practically impossible, for example, to get free of the connotations of the worst elements of the whole field: the moment the subject comes up, we're associated with all the history of mediumship in the most banal of terms. This fact is indicative of both Poett's own

inexperience, and the way association works generally. To have Jane's work studied and respected for what it is, on its own, is evidently asking the impossible of most people. It appears that intuitively at least Jane has made the right decision, to concentrate upon the books; at least they offer something the way she wants it to be. Unfortunately, I suppose, this also means that we set ourselves outside the mainstream of activity in the field, and that our readership is likely to be pretty much confined to the "average" individual. The "authorities" aren't going to pay any attention.)

I cannot say anything simply about the *Voice.*

("I don't care," I said, meaning that I had the time.)

(10:10.) Give us a moment.... The *Voice* has artistic pretensions. It is read by the "professional" nonconformists. To read it is a badge of individuality in the city. It is sardonic, coolly critical, hip, righteous for the underdog, and with all of this a carrier now and then for new ideas of format for initiators. It is intellectual, yet carries the underlaying thrust of emotional hope—the distorted voice of the beleaguered, weary, ironic idealists.

This means of course that deeply felt hope must be sardonically examined, that deeply buried faith must be stated with parried thrusts, and to that extent the paper speaks for a <u>concentrated</u> portion of your population so that our Jim Poett, who is a poet at heart, must appear in the slightly worn cloak of the skeptic. He must show that for all of his youth he is world-weary, not easily taken in, that he is objective—and only then can he allow his creative abilities to flow.

But he must dress his dreams in fashionable cynicism, while all the time trying to hold them safely clear, and gracefully allow some faith, some hope, to show in an uncontested manner.

Now innovators are not conformists. Creative people do not fit into <u>your</u> society, so often they will indeed <u>appear</u> as the eccentrics, the disinherited, the mad, the obsessed, or whatever—because their desires and intents, their imaginations and their wills, are not satisfied by the tenets or organizations of the conventional world.

They are trying things that other people will not try—being creative in whatever area is open to them, so that often the creativity itself has a strained or even grotesque air. Some people who write you are like that. They are looking for a rational pattern large enough to contain and explain and focus their own misunderstood creativity.

The *Village Voice* is probably read by more creative young people, and more people in the arts, than any other New York paper. To those people the new journalism is transparent. They see it as the current necessary way to write—the in things, but most of them unconsciously understand the reasons behind the techniques, as I explained them earlier.

Ideas are used in astounding fashions by creative people, and so many who read the article will in their own way use it as highly creative material. You both think that Ruburt's position is a poor one in society — that people regard mediums as spooks, or weird. Those beliefs <u>helped</u> give you your photographs, because, while you don't like the idea, you believe it.

Poett and the photographer, however, believe the same; only they regard "spookiness" and strangeness as highly commendable qualities that contrast with what they think of as the blandness of the common man.

End of session.

("Thank you.")

And a fond good evening.

("The same to you.")

(10:28 PM.)

DELETED SESSION
OCTOBER 18, 1978 9:20 PM WEDNESDAY

(Jane's physical condition continues to change and improve. She's now walking again with the table, two or three times a day, and seemingly better each time. Tonight she did very well. We seem to be doing things much better these days. I'm typing Session 741 for "Unknown" Reality. She's finished with Seven Two, etc., so I think these events have also helped initiate changes.

(At times Jane wakes me up at night; she's very nearly crying in discomfort, yet now we understand that those feelings represent her muscles wanting to be used; so far, though, we haven't managed to get ourselves out of bed at such times, which usually develop perhaps an hour before the alarm is to ring; these bouts, then, happen after she's usually slept for several hours, and the body wants action. I do think Jane has signaled to the body that it's time for changes to be made, which marks a learning point for her.

(After supper tonight she walked twice—both times much faster than she has in years—a very surprising and heartening sign. This shows the body can do it. She was exhilarated. She also had other rapid bodily movements, in a more extended fashion, in the arms and legs. Seth said that when the body began to recover, it would be an overall development. At the same time, Jane has been exercising a lot lately, and I'd rather she didn't overdo this activity.

(Last week the second and last installment of the Village Voice *article came*

out. Everyone agreed that it was much better than the first of the two, so that's taken
care of. I think both of us had some excellent quotations in the piece, and I'm happy
that a lot of people at least had the chance to read them.

(Jane didn't know whether she wanted a session tonight or not, but I suggest-
ed she have at least a short one, so Seth could say something about her moving abil-
ity.)

Good evening.

("Good evening, Seth.")

(With humor:) I see that the October fest begins.

Now: there is one main issue in particular that mitigates against a full life,
generally speaking, and that shows itself in many instances in either physical illness, or in the "illness" of poor relationships, or lacks of fulfillment.

It shows itself particularly in any kind of obsessive behavior, mental or
physical. It is the <u>overly</u> developed, exaggerated, "unnatural" <u>need for safety</u>.
Such an exaggerated need for safety is quite rampant in your society. It leads to
the setting up of barrier after barrier, to protect the self both against the <u>self</u> and
against the outside world.

Briefly—for I have said this before—all of your disciplines have seen the
natural self as unsavory in its basic character. You cannot be afraid of yourself
and not be afraid of others. Such attitudes lead to overcontrol of body or environment—or of other people. A family tyrant, for example, may have no physical symptoms at all, yet be quite obsessed with controlling the family members,
stuffing the household with regulations, limiting the family's freedom, or whatever.

No <u>un</u>predictability is allowed. Life becomes a series of habits, and in the
mentally ill, for example, you may have seemingly meaningless habits, compul-
sively performed.

People generally in your society find little opportunity to work with the
natural self, to explore its characteristics, much less be convinced of its good
intent.

Tonight Ruburt has evidence for the good intent of his natural self. <u>It sur-</u>
<u>prised him because he allowed it to</u>. He treated his body like a tyrant treats his
people, and the body strenuously objected. But the body does not hold a
grudge, and so it has begun to respond to Ruburt's new attitude—and the new
attitude allows him to allow the body's expression.

(9:33) I have said—too often—that the body was not diseased, and it is
not. The speed, the normal agility, is there to be unlocked. Forget what you have
heard, again, about what the body can and cannot do, or what must happen
before such and such a performance appears, for the body itself exults in creative

unpredictability, and given the chance loves to perform.

Habitual patterns can be broken overnight with creative unpredictability, and creative unpredictability is of course one of life's greatest characteristics. It sprouts everywhere, at any age, with seemingly new opportunities and fulfillments, whenever it is given the chance.

A few old hangovers, simply to be aired so they do not remain underground—this is old material—but Ruburt's mother used to tell him that he destroyed everything he touched. So when his books began to sell well, and for reasons given, he worried about this energy of his. Since his work was new, he had only faith in himself to go on, and that faith was indeed shaky at times.

Keep that in mind, then, and discuss it.

He has decided to walk. The body instantly knows when the decision is made. A prudent understanding of the need for safety is wise, and built-in— but no animal or person can operate fully under constant implied threats. The sense of safety can be amplified by a concentration upon the moment. And by the realization that those feared threats are indeed imaginary, and self-created.

Ruburt might go on television for example 50 times—to be met by applause, acclaim and understanding, but in his reality, imaginatively, he would be met by scorn and derision. He need never go on television, but he must understand that the safety factor is built-in, and is dependable

If he understands that, then he has full freedom and full safety.

Again, he does not have to feel—and he should not feel—that ideally he should be a public personality, going abroad to sell our ideas. That kind of personality would not be the kind to get this particular kind of information, or this kind of particular session to begin with.

(9:45.) Ruburt's fears gave him a black-or-white attitude; he must be public or private. There are many gradations between the two that would suit him quite well. What he is feeling now is the natural energy that comes through his physical being.

A few remarks, before we close for the evening.

There is no doubt Ruburt has made a breakthrough—and so have you, in terms of your ideas—for what I call illustrated Seth material. For you will find that you are uniting abilities, so that writing and painting no longer seem "opposing" abilities, with a distance between them. You will find that they are both creative arms of your basic psychic being, and that both abilities will be sharpened and fulfilled as a result.

Have Ruburt continue reading the session each morning as he has been doing, and look forward to further events for your autumn fest. You will also find your own dreams giving you material.

End of session and a fond good evening.

("Thank you very much, Seth. Good night."

(9:51 PM. Jane ended up glad she had the session. I suggested she read it daily for a while along with the others she reviews.

(Seth's reference to "illustrated Seth material" stems from ideas I've mentioned to Jane recently. I've had them for some time, actually, and they involve either black-and-white or color illustrations for some of my own psychic adventures, perhaps to be used in a work like Through My Eyes. *I wouldn't mind doing some work on the project when I finish "Unknown" Reality this weekend, along with other things in the works. One advantage would be that it would unite the art and writing aspects—particularly paintings of some of my dreams.)*

DELETED SESSION
OCTOBER 25, 1978 9:26 PM WEDNESDAY

(Last Saturday I mailed the last four sessions for Volume 2 of "Unknown" Reality to Prentice-Hall, and this week I've already finished up Chapter 1 for Psyche.

(Yesterday at the dentist's I learned through X-ray that I have two bad teeth on the lower right jaw that must be taken out. This after the pendulum had insisted many times over the past few weeks that the teeth were perfectly all right. At the same time, they've bothered me fairly often. My pendulum told me often that the teeth were responding to my negative projections that the two volumes of "Unknown" weren't going to make much of an impression in the mundane world, no matter what we said or did.

(In view of the massive contradiction here, I asked that Seth explain tonight what happened. I also wanted to do some pendulum work with Jane, and wanted to understand the situation before we started with her. I still had faith in the pendulum, since I've obtained many good results.

(Jane hoped for some material on herself. She's kept up her walking daily—six times each day—and also exercises twice a day on the bed. She reports feelings of progress on both counts, although she gets depressed sometimes. Her performance in the bathroom is also considerably improved.

Now *(rather loudly:)* the pendulum.

The pendulum can be used effectively under certain conditions. It allows some communication between the conscious and the "unconscious" portions of the self. It allows a <u>certain kind</u> of black-or-white, yes-or-no communication, with a little leeway toward a "maybe" now and then.

It does not allow of course for a full range of communication. It responds to the questions as they are asked, but it responds even more to the unspoken questions or feelings beneath.

For one thing, dependable overall use of the pendulum would <u>ideally</u> entail some moments each day, so that rapport could be established under even circumstances, without the pressure, say, of wanting to know about a problem or a symptom. <u>Ideally</u>, you should relax yourself as much as possible first—a light trance, for example, gives much more dependable results – but the mind should be stilled. You should go into a kind of neutral drive.

The pendulum has been used for a variety of purposes in various cultures —where, however, diviners from childhood have been trained to use such an instrument. When your mind is confused, and when you are quite concerned over a given problem, then you do not dip down far enough, say, into the psychic level.

You did not want the teeth to be bad—natural enough. The level you reached was one that responded to that fear, that perhaps the teeth were bad. You say that of course you wanted to know the truth—but the pendulum responded to the part of you that was afraid, by trying to soothe your fears, as for example a mother might say "No, do not worry, everything will be all right," while on the other hand she might be making rapid calculations as to what should be done, but first she will soothe the child.

Had you been more relaxed when using the pendulum, "it" would not have needed to soothe your fears, and would have realized that you were quite capable of learning the answer. The fact is that a "yes" answer—<u>at that point</u>— would not have particularly helped you—a fact known to the unconscious, of course. When using the pendulum, it is a good idea to mentally place a distance between your conscious mind and the pendulum, in which fears are allowed to dissolve, so that body and mind are smooth-enough. As far as the teeth are concerned, you are, as you said, surrounded by a sea of beliefs, so that the teeth are considered not long-lasting. If you can think of your body as existing <u>primarily</u> in Framework 2, that might help you separate yourselves from negative beliefs connected with Framework 1, for by such a mental change of view you take the body out of that context.

(9:45.) Addressing a question to yourself, writing it down after relaxing as earlier specified, can often bring excellent results. You write down, then, whatever comes to mind without questioning it. It may be a straight-forward answer —or a poem or a phrase that at first seems to make no sense.

Here, however, you are allowing the subconscious a greater range of expression; or you can ask for such writing to give further background on a yes-

or-no pendulum answer. It does take some time to understand why the pendulum answers as it does, but it will be responding not only to your question but to the greater framework and the emotional circumstances connected with it. It is very difficult, when you are honestly concerned, to then be <u>unconcerned</u> as you work with the pendulum—and yet, for the best results you must attain the state of mind in which you let the answers flow, unconcerned as to whether the answer is yes or no. Otherwise your very concern affects the results, of course, and the pendulum will "treat" your fear first.

In the case of the teeth in particular, the pendulum's answer was not "devious." Had there been considerable danger for example, that danger would have overridden other circumstances in your case. Sometimes, however, fear is so great that the unconscious begins soothing processes, for the healing process depends upon them. Do you understand the difference?

("Yes."

(9:50.) Now give us a moment.... (Eyes closed.) The letter I wrote to [Michael] Kosok does indeed apply, and in its way so does the article about the psychologist that Ruburt was telling you about.

Your assumptions about reality become reality. As long as you are dealing with Framework 1 only, there will seem to be no platform of an objective or subjective nature that will allow you to view reality in any other way than the way it appears to be. You do indeed have to change all of your assumptions—and while living in a world that <u>seems</u> to work by different rules than yours—nor can you as yet make all of your own rules work, so to speak. Only here or there do you see a window of insight, a clearing of the fog.

The psychologist believed most heartily in his theory of mental disintegration with age, and he set out to prove that he was right, bringing about self-predictive difficulties. Yet the theory, more or less fit into Framework 1 beautifully. Psychology did not challenge him. No difficulties were thrown in his way. The ideas that I am advocating find challenge on side, and you try to implement them—again—amid a tumultuous ocean of counter-beliefs.

Yet the way of your own growth and development demands and yearns for such expansion, and your experiences serve to point others in the proper direction.

(10:04.) Give us a moment.... It will help also if once a day you mentally place your existence in Framework 2. Simply state that you do so—but the reminder will serve as excellent suggestion, and put a mental distance between you and the world's beliefs.

There will be some acceleration in the popularity of our books in the next few years—but more than that, you should both be ready to gain a greater understanding of Framework 2 and of the Codicils, which are highly important. It takes some considerable psychological footwork, and yet the direction of your lives is now leading toward certain developments that were inherent from the beginning. This has to do with cycles of learning and understanding, in which maturity is highly important.

Ruburt's follow-up of the experiences in *Politics* will continue. But he needed the time between.

I am pleased with his progress physically, and with his determination. You are both finishing one cycle and beginning another, which will be most satisfying and creative.

In like circumstances with the pendulum, you might ask it: "Are you saying this to calm my fears?"

(*10:10.*) Give me a moment.... You will have breakthroughs in all areas of your private and joint concerns. I would like you to try to feel the energy of Framework 2 in your daily lives, by reminding yourselves of its existence rather frequently—and again, by <u>looking</u> for hints and clues of its existence, for when you do they appear. When you do not, it can <u>seem</u> as if you are locked in Framework 1. Look to all events then, and for their interweaving quality.

Do you have a question?

(*"I guess not."*)

Then I bid you a fond good evening—

(*"Thank you, Seth."*)

—and do not be bothered by your pendulum-itis.

(*"Okay. Good night."*

(*10: 14 PM. Seth wrote the letter to Michael Kosok on July 28, 1975, in the 752nd session. Coupled with the letter is a treatise written by Jane herself, which contains excellent material on how our perceptions form our reality, from that of electrons on up. It is really very good, and a work that I'd completely forgotten about; I see now that it should have been incorporated into "Unknown" Reality somewhere. It concerns the ideas that concepts, as well as our senses, act as programmers of reality. It deals very well with how we create our scientific views of the universe. Jane told me yesterday, when she found it in an old notebook, that although she wrote it, it "certainly came from Seth."*

(*The article about the psychologist creating his own reality, featuring his own mental deterioration, is in the latest issue of* Human Nature *magazine—November 1978. We've heard of him before—Donald Hebb, now 72—and his own story is a classic case of self-suggestion over the years.*)

DELETED SESSION
NOVEMBER 1, 1978 9:11 PM WEDNESDAY

(Tomorrow I mail to Prentice-Hall chapters 7 and 8, plus the Intro, for Jane's Psyche. *I've already started work on Chapter 9, out of the 11 making up the book.*

(Jane had no questions, relying instead upon Seth to come through with pertinent information about her present physical condition, which continues to show improvement. She continues and extends her walking each day, her exercises, etc.

(Today we received probably 30 letters from Prentice-Hall, some of which were dated in early October. We don't know why the delay, but the batch makes up for what we'd taken to be a drop in the volume of mail over the last month; Jane had worried about falling sales, or some such thing. She wrote impressions on the back of each envelope, and of the first few she checked out, found some good "hits." At the same time, by session time she was quite upset and irritable—appalled, really—at the content of some of the letters she'd read—this, we agreed, because we usually would focus more on the one negative letter compared to the ten positive ones—and by far most of them were very positive, friendly, sometimes even adulatory. A few mentioned the articles in the Village Voice.

(Seth goes into a couple of other topics also, which I'll do notes for at the time of mention.)

Good Evening.

("Good evening, Seth.")

Now: Ruburt once went door-to-door selling cosmetics. He wrote about his experiences in an unpublished novel.

Anonymously, he visited many homes, and saw the dissatisfactions, the panics, the difficulties that he knew no cosmetics could remedy.

You are not selling cosmetics now, and now Ruburt does not go door-to-door, but people come to you either physically or through their correspondence, and now you have far more to offer. You are not trying to pretty-up the world. You are trying to <u>restructure</u> the daily experience of the people who live in it.

Ruburt once received a few interesting pages from a world view, in which the author spoke, in archaic terms, of being a person who was a "life-taster," sent by God to taste the quality of man's experience, so that God might know what new ingredients might be added.

Now the species does have its life-tasters, rising always out of any given time to check on the overall quality of life, to see what new ingredients should be added—what new directions should be followed, what new ideas or inventions must be planted for future harvest.

Some people write to you in their triumphs and in their despairs, giving you, all-in-all, a library of unique, private reading matter, capsule biographies of the people of your time and country. This provides you with a far more comprehensive picture than, for example, any TV series could, or any <u>neutral</u>, scholarly study of hypothetical human beings.

The private letters, while indeed private, are in a strange fashion also a public outpouring of emotions, for those people of course make up the public. They write to you, or to me, but the questions are really addressed to the universe via this address.

They represent people's deepest yearnings, exaltations, and hopes. They are meant as samplers, spread out before you, examples of the varieties of present human experience. Most correspondents do not really expect you or me to solve their problems for them—but the hope is there that somehow the problems <u>can</u> be solved, and that the problems themselves are important.

(9:27.) Your evolutionary science, combined with your psychologists, so served to rob men and women of a sense of dignity and meaning that their problems and difficulties were <u>in a way</u> depersonalized. For example, they became part of the species' natural aging processes, as per your psychologist's article. It would make no difference who or what you were. The problem, say, of senility, would be an objective phenomenon that happened to you as a result of the body's slowing down. Certain mental problems would be called schizophrenic —period—with little attempt being made to understand that a certain unique individual had drastic problems differentiating between realities.

(Here Seth refers to an article by Donald Hebb, a Canadian psychologist, who wrote in Psychology Today for November, 1978 about the decline in his own cognitive abilities. He was busily tracing these out as he aged—he's now 74—in order to <u>prove out his own theory</u> of aging and senility, about which he's evidently written extensively. He makes no reference in his writing to the part the negative suggestions he constantly gives himself may have to do with his growing forgetful state—rather amazing, we'd say. The man is regarded as a leading authority, unfortunately; we wonder how many students he's inculcated with the same negative thinking over the years of his teaching career. The article is on file.)

People felt depersonalized beneath labels, so that they were told: "Oh, yes, you are a victim of ulcers, or anxiety attacks, or whatever," while the very personal suffering portion of their beings was ignored. So to some extent many people write for an acceptance of their individuality—even if that includes severe problems—and you both must indeed be struck by the vitality and uniqueness of human nature. It does not mean at all that you should concentrate upon the problems people write you about. Yet even those serve as a stimulus to these sessions, and spur you to seek further answers.

It is highly important, again, that you remember the context in which the letters are written, and the great thrust of creativity that supports the world. I must remind you both that peoples' good intent, their constructive creativity, their desire "to do better," is far stronger, far more vital and all-pervading than any of their negative qualities—or, quite simply, you would not have a world, in your terms.

The honesty and the good intent of most of the people holds the world together. The letters are meant as an education. Learn what you can from them.

(9:41.) Give us a moment.... Ruburt is doing very well. His intent is to walk, and finally to walk normally. He has handled the discomfort well, as the various portions of the body come into use again.

There are developments nearly ready, and I want him to remember once again the playfulness of creativity at all levels, including the physical. Peoples' problems may be source material, but you must not dwell on them. They must be turned off, so that the creative abilities can transform them in their own way.

(9:45.) Give us a moment.... You should also remember that each person is also immersed in Framework 2. The good intent and the creativity that individuals may at times be unable to express adequately, still exists and enriches the psychological atmosphere.

Now *(President)* Carter is a man of good intent. He is very cleverly trying to appeal to the <u>misdirected</u> good intent of Sadat and Begin, and by doing so to redirect the policies of the world. At the same time he must deal with the chicanery of politics itself, and the face-saving devices known so well to religion and politics both.

Carter was a cardinal in the 13th or 15th centuries—offhand, I am not sure which—then creatively unprincipled, comfortably lecherous, but he knew how to deal with politicians. And now he dons the psychological garb of a prince of the church.

You are lucky, in that his character is not given to fanaticism, but is tempered in that regard. He will have his finger in too many pies, while a fanatic concentrates unduly on one.

I expect more creative developments at all levels on Ruburt's part. I suggest he does some poetry. Do you have a question?

(I thought for a moment. "Why was Tam so upset about "Unknown" *Reality being too long?")*

Give us a moment.

He was not upset in that regard. He was upset with Prentice on some other matters, and then began to worry that *"Unknown"* might be too long — might run into difficulties. Tam likes to please, so often he runs into problems if he tries to please too many people at once.

End of session —

("Okay.")

— and a fond good evening.

("Thank you. The same to you."

(9:58 PM. "Jesus Christ, that was short," Jane exclaimed, looking at the clock, "but it doesn't feel short...."

(Seth's information on President Carter was unexpected by us, since we hadn't asked for anything like it. However, it fits in with much of our questioning of late, in connection with the Middle East peace talks these past few months, and the behavior of the three who met at the summit, held at Camp David: Carter, President Sadat of Egypt, and Prime Minister Begin of Israel. Recently Jane and I found it the height of irony that Begin and Sadat were jointly awarded the Nobel Peace Prize— evidently, we sarcastically concluded, because after thirty years of fighting Israel and Egypt weren't shooting at each other—at least for the moment.

(Perhaps the most upsetting or enraging part of such behavior is that the best our society can do is to reward men for such actions. A clear indication of where we're at as a world society, and of how far we have to go.

(Another point I want to mention in connection with Seth's material earlier in the session on psychology: His reference on page 3 to "evolutionary science" stems probably from our reading lately an article on Robert Jastrow, an astronomer connected with NASA. Jastrow cites the big bang theory of the creation of the universe as a proven fact, whereas it's only the latest theory, as far as we know. The article, in Penthouse *for November 1978, is on file. In it Jastrow goes on to talk about how silicon-based computer life is going to replace man and his messy emotions—theories quite in keeping with current "scientific" thinking about man's innate worthlessness and his accidental creation. Jastrow thinks we've reached a dead end in terms of evolution. A note: Seth gave an excellent answer to Jastrow's kind of thinking two years ago in either chapter 7 or 8 of* Psyche.

(Both Jastrow and Hebb are brilliant men, I told Jane as we lay in bed after the session last night, and this brought up once again a basic question I have. Simply put, it concerns the fact that our world society is now run by these brilliant men who think that way. I wondered aloud why other brilliant men weren't around who questioned people like Hebb and Jastrow, who told them their ideas were severely limited and distorted, who made a case for the kind of thinking Jane and I believed in. Most discouraging, I tell myself, to see that in our society at this time that's the overwhelming, prevailing view—with no one of stature asking any embarrassing questions. I wanted to know what happened to the loyal opposition, I told Jane. Did it disappear when it found itself badly outnumbered? Did those who could have made

a dent in such mechanistic thinking simply drop out of such fields when they real-
ized what the score was? Or hadn't they ever existed to begin with? Much could be
written about these questions.)

DELETED SESSION
NOVEMBER 8, 1978 8:43 PM WEDNESDAY

(Today I finished editing Chapter 11 of Psyche—Seth's *latest completed book,*
and wrapped it, with Chapter 10, for mailing to Prentice-Hall tomorrow. I am now
caught up with Seth's work, except for whatever may lie ahead with Mass Reality—
but we regard that as current work, still in progress, of course. A strange feeling, after
three years....

(I asked Jane if Seth would comment on my throat difficulty. Lately my throat,
or the roof of the mouth, has been uncomfortable. The pendulum told me yesterday
that it was because I was concerned that our finishing Psyche *this year would give*
us more money, which in turn would mean that our taxes next April would be high-
er —a ridiculous worry, I agree, and quite in keeping with my past attitudes about
money and taxes. I did think I'd learned some things about money and taxes, but
this latest hassle makes me wonder. I was also hesitant to take the pendulum at face
value, after the results achieved regarding the tooth data recently. But I figured I'd
learned from that episode, so decided to try using it again.

(We also agreed to try to get something for Frank Longwell, who has embroiled
himself in a bind with taxes, business, "the Edgecomb affair," and related troubles,
mostly unknown to us until very recently.

(Jane continues her physical improvements—especially in the walking area,
which has improved noticeably just in the last week. She hoped Seth would comment
further.

(A few notes, rather than at the end of the sessions:On Thursday, November 9,
I had the two teeth extracted by Paul O'Neill—a difficult time indeed, but after an
uncomfortable night and morning, am recovering as expected. I am glad it is over,
needless to say. Further restorative, "positive" capping is planned.... Tam is due next
Thursday, bringing the copyedited Seven *with him.... No sooner had I returned*
home Thursday after the extractions, than Jane told me Eleanor Friede wanted to
visit this Saturday. We said okay, hoping I'd feel better by then. So it's Friday night
as I type this material. The face feels better. Jane and I hardly think it coincidental
that Tam and Eleanor will be here within a few days of each other. Besides books
both have in the works of Jane's, what other reasons could have caused them to decide
on almost simultaneous visits, we wonder....)

Good evening.

(*"Good evening, Seth."*)

Dissertation: taxes, indulgence, age, and beliefs—that is the headline *(with amusement)*.

Now: in your country, generally speaking, rich and poor alike are provided with a multitude of services—many of course that are taken for granted.

The rich cannot buy a better light bulb than the poor—though they may have chandeliers galore, and electricity flows in your country through the poorest and richest areas as well. The rich and poor alike are provided with fire protection and police protection. The rich do not have purer water than the poor. Rich and poor alike walk down the same city streets. The same street does not suddenly become gold beneath the foot of the rich man and woman—and potholes in city, state, or government roads are felt alike by the tires of the Cadillac and the lowly Volkswagen.

The sewer pipes carry away drainage from apartment houses and mansions and from trailers as well, eventually, and all of that must be paid for by the people.

When you were a young man in New York City, bringing in the cash, you paid your taxes without a qualm. After you and Ruburt met, you had little-enough money for some time, as you tried to find your way, and you had little taxes at all. You had enough to eat, and a warm apartment, so you were hardly deprived—either of you.

Though you paid little taxes, the fire and police protection were not withdrawn, and all of the services continued. Later it seemed that the two of you made your way alone almost as aliens in your society, couched only by your own joint courage and determination. Then, when you began to make decent money, you resented giving it to the government—for the reasons just given, and because the government, it seemed, was built upon beliefs with which you could find no accord. So why should you so support it, when all that you had achieved was gained in spite of your society?

Yet that government did indeed couch you, and now through your taxes you couch other younger people, who cannot contribute as yet. There is no doubt that the very wealthy abuse the system, and yet all in all it is a good one, couching the young while they learn, and is so doing, providing a basis from which new beliefs can indeed emerge.

There are many on the edge of the system who are being carried, of course, and who also misuse the privilege. Despite that, however, at a physical level, your money is turned to help others at one level, while your work allows you the freedom of creativity, and the <u>privilege</u> of helping at a still higher level.

(9:00.) Ruburt rather good-naturedly appreciates being in the position of paying taxes, since his upbringing was at the taxpayers' expense. I know you understand this—but carried to the extreme, that resentment would allow you barely enough to live on, and you actually would refuse to make money, because you so resent the high taxes connected with a good living. Yet financial security is important to both of you, because it allows you the freedom to create as you choose, and to follow this path. Yet remember that for all of its failings, your peace of mind is also the result of the American services that were available when you did not have much money, as they are now.

Let us change our viewpoint, and consider someone who thinks of financial security as a threat—or rather, believes that overall it is damaging to initiative. We come then to Frank Longwell.

He battles his beliefs about age, yet he is frightened that with age comes complacency, stagnation. All of his life he has sought comradeship with others. He enjoys the easy commerce of the marketplace, the unpredictability of being a contractor.

He has, particularly in the past, been almost contemptuous of those with regular habits, regular ways. He has sought out to some extent the strange and the bizarre, and he believes, now, as he did earlier, in the importance of conflict as a way of keeping a man on his toes. One part of him loathes the idea of security. As he reached 50, his beliefs about age rose to the forefront. This was the time of caution and danger, when a man could retire, settle for security, give in to complacency—or even become a gentleman farmer—as he was at times tempted to do *(with amusement)*.

Now what does youth mean to many? A time of conflict, and emotional turmoil. Certainly the young are usually poor, rather than rich, and what is best to shock a complacent mind out of its complacency—its <u>feared</u> complacency? For Frank was not complacent, but feared that age would make him so—hence a conflict. Its very emotional vividness tells him he is <u>not</u> old and complacent, and its financial elements certainly make <u>clear</u> to him that he is not seeping in elderly security. No indeed—he is pushed toward action.

(9:16.) He likes the farmer image, but he is afraid that being a farmer would cut him off from the commerce with the marketplace that he now enjoys, and the hearty comradeship. His feelings about money are mixed. He is slightly contemptuous of it, while liking what it can buy. He is slightly contemptuous of the wealthy, or those in social positions. He enjoys needling them, while at the same time traveling in their circle.

He has the same feelings toward authority, which is connected to past feelings about his father. So not paying the taxes allows him to give the boot to authority, while it still seems he has a good excuse.

Rest your fingers.

(9:22.) He lives above his means for certain reasons—because he enjoys a certain kind of self-indulgence, and the immediate satisfaction of desires, but also a kind of backhand slap against the socially prominent or wealthier associates—that he can live as well as they.

He is overall good-natured, of good intent, as ready to serve the indulgences of others as his own. But he is not what you call a businessman. He is too warm, in this particular context, now—he wants to be liked and approved of, so he lets others take advantage of him—and when he knows this it makes him angry. Yet he continues on the pattern.

That is enough for now. I hope it will be some help to him—but he need not "scare himself to death" in order to prove that he is alive and vital. He is at his prime of his life.

(9:28.) Now: Ruburt's ribs and shoulder blades have bothered him simply because they are being stretched in new ways. His attitude has completely changed for the better. It is this of course that makes the walking possible, and that is releasing new energy from Framework 2. You can indeed expect more frequent improvements, and I will give you whatever current information is helpful. I will also shortly, with <u>everyone's</u> permission, return to our book.

Do you have questions?

("Why did I translate the tax resentment into the voice or mouth difficulty?")

Simply a beautiful symbol of communication, for you wanted to voice your resentment again, but covered it over. And with Frank in terms of probabilities, the Edgecomb adventure may still go through—but Frank and his brother each gave the gentleman permission to act as he has. Frank wanted that excitement. To a lesser extent now, the same applies to Eve, for she likes her unpredictability coated just a bit with some security. But this time of emotional turmoil takes their minds off the fact that their children are grown, and adds a new challenge—one that convinces them that life is still exciting, that you must be on your toes. It even brings them closer together.

End of session, unless you have questions.

(I told Seth we had no more, and he bid us a "hearty good evening" at 9:43 PM.)

DELETED SESSION
NOVEMBER 15, 1978 4:00 PM WEDNESDAY

(I've spent perhaps one of the most uncomfortable weeks of my life, since I had the two back teeth extracted last Thursday, as noted in last week's deleted session. I've learned some more about the whole situation through the pendulum, and asked Jane if Seth could comment in what I expected would be tonight's regular session.

(Eleanor Friede visited Saturday and Sunday, as planned, and went over parts of Emir *with Jane. We've learned that Jane doesn't take to justifying each line of her work, so we'll see what this means for future books with Delacorte, if any. Tam is due tomorrow afternoon, Thursday, and is bringing with him the copyedited* Seven Two, *as far as we know. We expect his visit to be pleasant.*

(In the mail today Jane received a book I'd sent for at her request a few days ago; then we'd both forgotten about it. It was advertised in the National Enquirer: *"A Doctor's Proven New Home Cure for Arthritis," by Giraud W. Campbell, Doctor of Osteopathy. Jane began to read through it at once, out of curiosity if nothing else, and discovered that it called for a very rigid diet. Were she to follow it, practically all we eat would be forbidden. It contained nothing about beliefs—and yet had evidently helped many. We discussed it to some extent. Later this afternoon, Jane said that she'd been getting feedback on the book from Seth and that she could have a session....*

(With amusement and surprise:) Good <u>afternoon</u>.

("Good afternoon, Seth.")

Now: each body is of course individual, and while there must be similarities in the ways bodies utilize substances, still there are differences—and sometimes the differences can be more than considerable. Not only in the case of a given substance in many bodies, for example, but any given body may utilize any given substance in quite diverse fashions, according to varying circumstances.

The dietary methods given in the book Ruburt read have indeed worked for many, and for the following reasons: as you suspected, a kind of conversion was attained. The people involved first of all had been told by doctors—medical doctors—that they themselves had no control over their own disease, that the symptoms could be lessened somewhat—<u>perhaps</u>—but that there was no hope for recovery.

They were frightened and angry, their condition such that they were often in constant pain. When they visited the author, however, he was optimistic and brusque. He said "You do indeed have control," and his personal manner was such that he convinced them. Now that was all to the good. They were given hope and thrown back to a feeling of self-reliance.

Now, however, the story becomes trickier. The patients had various beliefs, of course, behind their conditions. Many felt unworthy. Because of this many were unable to express normal aggression. Some were frightened of the world, and so forth. The author gives such people a specific enemy, or evil: no more must they be battered with formless fears, but these become gathered together and focused into the dietary area. Unhealthy foods become the villain.

This means that there is nothing intrinsically wrong with the person, which many of them have believed. They are good (as of course they are). The trouble is what they take into their system. Those who are cured are at a certain state when they approach the author, as mentioned earlier, feeling helpless after medical treatments that did not work—feeling that there is something wrong with them. They are in their own eyes "bad"—and in one way or another that kind of belief was behind the condition to begin with.

(4:13.) To that degree, the author offers them salvation: "You are good, but the food is bad." The fasting is symbolic, as is the emphasis upon enemas and elimination, for these are meant to flush the impurities from your system.

You are as empty, symbolically, open and vacant, as a newborn child, ready now only to partake of God's pure foods, determined to avoid technology's poisonous effects. You are taking in goodness, then, and becoming better and better. You accept dietary limitations—say a limited environment of food—rather than the limitations earlier felt in motion. The exterior environment opens up. Oftentimes the previously withheld normal aggression now can be legitimately expressed—against the food companies, the technological environment, the medical profession, and so forth.

The cured person becomes a convert to a new way of life. When there are no cures, or patients do not respond, or they slide back into old ways, the doctor-author simply says they are not ready to take the steps necessary, or they have taken them half-heartedly. And many who are cured, of course, come down with other conditions if they have not succeeded in identifying their own fears sufficiently with the author's.

The body is amazingly capable of turning what seem to be toxic substances into beneficial ones, and any body carries within it quite harmlessly all kinds of seemingly deadly viruses that in a healthy person add to overall body balance and health.

(Intently, and with humor:) I am somewhat familiar with food before canning and refrigeration, and there were maggots everywhere, and feces and dirt, and sanitation was largely unknown. So in certain terms God's fruits and vegetables are not entirely pure in spiritual terms, as many food faddists imply.

All chemicals are natural. They come from what was already available to you—you cannot make a chemical except from substances or elements you already have. In certain terms, now, some natural diets of five centuries ago could kill you today, though they lacked any technologically produced chemicals.

You tell your body what to do with the food you eat—and when you are in a technological civilization, it is rather foolhardy to convince yourselves that your food is poisoned.

Such attitudes may be part of your methods of learning, to show you that technology should only go so far. Period.

(4:28.) Now give us a moment.... Your diets are adequate. You could stand more green vegetables. Fresh potatoes are good. You do fairly well, however, with a moderate diet. Ruburt does not take to citrus fruits. That is simply characteristic of his body.

He started off very well with the walking and exercises and you have helped him. You both hit a period when for the moment your work was done —a time of creative regeneration.

(To me:) You needed some rest, but you do not really approve of it, the idea of playful free time seems to you somehow unvirtuous. At certain levels— not all—you resented Eleanor's visit, and Tam's, because you wanted so to begin new projects. You felt that Ruburt was coming along well. And you did not want anything to upset the apple cart. This simply fills out your pendulum material.

The difficulty after your dentist visit was partially natural enough, but exaggerated for these reasons, so that the discomfort gave you an acceptable reason for resting—while still being virtuous in your own eyes.

Now Ruburt is doing well. The sudden easy improvements you noted, however, as with the speed (in walking), came when he allowed himself some playful rest, and when he kept his spirits up. The point of power daily was of much benefit. These improvements will continue. He has determined not to backtrack, for example; but both of you must remember that creativity is playful—that is, that you must not try too hard, that you mentally look the other way now and then, and not watch the pot boil all of the time.

Let Ruburt write something—anything—as a creative playful exercise daily, without caring whether or not it will develop into a book.

(4:35. We were interrupted by a UPS delivery of books from Eleanor Friede— so quickly had she gotten them on their way to us after her visit over the weekend. Resume at 4:43.)

You forget many of the things I have told you, or you ignore them.

Healthy bodies do not need 8 hours sleep, and after 6-and-a-half hours many become quite restless. In Ruburt's condition this tendency is exaggerated.

When you sleep longer than 7 hours in particular, his muscles protest, and this causes much of the morning difficulty. He ignores the message, and sleeps, muttering in protest at the discomfort, and then it takes him another hour or so after breakfast, simply because he did not move the body when it was ready to move.

The sensations in the hips and the legs represent that urge toward motion. Energy wants to be distributed through motion down through the legs. Standing up will help, stamping the feet, or whatever. He should feel free any-time to walk, and if it is ten times a day, the both of you should be grateful—for he continues his progress. Before long he will begin to navigate somehow alone.

The entire rib area is stretching because of his exercises and walking. The discomfort there will gradually pass, as indeed other symptoms <u>have</u> since he began his walking. Standing by the breezeway table, leaning on it, is excellent, though this should be gently done at first.

The point of power should be continued. The companionship of proof-reading will help you both if you do it together. You became anxious and breathed quicker then through the mouth, as you became worried about your teeth—and the habit causes the difficulty in your mouth.

Unless you have questions, that is the end of the session.

(*Both of us dreamed about* The Word *last night—we saw the third episode on TV.*

(*I simply wondered if Seth had any comments.* The Word, *by Irving Wallace, is a book on the discovery of an unknown gospel by the brother of Christ, James the Just. It's a powerful story, although evidently written by Wallace in the contemporary genre of popular fiction these days. We thought the television adaptation contained many fine things, though—a number of excellent individual performances, although the story line was hard to follow over four episodes. Certainly neither of us had fig-ured on following the series through the four nights. Many of the scenes, filmed on location about the Mediterranean area, were very evocative to us.*)

I have nothing to say—though you may note that we are having an early session, so that you can watch the program if you want to. For you both, it has implications about the distortions of religion in its organized format, and other implications that will come to your own minds.

End of session.

(*4:54 P.M. I thought it rather humorous, now, when Jane denied having the session early so that we would be free to watch the last episode of* The Word *if we wanted to. Actually, I didn't think that <u>was</u> the reason.... but rather the strong feed-*

back from Seth that had resulted from her reading the book described at the start of the session.

(The talk about the Wallaces reminded me, however, that a few months ago Irving Wallace's daughter, Amy, had sent Jane a copy of her new book on psychic phenomena—particularly on healing.

(It's now Friday morning as I finish typing the session. Tam has been here and gone, leaving the copyedited Seven Two *with Jane. My mouth feels somewhat better, although still tender and somewhat swollen in the lower jaw. I still feel quite tired at times, interspersed with bouts of energetic activity. We're kicking ideas around.*

(Seth's comments about my breathing are very interesting. I've begun keeping my mouth shut, and the throat difficulty has lessened, although not disappeared yet.

(Besides helping Jane go over Seven Two *I am going to make a chart for her to keep records of her walking, exercising, and "free, playful, creative writing," as Seth put it.)*

DELETED SESSION
NOVEMBER 22, 1978   9:00 PM WEDNESDAY

(I asked that Seth comment on my tooth-extraction hang-ups—involving the attendant soreness and my reactions to the whole affair—as well as the mouth-breathing difficulty. The latter is much improved, incidentally, and the gum is healing okay as far as I can tell. Yet I still wondered whether I wasn't asking that the healing take place too rapidly, considering the large cavities in the gum to be filled.

(Jane wanted Seth to discuss her own progress—which continues, if too slowly for her. Tonight, using the typing table as a "walker," she walked the fastest yet during her exercise period with it. A good sign.

(We also speculated that Seth might refer to what may be called the "Jonestown Affair," or something like it. This had erupted in a mass suicide, involving over 400 Americans, in the community of Jonestown in what was formerly British Guyana, in South America. A US congressman was also murdered, along with media network people, etc. The sect, called the People's Temple, had been created by Jim Jones, a charismatic fundamentalist who had eventually been hounded out of the U.S. for many reasons, to then set up his town for his devoted religious followers in Guyana. The whole thing had a weird unbelievability about it, as Jane and I watched the TV reports and read—and saved – the newspaper accounts.

(Actually, the affair is a perfect example of much of the material Seth has been going into in his latest book on the mass culture and mind. To Jane and me, it seemed as if his material was being enacted in real life as the ideal demonstration of Seth's

material. The tragedy, if one wants to call it that, would make an excellent book in itself, and many probably will be written about it. It certainly furnishes ideal subject matter for the media. We also think that these books-to-come will not manage to penetrate the forces behind the phenomenon nearly as well as Seth could, but that Seth won't be carrying out such a project, either.

(I haven't started any new creative ventures yet, although I've done considerable work filing, organizing records, etc., to set the stage for whatever develops. I will soon be painting again. We expect to receive the copyedited Volume 2 of "Unknown" Reality *by December 7, and this is to keep us occupied until Christmas. At least, Tam doesn't want us putting it in the mail until after the Christmas rush is over.)*

Good evening *(whispering.*

("Good evening, Seth.")

Now: the message is clear: fanaticism can lead to mass suicide and murder.

Social injustices can cause circumstances in which people will give up reason, logic, and personal responsibility to follow a leader who offers them protection from an unsafe universe.

The message is meant to make all question who call themselves religious people. It is there for *(Prime Minister)* Begin *(of Israel)* and *(President)* Sadat *(of Egypt)*. It is there as an early Christmas present for those who use Christianity in fanatical ways. It is there also for all political leaders.

The message blazes across your television screens at a time when fundamental religion has begun to sprout again, both eastern and Christian. The warning points in particular to young people, showing in capsule form and in exaggerated horror the ultimate ends of such fanaticism when it is allowed to play itself out.

Capitalism has its faults, and democracy has its potential dangers, as has <u>any</u> kind of government. Often mere lip service is given to the beliefs, but they exist. There has been a strong distaste among your people for the blind following of public figures. Your politicians are scoffed at as often as they are honored, and their human failings are examined sometimes with glee—overall, a good healthy policy on the part of the people.

Your religious leaders have freedom to say what they want to, and they have all of technology's advances in communications at their service. As per James, when democracy does not work, people look elsewhere. Jones's followers were the disinherited, the disenchanted, the poor and struggling, yet many of those people were intellectually gifted and felt their promise cut off.

They were bitter—but more. They were frightened. They could not free their native abilities—many, now. Jones seemed to be their key to the establishment. He was the opener of doors. He had his picture taken with celebrities, and because he was "a religious man," the establishment took it for granted that his aims and policies were good, and that he spoke for those who had no voice otherwise.

He was, of course, a despot, and he did indeed set up his own alienated kingdom. Those that followed him pretended to themselves not to know what they were doing. You make your own lessons, so that these mass suicides and murders are an objective culmination, on those peoples' part, of other, lesser psychological suicides committed on the part of millions who abdicate their personal responsibility in such a way.

(9:20.) Since so many were involved, and since the temple people were their own community, then the symbolism also involves nations. Around the area there was a land of law, so that the situation was contained, and the temple people were aliens in that land. There are international implications, however.

The fact that these were Americans is indeed a shock, and a shock that will make religious Americans question the nature of their own beliefs.

The individual either exists for the sake of the society, or the society exists for the sake of the individual. So it seems. Either road, however, brings its own difficulties. An enlightened position would be somewhat different, for a reasonably free individual will automatically want to aid his fellow man, and you will have a society of individuals fully functioning, and that would mean you would have fully functioning social organizations.

Religious concepts that stress obedience over expression can also bring about civic disorder.

(9:27.) Ruburt has had many excellent signs, particularly in his bathroom behavior, this week—as old patterns of posture were broken, and new methods of walking and so forth were tried out. There is some anticipatory motion, in that while in one position the body anticipates new motions—better ones—that it cannot as yet take.

Those motions may be taken a few days or a week later in actuality. Ruburt feels the sensations, however. Certain portions of the body have been carried along, so to speak. They are now coming into better motion. The main point is for him to trust the process of healing—and for you to reinforce that belief, for it will in itself accelerate the process. That should be underlined.

(With some amusement:) You are both experiencing what should be a natural time of rest—not a low point. Had you been working on "Unknown," you would have had far less difficulty with your extractions. Your mind would have been on the book, and the extractions considered distractions—annoying and to be put aside.

Again, you equate—both of you—the time of rest as somewhat danger-ous. As if it could lead to all kinds of extravagant leisure, laziness, or as if it made you like everybody else *(with even more amusement)*, for when both of you are not "working," you feel lost without your badges of superiority. You want to show you are too good for creature comfort.

This is an excellent time to try the library together, to lie down on pur-pose to try out-of-bodies, or psy-time. It is an excellent time to see how many enjoyments can be found in the day, to putter creatively. Let Ruburt <u>forget</u> a book for a change, so that creative ideas of all kinds can surface. Be more play-ful in your lives.

Do you have questions?

("No. I guess not." I figured that Seth must be giving a short session for a rea-son, or reasons, so I didn't ask any.)

I will return to my book at your convenience. If you want something to <u>do</u>, sometime, I will do a quickie for you—say four nights a week, of questions and answers—<u>and I will even provide the questions</u>.

I bid you then a fond good evening.

("Thank you very much, Seth."

(9:41 PM. Seth's "quickie" sounds very interesting. I dare say that Jane and I could come up with some questions of our own, too.

(I might add here that the Jonestown affair reminded me at once of the mass suicide of the defenders of the Jewish stronghold of Masada, in the First Century AD, in Israel. But those people had a strong uniting religious faith and tradition behind them. But wait—it gets tricky; The Jonestown people <u>didn't</u>? A death is a death, regardless....)

DELETED SESSION
NOVEMBER 29, 1978   9:07 PM WEDNESDAY

(My two questions for Seth concerned the small lumps on the underside of Jane's left arm, including one on her elbow, and the bright redness of the palms of her hands that I noticed the other day. The color was much subdued at session time tonight. I've noticed it at times before, as well as the lumps or nodules that seemed to move about in the muscular structure of the arms. They seem to be muscular knots. I asked that Seth comment.

(Jane had no specific questions, as usual. She merely wanted Seth to discuss "the whole thing."

(Part of the session grew out of our recent reactions to the televised newscasts,

as well as what we've been reading lately, concerning the mass suicide in Guyana, the shooting of the mayor of San Francisco, problems with inflation, the Middle East — any of what seemed to be an infinite number of ills the species has created for itself. I must remember that my own caustic reactions pass rather quickly—even if they do return—but that they have a considerable effect on Jane. In some fashion, in order to maintain sanity, I end up laughing at what goes on in the world—probably a last resort. But I'm afraid some of my responses affect Jane more deeply, aside from her problems with her own reactions.

(However, I do keep much of what Seth has said on such troubles in mind, even if it doesn't show too well, often. In fact, I think his material and insights into the species' behavior is the only sensible body of material on the subject that can stand questioning and understanding—no small achievement, as I often remind Jane. Yet she can respond deeply to my remarks, which I do curb much more than I used to; then she ends up blue and depressed, which I suppose is the last thing she should do.

(By the same token, I try to keep Seth's material in mind concerning her own challenges and problems, and this has helped enormously. It has certainly freed us from a good amount of worry, no matter what residue is left.

(Whispering:) Good evening.

("Good evening, Seth.")

Now: I have spoken about this before. When you watch, say, the news on television, you must keep in mind several important issues. Despite the perhaps deplorable conditions being televised—whether of wars, massacres, graft, or whatever—the great inventiveness of man's mind is responsible for that technological achievement. And it is an achievement of great import, for the world can no longer hide one portion of itself from another.

Events that appear senseless demand some kind of explanation, and the explanations of the official world no longer content its members. The massacre of the Jews in the Second World War, in the numbers that existed, would not happen now, for the eyes of the world could not be kept out now, as they were then.

The selected newscasts shown in theatres in the Second World War were quite censored, but the aggressive press and its corps do now indeed serve in their own way as an invisible "police force." No country can really keep them out. There will be a television camera somewhere, and the most secret atrocities will find their way into the public eye. There is no longer any assurance of secrecy in the broadest terms, for nefarious acts of politics or government. Man's inventiveness, often a partner to his duplicity, has also invented, then, a method to insure that no crimes can be hidden, and has taken steps to shine a spotlight upon those areas of life that blot man's experience.

Those for example at Jonestown become symbols of social, religious, and political unrest. They died, quite simply, knowing beneath it all that they were not annihilating their consciousnesses, but bringing a given life to a conclusion in protest against certain conditions that exist to some extent among many others.

(Here Seth refers to the mass suicides in Guyana, mentioned in the last session. See the Time Magazine *on file.*

(9:20.) The flaws of religion in its organized form are often far more hidden than those of government. They are here brought into the light—flashed into millions of living rooms. Your sciences, religions, and your culture, has brought you into a peculiar position: "Forget your problems and they will go away." This is considered the most intellectually asinine *(amused)*, Pollyanna-like statement. At best a misleading phrase, encouraging laziness, and at its worst it is considered a cruel misstatement of fact.

How do you solve the problems? Your culture says that you concentrate upon them. Look for evidence of them everywhere. Contrast man's position with an ideal state. Curse your ignorance, and search for evidence of man's sinful nature. And many who do not believe in religion per se certainly believe in man's sinful nature—though perhaps giving it a more scientific name. So your culture believes that by publicizing crimes of whatever nature, you will somehow eradicate them.

Now to some extent, because of beliefs, because of the public's new knowledge through television of new nefarious acts, some governments do refrain from the more spectacular crimes. Overall, however, the concentration upon any problem, upon its negative aspects, automatically increases the problem.

(Heartily:) To concentrate upon probable solutions is something else again.

I say the same thing to you so often because in one way or another I hope to get through the opposite accumulation of seeming evidence to the contrary, for you are everywhere surrounded by it. Forget your problems and they will go away. That almost sounds like the babbling of a child or an idiot.

It certainly sounds <u>un</u>intellectual, like wishful thinking of the most sentimental variety.

Mothers tell children to forget their troubles. The children, not realizing how dumb their poor mothers really are, often do just that—and discover that their problems do indeed disappear. If you worry about the world, you can somehow perhaps save it—or so many people think. If you <u>don't</u> worry about the world, you are considered unfeeling, and it certainly seems ridiculous to imagine that the world can somehow take care of itself, and even remedy whatever damage it seems man has done to it.

But no: it seems that worrying will get you someplace. It provides impetus, and so it does—by promoting further problems.

You are used to thinking, however, that worry is an acceptable method of showing concern for private or public affairs. The best thing you can do for yourself, or your loved ones, or the world, is to stop worrying, and hence release all of the negative thoughts therein generated.

(With much amused irony:) The foolhardy, the brave, the utterly courageous, might even take a step further, and imagine that whatever problem is involved no longer exists, or to pretend that "it will go away," for in any case "it is not as bad as I thought."

Some other more courageous souls might decide to balance their input, and if the news is bad to turn their attention to the joys of the day, which are indeed immediately present.

(9:42.) Now: I can't—nor would I want to—turn you into children again, but you have a natural optimism, both of you—a creature optimism, with which all are innately equipped. That natural optimism is a power in the individual and in the world. It believes in triumph, in pleasant, unpredictable surprises, in unexpected solutions, joyful occurrences. It is like the child's anticipation of Christmas Eve, and it is biologically ingrained.

I have said, again, much of this before—but this is an update. Neither of you do yourselves service by worrying about Ruburt's condition, <u>worrying</u> that it might worsen in the future, or in your old ages, or by stressing its negative aspects.

You might each secretly believe that such worrying will frighten Ruburt enough "to make him do something," and that is hardly the case—for worrying always increases stress. Whenever possible, minimize the impediments in your minds. Now Ruburt has started doing that. At least keep in mind what I have said, for it is true. <u>To the extent</u> that you forget the problem, it will vanish. Physically, Ruburt is improving, as you can see—but he used a stimulus of fear —the fear that otherwise he might be bedridden.

Whenever he remembers Framework 2 there are sudden, significant improvements. I want him to imagine a box. And each day simply to imagine he puts into it a sheet of paper that says "Of course I walk normally." Do it as a joke, or whatever.

Now you remember his ribs hurt him for ten days or so, and that then that discomfort largely vanished. For a while he had trouble in the morning getting the chair out of the bathroom because of the difficulty with the left leg, and that vanished. This is since the exercises began. The left arm for some time was considerably "tied in knots" from the elbow down. It was one hard mass, say, that has largely broken up, leaving you with only the two lumps that change sizes. They are knotted into masses, loose and disintegrating, but presently aggravated by strain as Ruburt's weight on the walking table "bruises" those ligaments and muscles.

The entire area, however, began to release with a large mass breakup after the soreness in Ruburt's ribs, for the ribs "expanded," relieving pressure on that arm.

He will shortly be able to add other exercises in straightening out the knees further, and though he did not tell you, he has now and then tried and felt new loosening. He places his weight often upon his hands, increasing circulation there, bringing about the flush of color, but this only occurs with certain arm motions that suddenly release blood to the hands—that is, that release it more suddenly than he is accustomed to.

Now his sight has not deteriorated. It is potentially as good as ever. People use certain portions of their bodies to reflect stress, and Ruburt did this with the neck areas in particular. With his astigmatism the slightest variations of muscular activity become apparent, so that vision is affected one way or another.

(10:02.) The attitudes I am recommending this evening will greatly help (amused), for the neck area is extremely important, both in the eye condition and the walking. As soon as Ruburt cut down on his worrying for a day or so, he was crowded with creative ideas. He needs your help there—not in ignoring, say, the condition of the world, but by putting that in perspective, and by balancing it out by a determined effort to enjoy each day and to not let your worries minimize simple pleasures. Enjoyments are health-promoting.

Ruburt's box is his box in Framework 2, of course, with a slot for his suggestions. (Louder:) Did I answer all of your questions?

("Yes. Very good.")

I bid you a fond good evening.

("Good night, Seth. Thank you." 10:07. A moment later:)

One note: Framework 2 shows itself in your frame of reference through play, unpredictability, surprises. Now you know that people who simply refuse to accept the existence of clairvoyance, say, will not find any evidence for it. They will not allow it to invade their world, even though they may say they seek such evidence. You must. Therefore, remember Framework 2. Look for signs of its existence, for surprises, for unexpected solutions in any and all areas.

Otherwise you will only be left with the world's "official evidence." You must be prepared to change, to grow, even to give up habits. The old world view, the official one, may still be comforting you, for it is shared by millions. End of session.

    ("Thank you, Seth." 10:12 PM. As I explained to Jane, I too have been making good efforts not to worry....)

DELETED SESSION
DECEMBER 2, 1978 SATURDAY

    (Some members of Jane's "old" ESP class gathered at the hill house of Jane and Rob in Elmira, New York.
    (Dickie read his essay about creativity and commitment.
    (Seth:) Now. The sun shines, the writer writes, the artist paints, the thinker thinks, the dreamer dreams, and each of you, whether you know it or not, naturally follow your own natures. You bloom whether or not you recognize the pattern of your petals. You sing. You are like a trans-species, as Ruburt would say. Something happens when you meet the world, something happens when you meet each other, something happens when you have a child, when you think, when you look at each other. Something happens the moment you are born and the world is different. Because you are, the world is different. It is a world of individuals, and distorting an old historic statement: God must love individuals because he never made anything else. You are not born as members of a nation tied tail to tail. You each are aware of the difference of your thoughts. And when your thoughts meet the world, you change the world. Now, you are also changed by the world since you are not made of concrete. But if I have taught you anything, I hope I have given you the grace to know yourselves to some extent, to recognize that you are indeed, in your way, world changers. For as you change yourselves, as you grow you change the world. The world changes because you are. Now if you listen without listening too hard, in any intimate moment you can hear your molecules shout, if you will forgive me, with their own optimism. Each molecule is its own world. Each molecule is its own world. Your thoughts form worlds. I say what I say and I say more than you hear and yet you hear me silently. When I speak of responsibility, I speak of the cat's responsibility to lift its tail or twirl its ear. No cat says "I must hold my backside in such and such a fashion or I must play with catnip." And yet a cat is a cat, a perfect cat, whether it is flawed or has a broken foot, or whether it can hear or not hear, or whether it is ancient or young. A cat is a perfect cat. Now you can understand that. But in the same way you have a responsibility to be yourselves as a cat has to be itself. To express the joyful creature nature that is your own. And through that expression your spirituality will flower. For it will not flower

if you pretend that the spirit is elsewhere and you are here. So those of you who speak on my behalf, let there be times of boisterous activity. Let there be play. Let there even be time for discord if that is what is needed, but never, and I know you would not, never impose an artificial ceiling of peace. For peace is active *(to Sheri, Rick and Van Zandt.)* And so if there is any message that I have for your students, as usual it is not a quiet one. When you feel your own vitalities fully then that will be understood by your students. And when each person feels and releases their own creativity, *(to Sue)* there will be no need for books about Seth classes, but now there is such a need.

So you have all begun something, have you? And when was it begun? Now in my books and when I speak to you, I use simple words usually. And the people sometimes write asking why I do not give proper methods, that is, more and more instructions as to how to do this and that. So when I say to you let your classes thrill with quality, it is up to you to discover what quality means to you. And when I say to each of you, classes or no, that your lives be lives of quality, of beauty and of truth, I am not about to define beauty or truth for you. That is your challenge. So you will listen to my words and read them through your interpretations. And those interpretations are highly important. *(To Rob:)* Now if there is anything in the universe called good intent, then you have it here.

(Seth withdrew.

(Rick talked about a suggestion for a dream from the Gates of Horn, and that he felt his dream had related to the City. Discussion of Anita Bryant and of the mass cult suicide in Guyana.

*(Seth:)*Now, subject: Anita Bryant. Subject: Jonestown. Subject: Communication of the official consciousness and what it has wrought.

If it were not for television, you would not know much about Anita Bryant, you would not know much about the Reverend Jones, who believed he was God and led (in quotes, out of quotes), "his followers into folly". If it were not for television and technology and the official line of consciousness, you would not know of the fanaticism of Anita Bryant and our Miss America, American apple pie, good religion and all the rest. Now Anita Bryant serves a purpose for all of her distortions, for she presents each person with an exaggerated picture of certain beliefs. She makes each person question the nature of their own beliefs concerning sexuality. And sexuality is not only a personal question. It is not only a question of when to do it, with whom and when and how. Sexuality in your time means what is American. Is it American to be a football hero and a gung-ho male? Is it American to be a homosexual and love poetry or dancing or music or children? Is it a cliché to think that all homosexuals are sensitive and love music, and children? Are there no violent homosexuals and no bastards? Are all stereotyped masculine men that way because they want to be that way, are they forced to hide certain feelings? What are women? How do men consider them? Now Anita Bryant with orange blossoms presents you with all of those questions. And each person who views her on television must look into their own beliefs. And the same applies to our Reverend Jones, and to any fanatic, for the fanatic speaks in exaggerated terms, but he or she speaks beliefs that to some extent each of you hold, but to what degree? And so they are teachers in their way. You may hate them or deride them. And you may say they are fanatics, which they are. But they frighten you, because you know that in your hearts some of their beliefs exist in weaker terms, and where do you draw the line? So even the fanatic serves good purposes. And I will tell you that no one and no fanatic leads masses of people. People follow because they want to and no one leads them. And if you think you are a leader you misunderstand the people, for they are taking you where they want you to go. Only you are taking the responsibility and not them. You form your own reality. All of this, you see, is much trickier than appears at the hundredth or second hundredth or thousandth glance.

(*Van Zandt, who earlier had said he doesn't use Florida citrus juices, was relating Seth's comments about Anita Bryant to Jane.*)

(*Seth:*) Now I wouldn't drink her goddamned orange juice either!!!!

(*[Van Zandt:]* "Good for you."*)

(*When Seth's earlier comments were being related back to Jane, someone remarked that Seth said to look at the Guyana incidents at a thousandth glance.*)

(*Seth:*) You are mistaken; I was speaking about our sessions.

(*[Sheri:]* "Seth, are you still with us, because I waited to express this for a very long time.*)

(*Seth:*) I am indeed.

(*[Sheri:]* "I must express to you how much I love you and say thank you for all that you've done for all of us."*)

(*Seth:*) Now I love you and all of you, and I know that you love me. And I hope that that love is somehow distantly able, distantly, distantly to contain some, some, some, some kindly feeling for people like Anita Bryant. And say for roses who are blighted. Remember, and I do not expect any of you practically in daily life, to hold this as a rule. But remember. It is because you expect so much from people that Anita Bryant and fanatics fall so short. And that is why you are so angry at them. Your love for humanity holds. And you become angry when people do not live up to your expectations of their capabilities. You want them to be better, as you want yourself to be "better" (in quotes). You do not hate anyone that you are not capable of loving. Remember that. I do not expect any of you to be saints. For if you were saints you would not be here. And if I were a saint I would not be here either. But in the vast range of your emotions, leave room for loves that are very distant, so distant and so alien that you do not recognize them. And hold room for the feelings of loss and bitterness and anger that are behind Anita Bryant's statements. And the feelings of lack of worth that power her statements and feelings. It is as if she were a meadow upon which no rain had fallen. Then certainly would she be bitter and cry.

([Rick:] Seth, this is a little changing the subject just a bit, but I've been very interested about your comments about the dream art scientists and mental physicists as being some of the careers that I have been interested in.

(Seth:) Lots of luck!!!

([Rick:] Do you have any other suggestions that you might....because I've been considering this for a while.

(Seth:) Since there are no physical universities, and since I threw out those statements with my own purposes in mind, then it follows that those who are interested must find their own way; and that their imagination and will must drive them to find their own methods. But then people who spook out the universe usually find secret and hidden corners where they can play and work to their heart's content.

([Van Zandt:]: "Could I just say one thing before....?"

([Jane:] "Hold it Van Zandt; I'll get back, okay."

(Seth returned.

([Van Zandt:] "I just want to say that while we were discussing quality earlier.... now I want to say that since I began studying the books the quality has definitely increased in my life, and I want to thank you for that."

(Seth:) You thank yourself, for the quality was there all the time. You simply did not recognize what it was, and it will grow. And try some composing on your own. And use your own unique sensibilities to do that. Do not hassle it. Just think of it as a joyful game.

(Seth's remarks were related back to Jane.

(Seth:) You forgot the part about trying to love Anita Bryant, significanly.

([Rick:] "We were about to say it."

([Van Zandt:] "It's on the tip of our tongues."

(Seth:) Just a tiny, tiny, distant love.

(Seth's remarks were related back to Jane.

([Dickie:] "Sue, what is greatness?"

(Seth:) Sue is greatness. Dickie is greatness. Joseph is greatness. Ricky is greatness. Roni is greatness. You are all greatness. To know you are greatness is quality. Then your expressions are true expressions of quality, and they are not marred. Whatever they are, they are not marred. You recognize quality. Instinctively; whether or not you can say what it is. It inspires you. You run away from things that are not of quality, whether you can say why they are not or not. Your dreams are quality. Your dreams are quality. No one need tell you how to dream. You dream instinctively, automatically, and beautifully. You commit a beautiful dream each time you dream. And each dream is a dream of quality. Each breath you take is a breath of quality. All you have to do is to realize that each breath you take ultimately reaches to the ends of the universe and helps withhold your world. You are alone and not alone. Now that statement is far more important than it sounds. For in your aloneness, and in your togetherness, and between the two there is the meaning of your humanity. And there is the meaning of your life and your death. You cannot be completely together. You cannot be completely alone. Yet always must your existence flit between the two; between the desire and the ideal; between the dream and its execution; between your love and your expression of it. There dwells your reality and your meaning, and therein lies the validity of your soul.

(Seth withdrew.

([Jeff:] "He was talking about quality and how all of us have quality in everything we do, in everything we dream...."

(Seth:) Now, if you really believed what I said then, then you would bank upon yourselves. You would really trust yourselves. You would really know that you are an intimate part of the fabric of the universe; you would trust your abilities and bet upon yourselves. You would, without repressing anything, experience your own reality without impediments. You have a way to go. But you have support. You have biological support. For your atoms and molecules are not imbeciles. You could learn from them. The pupils of your eyes see far more than you see visually. And when you listen to this session think about that sentence. As Ruburt said earlier, I am not telling you you can have a heaven upon earth. For one thing, there is no such thing as heaven, and for another, if there were you would be bored. You need a challenge. Any flower uses it. And I am not talking about problems and challenges being the same thing. I am speaking of initiative, and desire and accomplishment. The need to use your abilities. They need to be used as a stem needs to grow. That is what I am speaking of. Now all of you this evening tell yourselves you will have a true dream from the Gates of Horn and we do have a City building. A City. Highly impractical, it seems at this time. A City that does indeed exist mentally. But all things must exist mentally first or they will never be materialized. And someday, that City might exist physically. But it will not be when you are here. Yet your memories will be in it and your desires. And to that extent you will be founders. And you forge such dreams in your sleep and in your private imaginings, and in your inspirations. For when one member of a species dreams such dreams, those dreams are transmitted to all other members. They do not die. When a runner at the Olympics does better than the runner before then all the sportscasters say, "How grand! We did not know man could run so fast." And so now records are being broken all the time. And mentally the same thing applies. Dream a grand dream. For when one member of the species dreams, all members, to some extent, participate. And the psyche, and the soul, and the heart of man takes new leaps, in your terms, not taken before. So trust yourselves, and trust your love and your dreams *(to Rick, Sheri, and Van Zandt, looking at Rick)*, and tell your students I said R-A-Y!!!! which means hooray. HOORAY!!!!

([Rick:] "Will do, Seth."

(Dickie was discussing Seth's remarks on the inner City when he noticed Seth's return.

([Dickie:] "Seth, how do you interpret that....?"

(Seth:) I never interpret myself.

I am dead, in your terms. And when this City is physically constructed, you will be as dead or as alive as I am.

([Dickie:] "But will we be living in that City?"

(Seth:) That is up to you. You will be a part of it whether you are living in it or not. It will be a part of your psychological geography.

([Anne Marie:] "Will that be related to the Third Christ at all?"

(Seth:) No.

The City simply represents, in your terms, an idealized version of a reality that can be physical. And that hopefully will be. And if it is, it will be created in your terms now, through your dreams, your love, your desire and your intent. And then it will seem to be given to its inhabitants, even as it seems to you the earth is given to you. For when you are born everything is here for you. It is given. But by whom is it given? And how is it that it has come? Can I say to you that your Earth originated in a sphere of dreams? That it is a mental creation of others, to some extent, in which you participate. That is indeed what I am telling you. *(In a whisper:)* Think about it.

(Seth withdrew.

(Group discussion.

(Seth:) Now.

Nothing is wasted. Nothing is wasted. Creativity least of all. So your thoughts are not wasted, your dreams are not wasted, and neither are the thoughts and dreams of others who have psychological realities perhaps completely different than your own. Nature is luxurious. It uses everything with a grand and riotous display.

([Ingrid:] "Seth, isn't it somewhat of a waste if people have abortions all the time? To me it just seems like a waste to become pregnant when all along, whenever you just thought of becoming pregnant, to have an abortion. It just seems like a waste."

(Seth:) It may be dumb. I do not know if it is a waste. For the consciousness will come to life if it wants to. And if the consciousness picks a mother who wants to abort, then the consciousness is only here for a short trip. A look around. It is like the seed from an apple tree who travels into the next yard but does not mature. It looks around and tries again. Any consciousness that wants to be born is born. And it picks a mother that wants to carry a child all the way.

(Seth withdrew.

(During discussion Sheri was talking about how much her students appreciate the Seth tapes.

([Sheri:] "The accent, at first, is a little hard to understand...."

(Seth:) My accent isn't difficult to understand. Now all of you have different accents. I have an eternal accent. It is always this way.

(Seth withdrew.

(Sue was concerned about the reaction of people in Dundee, NY to her book.

(Seth:) Now. Sue, if you speak of life and death and if you speak of men's dreams and aspirations, then some people in Dundee will understand. Do not think in literary terms. The literary terms can divide you from the people. But what you know intuitively can only connect you with the people. You will only vocalize feelings that they have but do not understand. Speak simply. Be aware of your own doubts and hesitations for they can relate to those. They are not creatures of habit. They are not opaque to these ideas. They are not as dumb to them as you think. To the ideas. Now I am indeed a strange animal to go into any farmer's barnyard. And I moo loudly indeed. And yet I am not all that strange to any of them. The strangeness is only at a surface level. Ruburt receives letters from people all over the country. In every walk of life. From farmers and taxi drivers, teachers, people in any profession. So do not think of the people in Dundee as a group of people who do not understand what you are doing. They are all individuals with their own dreams and levels of understanding. Some will read the books and some will not. Some will understand and some will not. People in other Dundees will do the same. You must be true to your own feelings, whatever they are.

(Jeff was recapping Seth's previous statements.

(Seth:) You are doing a good job.

([Jeff:] "Thank you."

(Seth:) One other point however. Ruburt never said "Will the people in

Elmira understand what I am saying?" He wrote because he had to write what he wrote. Now if you *(Sue)* have to write what you have to write, write it. If you do not have to write it, don't. For that is the way that you must go. You must follow your feelings. And if you write what you feel it must not matter, for your message wilt reach people all over the world. And if you do not write what you feel then the message has no meaning.

　([Sue:] "I guess I was concerned about immediate hassles over it....")
　(Seth:) Talk to Ruburt.

DELETED SESSION
DECEMBER 6, 1978 9:25 PM WEDNESDAY

(Neither of us had any specific questions for Seth.)
Now: a brief-enough session.

So much of a man or a woman shows to others. So much of a person shows to the person, but much of an individual's world view is hidden. It is hidden because people pay attention to the official areas of life.

(To me:) Your world view, for example, involves your knowledge and comprehension of government and politics as you perceive them, through reading or television. You interact with that invisible psychological climate, so that it becomes part of your mental environment. Your world view includes paintings that exist in your imagination, as well as paintings done in your terms "so far."

Your aspirations are a part of your world view. But they exist also amid your attitudes concerning the culture, your age, and the time that it seems must be involved with painting. Your world view includes your attitudes toward your parents, and toward their parents. It also includes your own attitudes toward your parents' aspirations, and your views of your brothers and their families. Your world view must include your beliefs about the body and the mind, about religion, history, and philosophy—and you stand as an entity, a psychological entity, in the center of this inner world.

You accept certain ideas and beliefs as a part of your world view, as everyone does. As a youngster, you—and also Ruburt—challenged many of "the world's" beliefs, and refused to accept them as a part of your personalized world views.

You threw out conventional religious ideas first, and then conventional scientific ideas, so while these may be a part of your society, they are not a part of your personalized world views. Some ideas fall by the wayside easily. Others either escape your notice, or do not seem vital enough at any given time to question. It is rather futile to ever wish that you were both "at one with the world," or to imagine yourselves following its beliefs blindly, but in blissful ignorance.

That would mean that you were wishing away your own intelligence, intuitions, and wit. There are strains connected with the route you have chosen, but at least you have the hopes of accomplishment—and, if you will forgive me —the creative joy of an honest pursuit. Those who follow the official lines of consciousness right now have no such support to fall back upon, while the results of their course becomes more obviously muddled.

(9:40.) Again, what I tell you does often run counter to beliefs deeply ingrained in both of you. Your achievements lie in the fact that you have indeed managed to free yourselves of the dogmas of your times, and of times before you. It is impossible for you to compare the richness of your world views with those of others—yet there is, as you know, room for improvement.

The improvement can come by casting aside as facts even more of the world's mental baggage. You understand many issues intellectually, but have not gained their emotional comprehension. My last session in particular mentions those issues. They sound simple enough, and yet they are right. Worry does not lead to action. In fact, it inhibits the intuitional insights that allow constructive action to occur.

You must be more understanding and compassionate toward yourselves than you have been. The matter of a bad tooth, or teeth, is not to be overlooked, but it should not be an occasion to put the self down, the cause of self-accusing thoughts, or bring about unfortunate feelings of inferiority.

The body is always an alive, alert, responsive, ever-changing framework, fully focused in the present. It will not live forever—nor does it want to. It knows pain and pleasure. You grow toward pleasure. And the desire for it propels you and the body. Pain often acts as a teacher, saying "This direction is not for you" as it reflects painful thoughts. Practically speaking in your world, there is going to be some wear and tear. To deny that is asking too much.

People have difficulties with their teeth in modern times, particularly, for many reasons—but mainly because it is one accepted area for the difficulty to show itself, and because the dentist's cosmetics can indeed repair the appearance. At least in some historic periods, people kept their teeth longer, knowing that nothing could be done to repair the damage.

Ideally—and this is a big ideally—there would be no such damage to the body. Your attitudes have been along the lines of self-accusation at any such problems. Any health difficulties will flow into the pool of your beliefs— but the body is not meant to be more than the reflection and materialization of your inner reality as it appears in space and time. Its problems are the results of your own inner ones, and meant to lead you toward inner comprehensions. In the same way, the Jonestown suicides lead the society to face its inner problems.

Briefly, all portions of Ruburt's body are gaining strength, and are rapidly changing. What he experiences sometimes as painful sensations, the <u>body</u> experiences as new signs of activity.

Last week's session should be read often by both of you, so that you make certain leaps toward emotional comprehensions that you need.

Do you have a question?

(I shook my head, no.)

Then I bid you a fond good evening.

(10:00 P.M. "I almost have that sickly feeling I get after some sessions," Jane said.

(Notes: On December 2 we were visited by a group of Jane's students from NYC – Richie, Ricky, Sheri, Jerry, Jeff, Van Zandt, etc. Jane gave a long session interrupted often by "class" discussion. We're to receive a transcript of the material soon, and it will be incorporated in the deleted notebook.

(Seth talked about teeth tonight because of my visit to the dentist today, in an effort—apparently successful—to save a front capped tooth which had suddenly begun to act up. I regard it as a very close call, and hope the filling put in will save the tooth. In addition, Jane also has tooth trouble—one of her bottom teeth is loosening....)

DELETED SESSION
JANUARY 1, 1979 9:10 PM MONDAY

(Note the date for this evening's session. It's the first one since December 6, 1978. Now with the New Year we want to start up a schedule for the sessions, and stick to it for the most part. The holidays are over. The Christmas tree and all the decorations have been dismantled; the house is cleaned to some extent, and the copyedited version of Volume 2 of "Unknown" Reality has been returned to Prentice-Hall. Jane and I spent two hard weeks erasing most of the suggested changes in the manuscript, and it is now headed for the printer for page proofs. I mailed it December 26, and just today received the return receipt.

(For the record: "Uknown," it seems, appears to be one of those jobs that won't go too smoothly, even though now we're reaching the end of its cycle. Even today, the day after this deleted session was held, I received a call from Tam at Prentice-Hall, wanting to know about cutting the length of the book. Both Jane and I refused.

However, the call evidently helped trigger a "panic" attack, as I call them, on my part, involving palpitations in the chest. The pendulum agreed. Naturally this is brought about by my own reactions to whatever the trigger happens to be, but still "Unknown," and other creative endeavors have often been involved, when conflicts between what I think of as useful creative work run into doing things like shoveling snow, or other household items that I seem to think of as "chores." None of this is new, although I have improved greatly in my reactions during the last year. The long working time—perhaps three years—spent on "Unknown" evidently allowed that project to accumulate strong psychic charges on my part; when doubts or challenges arise in conflict with the work on the book, I would react in uncomfortable ways occasionally.

(Jane is still faithfully doing her exercises twice a day, and walking more than ever; I am starting a chart. She is making her own list of things to do for 1979, including the point of power. I am still concerned deeply about her condition, and for the most part we seem to move along from day to do as we always do. In the holiday interim the sessions seemed to fade far away into the background. When we reach that state, I personally find myself thinking that the sessions make little difference one way or the other. Then when we resume, it seems that a key unlocks doors. I'm afraid that Seth has spent years encouraging us to do things that for whatever reasons we either don't do or can't do, simple as they appear to be.)

Good evening.

("Good evening, Seth.")

Now: I wish you a merry new year into which I hope you manage to insert a touch of lightheartedness now and then.

Now if I were you two, making a list of resolutions, my list would include feelings and attitudes. Things to do are well and good—very good indeed—but the feelings and attitudes are, shall we say, at least as important. I would not presume to make a list of resolutions for you, but in an imaginative endeavor this is what I pretend I would list if I were you—meaning you both. Though this is a new year, there is nothing really new about the list.

(Throughout this delivery Seth's voice and manner had contained more than a little gentle irony.)

One: I will approve of myself, my characteristics, my abilities, my likes and my dislikes, my inclinations and disinclinations, realizing that these form my unique individuality. They are given me for a reason.

Two: I will approve of and rejoice in my accomplishments, and I will be as vigorous in listing these—as <u>rigorous</u> in remembering them—as I have ever been in remembering and enumerating my failures or lacks of accomplishment.

Three: I will remember the creative framework of existence, in which I have my being. Therefore the possibilities, potentials, seeming miracles, and joyful spontaneity of Framework 2 will be in my mind, so that the doors to creative living are open.

Four: I will realize that the future is a probability. In terms of ordinary experience, nothing exists there yet. It is virgin territory, planted by my feelings and thoughts in the present. Therefore I will plant accomplishments and successes, and I will do this by remembering that nothing can exist in the future that I do not want to be there.

A certain Mr. Butts, I believe, spoke earlier today about his parents, and mentioned the accomplishments that were present but not appreciated. The list I just gave you is important because if you do not value your abilities or approve of yourself, then you cut yourself off from using your own abilities. You deny yourself their help and aid because you do not recognize your own abilities as such in the true sense of the word.

You question your own characteristics, and so your accomplishments fade in your eyes. I do not want to be severe, and yet you do indeed show ingratitude when you "wish you were like other people." People of ordinary ways wish deeply "that they were different," that they possessed qualities that you both possess.

(9:27.) When you feel that way, you deepen a sense of isolation, while at the same time robbing yourselves of the true pleasures of accomplishment and creativity that a light isolation provides. The points I have mentioned are the ones that can literally work miracles in your lives, and they can begin tomorrow. Ruburt should definitely resume the point of power. It will vastly increase the effects of his exercises and walking. For it will add the miraculous touch of Framework 2 to those activities. That last sentence is highly important.

Begin the library—the two of you or Ruburt alone if you prefer. Read over the Framework 2 sessions, for both of you have largely forgotten to focus in that direction, and to look for hints of its activity. The looking-for creates the activity also, you see, for it serves as a psychological focus.

Do not be so severe in your dealings with yourselves, but be more indulgent. The both of you do know the meaning of the word.

I will begin book sessions again Wednesday, and we will resume our two sessions a week. Those sessions will help in other ways also, for they also provide a certain psychic boost at certain times.

Do you have questions?

("No, I guess not.")

Then Wednesday we will begin our usual sessions, and I do bid you a productive and enjoyable new year—

("Thank you. Seth.")

—and a fond good evening.

(9:34 PM. Seth's reference to my parents stemmed from an insight I expressed earlier today—that is obvious once thought of: that often as a youth I deplored my parents' constant arguing and disagreements, thus judging them, but never gave a thought to how they <u>felt</u> on a daily basis while living such lives. Obviously—again —they must have been most unhappy much of the time. Such a simple understanding did not come to me that I remember, nor to my brothers—both of whom I think still have primitive ideas concerning father especially.

(At the same time, I now realize that my father did accomplish much that he and the other members of the family were blind to. All of us certainly were more than happy with some of his contributions—simply those revolving around camping, for example—while misunderstanding or missing out upon many other facets of his life, and our own individual lives as they functioned within the family framework. I suppose everyone feels later that there were innumerable things they could have done to help others....)

DELETED SESSION
JANUARY 3, 1979. 9:35 PM WEDNESDAY

(In the last session Seth promised to begin dictation on his latest book after a long layoff, but as things turned out the book was not begun anew. Instead I asked that he deal with the challenges Jane and I still face, and apparently are unable to resolve—her symptoms, and my own feelings of panic, and related symptoms, as mentioned also in the last session.

(I also planned to start reviewing the first deleted sessions Seth gave on Jane's symptoms, for I've never really forgotten them and always felt they were as good as any Seth has ever given on those subjects. The main one, the breakthrough session as I think of it, was the 367th for October 1, 1967. I read it over just before tonight's session began, and was able to reaffirm my opinion that it's still one of the best; at the same time it aroused questions, for it deals with causes in the past. According to Seth's suggested use of the point of power, and his late deleted material, one isn't supposed to dwell on the past, but go forward from the present—two major blocks of material, I told Jane this evening, that at first glance seem to contradict each other.

(I added that I doubt if they really do, but that the views need integration for us to understand it all clearly as a unified theory—sort of like field theory in physics, perhaps. I assume it will take lots of work to accomplish this, but am inserting these

thoughts here as a remainder of one of the things I want to accomplish this year in this area. Jane and I also plan a list of questions for Seth on the whole situation, and I see these as accumulating into a notebook to accompany these sessions. I think we've already achieved some insights that we've let slide or didn't understand.

(At this writing at least I plan to spend evenings typing new session material, and in the time left over to restudy the past material in the hopes of putting it all together with and/or without Seth's help. But out of this work I expect our questions for Seth will come. I'm deeply troubled by Jane's condition, and by what I regard as her strange passivity in the face of it; clues to this attitude exist in the 367th session. I'm sure my own role in the whole thing is a strong one, and that in my own way I'm as badly off as she is, although it may not show physically.

(I especially think Seth's remarks in the last deleted session—for January 1, 1979, to be apropos: "You question your own characteristics, and so your accomplishments fade in your eyes." I suppose what I want to know is why we must question those characteristics—or at least why we, meaning anyone, cannot live in harmony with them. Then at least we'd know some little peace of mind. As it is, that quality is very rare to us.

(Jane too read over the 367th session before the session this evening. It seems that essentially our situation is unchanged, 12 years later, which doesn't say much for our learning capacities, I'm afraid. When the session began I half expected Seth to tell us to stay away from old deleted sessions, since as mentioned delving into the past can cause too intense a focus there, and reinforce problems, whatever they may be. But he didn't. I said to Jane later that it seems Seth will tailor his material to suit our needs and/or moods of the moment, which may be one of the ways to integrate blocks of his material into a larger whole, which can display many facets or approaches.)

Now: Because of your frames of mind, this will be the first of several sessions dealing specifically with your problems.

Before we begin, let it be understood that your problems are no more upsetting, disagreeable, or exhausting than other people's. Many do not even reach your ages. Problems are a part of human life—a condition of your existence. They are challenges, highly characteristic of all living matter.

Your own problems can appear so large that you forget this. You are not inferior because you have problems. You are simply human, and if you need any proof that you are a part of the human species, and not so isolated from others, that is it. Again, however, creative challenges are set by each individual, challenges that involve achievements, of course, of one kind or another, simple or sublime. You are not inferior because you have problems.

Perfectionists, however, not only take a dim view of problems, but consider each one a blot, a proof of inferiority in themselves or others and they see such blots everywhere. They are in a certain fashion overly conscientious, and they fear spontaneity lest it be less than perfect. They fear flaws.

Now in close marriages or those of long duration, there is a kind of super-imposed family personality, a composite, to which each member contributes, and to which all members respond. In a relationship like yours and Ruburt's this applies in a very intense manner. What you read in the old session this evening still applies to a large extent. It should be noted, as Ruburt said, that the pover-ty angle was largely eradicated—yet you *(to me)* preserve it in your worries about taxes, for example—for those feelings of resentment still help you continue to feel impoverished and virtuous. They serve to disconnect you from any opulent income status—put you back with the poor where you feel you belong; and hence you imagine the greater, the far greater incomes of other people, and in that comparison you come out put-upon—but again, virtuous.

Before you moved here you imagined, both of you, what oddities you would be in the neighborhood, and exaggerated your differences from others. Ruburt did not mind spending the money for the porches. Since he would be "increasing the value of the plant"—the working establishment. He would write on the back one *(humorously)* to show the porch was not after all for pleasure.

This session you read *(the 367th)* applied mostly to Ruburt, yet you also have what I will call an overly conscientious self in battle with the spontaneous self *(a fact I'm well aware of, and had discussed with Jane before tonight's session).* You have actually grown somewhat more spontaneous. Why not—since Ruburt was nicely expressing the overly conscientious selves of both of you?

No one can completely do that for anyone else, of course, so you have your own struggles with spontaneity. Ruburt's spontaneous self was by far the most active, and so his defenses against it, as the overly conscientious self, were more obvious than yours.

Your struggles earlier, before you met Ruburt, involved relationships, in that you had no deep ones, allowing yourself to become close to no one. When you fell in love with Ruburt, a part of you was appalled, for it felt it must hold itself ever aloof—and in those days Ruburt's spontaneous self often met a response from your overly conscientious self, so that you appeared cold to him, and in repelling his spontaneity you were of course frightened to reveal your own.

(9:55.) You showed him often the face of the overly conscientious self.

Now: you had of course other problems that he was not experienced enough to see, and at the time the sessions began you were both at a low point. The release of psychic energy involved, regardless of me, was literally a new birth, bringing forth an impetus for change and creative activity. In an important sense, Ruburt's abilities as a writer found their forte. He had found his direction —though that direction did not follow his beliefs. He was naturally meant to go in areas that would confound his earlier upbringing.

His concern about your health also operated as a strong impetus, allowing him to break through usual frameworks, and the sessions did give you the knowledge you needed to recover.

Both of you realized from young ages that you were different from others, relatively speaking, and you gloried in the differences. When you came together you wanted to be alone together. You wanted to be alone and to work at your pursuits.

You set up, little by little, certain barriers against the world. As you grew older the failings of the human condition became more noticeable. Your own differences from others became more apparent. As the books became more popular, you were suddenly threatened in terms of privacy, of exposure personally— and perhaps, Ruburt felt, being forced one way or another into that other world in which, after all, the two of you did not belong.

To skip ahead: it is true that Ruburt has not asked you to take him for a ride, and it is equally true that you have not offered (*although I mentioned it last week*). He would have gone to the party (*at Bumbalo's on December 29*) with some encouragement from you, and you gave him none—for cleverly, when one is ready to move the other is not.

Your perfectionist tendencies tell you not to go out into the world until Ruburt can walk normally and proudly. Your perfectionist tendencies—I refer to both of you—tell you that it is a crime for either of you to have a problem, whether or not the rest of the world is filled with chaos.

You gloried in being alone. It was what you wanted. Now it seems that aloneness is a trap. You think of isolation and being cut off from the world, while at the same time you want little to do with it.

Ruburt's condition, in a way, stops you from hurting others. If you close the door in the world's face, it is because Ruburt cannot walk properly. The overly conscientious self on both of your parts to a strong degree becomes a composite personality. Its beliefs are invisible because you accept them unthinkingly. The next few old sessions should be read. You have both largely, except in your work, now, cut spontaneity from your lives; your habits are so set.

In that regard you do not challenge yourselves, and to that extent your work also suffers. Instead of (*hypnotic*) advisors, try to set up a dialogue, each of you, with the overly conscientious self, reminding it that spontaneity knows its own order—and that its defenses are overdone, with the best of good intent.

You must think in terms of surprises, of spontaneity, of changed rhythms. Between now and our next session, read that group of old ones, and each of you attempt to reach your own overly conscientious self.

Behind all of this is the feeling that exposure is dangerous, that your true feelings must be hidden, and that the world is unsafe—hence your need for defenses. Read this session also over together, and follow all the suggestions I have given you.

That is all for this evening—but hardly all.

("Good night, Seth.")

(10:14. I was surprised at the early ending of the session. "I probably had more," Jane said, "but I was feeling so sickly by then that I just quit...."

("Well, take a break then and see what happens. "

("I'll come back briefly because I hear a few sentences in my head." Then at 10:15:)

Ruburt's reaction to my following simple suggestions shows how badly they are needed, and you will doubtlessly experience your own weaker version.

You need the idea of change—an idea that Ruburt once used to find exciting. Change your living room furniture, your bedroom, your kitchen or whatever you can—simply to symbolically and slowly break you in to the idea of change, and to break up the invisible bulk of mental patterns that are connected with your present state.

I do not care, for example, what you change. Change your hours—but think in terms of change—and now for change's sake—to show that you can operate quite well without rigid patterns of behavior.

What you simply need is a change of scene. You could indeed take a van and make it to Florida. I do not see you doing this now. You must increase your view of your own operations.

What I want to say will wait, for I want you to read those old sessions first —and in all of this remember Framework 2, which deals with creative change, which is growth. End of session, and a fond good evening.

("Thank you, Seth." 10:27 PM. As usual, I think the material is excellent.)

DELETED SESSION
JANUARY 5, 1979 8:35 PM FRIDAY

(After supper Jane offered to have a session for me because during the day I'd had a number of recurrences of the panic feelings in my chest. The first one came early

this morning after I'd shoveled but a few scoops of snow in the driveway—no work involved at all, really, but I had to quit for fear of having an "attack" of some kind.

(Then this noon we received from Prentice-Hall copies of the revised index for Volume 1 of"Unknown," plus new page proofs of the type chosen for Volume 2— a matter we'd thought already settled. We liked everything except that I thought the italic type looked rather crowded compared to that used in Volume 1. Jane thought it looked okay. After lunch I had her call Ethel Waters at Prentice-Hall to tell her everything was okay, simply to get rid of the worries about the book.

(However, the feelings of unease and/or panic returned after supper, and Jane offered the session. I explained to her my reservations about the italic typeface, and my attempts to free myself of book concerns. I finally had to choose to place my physical condition first, thinking that more important than anything else. Many others had obviously thought the typefaces chosen for Volume 2 were okay, I said, so what was I doing, worrying about something like that, wanting to tell others how to do their jobs?

(I finally concluded it wasn't worth it, and hoped Jane would adopt some of this thinking for some of her own challenges. The pendulum, incidentally, agreed that my concern over the typeface caused my concerned feelings after supper.

(Jane surprised me by mentioning a session at about 7:40. By the time she called me to sit for it, it was 8:35—and her mood had changed. Before she'd felt "clear-headed." Now she had questions, and wished we'd gone right into the session as soon as she had mentioned it. As we waited for the session to begin, I read her the first questions I'd noted down from rereading the 367th session—Seth's first comprehensive session on her symptoms, and one that's been referred to rather often lately. I still want to study all of those early personal sessions, but haven't progressed far because of all the new material we've been getting lately. But they're always there, waiting. I didn't expect Seth to go into my written questions this evening, although he did refer to several of them, if rather obliquely....)

Good evening.

("Good evening, Seth.")

Now: the overly conscientious self is opinionated, closed-minded, pedantic. It believes it is right.

It is possible to be opinionated at times, closed-minded, and pedantic, in good normal behavior—but when certain characteristics <u>group together</u>, then you have the formation of an overly-conscientious self, which acts in a repetitive manner, always showing these fairly rigid characteristics.

<u>In your culture</u>, this portion of the self is formed in childhood and early school years. Often as a result of the conflict between the need for obedient behavior toward adults, and the need for independent growth and activity that

might well be judged as rebellious by the elders.

When I said it was not rational *(in the 367th session)*, I spoke relatively speaking. Of course, communication is possible. The conscientious self groups about ideas of right and wrong. This portion of the self is often altered, its characteristics becoming less apparent as individuals move through the various social groupings of work, church, or community, where it is obvious that the standards of behavior are hardly rigid, but adaptable.

You two have largely worked alone, and your work goals involve of course the development of personality characteristics that must apply to artistic work. You are aware of the fact that a great painting can still be great despite depicting, say, acts of violence that are "bad." In a certain fashion you began to apply the "wrong kind" of moral judgments. I will try to explain, though you may, Joseph, at first, disagree.

The material that came from *"Unknown"* today—you disagreed with the type of lettering, if I understand properly. <u>Now, that is legitimate as an artistic judgment—but it is illegitimate as a moral judgment</u>. There is nothing wrong or inferior about the people at Prentice, who made the "improper" artistic decision. It is not <u>immoral or wrong</u> not to have excellent artistic judgment. The people involved <u>are</u> in an art department. They are individuals, doing their best to develop their abilities and their lives—but your indignation was <u>moral</u> in narrow terms, rather than in quite acceptable artistic ones. You do this often.

Ruburt does it when he reads poor material. He immediately makes a moral judgment against a poet whose material is artistically poor. The person involved may indeed have difficulty artistically in expression, and an artistic revulsion can then be quite acceptable, but not a moral one.

Now you have even made—both of you, now—the same kind of moral, or I should say immoral, judgments about Ruburt's condition, which with your joint perfectionism is doubly appalling. You see it as morally wrong, not simply a physically poor condition, but a morally reprehensible one, reflecting upon Ruburt's integrity, his knowledge, his understanding.

(8:52.) You judge the world, but in far more rigorous terms morally than either of you really realize. Your beliefs exist in the present. I will always go into back material, or the past when you request it, for it is important that you understand I am never evasive in that regard. But the overly conscientious selves are not separate versions of you, really. The division is one I use to make certain points.

Those ideas are quite conscious when you allow them to surface. Again, they are beliefs that you least examine. The overly conscientious self is not creative, particularly—meaning innovative, but it does have great sustaining qualities and power.

Dialogues with yourselves may bring those beliefs more into the light, but I have often mentioned them in many sessions, and in different ways.

Now: you panic yourself. What body would not be panicked by some of your worries and thoughts? Again, I have covered this. If optimism seems to be such a simple-minded, idiotic attribute, then listen. It is indeed foolish enough to take it for granted—at least part way *(and with irony)*—that everything—All That Is, the important things—will somehow work out all right. The foolish body, not realizing that such a philosophy is a food for idiots, replenishes itself for good activities, and in an animal fashion anticipates comfort and exuberance.

Such an optimist will of course not be blind, and he will see that there are indeed many blemishes in the world; but his overall faith not only sustains him, but because of his own state of mind his creativity blossoms to whatever degree he has it. And he manages to wipe away a few of those blights.

The pessimists insist that nothing will work out right in the everyday world, and that is where you live. Illness will increase. Poverty is certain, depressions, and old age with the worst of imagined terrors. Of course, his body does not realize that the pessimist's views are the most intelligent, proper, sane and reasonable, and so it falls ill because the mind tells the body it has nothing to look forward to.

Now let us take a peek at something else.

I have told you time and time again that but for a few exceptions you have not used your creative abilities to help solve your problems. I suggested some changes. I will see how many you make. You suggested going to Sayre. Ruburt first of all thought of how he could get his socks and shoes on, but then he tried to overcome those thoughts, and imagine the trip. *(Sayre, PA—my home town.)*

The idea of a van to Florida led Ruburt into daydreaming, though he was very frightened of the idea, but you immediately thought of the difficulties, that it would not work, and overall neither of you have applied creative, imaginative, positive thought, steadily. You pick up each other's thoughts and feelings. Ruburt has made progress, but both of you still believe that worrying will somehow lead to positive action, that fear will be an impetus.

I know the extent of your creative abilities. There were occasions in the past when these were applied, and Ruburt improved considerably. His improvements of late have been largely the result of work in Framework 1. They have been steady since he began walking, but slow. Imagining a trip to Florida, for example, or anyplace he wants, planning for it, is a far more effective method of therapy than any worry, for such plans activate body and mind.

The resolutions I gave you would automatically seep through to the over-ly conscientious selves if you kept them in mind, and resolved to live by them. Ruburt does need some kind of class or such activity, but he has grown fright-ened. You have not encouraged him. He can see people more when he is better, but you must indeed act at least mentally as if.

You have the resources. Ruburt is determined to get better. You are both saddled with old habits of thought that you really do not examine, and that is why the overly conscientious self still rules the roost.

Creative change, some playful indulgence, the use of the creative abilities, and some simple reasoning with yourselves, will be of great benefit. Worrying is the opposite of mental healing, and will get you nowhere. Try to take this to heart—and again, in a larger framework. You are to concentrate upon the cre-ative suggestions I have given you, and not upon the difficulties.

End of session for now.

("Okay. Thank you.")

A fond good evening.

(9:15 PM. I might add that I don't think I for one believe any longer that worrying is the answer to very much, as Seth says Jane and I still believe, nor do I think that fear is going to act as a stimulus to positive action. I've disabused myself of such thoughts, with Seth's considerable help. I still worry, obviously, but have no illusions about it helping anything. The call to Prentice today was an effort to free one area of life. I told Jane today that this week I'd pay our taxes a few days ahead of time—another effort to get free....)

DELETED SESSION
JANUARY 8, 1979 9:29 PM MONDAY

(As I mentioned doing at the close of last Saturday night's deleted session, today I paid our NY State and Federal income taxes a few days ahead of time, hoping the action would contribute to my sense of freedom, and perhaps Jane's too. I've felt pret-ty good today, although a trace of the panicky feeling returned after supper this evening.

(Both of us have been rereading Seth's own resolutions for the New Year fre-quently, as given on January 1, 1979. Before tonight's session Jane read over the ques-tions I've written out, derived from my reading of the 367th session. We discussed them briefly. I could list many more, but probably won't. I still don't think Seth would want to spend much time discussing that old material in any detail, since he's said many times that focusing on what was wrong in the past is negative and self-

defeating.

(Starting yesterday, Jane began her walking exercises with the typing table by using a pillow under her arms. This has the effect of raising her posture an inch or so, and seemingly has produced immediate results in terms of a much-improved posture, better balanced and freer. She must have been ready to make the suggestion about the pillow, we thought. Already she's talking about using something on the table to help her stand even straighter. Her devotion to the exercises is certainly showing results.

(Willy kept bugging me as I tried to make notes for this session—sitting as he does close to me on the couch, wanting to stare at me and be petted at the same time, while I try to accomplish something. "I hope Seth doesn't talk too loud," Jane said as we waited for him to come through, "or I might lose that tooth." It was loose.)

Now: it is fruitless to go back to old sessions seeking to find out what is wrong, or what was wrong and self-defeating. It is an excellent idea to look at old sessions with a view toward picking up suggestions that I have given for constructive action, and following them.

Some things are simply difficult for me to explain, and for you to understand. The ideas of your society often make certain ideas invisible to you, though they are given in black and white. I use terms like the overly conscientious self to help you. And then of course you want to know why it does not know when to stop in overly protective devices. *(One of my questions.)*

"It" simply represents certain attitudes and beliefs that you possess, or that Ruburt possesses. They mix and merge with your other beliefs and ideas, and color your actions. When I speak so, I am isolating a certain portion of your subjective reality, and labeling it for convenience. "It" never really goes against your wishes. If Ruburt's main goals in work, for example, had directly involved and mainly concerned immediate contact with others, through university work or whatever, his mobility would not have been tampered with.

Many needs were seemingly met by the physical condition. A lack of understanding is behind the issue, of course, but the spontaneous self was also taken into consideration, so that inner mobility—the acceleration of ideas and experience—was allowed for. Some dampers were put there also, but not because one part of the self conspired against another part. It was a give-and-take situation; protection being used where it was felt it was needed.

You had a strong drive to use abilities, and not usual ones, where rules of conduct or professionalism were outlined. Because of both of your attitudes, you felt that a method should be cautionary. You were saddled with the usual beliefs of your times, and yet trying to understand new ones. The ideas I have tried to give you—outlined, say, in the New Year resolutions—have not yet gotten through to you.

Ruburt's codicils represented a point of intuitional understanding, but he has not caught up to them in practical living.

When you disapprove of yourselves, for example, again you rob yourselves of comforts meant to support you. The psychiatrist's letter *(Dr. Beahrs)* represents but one communication, but many others read the material and use it, and do not write you, any more than you write to other authors. And again, a book may sell in the millions, and still go in one mental ear and out the other while our books literally do change lives—and to that extent the world—for the better.

(Interesting, that this afternoon, the 9th, we were visited by Marian Merrill. whom we haven't talked with for perhaps a year. She dropped in for a visit, bringing a pudding cake and a Christmas card to her from an old friend-classmate of Marian's; Marian had seen her friend last year for the first time in 15 years. On the card the feminine friend asked Marian to tell Jane that "the books" had changed her life for the better. Marian had laughed and said that now she's going to read the books also, to see what had so moved her friend. Marian knows of the Seth thing.

(The little episode certainly seemed to have overtones of Framework 2's operations.)

A man who makes shoes may see his customers, but he will not know what roads his customers walk in his shoes—and you cannot know the mental and psychic changes for the better that the books are making in parents and their children. When you disapprove of yourselves, such factors escape you entirely, or become lost in other worries.

You must remember also that greater context in which you live. When you do this, you can indeed see the overall purpose of your life—but you cannot do so until you approve of yourself, and recognize that you as an individual are unique, and uniquely a part of all reality.

You have been taught that so many of your attitudes are unconscious, that this prevents you often from consciously putting together a picture of your conscious beliefs. Again, they appear invisible.

(9:48.) Give us a moment.... You must always remember that the self is not static, but a living gestalt of experience. It is best not to say, for example, "I have always been thus-and-so," or whatever, and still better not to identify yourself with any characteristics that you deplore. Your purpose is in what you are, and when you do not approve of what you are, you cannot see it. You can then, as I have said, lose sight of your own grace, but you cannot fall out of grace.

It would help you both considerably, if when you have the feeling of self-approval really, to sit quietly and try to feel your purposes. Think, however, of feeling, for this is your best clue, and it will bring you some answers.

To paint pictures or write books is only the topmost cover for a life's purpose, for the paintings or the books contain the purpose, but are not the purpose itself. The meaning is within the paintings, but the paintings are not the meaning.

I have a suggestion, and it is that you mentally speak to what I will call "the basic creative self"—and remember, these are terms. That "self" is a portion of your being that creates all characteristics, and that can therefore help unify them. It is also the Framework 2 self, but the word "creative" is more potent for the two of you to use. It knows of its innate goodness.

Now these are psychological manipulations, but manipulations that work. You must also realize that I must deal with you as you think you are—that is, with both of you, and for that matter with the world at large. In my greater viewpoint I see your lives—many of them, and the emergence of overall patterns of achievement and challenge, and I hope that you will progress to your own visions of such realities—at least in dreams, for they will sustain you.

(A note: Seth's material reminded me of his comments in the deleted 371st session for October 11, 1967. I read it last night; Seth answered my questions about what he sees when he looks at me, both as himself, and through Jane's eyes. Very interesting, and material both of us had forgotten many years ago.)

Ruburt is near a breakthrough, but that is all I will say on that.

Indirectly, I have answered several of your questions. Do you have any you want to put to me?

("Why has he waited so long to resume work on Mass Reality?")

The answer to that is simple. You both insist upon applying quite intellectual concepts to creative work, and ignoring Ruburt's natural rhythms. He works in great bursts of activity, but instead of understanding this, and trusting the quiet periods and the creative self, he is up in arms. The creative self is playful and spontaneous. It follows his natural rhythms. The fear of not producing, however, can inhibit his productivity, and wear him out with worry.

I suggest that each day he write what comes to mind for a while, for his next book is here as surely as the past ones are.

End of session.

Make up a new list of questions for the next session if you want, and I will answer them in my own way. A fond good evening.

("Okay. Thank you."

(10:40 PM. Jane herself had just enough time to comment on the brevity of *the session when Seth returned:)*

P.S.: In those old sessions filed away, there is also material in which I stressed the importance of making love. Your experience last night reminded me.

In lovemaking, when you forget yourselves to some extent, spontaneity is also aroused, and the healing processes brought into play through the touch of hand and caresses. It is the most therapeutic of practices in all cases. It reassures both individuals in the basic worth of the self. It increases all healing functions, and despite churchly tales to the contrary, it regenerates and inspires the creative abilities.

Now—end of session.

(I raised a hand before Seth could slip away. "How about his dream last night? Did he remember enough of it to interpret it correctly?"

(Jane has written an account of her dream. It concerned fur coats, among other things, and she's been getting flashes of understanding about it throughout the day.)

Ruburt did an excellent job with that, and the dream also shows that so-called unconscious material will come to the surface of the mind when it is requested. Those beliefs, however, were not really unconscious at all. His interpretation was correct.

("He's been trying to recall the identity of a certain individual in the dream, but can't quite get it.")

I believe it was Richard Wolinsky.

Follow my suggestions.

("Okay. Good night.")

(10:11 PM.)

DELETED SESSION
JANUARY 10, 1979 9:27 PM WEDNESDAY

("Home, sex, power, you and the driveway, hay fever, the impulsive selves that we were talking about earlier tonight"—these are all words dictated to me by Jane abruptly as we sat waiting for the session to begin.

(I'd been commenting on her call tonight to a psychiatrist—Dr. Beahrs—who'd written her recently from Washington state, and of his informing her that another doctor out there is also using the Seth material ideas in dealing with her patients. I talked about the doctor reporting that Jane's books were kept in the occult section of the bookstore, thus causing her to lose readers; I used the incident as an

example of how stereotyped ideas can limit something becoming better known— breaking out of its specialized field to reach a much wider audience, as I think Jane's work deserves. I used political activity as an example of a field reaching many people. Yet, I added, the fact that the two medical people had discovered Seth was, in a small way, a sign that the material had at least managed some sort of transcendent movement.

(Then in today's mail Jane received a letter from another doctor, as well as from a professor of mathematics – also signs that the Seth material was capable of wider appeal. I said that we should be grateful for these signs, and that they may be more widespread than we realize. Then Jane dictated the words quoted above, saying Seth would probably cover them in tonight's session.

(This afternoon, incidentally, she lost the loose tooth that has been referred to recently....

(It happened shortly after Frank Longwell's visit at lunchtime, during which we discussed a new arrangement for the stove/cooking area of the kitchen. This would be a sign of the spontaneous change Seth mentioned in a late session. Then the day after this session was held, Frank returned at noon with literature on what stove units are available, prices, et cetera, so the discussion proceeded further.)

Good evening.

("Good evening, Seth.")

Now: I have given some—not all—of this material before, but now you can put the understanding to better advantage. Ruburt's "overly conscientious self" was indeed built up in response to his belief that he was, to begin with, overly enthusiastic, overly impulsive, overly spontaneous. He was naturally expressive and open with people. He was creatively gifted—but an overly impulsive child does not care for an invalid mother, conscientiously, for 21 years.

He did not run away. He did not get into any serious difficulty. The very consistent writing of poetry through those years shows its own kind of discipline, but people are not used to bursts of creativity. They were not used to Ruburt's very quick insights.

He thought of himself as overly impulsive. Very seldom did he yell back at his mother. An impulsive child might have done far more. He refrained from heavy sexual encounters—certainly not the behavior of a sexually impulsive person. He knew he didn't want a family.

Here we see purpose, strong intent, and despite the ins-and-outs with mood, and the youthful wandering, the same purpose to write, to express oneself, to observe, and to stand apart from the mainstream of American life.

You considered yourself not impulsive, yet it is you who wrote "Make me a galaxy, Jane," took up with Ruburt after a very brief acquaintanceship, and brought him home to your startled family.

It was you who suggested the ESP book, and you also early decided not to become a part of the American mainstream of life. You did not have a strong drive to have a family. You avoided heavy sexual relationships also. Both of you, before you met, knew that you wanted to study and observe from your own viewpoints. You <u>felt</u> that a family life would automatically plunge you into the kind of living that would not allow you such luxury. At the same time, both of you to some extent feared <u>what you thought of</u> as the power of sex. Again, Freudian beliefs that filled the books and movies led you both in your own ways to fear that your energies could be "swallowed" by sexuality—that to some extent you had so much energy, and that most of it must go into creative work.

More than this, the Freudian concepts said more or less that each person, regardless of their individuality, was driven by sexual energies of great force. There was in such a system no room, literally, for individual differences, but a norm set so that you must behave thus and so.

Now. If you did not express your sexuality through sexual experience, as prescribed, you were in for trouble. So went the tale. You found yourselves married. Ruburt as a woman, with those beliefs in the background, determined not to betray the writer, Jane, or the artist, Robert—thru becoming pregnant, or making too many sexual demands. Ruburt, incidentally, had a natural abortion because the message was already in the body, and all of his worries and concerns were unnecessary.

There are bodies, in those terms, who do not want to have physical offspring. They are not faulty. They fit in with nature's plans, and with the psychological plans of the personalities involved. You were rather repressed at that period, frightened about your own work, and sometimes you would ignore Ruburt's occasional sexual advances when you happened to be in your studio. He felt he was too spontaneous, again, too impulsive—but then in that belief system he worried if his sexual needs could not be properly squashed, supposing someone else aroused them, and he "fell in love" with someone else as quickly as he had fallen in love with you. Or worse—supposing your repressed sexuality was repressed because of your joint work, and supposing you fell in love with someone else, and became sexually aroused for another?

(*I can safely say that such ideas never occurred to me.*

(*9:50.*) The entire premise is highly faulty, for the species deals with value fulfillment and quality, as do all forms of life, and not with mere physical reproduction. The sexual aspects of men and women do not exist apart from their individual psychological make-ups, but connected with all of the other unique individual characteristics.

Now give us a moment.... Those beliefs at that time helped give rise to further conservatism on Ruburt's part. Now: in certain terms physical activity—sports—intrigued you. They were highly acceptable masculine pursuits. They were mainstream America. They allowed you to participate with others. To communicate with them on one level, while at other levels you preferred solitude, painting and writing; and you always observed.

The hay fever began early, the example set by your father, and you used it to temper your activities in terms of sports in particular, because your intents overall did not want you to go in that direction. You kept those physical abilities around, though—the feeling for sports—in school, with the idea that you could fall back upon them if need be. But you would have considered that a partial failure. Your high-school art teacher, Miss Bowman, lent you the money to study art in New York City.

The comics acquainted you with what I will call a kind of surface art, and also in a way acquainted you with caricatures of social reality. Also involved however were folk dreams, as for example with Captain Marvel. While you happily worked and caroused quite innocently, you also began half unconsciously to further question the nature, not necessarily of society, but of the individual lives you met within it. The deep drives of your personality began to make their way known.

Simple-enough incidents, like shoveling the driveway, can bother you because they arouse old conflicts having to do with your earlier situation and the decision, say, to explore your mental and creative abilities rather than to pursue the physical ones in the excellence of sports.

The excellence in sports, however, also involved the accepted thing to do. Sports even then were looked up to. Rewards were instantaneous for good performance. This involves black-and-white thinking again, however, for you thought of "perfect performance" in sports—high excellence. Something like the driveway usually involves an inner dilemma: "Shall I do creative work or physical activity?" in rather absolute terms.

The driveway involves the sports situation, and also the mainline-America theme—for shouldn't you be shoveling the walk like your neighbor? This involves questions like "How different am I from my neighbor? What does he think of me, working at home?" et cetera.

(10:10.) Give us a moment.... The issue is obviously then clouded by current ones, so that different details in a day can contribute, or serve as triggers.

When you do not approve of yourselves, then you do not approve of your own power, and so you pretend that you have none. Often the word "power" has bad implications: power corrupts, for example. Often you both pretend that you have no power in the society, and this is not the case.

Give us a moment.... Because you have not seen yourselves clearly, you cannot see or judge the difference in your quality of thought from your early adult years, for example, or perceive what you have learned. But all of your difficulties are based to one extent or another on self-rejection <u>that has gone unquestioned</u>.

There is nothing wrong of course with having your driveway plowed because you have other things that you want to do. That is a simple, excellent, choice.

Give us a moment.... When you feel at the same time that you <u>must</u> and should plow the driveway out yourself, to <u>prove</u> that you are the same as your neighbor, or to <u>prove</u> that you are physically agile, and on the other hand <u>if you feel that you do not want to plow out the driveway at all</u>, then you are in a quandary—and when you shovel, you tell your body to shovel and not to shovel at the same time, setting your muscles against each other.

Taxes or whatever might serve as a trigger, but the basic point is that you do not approve of what you are doing. If you shovel the drive, you think you should be working, and vice versa sometimes. The session should help you here.

Give us a moment.... In all cases, overexaggerations are involved. If you shovel you are not suddenly going to decide to devote yourself to a life of physical chores, and "meaningless" activity, and ignore your creative work. You are not that kind of person. If you paint or write steadily, that does not mean you will let all chores go. You are not <u>that</u> kind of person.

If Ruburt walks, he is not suddenly going to turn into a television personality and ignore his inner work. <u>He is not that kind of person.</u> Misunderstandings of your own abilities and characteristics are responsible for such unfortunate conclusions. Again, the New Year resolutions, really understood, can help you, for they will dissolve such thoughts.

Do you have questions?

(*"Well, we're making progress, I think. We read the resolutions over several times a day.")*

You have made progress.

(*"Jane continues to improve."*)

Indeed. The session should also help there.

(*"Okay."*)

I bid you a fond and hearty good evening.

(*"Thank you very much."*

(*10:25 PM.*

(*Jane wanted to know if Seth had covered all of the topics she'd listed before*

the session—then realized that he'd missed just one: Home. "But I can't get it now,"
she said. "He's gone.... I felt like we got a whole lot of stuff, though. I can't believe it;
you mean I was only out for an hour?"

(This afternoon, by the way, I made arrangements to have our driveway
plowed. It's now clear. It's also going to be plowed by the service station operator who
takes care of our car; whenever the snow accumulates to three inches or so, the clear-
ing-out will be automatically taken care of.

(I for one think the session of great benefit. I've felt quite a bit better. Seth's
insights in the session carry further the various hints and clues I've uncovered by using
the pendulum at different times—in a not very efficient way, I'm afraid, considering
how much the situation has bothered.

(It's my hunch that Seth's New Year's resolutions are perhaps the most potent
material we could get, provided we keep them in mind as time passes. I have a copy
of them up on the wall of the studio. So does Jane, in her work area.)

SESSION 831 (DELETED PORTION)
JANUARY 15, 1979 9:22 PM MONDAY

(The following material is from the 831st session.

(10:27.) Ruburt will have no difficulty with his teeth *(on Wednesday).* His
body is vastly releasing in the head and neck areas, and he is using the symbolism of the teeth to rid himself of several important problems.

Tell him to forget publishing for now, for he worries overmuch. His creative self knows he wants to publish another book, and will easily provide the
means when it is given some freedom and not told what it must do.

Let him simply write what comes into his mind. Try the library <u>playfully</u>
—or even paint. Physically he is indeed making strides, and Framework 2's
activity is helping, and will more. Do help encourage him in a more playful attitude.

(To me:) You are already collecting material yourself, but that will be your
own surprise to you.

End of session, and from now on we will have regular book dictation, and
personal information as well.

("Thank you very much, Seth.")

A fond good evening.

("Good night."

(10:34 PM. "I'm so unsure of myself it must be terrible," Jane said. "I'm so
glad he's back on the book again. I keep asking, 'Is it good; is it good?' I've got that

sickly feeling again.... Don't look at me like that...."

(A few notes: This session was held on Monday, January 15, 1979. On Wednesday Jane had several lower teeth extracted here at the house by Paul O'Neill. No problems. The next Wednesday, January 24, she had the last two out—again, no problems as I type this on January 25.)

SESSION 832 (DELETED PORTION)
JANUARY 29, 1979 9:11 PM MONDAY

(The following material is from the 832nd session.

(10:35.) Ruburt has been responding to new beliefs, and his walking and exercises, beautifully. The resolutions *(given in the deleted session for January 1, 1979)* have helped. The first very important change has been occurring; for he has progressed to a point where the knees' positions have altered. They are loosening. Ligaments are moving far more than, say, two weeks ago when the process began.

He felt this today in certain positions, but that period is just about over, of discomfort.

My prognosis is excellent, so I wanted you to know that. And *Seven* will be easily accomplished. And I bid you both a fond good evening.

("Thank you, Seth.")

(10:38 PM. True, Jane's knees have been changing quite a bit lately. Some of the changes have resulted in very painful moments for her, as today; at other times she does well. Today is one of the few times she's missed walking since she began her exercises.

(Added the next day, as I type these notes: The discomfort returned at times, but not to the extent of yesterday. It has the unfortunate effect, of course, of making Jane hesitate to try getting on her feet each time, whether to change chairs, go to the john, or whatever—an effect she tries hard to counter each time. Usually she is able to move sufficiently well without great discomfort. But she reports that there's no doubt the knees are more flexible—and noisier—than before.

(Seth's reference to—concerns a new Oversoul Seven book Jane has just begun. Ironically enough, the first episodes are built around a dentist, and these stemmed from her own recent experiences with extractions, as given in the just-previous deleted sessions. Already, Paul O'Neill has loaned her two books on the history of dentistry....)

SESSION 833 (DELETED PORTION)
JANUARY 31, 1979 9:21 PM WEDNESDAY

(The following material is from the 833rd session.

(10:10.) End of dictation. A few remarks. Ruburt is doing well. The entire area from the right side to the pelvis to the right foot is in the process of being newly released. And his discomfort will only be a memory in a few days.

I do not know how to explain this—but there are connections with different portions of the body that are not physical in your terms: correspondences. Ruburt senses some of these. The temples are important, and the relaxation there <u>did</u> help trigger the knee releases.

Your own material is excellent and valid.

We will continue the chapter at our next session. Do you have questions?

("Well, I was going to read Jane the page I wrote just before the session started, but I can do it next time.")

That is what I meant when I said the material was valid. I can discuss it next session.

("Okay. Seth. Thank you.")

Then I bid you a fond good evening.

(10:15 PM. Jane was more than a little surprised at the quick end of the session. "Gee, I felt like there were reams of material—just reams," she exclaimed. "I also felt like I was getting into the Guyana thing, without mentioning it by name. At least I thought I was."

(See the 833rd session for the proper connections with some of Seth's material here. His references to my own material being valid concerned my insights that many of the heads I paint represent my own psychic searches, or efforts, to obtain understanding of the dimensions of the psyche through reincarnation and counterpart depictions of those various personalities.)

SESSION 834 (DELETED PORTION)
FEBRUARY 5, 1979 8:59 PM MONDAY

(The following material is from the 834th session.

(9:31.) Now: much of Ruburt's problem was centered in jaw tension. Beliefs, as you know, were the cause of the tension. He used the occasion of losing the lower teeth completely to begin an overall release of tension. This was made possible through changes in beliefs—the resolutions *(given by Seth on January 1, 1979)*, and his own intent.

The back leg muscles are considerably released from what they were, say, a month ago. This is allowing the front leg muscles to release. The further release of tendons and greater mobility of the knee is following, and, just beginning, certain portions of the right ankle.

In certain positions, those areas hurt when his weight is on them in a certain way. This has frightened him. But he has done well with it. And he can do far better. The main thing is to remember the body's good intent, and its ability to follow through because fear of course increases tension on the muscles.

The legs are extending further, however, and sometimes when he walks in the bathroom this is quite obvious. Have him try walking to the couch, as yesterday, to begin with, but these changes definitely mean that the important alterations in the knees are happening.

Take your break.

(9:38. This was the end of the personal material.)

SESSION 835 (DELETED PORTION FEBRUARY 7, 1979 9:11 PM WEDNESDAY

(Seth's deleted material this evening is very brief, but it's presented separately so that the notes that follow can be presented in our private material.

(The following material is from the 835th session.

("I'll tell you something," Jane said as we sat for the session at 8:55. "I want to have a session, but ever since supper time I've had the greatest feelings of healing and relaxation—especially in my legs. Things are really changing.... Those feelings are stronger than anything I've had. I noticed them in the bathroom tonight too. So I'm telling you about this ahead of time, just in case I conk out or something. I want to have a book session, though."

(She's resumed walking a little bit both yesterday and today, and in more comfort than she'd had since the leg changes became more pronounced recently, and feels better about that. This afternoon I watched her do some of her exercises on the bed, and saw a noticeable improvement in many of her movements, especially those involving the knees—a most hopeful sign.

(Then at 9:04 Jane discovered a sudden freedom in bodily motion: She could reach across her chest with her left arm, toward her right side, at the same time that she turned to the right from the hips—a movement I hadn't seen her execute in years....

(It had been snowing for several hours by the time the session was due. The fall was very fine and light, and several inches had accumulated. I'd managed to shovel in the driveway twice, without reactions—a great relief. I'd reread the material on

myself in the deleted session for January 10, and plan to continue to do so.

("I guess I'll be all right...." Jane said just before the session began, "but I don't know how long it'll be."

(As things developed, she did fine in the session. Most all of it was book dicta-tion. When Seth asked at its close if I had any questions, this rather humorous exchange took place:

(10:17. "Do you want to say something about Jane?")

Ruburt is finally learning to trust the nature of his being—the self that is. His body will walk normally again, and his eyes will clear. End of session.

(10:18 PM. With a laugh: "Okay....")

SESSION 836 (DELETED PORTION)
FEBRUARY 26, 1979 8:33 PM MONDAY

(The following material is from the 836th session.

(9:46.) Some of the material *(in this session)* on pain should help clear Ruburt's mind, but the past week's blue periods and so forth simply represent-ed one more example of a situation in which he tried to make himself get bet-ter by "realizing the gravity of his condition"—by contrasting his performance against "normal" performance, and by the old beliefs of not trusting the body. These automatically bring forth feelings of hopelessness.

Your communication, however, is much better. You can help most by reminding him of our resolutions <u>when</u>, say, he feels blue—for when he remem-bers them he does not need the reminder *(with amusement)*—and simply by reassuring him of his body's good intent, and in its ability to follow through.

Whenever you can give it, then, reassurance with <u>tempered</u> sympathy.

His legs and thighs are releasing. <u>He should forget any past behaviors</u>, and start from the present, so that improvements are recognized and not lost in dis-satisfaction.

(9:51 approximately. From here on Seth returned to the regular session, saying good night at 9:54 PM.)

SESSION 838 (DELETED PORTION)
MARCH 5, 1979 9:14 PM MONDAY

(The following material is from the 838th session.

(9:59.) Do not forget the resolutions, either of you, and for Ruburt the

point of power. Trust in the body, for it is improving, and the feelings in the legs <u>are</u> caused by greater activity and circulation.

When you are clear of your galleys (*for Psyche*), then encourage more walking. (*10:00 PM.*)

SESSION 840 (DELETED PORTION)
MARCH 12, 1979 9:28 PM MONDAY

(*The following material is from the 840th session.*)
(*10:25.*) Ruburt is doing well. A small note: With more physical activity, let him talk to you anytime he feels conflicts between writing and physical activity—and I will speak about that next time.
(*"Okay. Good night."*)
(*10:26 PM.*)

SESSION 841 (DELETED PORTION)
MARCH 14, 1979 9:08 PM WEDNESDAY

(*The following material is from the 841st session.*)
Now let us look briefly at Ruburt's old man.
(*Here Seth refers to an article in the* National Enquirer *that has intrigued Jane considerably. It was printed in the issue for March 6, 1979: "Miracle of 80-Year-Old Marathon Runner." I think she's using it as quite an effective inspiration for herself.*)
He was indeed near death. He had severe heart disease. His circulatory system was affected, and he had breathing difficulties. He was 78. To that point, he had believed that his thoughts had no effect upon his body. He believed he could not get well. Then his own inner resources came to his assistance.
He decided to trust his body for the first time in his life, and to trust his mind. Almost overnight, relatively speaking, his heart regenerated, and two years later he ran the 26-mile marathon.
There is the other side of the picture, for his new thoughts physically regenerated the body, or allowed it to regenerate itself. Overnight—almost—he managed to completely change his picture of himself—and all of the physical evidence that before had confirmed his condition vanished. The social weight of other people's beliefs about him and his impending death, dissolved.
Ruburt is using that information well, and you have been excellent in your response and encouragement—and that, of course, is no coincidence. Your

thoughts about him to some extent also changed, and telepathically he becomes aware of that alteration.

The old man could have healed himself no matter what the physical difficulty had been....

The old man changed probabilities, you see, moving into another, and your thought patterns deal with probabilities all the time, at one level, as your c-e-l-l-s *(spelled)* do at another—so perhaps that will help you see more clearly the connections between health and illness, and the directions that your thoughts take.

All probabilities exist first in the imagination.

DELETED SESSION
MARCH 19, 1979 9:31 PM MONDAY

(Yesterday I finished typing up the 841st session, so now I'm all caught up on the sessions that had piled up while Jane and I worked checking the page proofs for Volume 2 of "Unknown" Reality, Psyche, *and similar matters. Now I'm organizing my files for new work, doing some painting, and making a few picture frames for both of us, a very pleasant interlude for a change. Today I picked up the lawnmower from the dealer who services it; tomorrow I take the cats, Billy Two and Mitzi, to the vet for their first encounter with Doc Davidson.*

(Two notes: 1. Last Thursday, March 15, Frank Longwell brought a two-day-old lamb with him when he visited us. Remarkable, that a creature that young could navigate so well, as well as possess a kind of beauty Jane and I were so unaccustomed to. 2. Last Saturday afternoon, March 17, Bob McClure visited us unexpectedly. His cancer had reoccurred; he had taken a new series of treatments for it, and was again in a state of in-between, or perhaps remission. We had an enlightening talk, and by the time he left Bob said more than once that he's "learned a lot" from Jane. Jane on the other hand was surprised at Bob's lack of insight into the challenge of cancer that he's taken on. But he seemed open to her ideas.

("It's liable to be a short session," Jane said at 9:15," I'm just doing it because I don't want to miss a turn." She was very relaxed, and had had a pleasant day. "I'm just waiting now," she said at 9:25. "I hate to do that...."

(As for myself, I have yet to add new questions to the list Seth suggested I make up, concerning his current material. This will take some study.

("I almost feel him around." Jane said at 9:26. Finally:)

Now: you read an article about a child suddenly cured of arthritis by a healer, and you wondered about it. *(See attached clipping.)*

You mentioned telepathy. And wondered what the child was picking up from the parents. Here I want to emphasize the importance that telepathy can play, and the vital role of suggestion.

(My remarks came about in response to Jane's wondering comments about what, if any, part beliefs could play in one getting so ill at such a young age. I thought our frame of reference wasn't large enough. If one wanted to consider telepathy, that could have an effect. So could the idea of reincarnation, and of counterparts, I added — three situations not considered within our ordinary contemporary scheme of things.)

Children are extremely sensitive, of course, to their parents' feelings and beliefs, particularly since they are dependent upon the parents to meet their needs. They can accept roles in somewhat the same way that children play at being sick, and in extreme cases some children find the game becomes only too real.

In a way the child allowed itself to be hypnotized into the condition, the symptoms becoming potent physical "posthypnotic" suggestions. The parents did not want the child to suffer. But on the other hand the mother was early frightened by the idea of a vital male baby, who might be overly rambunctious and difficult to control. She was overly fearful, ironically enough, for the child's safety—and hence he developed a condition that kept him under scrutiny all the while.

The child would not be run over by a car, for example, or pick up diseases from other children in school when he grew. He would be protected.

The disease showed itself early. The mother wanted the child to stay still, was worried lest it fall. It was actively motivated toward lack of motion. Such exaggerated fears, of course, were a strong element in the family itself, so that the family did not feel free to move. The woman was not easy in social life, and could now stay home to care for the small invalid.

(Pause.) The child wanted to please the parents. He received an over-abundance of sympathy, special treats, and so forth, so that his condition brought more and more rewards, even as he became more uncomfortable. The child responded in such a manner because of its own characteristics. Another child, for example, might have become overactive in rebellion. In a strange fashion, the pain represented heightened sensitivity – extremely unpleasant, but also represented a vital emotional bodily response of a direct nature. In other ways, the family behaved opaquely. Nothing seemed clear-cut.

Unfortunately, cries of pain brought the child instant attention, and they were often exaggerated. The child wanted out, finally, but did not know how, for he had allowed the destructive game to become real.

The healer was the hypnotist in reverse. The doctors had always acted doubtful, and professed pity, and the child recognized their feelings of hopelessness. The

Toddler Walks for First Time in a Year After Faith Healer Touches Him

By MARSHA MAY

Sobbing with pain, Johnnie Stevenson winced as his swollen joints and limbs were touched by faith healer Rev. George Fox. After half an hour of treatment — still in tears of agony — the 2-year-old boy was taken home by his parents.

The next day, the happy little tyke was walking — for the first time in more than a year!

"It's a miracle!" said the boy's father, Alex Stevenson, 37, of Uddingston, Scotland. "It was undoubtedly the work of God."

For a year, Johnnie, a victim of rheumatoid arthritis, had deteriorated. His tiny body swollen so badly that he couldn't even move.

"Johnnie was getting worse instead of better," admitted his physician, Dr. Gary Mearns, 28, who held no hope for the boy. "He just lay in bed, crippled.

"It eventually would have affected his vital organs such as heart and kidneys and almost certainly could have killed him."

Johnnie's mother, Marion Stevenson, 40, recalled: "They told me there was no hope of a cure. I couldn't stand seeing Johnnie in so much pain. His body was badly swollen and it was painful just holding him in my arms.

"So I made up my mind to take him to a faith healer."

Last October 12, the Stevensons took Johnnie to Rev. George Fox, a faith healer who was featured in The ENQUIRER's Dec. 13, 1977, issue.

"He was all swollen, and in great pain," said Rev. Fox, a Church of Scotland minister for 20 years. "I could hardly touch him because of the pain. I laid my hands on his swollen body and prayed for him."

Johnnie was still in agony after the half hour healing session, and his parents took him home, put him to bed and prayed for him.

"The very next morning — just 12 hours later — we heard Johnnie shout-ing," recalled his mother. "We couldn't believe our eyes. He was sitting up in bed — and there was no sign of the swelling.

"Later that day he climbed up onto the couch and was standing on his own. A couple hours later he walked for the first time in over a year.

"It was like something you read about in the Bible!"

Jean Shaw, 33, a neighbor, said, "The change in Johnnie is so remarkable. One day his hands were so swollen they looked like a pair of rubber gloves that had been inflated. But now he is running around. It is a miracle."

Dr. Mearns said: "I am amazed. There is no medical reason for this cure. It certainly can't be explained by our medical knowledge."

Johnnie's story is "remarkable," agreed Dr. J.T. Scott, head of the rheumatology department at Charing Cross Hospital in London. "There is no cure for this disease. The fact that the boy has gotten better so completely seems quite extraordinary."

Today Johnnie runs around like any normal boy, playing soccer, rocking on his rocking horse and pedaling his toy car. He takes no more of his medicine "because he doesn't need it anymore," said his mother.

Added his father, "We don't bother taking Johnnie to the hospital anymore. We took him back once and no one could believe the change in him, when three weeks earlier he had been crippled. Johnnie is cured!"

Rev. Fox

CUTE little Johnnie Stevenson can now play on his rocking horse.

(From The National Enquirer *of March 27, 1979)*

healer expressed confidence. The healer believed the child could be healed. Telepathically this was known. The man could stop the game.

(9:50.) The healer instantly reached the boy in Framework 2, whereas you know time is foreshortened—so in your terms results can appear far more quickly than in usual terms. The healer telepathically reminded the child that he was indeed full of energy and vitality. When this was fully understood, the previous suggestions vanished, with their results.

It is possible that such a healing can automatically give the family as a whole a new set of beliefs. If not, of course, one member or another may become ill, or the child might have a relapse. As probabilities go, however, the child's experience is enough to show it that such illness can indeed vanish overnight. Now that knowledge is a part of that child's experience, and the cure will be the great event of his life, in that it will always be in the back of his mind as he grows.

(Pause.) Get our friend some Pall Malls....

The child becomes a teacher for the parents, for the doctors who treated him, for the people who read the *Enquirer*, and for all the people who will meet the child as he matures. Remember the old man. Here the hypnosis, the suggestions, were self-applied, although many came from society's beliefs. The man was a contractor, given to physical labor in his younger years, but convinced that the minute he retired his body would begin to fail. It would deteriorate with age.

Furthermore. He believed that physical exertion <u>was</u> life itself, and he little appreciated the world of the mind, so little by little the self-suggestions took effect. His illness itself made him question, until finally he realized the great <u>mental</u> vitality he possessed. That mental vitality led him to trust his body once again, and to act in direct contradiction to those previous beliefs of the doctors, family, friends, and society that had so bound him.

(10:02.) Your friend Bob McClure believes that the self cannot be trusted, these beliefs coming from his parents' interpretation of Christianity.

Your friend then turned to other religions that still stressed the same beliefs, though in a more exotic form. To him sexual love must stand in direct opposition to spiritual love, so that his relationships with women put him in an impossible situation—and desire itself ultimately becomes a condition from which one must escape. *(Dryly:)* In the terms of earthly beliefs, there is but one escape from desire.

A man only gives up his soul when he has not met it face to face, and that is like bidding adieu to a stranger you have met at a train station: little loss, <u>for you do not know what you have missed</u>.

A note to our friend Susan: she is overly identifying as a woman who happens to be an individual, instead of as an individual who happens to be a woman

—and therefore finding herself involved in quite unnecessary dilemmas.

Ruburt is doing very well, removing the suggestions that have resulted in the symptoms, and finally beginning to trust the body, as the spring lamb trusted its body and its being. That trust is all that is required.

(To me:) When you consider your creative pursuits, trust the body of your creativity, and stop making judgments like this or that will probably never be done, or finished, and therefore limiting your probabilities. Remember Framework 2.

And now *(loudly)* I bid you a fond good evening.

("Thank you, Seth.")

(10:12 PM. Jane felt better. She's going to go over the recent sessions to see what portions of them fit into Mass Reality. *We agreed that much of the material is at least related to it.)*

DELETED SESSION
MARCH 26, 1979 9:49 PM MONDAY

(This afternoon Jane did her exercises on the bed as usual. Relaxing for her nap afterward, she asked for a message from her creative, spontaneous inner self, the part that keeps her body alive and gives her life meaning and inspiration. Then she fell asleep. Later, when she was getting supper, she realized suddenly that she'd had an experience after all, that "something had happened while I was asleep, and I was delighted with it while I was asleep." She couldn't recall any details, however. I suggested Seth discuss the experience tonight.

(Today Jane had been very upset because her control of time seemed so faulty that she wasn't getting all the things done through the day that she wanted to accomplish—writing, exercises, seeing an occasional visitor, using the phone—whatever she might have wanted to do on any particular day. I'd had somewhat the same feelings today, having managed to "work" at painting for but a couple of hours this morning. The rest of my time had been devoted to chores, it seemed, and both of us felt the day had slipped by without our knowing it.

(Before the session Jane showed me the paper she'd written this afternoon, on the direction she felt that Seth would be taking in Mass Reality. *I planned to attach it to this evening's session, but did not since this is private material. It may be added to the next, possibly the 844th, session.)*

Now.

("Good evening, Seth.")

Good evening.

(Pause.) Time. It takes so much physical time to perform any given number of physical activities.

The physical act of writing itself takes time. Basically, however, creative acts, the acts of insight, intuition, of revelation, do not take time in the same fashion. They often appear suddenly. A moment's insight, for example—a <u>moment's</u>— might carry you in a flash where your intellect alone could not travel in years.

It might take you years, possibly, to thoroughly discuss all of the ramifications of that insight, but the original creation comes from Framework 2 <u>into</u> your time. Taking it for granted, again, that physical <u>limitations</u> of time exist. Nevertheless when you become overly concerned with the seeming shortness or lack of time, it is almost always because you have fallen back to conventional ideas: you have only so many moments in a day. But the conventional version says, really, that those are surface moments; that you, say, run from one to the next, as if time were a moving sidewalk with the past moment vanishing forever.

In that version of events you must indeed be very careful of "how you use time." it seems that other people can steal your time away from you, prevent your use of creativity, when of course—literally, now—that is quite impossible.

No one can steal your time, or in any given moment prevent you from using your creativity. The <u>belief</u>, however, can certainly make that appear true.

In the first place, your intuitions are of course always working. Regular working hours can give you a time framework you need, in which those ideas can appear, but the ideas themselves, and the insights, often come to you particularly when you are not thinking of work. When you are doing any of a number of other things, encounters with others that often appear as distractions, are instead springboards for insights that you may not have had otherwise.

I am not saying that you should not have regular working hours. I am saying that you should change your beliefs concerning the nature of time and creativity—and for Ruburt, time, creativity, responsibility, and work. *(Pause.)* If you become more aware of those issues, the time that you have, all of it, will quite literally seem to expand. Ruburt in one moment is often mulling over and mentally arranging his time. Figuring out how he will get such-and-such done an hour or two hours from then—so he foreshortens the moment, in that it becomes far less full than it is capable of being for him.

Each physical moment is literally filled to the brim with the unceasing vitality of Framework 2. Regardless of what you are doing at any given time, the creative abilities are always active, and they seize upon the most mundane circumstances as well as the most profound, seeking to bring to the surface of consciousness the greater dimensions of awareness that are possible.

Ruburt has been thinking too much in terms of responsibility and work again. The attitude turns beloved projects into pursuits that <u>must</u> be performed along the surface of the moments. He has begun *Seven*, and so <u>it must be finished</u> (underlined), because, while he loves the book, he has begun to think of it as "work." So poetry lately, again, does not fit in, for he must have a certain number of pages to show "that he has used his time properly."

There is no way to use your time properly. <u>Properly</u> is not the way to use time *(intently)*. Left alone, your creativity knows its own rhythms, and drinks at the springs of Framework 2 at its own delightful leisure. That delightful leisure, that "loafing of the soul," from Ruburt's Whitman—the poet—is what ends up producing the kind of <u>great</u> creative "works" that Ruburt searches for.

(10:12.) What I am saying, again, is quite apart from your having regular working hours, but you would do far better to choose another word than "work." Your intuitive hours, perhaps, or your <u>creative hours</u>—even better—for in that kind of atmosphere the greatest works would result.

Framework 2 and its creativity takes <u>advantage</u> of your time—and <u>will</u> appear within it. But it operates according to the processes of association, and those processes dip in and out of time constantly.

(Amused:) I often break off book dictation also at certain <u>times</u> to help relieve Ruburt of feelings of responsibility, when he thinks that he should have book sessions because of the responsible work involved. Poetry, painting, and out-of-bodies are quite as much a part of his "work" as anything else he does. To some extent all of this applies to you also.

(10:18.) Now: Ruburt's body is responding far more than either of you presently realize, and this is because in that regard Ruburt's beliefs have been changing at a fast rate. Here the ideas of responsibility also have some application. He <u>does not</u> have a <u>responsibility</u> to sit constantly at his table, as if creative ideas could only <u>find</u> him there. This does not mean, again, that there is anything wrong with his sitting at his table five hours steadily if he wants to, but that he must loosen his beliefs about work and responsibility.

He did not remember this afternoon's message. The reason he did not is also the reason why people often do not remember certain dreams. The real communication is not verbal. It is not, say, a simple declaration, but involves realizations and insights of vital import that are given purposefully in such a way that they will gradually be sifted into consciousness because consciousness, the consciousness, would not be able to interpret the meanings in usual terms. This is not a good analogy particularly, but it is as if you received an important communication, say, three paragraphs of great import, with all the individual letters appearing, but not in their proper sequences, and gradually the letters would float together to form the proper words, and then the words would float together to form the proper sentences, and so forth.

In this case, however, deeper portions of the personality understand the message, and it will then in its own way rise to usual consciousness.

What I have said here tonight also contains material that will help Ruburt's physical condition.

(10:27.) Give us a moment.... Now: Pocket Books did not know what to do with *Seven. (See my question in session 842.)* It was fiction, and yet they were aware of Ruburt's psychic reputation. *(Pause.)* There were indeed problems within the firm, and the editor who liked the book was let go and unable to follow through as she would have liked.

Besides this, however, there are certain other elements working along with the *Seven* books.

Ruburt's books and my own—that is, Ruburt's psychic books—are considered nonfiction, clear and simple. The *Seven* books are considered novels, yet they are not science fiction. It is understood that the author is breaking new ground—but metaphysical ground. Some people who read our other books are afraid to read the *Seven* ones—for if Ruburt writes fiction, which means not fact, then they fear the line between fact and fiction blurs, and where is the Truth, in capital letters?

The mass reader is used to conventional science fiction. The metaphysical elements are actually quite at variance with the science fiction audience: the reincarnational aspects in particular. The book's very originality, therefore, to some extent has limited its readership. This is no simple Star Wars, for example.

At the same time all of this is known. The impact of all of our books goes far beyond, for example, the numbers sold, and it is in both of your natures *(with amused irony)* to send forth into your worlds books that are in exuberant opposition to its mass beliefs—*(much deeper)* so you can hardly expect the readership of gothic novels. Even I am more realistic than that!

The impact of the books is something else, again, and the steady sales and those steady sales will continue and accelerate. In terms of fiction, there are set categories, and *Seven* fits none of them. You are setting yourselves new categories. Enjoy the privilege, the ability, and the rewards, for the books do sell. People do listen.

Particularly in the beginning, for all of your joint complaints about Prentice, Prentice was innovative. *(With humor:)* I believe that Sadat on television this evening said *(louder)* that it takes time for old ideas to change.

You are working for a peace treaty of a different nature. I am not putting down the species in any way, yet it is true to say that *(pause)* people who are beyond their time, or ahead of it, cannot expect most people to accept their ideas so readily.

The mass best-sellers, for example: would you want to have the beliefs of the authors or the readers? I do not believe so. I meant to answer your question earlier. Have Ruburt read this session well. Do you have questions?

("Oh, about five million of them—but none right now.")

Then I bid you a creative and exuberant good evening.

("Thank you, Seth."

(10:44 PM. Seth's reference to President Anwar Sadat of Egypt came about because this afternoon Sadat, President Carter, and Prime Minister Begin of Israel had signed the long-sought-for peace treaty between their two countries. The event had been televised. We'd watched reruns of it on TV while we ate supper.)

SESSION 843 (DELETED)
MARCH 28, 1979 9:23 PM WEDNESDAY

(At 3:50 PM Jane told me that she'd just received from Seth a definition of cults. She repeated it as best she could: "....a closed, emotionally charged mental environment, in which the characteristics of individuality were purposefully undermined." Then a little later she picked up some more material while doing her exercises. Some of it drew a comparison between the paranoid individual, and an organization that contained the same ideas. The individual would be called ill for thinking the world was against him, but the organization's similar beliefs would be more unthinkingly accepted because of its sheer size and power in the society.

(In connection with that material, Jane wrote a paper on March 26, in which she briefly outlined the probable direction Seth would be taking in Mass Reality.

(While we waited for Seth to come through I read to Jane a couple of pages of rather disorganized material and notes I'd been working on this afternoon and evening. They'd been touched off by an article we'd just read in the March Esquire, *having to do with the supposed difficulty the male and the female have adjusting to each other. For the most part Jane and I regarded the article as a distorted jumble of various negative ideas.*

(I also asked if Seth could comment on my dream of Mrs. Johnson that I'd had last November, 1978. I showed Jane the pencil sketch of Mrs. Johnson that I'd done at the time. I've written my own longer notes explaining why I couldn't find my account of the dream—I believe I simply forgot to write it down—but since I remembered it well I described the dream to Jane now. I plan to do a small oil painting or two of the sketch I've done of Mrs. Johnson, plus another image of her that I hadn't drawn at the time, but retain well.

Mrs. Johnson
3/29/99

(I was surprised when Seth began this evening's session with material on the dream—but also pleased. A copy of his material is attached to my own material on this dream.

(Whispering:) Good evening.

("Good evening, Seth.")

Now. *(Pause.)* About your dream and drawing.

In dreams you often personify portions of the self. And meet them as if for the first time. Your Mrs. Patterson represents your own love for your fellow men and fellow women *(with gentle emphasis)*, and expresses a deep compassion for the situation of your species at this time.

Those characteristics are set in the form of an elderly woman whose pace bespeaks wisdom. She has no arms. However, her concern, her love and understanding, are seen only in the expression of her eyes and face. She cannot <u>embrace</u> the world, and so she is armless. Her concern and understanding also have a mental quality, as your own deepest feelings in those regards are expressed through art or writing <u>indirectly</u>, rather than through direct contact with others.

There are <u>indications</u> of arms beneath the clothing—indications only. For you embrace the world through, say, inner devotions rather than exterior acts. The woman is alone, with many empty rooms behind her, signifying that you set yourself apart from the many worlds of commerce in your day— meaning social commerce—and that such an understanding can also bring loneliness.

A certain amount of <u>comparative</u> isolation from the world is necessary if you <u>are</u> to understand man's condition. Yet the woman is not weak, but strong: nor is she unaware of some irony in the situation.

(9:34.) Give us a moment.... I believe the name Mrs. Patterson comes—

("Well, I'd called her Mrs. Johnson." I reminded Seth. In trance, leaning forward, Jane stared at me, momentarily quiet.)

Then give us another moment.... Ruburt's chain of association gave the name Patterson because of an old song. The *[name]* Johnson brings in the woman's sense of strength, and yet says that she is of ordinary heritage—a person of the earth, a powerful person in her way—and the connections with your associations have to do with the late President Johnson. Behind all of his carryings-on there was a strong quality of compassion that he found most difficult to express.

He was president of your country in trying times: rambunctious, at times crooked in his dealings. But with "common roots." In a way, the woman is the other side of that image. Her qualities are the ones you use to govern your psychic lands *(spelled).*

She is devoid of possessions of a physical nature, signifying that <u>she does not reach out toward</u> such possessions, but reaches with inner hands *(pause)* for other fruits.

The table is the one physical item, representing the domestic reality with which each person must deal. You could not have made the same points to yourself as well had the image been male, because of the beliefs that are ingrained in you. The portrait does represent then a portion of yourself—and a portion that understands <u>you</u> quite well, and took that form for your edification.

Take a very brief break.

("Thank you.")

(9:44. "Sorry about that." Jane said in reference to her substituting Mrs. Patterson for Mrs. Johnson while in trance. She said the Patterson connection was from an old song—perhaps a Beatle title—having to do with "Oh, Mrs. Patterson," or something like that.

(I thought the substitution of the names was more interesting than if it hadn't happened, I told Jane. "The ramifications may be endless. If I hadn't corrected him, Seth could have evidently interpreted the whole dream from that viewpoint, that of Mrs. Patterson, and the result would have been just as valid—different, maybe, but I'll bet with a lot of similarities." I thought the idea fascinating, and commented on the unexpected opening up of a new field of inquiry that ought to be most rewarding to follow—if we had the time. On second thought, I said, there may be few if any similarities in the interpretations through the two names, although each analysis could still be good.

(Return at 9:51 for a little more on the dream.)

There is a portion of each person that correlates with the meaning of that image.

It was created and interpreted according to your own individuality, but it will also remind others that within themselves they possess, each of them, the wisdom, <u>compassion</u> and understanding that exists, whether or not it is expressed in usual terms through physical acts.

(Pause.) Give us a moment.... When the dream gives you such an image, and the image becomes objectified, then you are of course showing a new part of yourself in the physical world, and bringing into expression <u>through your physical hands</u> the emotions that otherwise could not be expressed.

(9:55.) Now: Dictation.

I have just interpreted for Joseph a dream of his, in which he was able to express emotions of a rather profound nature, and I want to stress here that you are above all an <u>expressive</u> (underlined) species.

Your mental world is full of ideas and feelings that surge toward actualization. You have a need to express your <u>self</u>—and I am repeating the word "express" quite purpose<u>fully</u> *(with a smile)*. You must feel that <u>you are a self</u>, and that you can express that self in the world that you know.

(A note: I must write that not only was I surprised that Seth opened the session with an analysis of the dream, but that I was even more surprised with the generous connotations he ascribed to it: I may love my fellow man, but often times feel that that feeling is compromised by events in our world, even though I fully acknowledge my own part in helping create that world in the most intimate detail. Seth's interpretation of my feelings may be too generous. He may also be taking the larger view, as Jane often says he does. On that basis his material may very well express the content of that dream; from that wider viewpoint, I would feel the compassion he describes more openly. Perhaps it's all another reflection of that curious dichotomy I've often felt: One may rail against the world in general, and the behavior of its individuals in particular. Yet as one gets to know each of the individuals in his or her world in particular, it becomes more and more difficult to blame them for the state of the world, or much else for that matter: One becomes too enmeshed with their individuality and humanness. An understanding on a more personal level of the forces in their lives that push and pull them in often conflicting directions makes it very difficult to actively blame people for very much on an individual basis....)

In closed mental environments such expression is vigorously denied, and the very foundations of selfhood are attacked. I will use my own definition of a cult here, saying that a cult exists whenever a group forms a closed, emotionally charged mental environment in which the foundations of individuality are systematically and purposefully undermined.

In such situations you are taught that the self you have is not only flawed, but a facade—a fake self that cannot be trusted, and whose expression must be largely denied. You are told to give up the self to the leader of the group—the guru, the master, the father, the authority by whatever name.

Such systems distort the very nature of idealism by placing the ideal in such an exalted position that it can never be attained, for by giving up the self you have you are to attain instead a wholly pure, wholly loving, idealized, spiritual self. This self will love each other fellow being without reservations, distinctions, or judgment. This self is to miraculously appear as the old self is annihilated. The "annihilation" is accomplished by turning the will over to the authority. To act contrary to your own wishes or inclinations is considered a virtue. You are told not to make decisions, and to give yourself completely to the system of the cult.

(Pause at 10:10.) At the same time, there is much discussion about the good of mankind, ideal principles, goodness, charity and faith—but these are seen as possible only within the group, for the exterior world, you are told, is full of evil and corruption.

The group is always pitted against the world, which becomes its enemy. Paranoia reigns. Evidences of the world's corruption are collected, and any proofs of man's good intent begin to fade away. The end is seen as justifying the means. The hoped-for spiritual heaven on earth—in those terms (underlined) – is unattainable, of course.

The fundamentalist Christian groups, for all of their fanaticism, at least offer some kind of temporary relief for their believers; they are "saved" through prayer and good works. Many other sects, however, offer no such comfort, as for example the Guyana group. The concentration upon self-betrayal and worldly corruption offers no escape. Expression becomes meaningless under such conditions, not trusting the structure of the self, then the self's expression is denied. It is feared. Yet the new self never comes—not the promised, overly idealized self that feels a godly love without distinctions. And all good works appear meaningless in the terribly exaggerated picture painted of social and world events.

(Pause.) The concentration upon self-righteousness and evidence of corruption leads to its own fulfillment, and in that dark light the expression of the good appears powerless.

Such groups frown upon the questioning mind. They stress love of mankind, while at the same time cutting down on strong personal affiliations of a loving nature, so that love itself cannot seek its expression in concrete terms. Yet human love specifies, makes distinctions. It focuses with uncanny brilliance upon one individual. Such groups try to defuse that new *[true?]* focusing. They preach of love while allowing any given individual to love no particular person, and by forcing each individual to cut any bonds of love previously established.

Such people can love no one. All must be pretense. You are given your powers of decision for a reason. You are given the self that you know for a reason. Through fulfilling that self, through following your natural inclinations and desires, you will discover a spiritual and psychic fulfillment. You will expand yourself.

End of session, unless you have questions.

(10:29. "Would you say a few words for Frank Longwell?")

Give us a moment.... Only that he has learned much, and could not have considered taking his father in in this same manner, kindly and rationally, even a few years ago.

He still does not have all of the implications of the resolutions, but they will come to him. It is important that he and Eve not feel <u>martyred</u>, taking in the father, but I believe they both understand their positions there, and recognize they are forming their own realities and considering an act of kindness for its own sake.

His mother is enjoying being a young girl. That is, she is happily and knowingly hallucinating early girlhood experiences for the sheer joy of the freedom involved. She has made no decisions about rebirth yet, but is enjoying her freedom and keeping an eye out for her husband at the same time, thinking how enjoyable it will be for him to be lithe and free again.

The husband does not want it to seem that he is giving up too soon, however, which he seems to think would involve a loss of face. She is aware of her children, yet likes to appear <u>younger</u> than they are now for her own loving amusement.

End of session—

("Thank you.")

—and a fond good evening *(whispering)*. And I repeat: Ruburt's body is making considerably more beneficial changes than you presently realize.

("Good night, Seth.")

A fond good evening *(whispering.*

(10:36 PM. "I'm a natural stewer," Jane said. "I've just been wanting him to finish that chapter on the book. Maybe he can do one session a week on the book, and one on other stuff we want, or that comes up...." She's mentioned having Seth get back to Mass Reality *quite often lately, so we know that's what will happen soon.)*

JANE'S NOTES
MARCH 26, 1979 MONDAY

Today, Monday March 26, 1979 I briefly look over the start Seth has on chapter 6 of Mass Reality. *I'd been somewhat concerned about getting back to the book though the sessions have been excellent lately. Anyhow, got the idea when I put the book away that Seth would speak about things like the Moonies without mentioning them, idea being that the self as it is isn't trusted; as in the Jonestown thing. Such groups make people dissatisfied with the self as it is, and try to superimpose the idea of a superior self—realistically impossible. This generates more guilt of course....*

(There was some other stuff I got but I've forgotten it already.) Anyway the chapter was to be followed according to what I got, by one on frightened people who suddenly break out of old ideas, open their mental environments, and seemingly work miracles in their lives; like the old man, the old woman....

NOTES FOR SESSION 844 (DELETED)
APRIL 1, 1979 SUNDAY

(The last session we presented in Mass Events, *the 841st, was held on March 14. On the 19th we received from our publisher for checking, the proofs of the index for Volume 2 of* "Unknown" Reality, *then two days later the proofs for the front matter of* Psyche *arrived. Going over these two sets of material was routine; nothing had to be returned, and in each case Jane called Tam Mossman at Prentice-Hall to give her approval and to make a few suggestions for changes. She's worked each day at her third novel on* The Adventures of Oversoul Seven, *and has heard often from Sue Watkins about Sue's progress with her book on Jane's ESP class:* Conversations with Seth *and with all of her other activities. Jane has held four sessions since the 14th: two personal ones, and two [842-43] on matters other than book dictation.*

(Early last Wednesday an ominous development began unfolding at Three Mile Island, the nuclear-power-plant located on an island in the Susquehanna River below Harrisburg, Pennsylvania. It seems that through a combination of mechanical failures and human error, unit 2, one of the plant's two nuclear reactors, overheated and discharged radioactive water into the river, and began releasing small amounts of radioactive gasses into the atmosphere. [The entire plant is idle, since unit 1 had already been shut down for refueling.] By now the situation is much more serious, however: There's a chance of a catastrophic "meltdown" of the uranium fuel rods in the damaged reactor's core—the worst possible accident that can occur in such circumstances, short of an explosion, and a kind that proponents of nuclear power have long maintained "almost certainly cannot happen." If the meltdown takes place, spewing great clouds of radioactive materials into the atmosphere, several hundred thousand people could ultimately become casualties in one form or another.

(Now there's talk of evacuating up to a million people who live in the counties surrounding Three Mile Island. Some refugees have already reached the Elmira area, where we live, and upon checking a map Jane and I were surprised to see that we're only about 130 airline miles north of Harrisburg. We've driven the much longer road distance comfortably enough in one day. "Strange," I mused to Jane, "that of all the

nuclear power plants in the world, we end up living that close to the one that goes wrong...."

(Our region is supposed to be outside the danger zone—yet we see conflicting newspaper reports about whether the prevailing wind currents would make us vulnerable to the aftereffects of a meltdown. Even now local civil defense officials monitor the air several times daily with radiological survey meters—equipment similar to Geiger counters. Jonestown was far away, remote in another land, I said to Jane, but the potential mass tragedy of Three Mile Island hovers at the edges of our personal worlds. The whole affair has a sense of unreal immediacy, because there's nothing to see, and because I don't think most people really understand the probabilities involved. It would hardly be a coincidence, I added, that the mass events at Jonestown and Three Mile Island took place within less than six months of each other, and that they represented the two poles, or extremes, of mankind's present main belief systems: religion and science.

(Certainly we hope that as he continues with Mass Events. *Seth will comment extensively on Three Mile Island, just as he's in the process of doing about Jonestown. In fact, material on Three Mile Island developed in the session this afternoon— which is the main reason we decided to give these excerpts here.*

(Actually, the session might better be called a Jane/Seth session, in that Jane's own consciousness was often uppermost, riding upon Seth's underlying and steadying influence. This rather unusual situation came about because after lunch today she wrote excellent analyses of two dreams I'd had recently. As we sat at the kitchen table discussing her work, Jane felt that she could go into a trance state that was her own for a change, instead of being in "just" a Seth trance. She began delivering the material at a measured pace in her usual voice. As soon as I realized that she wanted to have a session I asked her to wait until I found my pen and notebook. Then Jane proceeded to come through with much evocative material on dreams—our second reason for excerpting the session for Mass Events. *Some of the more generalized dream material is presented below; some of the more individualized portions [which, in fact, came at the start of the session] are given in Note 2.*

(After drinking half a glass of milk during a break, Jane resumed her delivery at 4:30:)

This is just loose now....

NOTES ON SESSION 844 CONTINUED

(1. Sue has to do a considerable amount of research for Conversations with

Seth, *incidentally, especially locating, then interviewing—in person, by telephone or by mail, as the case may be—numerous class members. Many of them are scattered about the country by now, and some are abroad. Sue has also devised a very helpful questionnaire to be filled out by those cooperating in her study.*

(2. Much of Jane's trance material on how individuals use dreams personally came through in answer to a question of mine that we'd often speculated about lately: If most people do not remember their dreams most of the time, of what use can their dreams be to them? The question was really based upon our belief, indeed our certainty, that everything in nature is intentional and useful; therefore dreams must fulfill important roles in peoples' lives—but how, in ordinary terms? Here are quotations from the answers Jane gave while in trance:

"Even if you don't consciously remember your dreams, you <u>do</u> get the message. Part of it will appear in your daily experience in one way or another—in your conversation or daily events."

"Because dreams are such a perfect combination of stimuli from the inner environment <u>and the exterior environment</u>, other events are often used to trigger inner dream messages, just as the opposite occurs. And in a gathering of three people watching the same TV drama, say, each of them might be interpreting different portions of the program so that those portions correlate with their individual dreams of the night before, and serve to bring them their dream messages in ways they can accept...."

"Great discrimination is used so that, for example, one newspaper item is noticed over others because a certain portion of <u>that</u> item represents some of the dream's message. Another portion might come from a neighbor—but from the dreamer's <u>interpretation</u> of the neighbor's remark, that further brings home the dream message."

"In such cases the individual will scarcely be aware that a dream is involved...."

"You might dream of going away on a long trip by car, only to find that a tire blew when you were driving too fast. You may never remember the dream. One way or another, however, you will hit upon some kind of situation—a portion of a TV drama, perhaps—in which a tire is blown; or you will see an item of that nature in the newspaper, or you will hear a story, told directly or indirectly about the same kind of dilemma. The magnitude of the physical stimuli with which you are surrounded makes it possible, of course, for any number of like situations to come to your physical attention during any given day. Even then, you might not recall the dream, but the situation itself as it comes to your attention might make you check your tires, decide to put off your trip, or instead lead you to inner speculations about whether <u>you are going too fast</u> in a certain direction for your own good at this time. But you <u>will</u> get the dream's message."

SESSION 844 (DELETED)
APRIL 1, 1979 4:01 PM SUNDAY

*(This afternoon Jane finished typing her analyses of my dreams of March 29 and 31. The dreams were excellent ones and she did an excellent job interpreting them. The first one involved Bill Gallagher, the second one Jane's and my confrontation with a pack of large wild dogs. Some of the dogs bore human heads, and some human bodies and canine heads. This dream made a considerable impact on Jane— so much so that it's led us to some interesting new dream material that is dealt with in today's session. Both dreams are on file in my dream notebook, of course. An extra copy of this dream is attached to my own notebook that I'm letting grow all by itself into ideas that may be used in a work of my own, similar to Seth's original suggestion for*Through My Eyes.*

(Jane finished her typing the dream material at about 3:30 PM today. Next she got on her stool to do the dishes. As she sat at the sink she began to get more dream material, this time from Seth. She called me as I wrote my own dream material in my writing room. In the kitchen, she began to quote to me the first paragraph of what she was getting.

(I tried hard to focus on what she was telling me, so that I could write it down at once, but as she continued I saw that I'd inevitably lose a lot of it. I asked her if she could repeat her material if I got my notebook. She said yes. While I made ready for dictation she sat in her chair at the kitchen table. Neither of us had expected a spontaneous Seth session, but that's what developed. Jane started over. The first paragraph below substantially repeats what she first told me. She always kept her "own" voice, and spoke in a conversational manner throughout. Her dictation was a little fast, so that I scribbled notes at times. Although I worried about deciphering them later, I anticipate no problems.

(Rather often lately we've speculated about why most people don't remember their dreams. And if they don't, how can they make use of them? Since we certainly think nature has given our species—and probably most others—a dream life for a reason, we take it for granted that the dream material is put to good use in ways we may not understand. Dreaming could hardly be a useless creation on nature's part. Nor did we want to wait for science or psychology to explain dreams, since here we were having them all of the time. All of the material referred to in these notes, then, came together and furnished a foundation for the session to follow.)

Even if you don't consciously remember your dreams, you do get the message. Part of it will appear in your daily experience in one way or another—in your conversation or daily events. Our discussion about the Gallaghers not liking animals—really not liking them, was the exterior part of the dream (*of March 31, involving the dogs*). It brought up the same kind of questions, and Bill was in the dream (*on March 29*) before the one of the animals.

(*This material touched upon part of the discussion Jane and I had earlier today—that dreams should be studied in <u>sequence</u>, for additional meanings. A sequence of dreams, Jane said, would give a much better perspective on the dreamer's challenges, fear, etc., in life, and yield much better insights. Subject matter assumes a new kind of importance, then as does the relationship of one dream to another.*)

In the past, if people didn't remember their dreams, they'd project their dream events upon natural events, or read objective events as symbols that would actually express the dream itself. Now, even though people might forget their dreams, they often react to certain portions of TV dramas, or events that correlate with the dreams of the night before.

(*Consider all of Jane's material so far as the first paragraph of her material.*)

Because dreams are such a perfect combination of stimuli from the inner environment <u>and the exterior environment</u>, other events are often used to trigger inner dream messages, just as the opposite occurs. And in a gathering, say, of three people watching the same TV drama, each of them might be interpreting different portions of the program so that those portions correlate with their individual dreams of the night before, and serve to bring them their dream messages in ways they can accept.

Then earlier I got (*Jane said*), that when we're interpreting dreams, we should also look over groups of them, over a period of time, to see if you see yourself as a hero, a victim, a victor, bravely grappling with problems or whatever.

(*Laughing:*) I'm just getting some more. When you do remember your dreams, it can be quite effective to talk mentally with any of the dream images that are distressed or in difficulties, to bolster their courage or whatever, as you would bolster the courage of children for in a way these dream images are mental children.

It seems that your dreams are ineffective or unknown to you, or poorly realized, if you don't remember them. Or having remembered them you can't interpret them properly, meaning that in your terms you can't make sense of the dream message.

You have many other ways, however, of deciphering that dream message.

Dream memory and interpretation is the best, of course. It only occurs, however, under certain conditions, when the individual involved is at a certain state of awareness, in which he is ready to consciously accept such information as originating in dreams, and when the dreams are recognized by him as being an acceptable way of receiving information.

(More intently:) When dream information is also considered a <u>social asset</u>, or even a <u>political</u> one, when it is seen as one of the many tools of assessing private and national probabilities, then dream recall and interpretation becomes highly prominent, and can be raised to the highest of arts. When it is not recognized, or when the individual looks mainly to the exterior environment as the <u>provider</u> of information, then the dream's contents are projected onto objective events.

Great discrimination is used, so that, for example, certain portions of one newspaper item is noticed over others because <u>that</u> item represents some of the dream's message. Another portion might come from a neighbor, of course—but from the dreamer's interpretation of a neighbor's remark that further brings him the dream message.

In these cases the individual will scarcely be aware that a dream is involved. Before such communications, the normal world of social concourse and natural phenomena always provided a great backdrop, in which the dreams of the night before would speak their messages—and the exterior circumstances then become recognizable for inner insights.

You might dream, for example, of going away on a long trip by car, only to find that there were difficulties and a tire blew when you were driving too fast. You may never remember the dream. One way or another, however, you will hit upon some kind of situation—a portion of a TV situation—in which a tire is blown. Or you will see an item of that nature in the newspaper, or you will hear a story, told directly or indirectly about the same kind of dilemma. The magnitude of the physical stimuli with which you are surrounded, makes it possible, of course, for any number of like situations to come to your physical attention during any given day. Even then, you might not recall the dream, but the situation itself as it comes to your attention might make you check your tires, decide to put off your trip, or instead lead you to inner speculations about whether <u>you are going too fast</u> in a certain direction for your own good at this time. But you <u>will</u> get the dream's message.

(Approx. 4:22. Jane took a little break. "I was Seth then," she said, "but it was half and half there for a while. It was really funny," she laughed. "So I went into a Seth thing. It was more me topside, but he was definitely there at the end."

(I thought Seth's definitely at least influencing her delivery, too, for it had *"smoothed out" a bit compared to the slightly uneven manner in which she'd begun giving me the material.*

(Yet Jane had kept her own voice throughout, and I could tell that she, rather than Seth, was "in charge" of the session.

("Now I can get something on my own," she said. "Like you'll come across something in a TV drama, or see it in a newspaper or hear about it, and it has quite a charge for you—only you'll never connect it up with the dream you might have had the night before."

(Now she drank half a glass of milk. Then at 4:30:)

This is just loose now. But I've got a couple of points to make....

One was that because objects just originate in man's imagination anyway, there's always a strong connection between objects and man's dreams. They act as symbols of inner reality, so it's only natural that whether he's aware of it or not, man perceives objects in such a fashion that they also stand for symbols that first originate in his dreams.

This has to do also with larger events <u>that you might</u> for convenience's sake think of for now as psychological objects—that is, events seen and recognized by large numbers of people in the same way that objects are.

The Christ drama is a case in point, where private and mass dreams were then projected outward into the historical context of time, and then reacted to in such a way that various people became exterior participants—but in a far larger mass dream that was then interpreted in the most literal of physical terms. Even while it was, it also got the message across, though the inner drama itself was not recalled, and as the dream merged with historical events, and as it was interpreted by so many, its message also became distorted—or <u>rather</u>, it mixed and merged with other such dreams, whose messages were far different.

Look at your nuclear reactor troubles at the plant by Harrisburg *(Three Mile Island).* The entire idea of nuclear power was first a dream—an act of the imagination on the part of private individuals—and then through fiction and the arts a dream on the part of many people. Instantly, probabilities spun out from that dream in all directions with vast potentials and dangers.

It was hardly a coincidence that this particular situation <u>arrived</u> in the social climate first of all portrayed in a movie.

(The movie is The China Syndrome, *of course, with Michael Douglas, Jack Lemmon and Jane Fonda, which opened to rave reviews perhaps two weeks or so ago. The short story referred to above was reported on a TV program about Three Mile Island: Jane and I caught a glimpse of, I believe, a local newspaper or magazine in the Harrisburg area that had printed a short story about a nuclear accident at that plant, <u>on the same day</u> that the troubles began at Three Mile Island. We hadn't heard*

of the story. If I'm in error and the story was printed in a national magazine, for instance, we still haven't heard of it. Nor have we heard or read about this amazing "coincidence" since seeing that one mention of it on that TV newscast.

(I might as well use this opportunity to point up what I think is an obvious connection between the nuclear mishaps at Three Mile Island, and the mass suicide at Guyana [Jonestown] earlier this year. It could hardly be a coincidence, I remarked to Jane this noon that both mass events had taken place this year, and represented the two poles, or extremes, of mankind's present belief systems: religion and science. Then this afternoon Sue Watkins called Jane from Dundee—and proceeded to tell Jane about the "obvious connections" between Guyana and Harrisburg....)

Nuclear power stands for <u>power</u>, plain and simple. Is it good or bad? <u>It stands in man's dreams as belonging to God:</u> the power of the universe *(intently)*. Man has always considered himself, in your terms, as set apart from nature, so he must feel set apart from nature's <u>power</u>—and there must be a great division in his dreams between the two.

Nuclear energy in fact, then, comes as a dream symbol, and emerges into the world as something to be dealt with.

Fundamentalists think of nuclear power as a force that God might use, say, to destroy the world. That event in Harrisburg means one thing to them.

Some of the scientists equate nuclear power with man's great curiosity, and feel that they wrest this great energy from nature because they are "smarter than" nature is—smarter than nature, smarter than their fellow men—so they read those events in their own way. The probabilities are still surging, of course, and in private and mass dreams people try out all kinds of endings for that particular story.

All in all, millions of people are involved, who will be affected of course to one extent or another.

(4:45. "I've learned something this afternoon," Jane said during a brief unannounced break. "I've thought of it before, but finally I'm getting it through my head that the sessions are much better when I don't have any concern—and when I feel concern, I find it harder to get into it. I began to get cautious toward the end there, in some fashion... I think we'd have gotten more on the nuclear thing otherwise."

(She didn't think any fear of making predictions that might turn out to be wrong had anything to do with her concern.

("I remember he—Seth—even helped me out with stuff on the Christ drama in there," Jane said. "Oh-oh, there's more—" and she went back into "her" trance almost at once.)

There <u>was</u> a tie-in, and it's that the Christ drama happened as a result of man's <u>dream</u>, at least, of achieving brotherhood—a quiet, secure sense of consciousness, and a morality that would sustain him in the physical world.

The Christ drama <u>did</u> splash over into historical reality. Man's fears of <u>not</u> achieving brotherhood, of not achieving a secure state of consciousness, or a workable morality, result in his dreams of destruction, however they are expressed, and indeed, the present physical event as it exists now at the energy plant in Harrisburg can easily be likened to—and is—a warning dream to change man's actions.

(End at 4:47 PM. "Okay," Jane said. "I knew there was some connection between the Christ thing and what's happening in the world today, and that was it. I like it when it's fun, and that was fun. That was a nice smooth state of consciousness."

("I should mention a couple more things, though. This happened at a time of day when I'm not usually at my best – around four in the afternoon. And I'll often get things like I did the first part of this session, when I was busy with the dishes. I'll notice it, then say to myself that I'll tell Rob later.... So I wonder how often I've missed out on some good stuff by doing it that way, especially when I even forget to tell him about it."

("Well," I said, "you might have lost some things by doing that, but don't worry about it. You can't be turned on all the time."

(Now here is some material Jane wrote later in the day, following Sunday afternoon's session. She began giving it to me verbally after taking her nap before supper, but I asked her to write it down for this record. Involved is my dream of March 31.)

Jane's notes: Sunday, April 1, 1979.

("This afternoon I interpreted some of Rob's latest dreams, one in particular involving me, beating a black-haired dog on the head. The dog was my spontaneous self according to my interpretation."

("I finished the dreams and did the day's dishes. Suddenly I got some material on dreams that I knew was from Seth. I called Rob, and when I told him what I had, a spontaneous Seth session began—most enjoyable from my standpoint.... My consciousness seemed to be riding on top of his [Seth's] in a funny way."

("Later when I took a brief nap I mentally imagined myself beating the black-haired dog—and my mental right arm really went bang, bang, bang, banging wooden blocks on the dog's head really fast, and for a minute I couldn't stop it. Finally I did, and saw myself petting the dog, brushing it, and telling it I was sorry...."

(See the Harrisburg material on file.)

SESSION 846 (DELETED PORTION)
APRIL 4, 1979 9:30 PM WEDNESDAY

(I'd asked Jane today if Seth could discuss briefly two subjects in the session this evening: My recent hassles with the discomfort in my side and groin, and Jane's right hand. I hardly thought it a coincidence that my side began bothering me—as it had years ago—just when we'd finished our work on the page proofs for Volume 2 of "Unknown" and Psyche, *and I was free of that work load for the first time in a long while. I'd obtained what I thought was some good pendulum material on the problem, and wanted to see if Seth confirmed it. As usual, his material added more insights.*

(My question about Jane's hand, her writing hand, had been on my mind for some time now. For she's been carrying that hand with all but the index finger turned under more than ever; indeed, she cannot straighten the fingers, and I've worried about that situation. Especially am I curious about why the hand thing when her walking continues to improve?

(The following material, then, is from the 846th session.)

(10:22.) Your side bothers you when you want to be on the right side of yourself, as in the old term, getting up on the right side of the bed. In other words, you are perturbed over what is the proper direction for you to take—not trusting yourself to make the proper decision automatically, but wanting to force a quick conscious decision so that you will know what to do, and have it over with.

(Pause.) Your dog dream *(of March 31, 1979)* also somewhat symbolizes that dilemma: do you go with your head, forcing a conscious decision, or do you go with your instincts, symbolized by the dog's form? The question itself causes the dilemma of the dream—that is, the separation of the two in your mind, instinct and reason, causes the uneasy confrontation. There is no separation, of course, only a seeming one, for again, the mind's conscious processes are spontaneous, and the body's instincts are highly disciplined, so there is no need to vacillate between one side of the question or the other.

("It's the left side that bothers." I reminded Seth.)

In your mind, the left side represents the unconscious portions of the personality. Do you follow?

("Yes.")

The situation with Ruburt is such that conditions like the hand are transitory, as with other conditions that bothered him and left. Do you remember them?—

(I nodded yes.)

—and simply occurred as old balances were broken down, and new ones established.

I do not want to get into a long discussion on Ruburt this evening—but *(with much humor)* I will bring you an update shortly of a comprehensive nature.

("Okay.")

The dreams are as Ruburt interpreted them, dealing with your feelings about prominence.

Give us a moment.... In the first *(on April 3, 1979)*, you are with an exotic move star, who would not ordinarily appear in a grocery store or a supermarket *(actually a five-and-dime in the dream)*. She is exotic and foreign, an old friend. You greet her fondly. Ruburt should like this, for the actress stands for your idealized version of Jane, as a star however in a different theater. You are at her side, and the supermarket stands for the marketplace.

In the second dream *(on April 4, 1979)*, Bill Macdonnel, whom you do not consider an excellent artist, reflects your own sometimes confused feelings about what might have happened had you devoted your work primarily and exclusively to art, or played the artist, as Bill does. The work, however, would not have been right for you, but upside down in a fashion, because with your knowledge before, say, our sessions, your particular blend of psychic abilities and writing abilities would not have developed; your painting would have lacked, in a way that would be quite noticeable to you. In the dream you realize that your way is better.

Your brother *(Loren)* represents strong beliefs that you had and identified with, that could have been very limiting. You avoided them, or rather, left them behind. You do have a kind of prominence now, and your work is on a different kind of public mural.

The younger people represent versions of yourself, who wonder at your prominence in a different field, but you do not care. Your paintings now, and your best ones, you see, will evolve as a result of the psychic understanding you are learning. You cannot compare artists, for each is gifted in a different way.

End of session—

("Thank you very much. Very interesting.")

—and a fond good evening.

("The same to you."

(With amusement) I hope the atmosphere is calmer now.

("So do I. Good night."

(10:41 PM. "Gee, that wasn't long," Jane said, looking at the clock. "I told myself before the session that you're supposed to identify with your creative self, so I

just said I'd go along with whatever happened in the session. I didn't care what it was, I'd do it."

(She remembered Seth talking about my own hassles, and the dreams. She felt much better now. I felt good too, about getting the personal information. In a more penetrating way, Seth enlarged upon some of the pendulum information I'd picked up.)

DELETED SESSION
APRIL 9, 1979 9:18 PM MONDAY

(Before the session I burdened Jane again with my hassles about my side and groin. I'd felt somewhat better after Seth's information about those portions of my anatomy in the deleted part of the last session, the 846th, for the previous Wednesday. The feelings hadn't cleared up sufficiently, though, and today they had been especially bothersome. I was really uncomfortable by session time, I told Jane. She listened with a worried air. She didn't say a great deal, except that she'd try to get herself in a quiet mood in order to have the session, and hope Seth could help. I was personally quietly disgusted by the whole affair, and told her I'd cheerfully dispense with whatever was causing the upset, lest it turn into a chronic physical inconvenience. I also said I thought the whole thing was in my head.

(I've received various answers from the pendulum on the background causes for my upset; not really contradictory, by and large, but signifying to me that in spite of my concern I hadn't been willing to buckle down and really work at uncovering the beliefs causing the unrest. Interesting observation.

(I'll begin the private material with a paragraph that's not strictly private, in order to set the scene—although actually Seth says little enough to me.)

(10:17.) In man, again, generally speaking, reason and emotion become separated so that man can think about his emotions, or emotionally feel his reasoning thoughts. Now. In human health difficulties, usually, the paths taken by reasoning and emotions become, say, too divergent, so that the reasoning mind says one thing and the emotions say something else. Fears as emotions are not reasonably considered, and thoughts are not emotionally tinged.

In your case, I meant to mention *(in the last session)* that the time of taxes has some involvement with your difficulties, for reason tells you they must be paid, while your emotions are resentful. You are not sure whether your creative work will "pay off"—that is, whether you will be adding to the financial kitty. Hence your dilemma as to what projects you <u>should</u> do or not do.

As I mentioned, the creative spontaneous self knows of your entire situation, <u>so that</u> its unimpeded production will automatically meet all of your needs.

I believe I have answered all of your questions. And I bid you a fond good evening.

("Thank you very much, Seth."

(10:25. We thought the session was over at this point, but Seth did return a minute later for a little more material related to the body of tonight's session. End then at 10:29 PM.

(I was a little surprised at Seth's mention of taxes, since my pendulum hadn't brought this fact out. I'd thought I had fairly well put the problem of taxes in its place after a number of hassles over them in recent years; that is, I thought I'd learned <u>something</u> there....

(However, I did feel better by session's end. I went for a walk near midnight, slept well, and have had a better day today. The feelings linger, though in a much subdued form. I talked with our tax man, Jack Joyce, on the telephone today; we may get our forms Thursday. I want to pay the taxes by Friday to get free of them, and to see if this act helps set me free. I think that because of the Easter weekend coming up, an extension of the tax-paying deadline until next Tuesday the 17th is permissible, but I don't want to wait that long.

(At 8:30 PM, Tuesday, April 10, 1979, pendulum says:

1. *I <u>am</u> concerned about what to do next.*
2. *I worry that* Through My Eyes, *say, will take too long.*
3. *I'm mad at Prentice for various reasons, while not being blind to their good points.*
4. *I <u>do</u> resent paying the taxes.*
   [All of these contribute to the physical effects.]
5. *<u>My side bothers me because I'm not working on</u> Mass Reality. *[Related to 1 & 2, obviously.]*
6. *Note: Insight received at 10:15 PM: The feelings in the groin of "having to go" all the time, are nervous interpretations on my part of the urge "to go" ahead creatively in whatever way is chosen....)*

DELETED SESSION
APRIL 16, 1979 9:51 PM MONDAY

(I'm making an extra carbon of the session for my own records.

(Here's a copy of the paper I wrote on April 15, following the material Seth gave for me in the deleted portion of the session, the 847th, for April 9:

("We didn't get the tax forms from Jack Joyce until Saturday, April 14. This means we can't pay them until Monday, the 16th, the day after Easter.

("My side bothers me considerably as I write this, at 8:30 PM. Yet I went for a walk after supper. I'm distinctly uneasy. After napping Thursday afternoon [the 12th] I fell into a deep depression, not speaking to anyone any more than necessary. This obviously involved Jane more than anyone else. My physical hassles have waxed and waned—I'm hoping that paying the taxes tomorrow helps. [They amount to much less than I'd figured on, incidentally—including estimated payments for 1979 —so one would expect me to respond to that—but I haven't yet.

("The pendulum insists there's nothing wrong physically in the side-groin area, but I'm beginning to wonder. Pendulum tells me the side bothers because I'm not working on Mass Reality, *which will get us money, whereas* Through My Eyes *is a less-certain project, would take longer, and the time I spend on it is time lost on* Mass Reality. *In other words, I'm very concerned about my financial contribution, and paying all those taxes exacerbates it all.*

("The pendulum says I don't think I'll get money for Through My Eyes, *that it's a waste of time, that I don't want to work on it. I do want to work on* Mass Reality, *so as soon as I finish my filing for* Through My Eyes, *I'll start in on* Mass Reality.*

("The pendulum says my side started to bother me after I estimated $70,000 income for tax purposes for 1979, without seeing how Jane and I have any chance yet to bring in that much this year."

(I should note here that last Friday evening we were visited by the Gallaghers and Sue Watkins. As the evening progressed we became involved in some pretty heated and involved discussions about Three Mile Island, man's greed for money, his basic good intent, and related issues. Bill and Sue especially got going pretty good, and Peggy said she didn't like that. I think I made some good points; even Bill said he probably exaggerated man's greed, yet he wasn't about to change his views. Sue was upset. Jane was too, yet tried to take it all in. I probably spoke more frankly than I had in the past, yet was oddly unbothered by it all.

(I do wish I had on record some of my remarks, since in them I clarified some of my own ideas about man's behavior versus his basic good intent.

(Then while doing the dishes before this evening's session, Jane said she "got" that Friday night was the "playout" of my dreams involving Bill Gallagher and Sue, which had taken place separately. The playout wasn't literal, Jane said, "So I don't think most people would have made the connections. But I picked up that Seth would go into those dreams tonight, and I asked that he give the best information that he could."

(I'd temporarily forgotten the dreams about Bill and Sue, although I have

them selected for inclusion in Through My Eyes; *they're on file in that notebook. The one with Bill took place on March 29, 1979. Sue on March 31, 1979. This was a period in which I had a series of potent dreams that Jane has done a lot of work interpreting [including my famous dog dream of March 31, 1979], and which could easily make up several chapters in a book on the subject, if we had the time to produce it. These dreams have been operating as a series, as Jane has pointed out, which increases the value of a person's dreams in unexpected ways. I think some original ideas are embodied here. Jane has interpreted the Bill and Sue dreams, and Seth has commented on them also. See the 845th session. All of Seth's dream material has been excellent, by the way.*

(Now here's a copy of the paper I wrote tonight at 8:30 PM [on 4/16/79:]

("After supper tonight I told Jane that I felt as though I was "near a breaking point," that I might have to seek medical help. For what I wasn't sure—a hernia, something wrong in my side, stomach, or what. She was upset. We'd slept this afternoon from 2:30 until 6. I'd hoped I would feel better with the rest, which I seemed to crave, but it hadn't helped. Nor had paying the taxes this morning, although it could take the body a while to respond to any change in status or thinking, and I'd seen this happen before.

("The trouble appears to be in the lower left groin or side, with ramifications at times in the left testicle. I don't think the latter is the primary cause, though, even with the enlarged veins I've had there for many years. Today, my stomach began bothering; I've taken baking soda three times, and that seemed to help, if temporarily, each time. Walking also helps.

("Tonight the pendulum says just what it did yesterday—that I feel poorly because I estimated a high income when we don't have it in sight; that I think I should be working on Mass Reality *instead of* Through My Eyes *because the former will bring in sure money; that I think I don't contribute enough financially; that I feel lousy because I want something definite to work on —that at this time I'm not contributing enough. The pendulum also says I think I deserve the symptoms for the above reasons.*

("The pendulum also says I think my body is capable of healing itself, wants to heal itself, and that I want it to heal itself. It also says I do not think it's safe to get well. I don't feel bad because of Jane's symptoms, although I'm very concerned about them daily.

("The pendulum repeated my insight of a couple of days ago—one that may be very important: that all of my upsets over the years, the stomach, the side, the groin, the shoulder—the whole bunch—stem from my consistent feeling that I'm a failure in life, that I don't contribute enough, that I don't help Jane enough, that I haven't really made it as an artist or as a writer.

("The pendulum also says I <u>can</u> make it as an artist <u>and</u> writer, and that I'm too hard on myself. I've begun reading Seth's New Year's resolutions again, and these have helped."

(I read my paper quoted just above to Jane as we sat for the session. I asked that Seth comment, but also said I didn't want him devoting the whole session to my challenges, since I know Jane wants book material also.)

Good evening.

("Good evening, Seth.")

Now: let us return to your dream series. You know the one I am referring to.

Now: let us see how recent events reflect the dream, and how they appeared in the dream in symbolic form. The physical events I refer to are the encounters with the Gallaghers and Sue Watkins Friday evening—the discussion of philosophy, the sense of conflict and mixed emotions.

In the dream *(of March 29)* Bill Gallagher offers to take you out to dinner, and you say you have good food at home. Here the word "food" refers to nourishment. He offers the nourishment of the world—but the world as he perceives it, and instead you prefer your private nourishment. Bill Gallagher sees a dog-eat-dog world, and, as mentioned earlier, animals have an entirely different meaning to Bill.

The evening found you in a clash of ideas, as Bill painted the world through the most pessimistic of eyes. He saw man's greed for money everywhere predominate. The rest of you to varying extents objected, because he portrayed so clearly the darkest of your own fears and imaginings in exaggerated fashion.

<u>To some extent</u> (underlined) now, his beliefs stand for a certain conventionalized view of the world. <u>To some extent</u> (underlined) those views, colored by a different era, were those of your own father, concerning at least the world of commerce, business, and so forth. You all felt that those dire events of the cultural and social world were somehow transposed over the natural one.

(The phone began to ring at 10:00, much to my surprise. In trance, Jane stared at me. "Forget it," I told Seth.)

Now: Bill Gallagher, with his beliefs about that world, in his mind joined it. He felt that he betrayed himself, that he performed acts that he should not perform in order to fit into its context, and he felt that he must do so in order to survive.

You were astonished when Ruburt told you how much money the Gallaghers were making, for if Bill sold his soul, few it seems could have sold it for less. Bill, however, concentrated upon life's regrettable elements, upon the impediments, the dishonesties and so forth, until it seemed that even if he followed the world's way he could not succeed. His idea of manliness was such that he insisted upon a conventional job, clear-cut.

(As Jane spoke in trance, Mitzi jumped up into her lap. The phone had stopped ringing some time ago. As of this writing, the next evening, we still don't know who tried to call. Mitzi is our beloved cat.)

As the evening progressed Sue Watkins became more and more upset, as Bill pointed out the toll that society demanded, the impossible stakes and the penalties that must be paid. Bill feels that his business productive life is coming to an end, when he will retire. He spoke of the values that existed when he was young in the world, that now are gone. With all of that as background, then look back to the time clock you found, hidden in your dream in a closet.

It refers not only to the matters that I have mentioned in past sessions, but also to your ideas of age, and those are also connected to your ideas of manliness, for you want to be a provider.

(10:07.) Now: the route you chose was far different than your friend's. You did not choose a job as a life endeavor, where money would be clearly paid for acts specifically assigned, nor did you choose a route for which there was any conventional role for you to follow.

When you pursue new avenues, there are no such easy ways to assess success or failure *(intently)*. Thinking in terms of the conventional world, however, you feel sometimes at a loss, for you want to say, "What am I?" in those terms (underlined)—an artist, or a writer, or a combination of the two? Ruburt wonders, what is he—a writer, a psychic, a combination of the two? The books bear his name, so you feel that they are primarily his, and yet all of those feelings ignore completely the larger realities of your lives and of your work.

If you were just a writer or just an artist, or if Ruburt were just a writer or just a psychic, then neither of you would be involved in this endeavor, which is even in your terms, of such a creative nature that it defies definitions. It does not rest in either of you alone, but rises from joint psychological structures *(intently)* that you have formed together, each using what characteristics you could—psychological structures that you then can use to gain a viewpoint upon reality that is so unique.

Next to that kind of achievement, conventional ideas of success or failure are literally ludicrous in basic terms, though I understand the hold that cultural beliefs can still have upon you.

Those doubts, however, of course mitigate strongly against your feelings of self-approval, and undermine your natural stamina and courage. Ruburt was bothered by the same feelings in reverse in the past, but he has learned to understand quite clearly that our work is a threefold venture. It would not exist in its present form—and its present form is its best form—were it not for your own participation. In a fashion you are merging arts together, and laying the groundwork for new kinds of art that presently do not exist.

You succeed sometimes in spite of yourselves, for it does not escape the Gallaghers of course that you are very well off financially <u>as the very result of the very unconventionality</u> of mind that it seems you sometimes find at least <u>a bit</u> regrettable.

The ideas of age bring this kind of thing into focus. They make Bill Gallagher for example more bitter about his life, for he feels cheated of the rewards when he followed the system. Conventional ideas of age, however, can limit your own ideas of your own creativity. You start thinking "How much time is available?" when the very creative thoughts themselves make more time available.

Take a brief break.

(10:23. We talked about the dream involved with tonight's session material. I wondered if it was legitimate to say that the group of dreams was a precognitive insight into the one event—the Friday night gathering. Jane thought so. If true, it would be an original insight, I said. Not that the dreams presaged Friday night's event <u>*per se*</u>*, but* <u>*pointed toward some sort of event like it taking place*</u>*. I told Jane that I didn't remember reading any ideas like this anywhere.*

(Resume at 10:32.)

Now: beside other reasons, the taxes serve as a focal point, because you feel you must pay tribute to the world that is described by Bill Gallagher—<u>and in that world</u> you feel you have no <u>specific</u> (underlined) conventional role, as earlier mentioned.

Ruburt used to feel embarrassed because he made more money in those terms than you, and certainly this played some role initially in the symptoms. *(Does it still?)* You could not have a job, obviously. You had to take care of him, and it seemed you both saved face; but almost all of your problems come from the unthinking acceptance of conventional ideas that have been allowed to hold sway.

The discomfort in the testicle reflects the problem you feel with the masculine role. But the typical masculine role in your country, you must understand, is certainly not primarily that of an artist. If the male has natural abilities that happen to fall among those largely accepted by society, then there is little problem—<u>in that regard</u> at least—but if his natural abilities lie in other directions, then difficulties can arise.

You did what you wanted to do, in line with your own natural inclinations, and only when you judge your circumstances against convention's surface beliefs do you lack your own approval. You cannot rate the subjective growth of a personality, lines of comprehension, or the value of ideas given to the world. You are a success in lines that can be <u>felt</u> by the world but not measured. The books are more effective than any letter to a congressman, and you put the substance of your life into your notes.

(*Seth's reference to a letter to a congressman came about, I think, because during our conversation on Friday night Bill Gallagher said that no one present had done anything to protest the conditions in our world that we didn't like—forgetting, of course, that the books themselves are full of protests, and of suggestions for the better. But Bill doesn't read the books, and to that extent lives in a world closed off from such ideas.*)

Now give us a moment.

Ruburt's experiences (*of April 12; see the end of the session*) were excellent, and did affect you beneficially at other levels, by releasing comprehensions that will appear in your time.

The experiences also kept him from becoming too embroiled in your mood at the time, and by giving him an experience of your own joint greater subjective reality. The reincarnation dream (*see the end of the session*), however, had to do with Nebene, who resented any tribute paid to Rome, and was enraged by the crooked practices of all the tax collectors. He did not ascribe to Rome's religion, or really agree with its government, and he felt that taxes simply represented money given to rogues and thieves to enrich the pockets of the wealthy. He himself believed in austerity.

Ruburt thinks of taxes as money paid to society for leaving him alone. He pays his dues, so to speak. The dream did involve Saturday's visit with the tax accountant (*Jack Joyce*), which in a way was a re-creation of the dream. Ruburt knew a few moments before the man's visit that the taxes would be less than you supposed. He had been worried they might be <u>more</u>, and that you might become more upset.

(*10:47.*) The tax man is a well-meaning individual, far from a rogue, with his own problems, and in the dream this information is realized by you, and hence picked up by Nebene. Joyce, by his very characteristics, in his way stood for the confused but well-meaning-enough society. Ruburt felt he had paid his dues, physically speaking, and was done with that.

His body is definitely improving, but you must both examine your beliefs again about the conventional matters I have spoken about this evening, for they affect your behavior. You need to free yourselves in your work, allow for regular hours, but as I have often told you, arrange for changes of your own choosing—ordered change is excellent. You lack the give-and-take with others that jobs provide. You need solitude. Yet you must also provide for changes within that routine, for those changes give you a different view of your own subjective reality. And they can often help you solve problems, simply because old associations are broken up.

You usually do not follow through on such suggestions. Do you have questions?

("No, I think this is enough for one night. It's very good. Thank you.")

Then I wish you a fond good evening.

("Thank you, Seth.")

(10:49 PM. Now here are the "three exercises or experiments Jane tried in an effort to help me when I was in such a despondent mood last Thursday, April 12. She said later that when I evidently didn't get anything out of them consciously, that this made her question the value of similar things she tries to do for others.

(1. "Exercise: to send energy to Rob. Mentally see him in his studio, at drawing table. Imagine and visualize the energy all around the corner of the house and sky, rushing toward him; then am surprised when mentally the top of his head comes neatly off, like a lid from a jar. I see hands, mine I think, reaching in, straightening things out [as you'd untangle a telephone cord]. This upset me some. I was leery as if I didn't know if I could harm him, rummaging around in there like that; then realized that these images represented tangles of thought that were being smoothed out. A few minutes later Rob is in the living room and I think he was watering the plants really. I thought he was in his studio and that's where I saw all this. [About 9:30 AM.]

(2. "2:20 PM. Imagine Rob in writing room, soft, warm yellow light shines on him from Framework two, and though I didn't specify, the light lingers particularly on his shoulder. Then I see him quite clearly in miniature, jumping and rolling high in the air, throwing his arms out....

(3. "8:30 PM....Decide to.... do another exercise with Rob. Instantly I see him seated in writing room and behind him stands a transparent whitish woman's image, my astral self. From behind Rob, standing, she lightly soothes his forehead, then quickly is in his lap, facing him, sort of melting in with him; then they express their love.... or the actions express it....together in a fashion I can't describe of both of their astral forms entwined, fly off into space. They separate, doing ballets in the sky come together again; very free."

(Here is Jane's account of the dream of April 13, Friday, mentioned by Seth on page 97 of the session. Note that she had it the day before the tax man, Jack Joyce, visited us, and the day after she'd tried her three experiments for me:

("Before nap I asked for help from spontaneous self, and when I awakened I did feel better. Awoke several times during hour nap, realizing I felt rather good.

Toward the end of my nap: I presume, a dream.... I was having a Seth session, seated at my place at living room table. Rob possibly could have been sitting in my desk chair. Anyhow, he was facing me. He started to yell, throw up his arms, and he was remembering some reincarnational material that was unpleasant. Possibly Seth had just given it to him. I came out of trance though, telling Rob everything was okay to remember, let it out, and let go. Another figure sat nearby, taking notes, and I think this was Rob too; this figure was more distant and said nothing....very clear."

("Rob has no memory of this or of Thursday exercises either. Did they affect him in any way?")

("At dinner, vague thoughts that Nebene hated taxes of any kind, with the chicanery involved.")

DELETED SESSION
APRIL 18, 1979 9:42 PM WEDNESDAY

(Once again, as I had before the deleted session for Monday the 16th, I told Jane that I was close to a "breaking point." My side had bothered me all day today in the same old fashion. Although I'd felt slightly better yesterday I'd been taking baking soda often for my stomach for several days, and it seemed now that the feeling of pressure, or gas, perhaps, was getting the best of me. I took soda before lying down with Jane this afternoon. I woke up half an hour later so uncomfortable that I had to get up.

(The pendulum gave me the same reasons for my overall malaise, as well as agreeing with the fresh insights noted below. First, though, the pendulum said the soda did generate gas. It also insisted I didn't have a hernia or an ulcer, etc., although I told Jane that depending on what Seth said tonight I may seek medical help tomorrow. At the same time I swore off baking soda, which is an old habit with me, in favor of Maalox, which I found in the cupboard. The Maalox helped, and I ate a little supper.

(I'm naturally worried that I've created a physical condition, and so is Jane. She began some writing about me today, stressing my characteristics as I confront the world with a distance between the two. Her material is excellent; she said she doesn't know where it comes from, or exactly what state she's in when doing it. It's far from finished, but she finally let me see what she had after supper. She doesn't know whether she can "calm down enough to do more on the piece or not," although I'm sure she will. She also mentioned trying hypnosis with me, since I'm a good subject. I'd quite forgotten that art. At this stage I'm willing to try it. At this stage I'd try any-thing right now. At 8:15 PM my stomach bothers a bit, but the left side has subsided

to vague feelings of discomfort in the groin and testicle. The stomach does appear to be the primary seat of upset in all of this, and has for some years. I think it triggers the other unpleasant effects. Jane and I discussed the possibility that I may have an ulcer.

(Last night while we made love I broke down and cried for my worry over Jane.

(This afternoon Larry Dowler of the Yale Archives called to postpone his scheduled visit of Thursday afternoon to next Sunday. I hope to feel better by then. Now here are the insights I picked up starting at 11:20 this morning, as I went about daily business:

(1. My side/groin area bothers because I'm afraid it'll cost money to get sick. I equate money for medical expenses with money for taxes.

(2. Again, I don't think it safe to get well. I think if I get well I won't buckle down to work on Mass Reality.

(3. My side hurts because I'm afraid Volume 2 of "Unknown" Reality *won't be appreciated.*

(My side hurts because I'm afraid all of Jane's work won't be—and isn't—appreciated. Through My Eyes *isn't involved—my projected biography.*

(In the deleted session for April 16, 1979 Seth remarked that Jane "used to feel embarrassed because he made more money in those terms than you, and certainly this played some role initially in the symptoms." I asked that Seth comment as to whether any such mechanisms might still operate with Jane.

(Jane read these notes over as we sat for the session at 9:35. I explained that I hated to "put her on the spot" by asking if I had an ulcer, or a hernia, say, or gas or whatever. I realized my doing so frightened her. At the same time, I said, I was curious as to whether I did have an ulcer, for instance—that if so, I could see that I'd created that situation in order to contend with certain challenges.)

Now—

("Good evening, Seth.")

—good evening. Pretend that you have two men. One cares little for the opinions of the world. He wants to spend his days in contemplation. He wants the freedom necessary to ask whatever philosophical questions come into his mind.

Basically, he cares not a jot for time as it is generally understood. He does not care for position or power. He only asks to be left alone in his contemplations, and to express these in whatever manner suits his nature. Actually, he is <u>free of sex roles</u>, and refuses stereotypes of any kind. He views cultural and educational establishments with a clear questioning eye. He cares not a jot for position or for money, but only for the freedom. He wants to study the world and nature, and the nature of men and ideas, and to search from that vantage point for some greater order, and some greater context in which life must reside.

Now we have another man, who is also contemplative and determined—but this man is pursued by time. He must show that he produces so much work in a given number of hours, so that others will know that he is diligent and filled with the good male attributes of a provider. He is very concerned about the opinions of others, and he wants to see the effect of his work upon the establishments of the world. He wants to know where he stands, and he wants to fit a neat category, so that he can say to the world: "If you are a shoemaker, I am something as definite; or if you are a professor, I am a writer or an artist, or a — ?" He wants his contemplation to pay off, and he is very anxious about where his money goes.

These two men are one, of course. They represent your own opposing beliefs and feelings. At one time or another you do not agree, or approve, of either set, and so you are always berating yourself about being different than you are.

The greater portion of your nature belongs to the first man, and the second set of characteristics has been overlaid, so that there is a rub between the two systems of belief and feeling.

(Pause.) The two of you, having no children, cannot count upon children to fulfill your dreams, as many do, or to accomplish what you do not accomplish, as many do. Your "work" is in a way like your marriage: it must satisfy an almost infinite number of requirements and demands *(with humor)*. It must give you a sense of belonging, accomplishment, emotional support, at times exhilaration, be intellectually and emotionally satisfying, give you financial success, and some power in the world.

That "work," however, is in your case the natural gift of the first man described—and he, it seems, must work under the demands of the second man, taking all of his ideas of time, sexual roles, and social demands into consideration. You are not nearly as free of those as you might suppose—and I have mentioned that before.

Moving to this house, (any house), brought those hidden demands into some prominence, and then the second man's idea of a <u>householder</u> were further laid upon our first man's shoulders. There is nothing wrong, certainly, and much pleasure, in taking care of your establishment—but not because you must prove something to yourself or to others.

With your projects of the past finished, the "man who needed a job" had no job. It was as if he were laid off, and immediately had to find a new job. <u>That</u> man approves of creative projects <u>only when he thinks of them as jobs</u>, when they become acceptable as legitimate male pursuits. Commercial art is beautiful there, for at one time it allowed you to <u>paint because</u> *(underlined)* you were immediately repaid, and <u>that</u> made art legitimate. *(With some ironic humor:)* I am laying it on here. And forgive a bit of gentle—gentle—sarcasm, but to your puritan American soul, art for its own sake, or contemplation, still somehow goes against the grain.

Your basic personality, the first man is immensely pleased simply that the money comes. He is pleased with the time that has been gained, with the abilities that he has used and developed, and filled with a natural creative zest. You have not completely approved of him, however. The taxes bothered you more this time because they fell just after your projects were finished. You have a nervous stomach—and *(heartily)* I would have one too if I were forever taking sides against myself, and not approving whatever side I happen to be on at any given time.

(10:06.) You fall into the habit of accepting the disapproval as fact, instead of realizing that it represents a feeling you have at any given time that may or may not be justified. You can kick a dog, and if you disapprove of your act that is a justified disapproval of an act *(intently)*. You are having your physical problems because you are trying to leap over these limitations—that is, your body is saying "Stop taking sides with yourself, or rather against yourself." Your spontaneity is more than able to bridge such gaps, but often you will disapprove of it, if its suggestions go counter to negative ones concerning time that you have already given yourself.

(Pause.) Your worth is in what you <u>are</u>. Anyone's worth is in their own essence. That which you are will naturally produce acts or works of whatever kind. Your television news program *(on ABC)* is now producing a series about your nuclear power, and that of Russia. As in all such happenings, the worst probability is considered imaginatively, and steps taken in the physical world—using much energy and inventiveness—steps that are supposed to prevent this worst probability from occurring. Frightened people do not make wise decisions. In fact, they often take actions that inadvertently bring about the feared results, whatever the circumstances in the given case.

Often, however, in their private worlds people have their own versions of the feared probabilities, which they <u>then run through</u> the screens of their minds for good measure, so that they can take steps to avoid whatever catastrophe or near-catastrophe is involved.

In your own way you often do the same thing. Sometimes your body bothers you, and it is saying "You worry too much. You need to relax, so that I can relax." Instead, you then promptly worry about your body, concentrate upon its malfunctions, focus upon its problems. It is the overall approach to daily life that is important. The rules, again, appear too simple: refuse to worry. Trust that you know your next projects. Allow them to happen, and forget all projected limited suppositions, such as "I will never have the time to do this or that," for those limitations do not exist in fact. In fact, period.

The projects that <u>you</u> are meant to do can be done in your lifetime. The ones that are not done are not done for a reason, because <u>they do not fit in</u> with your nature, or because they can be handled in a different way, or whatever, but you must trust that the spontaneous self understands the overall shape of your life, and its creative contexts and contents.

End of lecture *(with a smile.*

("Okay. Thank you.")

I will hold another lecture whenever you want.

(I didn't want Seth to leave before I asked this question: "Do you want to say something about your remark that Jane's early symptoms were at least partly connected with her embarrassment at making more money than I did?")

You must understand, as certainly you do, the focus of your lives. Even before the psychic venture began, it was always your individual and joint work: in the beginning writing and painting.

You were both unconventional. On the exterior you broke conventions, but you were still tainted by conventional ideas. Even without the psychic endeavor, you both would have been bothered if, say, Ruburt succeeded as a writer of his own books, with no help from you of any kind, unless you succeeded as an artist. It was quite well known by both of you, however, that you disliked the marketplace.

That dislike, as much as anything, made you unwilling to do what is required to be a selling artist. You felt differently about commercial work. You have always had the sex roles to contend with in society to some degree. All of this did help contribute to Ruburt's symptoms, particularly in the beginning. He was afraid you would be jealous, that others would say he dominated you, and to some extent both of you felt the symptoms helped you save face in society.

(10:29.) The symptoms also served later to provide you both with a sense of separation from the world, a reason for not doing what you <u>thought</u> you should do in conventional terms: go out and spread the word, become television people, or lead groups, or give seminars—all things that largely went against the private portions of your nature, though otherwise you were both equipped to do so.

You would be very wise <u>to see the people you see</u> (underlined), because you want to see them when you do, while never using Ruburt's condition <u>as an</u> <u>excuse</u> for not doing what you do not want to do anyhow, or for not seeing peo-ple you do not want to see anyhow *(intently.*

(Long pause.) You are, because you have chosen it, initiating a new way of life. You have made it work in many important fashions, and if you could stop <u>disapproving of yourselves</u> a moment, you could see that this is quite true. There is no reason to feel ashamed of Ruburt's condition. *(Pause.)* You have a lifetime of beliefs behind you that you are in the process of discarding. The very cre-ativity that surrounds you should be quite legitimate proof of the practical nature that results from our concepts.

Now I bid you a fond good evening, with one footnote.

I have given, I would say, five or six sessions at a minimum on the impor-tance of touch or lovemaking, its importance as natural expression, as a creative act—and this apart from its physical benefits, release of tensions, and spiritual enrichment.

A fond good evening.

("Thank you. Seth. Good night."

(10:40 PM. "That was good," I said to Jane at once. "I feel better already."

("Thank God," Jane said. "I'm better at it now—remember how touchy I used to be? I'd feel my trance come right up to the surface whenever we got into anything personal. But I had no idea of what he was going to talk about. I'll have another ses-sion for you tomorrow if you want to." I said we'd see; that this one was excellent, a great help.)

JANE'S NOTES

(Attached to the deleted session for April 24, 1979.

(Last night April 23, Monday, Rob suddenly got super-relaxed and really flop-py before our scheduled Seth session. In the meantime though as I went into the john, I started to pick up some of the things Seth was going to discuss, and after Rob began his odd relaxation, I got more. As best as I could I told Rob what I was getting. We decided not to have the session—I don't think Rob could have taken notes anyhow; besides I wanted him to take advantage of what was happening.

(This is more or less what I was getting, and told Rob, though I've probably forgotten some things. That Rob was having a "body vacation" or that his body was taking a vacation, a rest; and that the contrast between his floppy state and his usual one would let him know how tight he'd been.... Something about us not taking vaca-tions....and even not wanting to rest between mental creative projects; that Rob had

his stomach troubles when he needed a rest....a vacation of some sort could have pre-
vented that....but since we prefer to do things differently, we should frequently
arrange changes in our lives....that we control....changes in the house, routine,
hours....or even a week off to do the house or yard or whatever.... The mind wears
the body out sometimes....and then the body sends signals of distress....

(We should consider such changes as a part of our working life, to provide
refreshment; otherwise we just stew because we're not "creative or working" or what-
ever....even furniture rearranging or changing whole rooms to different functions can
be considered a vacation of a sort, and while I've always felt guilty at involving Rob
in changing furniture—but do, anyhow. Seth said this was good sense and impulse
on my part....

(The idea being since we refuse to take vacations like other people [really before
I was physically bothered] we have to have our own equivalent which can be any of
the above mentioned at different times. I think there was quite a bit more that I've
forgotten.)

DELETED SESSION
APRIL 24, 1979 9:31 PM TUESDAY

(The first portion of these notes—as indicated—was written after supper on
Monday night, preparatory to what I thought would be the regularly scheduled ses-
sion for the evening. However, the session wasn't held. Let me explain.

(Late yesterday afternoon [Monday], we were visited by Larry Dowler of the
Yale Archives. He told us many things and answered—and asked—many questions.
Seth came through briefly several times, and very humorously, to handle certain ques-
tions himself. Among other things, he said that "there is no place for the Seth mater-
ial to be kept," that "you have to make a place for it, for it is unique." The interludes
weren't recorded, to my regret. Seth did express his own willingness to have the mate-
rial available to the public, but Jane and I are much less sure of that.

(We liked L. Dowler, and will see what develops. This morning I made an
appointment with Bill Danaher for tomorrow about a will. This morning Jane
received Tam Mossman's agreement to act as literary executor.

(Tam has rejected Stefan Schindler's book on Seth – he did so last week—so
this morning Jane called Eleanor Friede to see if she wanted to examine the work.
Again, no. Then Jane called S. Schindler with that news; he in turn has "a list" of
West Coast publishers he wants to try, evidently thinking the university press route
won't work.

(In the last three days I've learned a number of interesting things about my

continuing physical upsets—and will list some of my pendulum material should any portion of this session refer to them. The deleted session for April 18 has helped a great deal. My own insights through the pendulum tell me, for example, why Seth in that last private session said I have a "nervous stomach," but nothing about the other hassles like, say, the side or groin. [It all seems to stem from the initial stomach difficulty.] I need to study more. I still don't want to burden Jane with a series of sessions on my own problems. I know I can—and am—working them out. Each bit of information is bound to help.

(Jane was quite upset because of all the time she spent on the calls this morning, plus the visits this noon by F. Longwell and H. Wheeler. Nor did I accomplish much. I mowed some grass, worked with the pendulum, helped Jane walk—she's still taking steps—and wrote these notes. The pendulum insights may be most valuable, however.

(Now these notes are continued late Tuesday afternoon and night, before the session.

(They are much longer than they need to be for session notes, but I want the more detailed account for my own possible use in the indefinite future:

(Not long after finishing Monday's notes, then, we sat for the session. I didn't feel too well. Within a few minutes, however, I noticed that I was becoming quite relaxed. I sat with this notebook on my lap but didn't exert myself to open it. My arms and legs, and head and neck, began to feel looser and looser. "It looks like I picked up a suggestion about relaxation," I told Jane. "But I'll be okay. I want to have the session," I said in answer to her questions. She sat opposite me, smoking, waiting to go into trance. My head flopped back against the couch. "Wow...."

(I insisted I could take notes okay, even as the feeling deepened. The malaise became more profound. I didn't feel like writing the notes I wanted to about what was happening. Indeed, I didn't even feel like taking the cap off the pen. The sensations were extremely pleasant—and heavy, yet looser and looser. My eyes closed. I sat motionless for minutes at a time, bathing in a most beneficial, relaxed state. It was actually one I'd been trying to approximate ever since I'd begun to feel bad after finishing checking all the page proofs for the books we have coming out this year. But when I'd told myself I wanted to relax, I'd had no idea such a profound state could be obtained. I had approached it in a casual way through self-hypnosis: the same lax, heavy looseness in the limbs when I made the effort to move. I savored the experience now because I felt at a deep peace and my body was almost free of aches and pains. But at the same time I wanted to know more.

(Soon I didn't care, though. My condition became so totally relaxed that <u>any</u> conscious and deliberate movement was forgotten unless I made a strong effort to exert myself—to pick up a piece of paper, to lay this notebook on the coffee table, say.

Fortunately I'd put the cats in the cellar before the session so I wouldn't have to do it later. Jane was obviously concerned. "Are you all right?" she kept asking, and I hardly replied. This was easily the most complete experience of its kind I'd ever known, and it was deepening.

(As soon as she saw that I <u>couldn't</u> take notes, Jane began describing to me what she'd started to pick up from Seth about my condition. I was both very interested and so far out in my own world of sensation that I could hardly comment. I was taking a "body vacation," she told me. She said much more, which she wrote about briefly Tuesday afternoon at my request. Her notes are inserted at the end of my notes. Seth, Jane said, would explain the whole thing in the next session, whenever that would be held.

(Jane sat on the couch in her usual place to my left. By now I was far out of it: I doubt if I could have moved except in the direst emergency. As Jane talked I fell asleep a number of times. She said I snored so loudly that she had to turn the TV volume up in order to hear the programs. During half-waking periods I was conscious of my lower jaw continually dropping, so that I sat with my mouth gaping open in a most uncharacteristic manner. I slept through deep, immensely enjoyable and totally saturating periods of relaxation. After a while my arms began to twitch and jump spasmodically without my conscious volition. These reflexive reactions continued for some time, even later in the evening when I began to come out of the heavy sleep periods. But while they were happening I cared not at all.

(Jane, hungry, ate cookies and drank a glass of milk I'd set out for myself before the session. Lately during sessions she's been sipping red wine. When I could speak coherently, I offered her the piece of cornbread I'd set out with the milk, but she refused it. By now, I was conscious enough to sit with her through the balance of a dated mystery movie starring Rock Hudson. [He was caught as the murderer, finally.]

(When I finally tried to get on my feet to get Jane more milk, however, I realized that my situation was far from over. I staggered around in the kitchen, taking six-inch steps with more than a little effort and caution. My knees felt loose as could be, but the muscles in the legs were heavy and stolid. I poured more milk for both of us, and ate the cornbread, half asleep as I did these things. When we decided to retire I shuffled about the house, cleaning up and locking doors and windows as Jane made ready for bed. I could have cheerfully collapsed at any time. I bumped into walls and door-jambs, or leaned on tables for support for minutes at a time. I yawned deeply and wished only for bed, over and over again.

(When finally I stared at myself in the bathroom mirror, I was more than a little disoriented—for a face confronted me that I hardly recognized. It was almost that of a stranger. I finally figured out why that mirror image confronted me with

such an unreal quality: All the muscles and planes of my face were super-relaxed and smoothed out, so that the face at once looked both younger and older than its real age. My jaw hung. In the bedroom, I muttered to Jane that I hadn't recognized myself.

(My state persisted—so much so that I felt like a long-distance runner nearing the finish line. I was engaged in a contest to see if I could help Jane get ready for bed, set the alarm and the electric blanket, turn out the bedroom lights and open the curtains and a window—all before I gave out in a heap on the bed. Indeed, I lost my balance twice while helping Jane undress, and each time collapsed on the bed beside her, to her evident concern. Nor were those episodes painless, for in one of them I put an unnatural strain on the deltoid muscle in my right shoulder. [I'd injured the shoulder last summer while pulling on the starting cord for the lawn mower; it's bothered me ever since, although not steadily.] The pain was intense, although not as bad when I'd first hurt the muscle. I struggled to rouse myself enough so I could take pressure off the arm; I was afraid I'd re-injured it. So even in that state of deep relaxation, in which I could move only with effort and concentration, I learned something that I fully realized at the time: Even though I was far out on a "trip" of some sort, I could still feel pain. My muscles weren't magically healing themselves, nor was I undergoing any kind of overall healing that might confound my own beliefs, or those of medical science. Not that I'd thought I was....

(But nevertheless, I knew I was having a most beneficial experience, and one that might very well head off other, deeper troubles. This I understood quite clearly. I believed Jane-Seth's material about my being on a "body vacation." It was impossible for me not to believe it, considering that I'd felt so poorly since early in the month, and that I was so much better right now. I just hoped more beneficial results would flow from the experience, and I was appalled that I'd been that badly off, that "tight," so that my body greatly needed such a drastic kind of relief.

(I slept at once. although Jane lay awake until about 2 AM. I felt many reminders and remnants of the experience throughout the next day—Tuesday—especially in the arms and legs: They were often loose and floppy, with a peculiar lightness and ease of motion in the joints particularly. At my request Jane wrote her account of the non-session events of last night, and it's attached. I noticed more signs of the same sort of relaxation before tonight's session was due, and wondered if I could focus upon Seth clearly enough, or write fast enough. After a number of hesitations, which only confused Jane as to what I really wanted to do, I sat for the session.

(I'll insert here the note that we did see Bill Danaher about a will this morning.)

Good evening.

("Good evening, Seth.")

Now: a few remarks from several viewpoints.

First of all, a note of history: the material Ruburt got on you on his own was excellent, though unfinished. You looked at the world and saw that it was wanting. You yearned to give it some standards of excellence – standards, however, that could be applied to the entire area of living, to personal relationships, to politics, to social events, to philosophical thought.

You wanted to illuminate the world in some respect. You saw your family as a small sample of the world's peoples, and their interrelationships with each other, and with the neighborhood, as representative of most people's relationship with the world. You were sorry for your parents. You yearned to help both of them, as you yearned to help your brothers. That part of you existed quite intimately in your thoughts, while at the same time you found it difficult to communicate with the family [members] generally, and you were struck by the great gap of communication that seemingly existed between the most related people.

On the one hand, you pursued your version of what was expected of you. You went to school, became a commercial artist, and did very well at it. Now you liked that work, Joseph – not only because of the art, but because of the communication that was involved. Particularly when you drew animals, you could use them as symbols for noble virtues, but in any case it was the means of communication, a communication that to some extent could bridge the particular emotional troubles people might be having at any given time.

You became discontented, however, drawn yourself toward fine arts. Yet even these involved a highly specific nature. The world of art galleries is highly esoteric in its own fashion. Beside this, however, you were still searching for some direction that would allow you the greatest opportunity to provide at least a glimpse of the kind of excellence that you always carried as an ideal in your mind. That impetus was always with you in this life.

You sensed certain characteristics in Ruburt when first you met, and you knew intuitively that certain probabilities could bring the two of you together, both using your individual abilities in ways at that time unknown to you, but that those individual abilities, joined, could together produce a new kind of threshold—an overview through which that sensed excellence could at least be glimpsed, contained in essence at least, and communicated.

It is the communication of the ideal of excellence that is so important to you. You also initially, before this life, wanted to achieve some kind of overview that would unite the arts, and that would introduce a new kind of psychological art. You suggested the ESP book—hardly a coincidence. Hardly indeed, for intuitively you knew where it would lead.

(9:47.) The two of you do not have children, yet you do indeed not only

have mental children, but you are—if you will forgive the term—psychic or mental parents to many thousands of people. All of this cut directly across some of your ideas about success in usual terms, and your abilities fit together in different ways than you originally planned.

(Long pause.) The two of you mixed and matched your characteristics, and put them together in such a fashion that they would jointly form a completely new kind of creation, in terms of art and psychology, and this was bound to produce expansions of your consciousnesses, and stresses and strains, when you came across portions of your ideas that had not grown along with the rest of you. The sessions, as they exist, exist as they do because of your actions and Ruburt's.

Now: Ruburt's rendition of my absentee session last evening was basically correct. When you believe that relaxation means that you are limp, that you can do nothing, that you have <u>let go</u> *(with humor)*, then, of course, you experience it as such. Your body was activated so that it was naturally sedated. To both of you, however, relaxation means somehow to be <u>lax</u>, to shuffle *(louder)* rather than to be resolute and determined and forever at it; and so then natural relaxation can seem overwhelming, for you are afraid, both of you, that if you relax you will do nothing.

At a certain point your body does not care. It relaxes you anyway. Now Ruburt has much slighter versions, in which, say, daily or weekly tensions no longer collect as they did, which allows him some physical improvement—but he also feels that if he really relaxed he would only do the dishes or whatever. The world would hardly fall in if neither of you did anything for several days. The relaxed body, however, the truly relaxed body, can physically perform of course far better than the tense one.

Thoughts of the will and your approaching 50th and 60th birthdays have led <u>you</u>, Joseph, to look over you life, to ask, "What have I done? Am I a success or a failure?" But when you do so, you often ask the question through the cast of old conventional beliefs. If you ask "Is the world a better place to live because I live?" or "Have I helped the people in the world in any way?" or "Have I lifted men's hearts or minds in any way?" or "Have I affected others for the better?" then those answers must be yes, and there is no better measure of true success.

You have been a good and true partner to Ruburt – and indeed you have. Though you do not have children, the two of you do indeed possess a unique relationship, and that in itself is an achievement. You have each given meaning to each other's lives, because you have each sought for it separately also. You are an accomplished person in painting and in writing, and the characteristics that also give you those abilities merge together to form the framework of the sessions, and the excellent quality of the notes—in which, by the way, you communicate to others very clearly those ideas of excellence, and those visions, that sustain many readers.

I am not given to flattery. But these are statements of fact that you should recognize as such. End of session.

("Thank you very much, Seth.")

A note: I do want you to remember Ruburt's version of last night's session, and follow my suggestions concerning changes that can serve as variations—working variations—to allow you some rest and refreshment.

You work, for example, perhaps as many hours as you want, or can—but you completely change the hours, or you work as usual, but you change the furniture in the rooms, or turn the rooms to different functions—or whatever—but allow for such changes in the overall routines. They will refresh you.

("Okay.")

(10:09 PM. "Before the session." Jane said, "I told Seth I wanted whatever was necessary to help you. I didn't care what it was. I'd stay out of the way as much as possible. If you were sick of me, or wanted out—anything—I just wanted to know so you'd get better. I know you love me, but maybe you get sick of my running your life or something like that...."

(Jane said more. She was so emphatic and serious that I had to laugh, though in a subdued way, for I still felt lingering effects from my deep relaxation of last night. I was, for instance, a bit slow writing these notes—yet, oddly, I'd been able to keep up with Seth all right during the session itself.

(I want to note that Jane continues her steady, if slow, improvement physically. I told her that her knees especially now show a noticeable increase in flexibility. She does her exercises faithfully twice a day.)

DELETED SESSION
APRIL 30, 1979 10:15 PM MONDAY

(Before the session Jane read over the letter from D. R. Moorcroft, the professor of physics who'd written her such a fine letter on April 3. She divided the letter into questions; Seth may discuss some of them tonight. We thought Professor Moorcroft's letter was very well done. Seth does refer to the first question Jane had noted, and that material is also presented as the 849th session, as well as being included here.

(As for myself, I feel somewhat better than I have been so far this month. The

siege seems endless. I haven't asked the pendulum many questions at all since the last ones I recorded on April 21. My stomach still bothers, but on a much-reduced level; the groin/left testicle seems all but clear at times; occasionally the discomfort returns on a reduced basis also.

(What I'm trying to do is to let the information Seth has given in the last several deleted sessions for me, starting with that for April 4, sink in so that I can achieve a synthesis of it all both consciously and unconsciously. I think the material is very perceptive, and that I may have begun achieving some kind of equanimity between the two men, or opposing sets of belief, that Seth so aptly described in the deleted session for April 18. [I read these sessions daily.] It's essential that these conflicting beliefs be resolved by the personality, and I'm determined to do so. I think the physical improvements noted are first signs that I can get the results I want.

(As I told Jane last night, I didn't realize that I was so tight, so bound up with tensions and stresses, that I was ready to fall ill because of those basic conflicts with self-disapproval, the male-provider role, money, taxes, and all the rest of the daily paraphernalia of living. I've had several lesser encounters with relaxation effects since the massive one of April 24—the last one being last night. I've enjoyed them all. I've also slept well now for some time. My dreams, those I remember at least, have also reflected efforts at reconciliation of opposing beliefs, fears, and so forth. In the meantime, I've let myself go, not working hard in any direction, relaxing while working on the files, or in the yard, or shopping or painting or whatever. The line that's most impressed me in all of this, perhaps, is Seth's quote to me from my own body, given by him in the deleted session for April 18: "You worry too much. You need to relax, so that I can relax."

(The phone rang at 8:45 PM, as I worked on these notes. The caller was Larry Dowler, calling for the Yale Archives. They want the Seth material and related papers. There are many questions to be resolved yet, since we have yet to even see the will Bill Danaher is drawing up for us. We have to resolve the issue of public accessibility, and others. [Jane is not in favor of public accessibility at this time.] LD explained a few things, suggesting among them a committee, perhaps, to screen qualified applicants to the material. All will be resolved. "I can't believe it," Jane said a number of times as we talked. Certainly we hadn't expected such an outright acceptance so quickly after LD's visit last week [Sunday the 22nd]. LD or his secretary will write. He goes into the hospital for knee surgery within a few days.

(All of this delayed our sitting for the session until 10:07. By then, Jane said, she couldn't remember much of Professor Moorcroft's letter, but I told her it didn't matter. "I'm still wiped out about Yale," she said. She remarked more than once about her failure to win the Yale prize for younger poets in years past, Tam's attending Yale, and so forth. "Here I thought we were going to have a nice peaceful week,

with some sessions on Mass Reality, *maybe, but now, who knows...."*

(I didn't think anything immediate would develop, I told her, nor did I expect the session tonight would be on me. Jane, understandably, had questions about recognition, now that Yale had expressed willingness to accept her work. That is, at least rejection wasn't implied, but I must admit that both of us are very cautious about expecting any sort of real acceptance via academia; certainly not these days. Our main goal in wanting a home for the Seth material—or for a lifework, really—is one of preservation for future use. We don't think that Yale can have much of an idea of what's involved with Jane's abilities, or the subject matter of the Seth material.

(Finally: "I'm about ready...." Jane said.)

Good evening.

("Good evening, Seth.")

You make your own reality. Your finest abilities will seek to express themselves regardless of the misunderstandings you may have concerning them or the barriers seemingly thrown in your way by family or society.

Some portion of you rises up to say yes when your own finest abilities show themselves in whatever form. Later you might see that many of your own decisions or actions that once appeared disadvantageous, and for which you berated yourself, were in fact the very ones that helped bring your own abilities to your attention.

On the one hand, our sessions were something that you did aside from something else, that you thought you should do, both of you. You considered yourselves a writer and an artist. Yet once the sessions began you continued them, wondering often whether or not you should have—I am speaking of you jointly—not realizing that you had found the vehicle that would coax your best from both of you.

(Pause.) Your spontaneous selves in that area, <u>relatively speaking, now</u>, (underlined twice) were allowed their expressions. Creativity was not inhibited by a certain form but *(louder)*, in a unique way was freed from form. It was allowed to leap beyond the boundaries of painting or writing, to escape even the temporal frames of your present personalities, and to form an original psychic or psychological structure—a new psychological art, if you prefer—that could be contained in none of the arts as they are known. You were free enough to be daring, and you took this upon yourselves out of your own sense of curiosity and wonder.

(Seth's voice was still moderately louder than usual.)

I did not start out writing books, but speaking to you for your edification. Had I begun writing books, Ruburt would have been appalled, thinking that I was invading his province. In this area of your lives, however, and relatively speaking again, you have allowed your creative spontaneous selves some freedom. You have behaved gallantly *(with amusement)* and well.

In the beginning the sessions were private. They have attained other dimensions now, as they were meant to. But as far as the sessions themselves are concerned, I want to stress the ease with which they naturally occur, the lack of strain. You allow yourselves to be.

(Pause at 10:29.) Once begun, the sessions happen. Contrast this with your joint attitudes toward "your other work," with the hassles involved, the need to be absolutely sure of what you are doing, to have the plan there, and everything known in advance. Those ideas impede creativity.

(To me:) Your body wanted relaxation, but you believed that relaxation was, under the circumstances, wrong, and often when your body began to relax in the past you automatically tightened it, as another might straighten his tie to be more presentable. Relaxation leads to spontaneity. It allows you to be freely what you are. When you are tense you impede mental, psychic, and artistic spontaneity, when you relax you are open to intuitive events.

Your experience in relaxation *(a week ago)* allowed your body some release. The relaxed body sends forth hormones and chemicals of a balanced nature that influence the processes of thought, modulate moods, and also allow for moments of deep contentment, and moments of elation. When the body becomes too tense reactions are exaggerated in certain fashions, bringing forth dejection or depression. When necessary, such reactions are meant to show the personality that changes are due. You should have more of those relaxing periods of varying degrees, as your body becomes regulated again. You will find yourself at times wanting physical activity more than usual, and at other times wanting only to relax.

The mind operates in the same fashion, following its own rhythms, covering mental ground at an amazingly quick rate on some occasions, and on others desiring a change or a rest.

(10:39.) Give us a moment.... Rest your hand. *(A one-minute pause.)* Do you have questions on that material?

("No....")

You are doing well. Get our friend some cigarettes....

(10:42.) A very brief beginning on question one *(of Professor Moorcroft's letter)*. Give us a moment....

There are almost always hidden variables, but they are of little consequence here. Every visible or invisible particle has consciousness according to its own scale of reality. Each particle, visible or invisible, is awareized energy. This is most difficult to explain, but like, say, the units of some multidimensional computer, each visible or invisible particle carries within it the knowledge of all other particles, including their positions, and their probable positions.

Each operates within the field of probabilities, and "makes its decisions" on the basis of such inbuilt information. There is then an almost instantaneous flow of information throughout such particles. *(Pause.)* The position of one cannot be ascertained ahead of time with any certainty in your framework of reference, say in the situation of the proton, because the proton is receiving such a barrage of information that is not available to you at a conscious level, and that is not available to your instruments.

That same information *is* available on a cellular basis *(pause)*, and to the smaller particles that make up the bodies of the experimenters, and the structure of the instruments.

(Pause.) I am aware this is of little practical value to you.

(10:53.) Give us a moment.... *(Long pause.)* A very brief note in terms of significant but small connections with Framework 2: Ruburt's attempts to get the Yale prize, Tam's schooling at Yale, and your present experience with the papers—these simply hint at connecting clues involved with probabilities, an interesting subject that I will get into at some time.

Ruburt is flabbergasted. I am pleased, and I bid you both a fond good evening. Unless you have questions....

("No, I guess not.")

(As Seth, Jane nodded, closing out the session.)

("Good night, Seth." Jane was surprised at the session's quick end. After supper she'd felt Seth material on his book, the latter, and personal stuff, she said—all before the call from Yale. She could only speculate that the "Yale business" had something to do with the short session, even though she wasn't consciously aware of it. We'd been set for the session to run until midnight if that was the way it developed.

(And I felt another relaxation experience—a milder one than last week's— coming on....)

SESSION 850 (DELETED PORTION)
MAY 2, 1979 9:49 PM WEDNESDAY

(This material is from the 850th session.

(I continue to feel better, although not fully recovered by any means. My physical hassles disappear for fairly long periods, and then I'm conscious of one or the other of them. All is much more subdued, though. I still read the deleted material for myself on most days, paint a little, do chores, work on the files, the yard, help Jane, record

dreams—but I try to do all of these things at an easy pace while trusting that I'll con-
tinue to reconcile opposing beliefs, and see more physical and creative improvements.
At this writing I still feel an occasional, if mild, return of the first massive relaxation
of April 24: very pleasant. I've also developed the habit of repeating Seth's quote from
my own body, as he gave it in the deleted session for April 18: "You worry too much.
You need to relax, so that I can relax." Evidently I find this suggestion, given daily,
a very potent one.

(10:58.) Break is over. Remarks. You are quite capable of dealing with
your life's events, and with handling daily stress. It acts as a natural stimulus.

What the body cannot stand today is the stress thrown upon it by the
imagined stress or problems that it <u>might</u> be asked to face tomorrow, or next
week, or 20 years from now. Then, you are not allowing it to act in the present.
You are seeking from future probabilities unpleasant—or perhaps the most
unpleasant—circumstances, and actually demanding that the body handle that
stimuli <u>now</u> *(all intently).*

Again, significances are important. If one unpleasant event today automatically causes you to think of 20 more that <u>might</u> happen in the future and
you dwell upon those, then you hopelessly confuse your body. It finds in the
present no justification in fact for such interpretations, while your thoughts act
as if those situations were presently before you, to be confronted. Stress results
when the body does not know how to react, and therefore cannot react smoothly.

You are doing well, and I will devote some time to Ruburt—but we will
get back to the book once a week. For *(louder)* when we do not, that in itself
causes stress.

I bid you a most affectionate good evening.
("Thank you, Seth. The same to you. Good evening.")
(11:05 PM.)

SESSION 851 (DELETED PORTION)
MAY 7, 1979 9:39 PM MONDAY

(This material is from the 851st session. I suggest that the regular portion of
the session be read in conjunction with what follows, for the two parts complement
each other well. However, I didn't want all of the session filed under deleted mater-
ial, since that other portion has good general application.

(For the past few days I've done little "creative" work, beyond working on my
watercolor portrait of Mrs. Johnson, the subject of my dream of last November, for

an hour or two in the mornings; then in the afternoons I've typed these sessions and written the required notes for the record. I've done a lot of yard work—it seems to be a very therapeutic activity at this time—and worked on filing. I feel considerably better, to my great relief, although the stomach isn't cleared yet as much as I would like. The discomfort in the groin/testicle area is much less, at times absent altogether, and I believe that my steady rereading of Seth's recent private material for me has helped a great deal here. I've also taken to using mental imagery in this field, and will continue to do so for some time; I think there's no reason why that can't be effective also. It's something I've largely neglected in past periods of discomfort. I haven't gone back to the pendulum yet. I read Jane's prayer for <u>her</u>, and Seth's New Year resolutions for me. The more I study those, the more I realize how good they are.

(I think tonight's private material came through, at least in part, because I reminded Jane today of Seth's references to her in recent private sessions. I'm referring at the moment to his comments about her embarrassment, in the early days, at earning more money than I did [see the deleted session for April 16, 1979, page 97], and that in later years the symptoms served to provide us with a sense of separation from the world, for a number of reasons [see the deleted session for April 18]. Seth has already touched upon such questions in the deleted sessions that follow, especially those for April 30 and May 2, and extends his coverage of them this evening in response to my latest queries.

(10:06.) Ruburt is doing well with the walking, and he is more and more aware of relaxation of various portions of the body. In fact—in fact—his body can heal itself overnight. All of this boils down to what I have said unceasingly *(whispering)* about trusting the spontaneous self—for in the most simple of terms, you do not need poor mobility as a working method for <u>any</u> reasons, if you trust the spontaneous self in its dealings with the conscious personality and with the world.

Of course, to some degree the condition involves you both in your social dealings with the world. Ruburt believes in economy, and the condition <u>seemed</u> to take care of many different possible problems, for himself and for you also. You both knew you were different, and whether or not the sessions ever began, your minds were uniquely explorative. You kept the world at a good reach. Ruburt did not know, <u>as given</u> in the past, what the spontaneous self might lead to. The symptoms served to slow him down psychically, while he mentally considered his position.

As he became known, they served to keep the world away for both of you. They served to show <u>why</u> you worked at home, or did not sell your work at galleries: you had to take care of Ruburt. They saved you both from making endless decisions as to whom you would see, or whether you would go on tours.

They pared life down to its necessities. They were Ruburt's version of health foods, abstinence, and so forth, in the Nearing's way, and to all of this both of you to some extent acquiesced.

If you trust the spontaneous self, then automatically you do not need such a framework, but you must learn to allow it its expression. Ruburt's idea of seeing your psychiatrist *(Dr. Beahrs)* is good in that regard. Do not be so afraid, neither of you, of making mistakes, or spending a bad evening or two.

In this neighborhood *(gesturing)*, Ruburt's symptoms were a social statement also to the neighbors at large in the new environment: better than a note upon the door, that neither of you were to be bothered, but ignored. And again to some extent, both of you acquiesced.

(10:15.) Now: you can express the same statements in other ways, by being willing to make decisions on their own basis: "Yes, I want to do this. No, I do not want to do that," instead of providing yourself with a blanket excuse, as Ruburt has done. Neither of you have really wanted to be free to go on trips, to be in a position where you must decide whether or not you wanted to speak here or there. And beside that, Ruburt had his own concerns with spontaneity and discipline.

He is doing well. He can do far better, and the way to begin is to allow the spontaneous self as much freedom as he can in daily life, and to trust its expression—that it knows his psychic and creative needs, his physical needs, his social and financial needs, and all of these can be taken care of.

Again, to some extent now (underlined), both of you wanted a framework that would allow you what you thought of as freedom to work. Ruburt is learning that even he went too far, but I do want you still to think of the symptoms as a well-meaning but distorted structure that can dissolve—and can dissolve overnight when Ruburt understands it is no longer needed or wanted. It is a method that he tried, but it did not work because it defeated its own purposes.

I do not want him to feel guilty about it. You are aided and abetted, of course, because of previous beliefs of society, where illness is a quite acceptable method of procedure, where it is considered normal. It is a method, therefore, that belongs with those old beliefs, and should be discarded with them.

It worked for a while as a way of avoiding distractions, but the personality no longer needs such artificial "aids."

This session should be of value at this particular time, but I do not want you to dwell upon the reasons for the condition. I want Ruburt to stress instead the expression of the spontaneous self. There are many methods from your point of view, some better than others, of course; and what I am saying this evening is largely directed to you with my knowledge of your viewpoints. In still greater terms, each life experience is unique so that it is literally impossible to put labels, such as "positive" or "negative" upon any aspect of experience, so keep this in mind also.

In any case, there are some good things coming that will cheer you considerably—and in the meantime, have a good evening.

("Thank you.")

Do you have any questions?

("No, you've covered the questions I had in mind.")

(Whispering, with amusement:) I thought I did.

("Good night.")

(10:30 PM. I think the session could well be a very important one for both of us, and that it's hardly a coincidence that it came along at this time. Jane continues to improve in her walking—she's up to 12 times daily, with the aid of her typing table—so we seemed to have retreated from the prospect of her becoming so inactive that she stopped getting on her feet. That realization had to come before anything else could be done, of course—so tonight's session and the questions we've been asking lately about the symptoms certainly seem to have come about at the right time.)

SESSION 852 (DELETED PORTION)
MAY 9, 1979 9:39 PM WEDNESDAY

(The following material is from the 852nd session.

(10:41.) Give us a moment.... Have Ruburt read the last session again. Help him to trust the spontaneous self, and as you shall see, these ideas are indeed directly opposite to those of your educations, so do not be impatient.

Fear of the self, itself, can lead people to the horrendous experiences mentioned in tonight's session, so you are working with some revolutionary ideas, and trying to apply them to daily living.

(To me:) You are doing well and ideas and beliefs are changing places in your mind, to good import. And now I bid you a fond good evening.

(10:45 PM.)

SESSION 853 (DELETED)
MAY 14, 1979 9:46 PM MONDAY

(A copy of this session is also being placed in the deleted notebook, since I'd like it to be placed under both categories.) I think it contains some excellent general mate-

rial that, I told Jane, I was afreaid wouldn't be seen by anyone if it were filed exclusively under private material.

(Neither of us had questions for Seth in particular. That is, I said, "I could ask 5,000 questions, but I haven't planned any for tonight." Jane said we could have "just a question-and-answer Seth book"—one made up of just those ingredients, without the formal session format. "But the publisher would want it organized according to subject matter, or presented in some orderly way," I replied, whereupon she wrinkled her face at the work this might involve: "But you could do all that after we got the material...."

(Actually, this evening's session grew out of several insights Jane had given voice to in recent days, and osme relaxation effects that had followed several of those. "But right now I'm just waiting," she said impatiently at 9:40 PM, after we'd been sitting since 9:25 or so. "It makes me so mad. Here I was all set to go earlier." Then she amended: "It makes me mad because I feel like I'm in an odd in-between subjective state. It isn't comfortable—I want to be one thing or the other, maybe...."

(Finally, rather slowly but, strangely, with emphasis:)

Good Evening.

("Good evening, Seth.")

Dictation is for Wednesday.

I want to make a few comments. Generally speaking, creativity has feminine connotations in your society, while power has masculine connotations, and is largely thought of as destructive.

Your scientists are generally, now, intellectually oriented, believing in reason above the intuitions, taking it for granted that those qualities are opposites. They cannot imagine *(pause)*, life's "initial" creative source, for in their terms it would remind them of creativity's feminine basis.

In the framework of this discussion, now, only, you have a male's universe. It is a universe endowed with male characteristics <u>as these appear</u> in the male-female orientations of your history. The universe seems to have no meaning because the male "intellect" alone cannot <u>discern</u> meaning, since it must take nothing for granted. Even though certain characteristics of the universe are most apparent, they must be ignored.

(Pause.) You must understand I know that the terms male and female here are being used as they are generally understood, and have nothing to do with the basic characteristics of either sex.

In those terms, the male-oriented intellect wants to order the universe, name its parts, and so forth. It wants to ignore the creative aspects of the universe, however, which are everywhere apparent, and it first of all believes that it must divorce itself from any evidence of feeling. You have in your history then a male god of power and vengeance, who killed your enemies for you. You have a prejudiced god, who will for example slay the Egyptians on behalf of the Jews to retaliate against previous Egyptian cruelty. The male god is a god of power. He is not a god of creativity.

Now, creativity has always been the species' closest connection with its own source, with the nature of its own being. Through creativity the species senses All That Is. Creativity goes by a different set of rules, however. It defies categories, and it insists upon the evidence of feeling. It is a source of revelation and inspiration—but revelation and inspiration do not initially deal with power, but with knowing. So what happens often in your society when men or women have creative bents, and good minds to boot?

(10:03.) The Catholic Church taught that revelation was dangerous. Intellectual and psychic obedience was much the safer road, and even the saints were slightly suspect. Women were inferiors, and in matters of religion and philosophy most of all, for there their creativity could be most disruptive. Women were considered hysterics, aliens to the world of intellectual thought, swayed instead by incomprehensible womanish emotions. She was to be handled by wearing down her energy through continual childbirth.

Ruburt was highly creative, and so following the beliefs of his time, he believed that he must watch his creativity most carefully, for he was determined to use it. He decided early to have no children—but more, to fight any evidence of femininity that might taint his work, or jumble up his dedication to it. He loved you deeply, and does, but he always felt he had to tread a slender line, so as to satisfy the various needs and beliefs that you both had to one extent or another, and those you felt society possessed.

He was creative, and is. Yet he felt that women were inferior, and that his very abilities made him vulnerable, that he would be ridiculed by others, that women were not taken seriously as profound thinkers, or innovators in philosophical matters.

The trance itself had feminine connotations. Though he conveniently forgot [Edgar] Cayce, for example, who was a trance master. And yet at the same time he was afraid of exerting power, for fear it would be thought that he was usurping male prerogatives.

Now: you are creative, but you are a male—and one part of you considered creativity a feminine-like characteristic. If it were tied to money-making, as it once was, then painting became also power-making, and hence acceptable to your American malehood; and I am quite aware of the fact that both of you were, by the standards of your times, quite liberal, more the pity. You would not take your art to the marketplace after you left commercial work, because then,

<u>in a manner of speaking now</u>, understand, you considered that the act of a pros-
titute, for your "feminine feelings" that you felt produced the painting would
then be sold for the sake of "the male's role as provider and bringer of power."

The art of the Old Masters escaped such connotations, largely because it
involved so much physical labor—the making of colors, canvases, and so forth.
<u>That work</u>, providing the artist's preparation, now belongs to the male-world
manufacturer, you see, so the artist as a male in your society is often <u>left with
what he thinks of as</u> art's feminine basis, where it must be confronted, of course.

(10:20.) I want to make it plain that such ideas are rampant in society, and
are at the basis of many personal and national problems. They are behind large
issues, involved in the *[Three Mile Island]* nuclear fiasco, for example, and in the
scientist's idea of power and creation.

Both of you, highly creative, find your creativity in conflict with your
ideas of sexuality, privately and in your stance with the world. Much of this is
involved with the unfortunate myths about this creative person, who is not supposed to be able to deal with the world as well as others, whose idiosyncrasies
are exaggerated, and whose very creativity, it is sometimes said, leads to suicide
or destruction. No wonder few numbers of creative people persist in the face of
such unfortunate beliefs.

Indeed, these are some of the reasons why Ruburt distrusted the spontaneous self—because it was feminine, he believed, and therefore more flawed
than the spontaneous self of the male.

You run into many contradictions. God is supposed to be male. The soul
is sometimes considered female. The angels are male. Now let us look at the
Garden of Eden. The story says that Eve tempted the male, having him eat of
the tree of good and evil, or the tree of knowledge. *(Pause.)* This represented a
state of consciousness, the point at which the species began to think and feel for
itself, when it approached a certain state of consciousness in which it dared exert
its own creativity.

(Pause.) This is difficult to verbalize. *(Pause.)* It was a state when the
species became aware of its own thoughts as its own thoughts, and became conscious of the self who thinks. That point released man's creativity. In your terms,
it was the product of the feminine intuitions (though, as you know, such intuitions belong to both sexes). When the passages were written, the species had
come to various states of order, achieving certain powers and organizations, and
it wanted to maintain the status quo. No more intuitive visions, no more
changes, were wanted. Creativity was to follow certain definite roads, so the
woman became the villain.

I have given material on that before. To some extent, then, Ruburt became afraid of his own creativity, and so did you. In Ruburt's case the fear was greater, until it seemed sometimes that if he succeeded in his work he would succeed at some peril: you might be put in an unpleasant light, or he might become a fanatic, displaying those despicable, feminine hysterical qualities. *(With much humor:)* I hope this session benefits you both. End of session, and a fond good evening.

("Thank you, Seth. Good night.")

(10:35 PM. Jane's trances and delivery had been good. "I didn't know he was going to do that," she said after I told her it was an excellent session. "Maybe that's why I felt so uncomfortable before the session. Now I feel exhausted. I could go right to bed, but I won't...."

(Jane said she couldn't really describe them now, but she had "great emotional feelings" when she delivered the part of the session about my thinking that selling work made me a prostitute. "Some gargantuan feelings there, full of humor," she said.

(She laughed. "You are so strange," she said. "Here you won't go to the marketplace, but you think of saving all of these private sessions for posterity, to give them to the world. You're very close-mouthed: you don't blab our personal business, as you put it, but you'd do that.... Instead, I see us when I'm 80 and you're 90, out in the backyard, burning it all."

(Yet she easily agreed that this evening's session, whether private or not, cast much light on the regular, or published material, adding depths of understanding and background information.)

SESSION 855 (DELETED PORTION)
MAY 21, 1979 9:15 PM MONDAY

(The following material is from the 855th session.

(Before supper this evening Jane said she was tired of "trying to figure out the world," and so forth. Part of her pique stemmed from her difficulty in trying to get into her ideas on heroics. She has done some excellent writing on heroic themes in recent days, but hasn't plunged into her library yet. And to me: "Sometimes I think that you, whenever you get any idea that doesn't have to do with painting, ought to stamp it out with both feet, and just stick to that. You shouldn't ever have left it...." I admitted that the thought had occurred to me—that indeed I'd been thinking about it a lot since I'd had my physical hassles starting early last month.

(I told Jane that I'd long given up trying to hammer out my next writing project, as Seth had mentioned I was trying to do in one of these recent deleted sessions.

I was now simply trying to live each day, painting, working on the files, or in the yard, doing errands, and so forth. It's all helped, although I don't feel completely free physically yet. I've managed to come up with some new insights about painting, however, and have begun implementing them. I can already tell the difference in the work, and am very pleased with that. The insights, which seem rather obvious in retrospect, represent a sort of synthesis that I've been trying for in recent years.

(Today we received from Larry Dowler of the Yale archives a letter giving us his latest thoughts, as well as a form to sign. making the gift of papers to Yale legal, evidently. We have a number of questions to resolve first, though. At the moment I must be putting them off, but eventually we'll deal with them all. We haven't received our will from Bill Danaher yet, and we have more questions for him, also. I told Jane that I regretted starting that whole business, but she responded by saying that we'd have to do it sometime, probably, so we might as well go through with it. I'm somewhat dismayed by the work that might be entailed – that is, if I carry through with the original idea of checking through all the material, putting it into notebooks that match the originals, and so forth.

(9:53.) To some extent both of you, and by your own choices, have established your own laboratory of the mind, in which you live your lives and examine them at the same time—and in which you try to view any maladies and dissatisfactions by different standards; and in a light that requires more of you, so that you do not rely as others do upon the comforts of conventionalized knowledge in any field.

You are, it seems, denied the easier satisfactions of accepted answers *(pause)*, and to some extent denied the cozy comfort of shared beliefs. *(Pause.)* You are also, however, as Ruburt wrote, hampered it seems by old beliefs that still exert their hold. You are throwing out, to some extent, now, much of the accumulated nonsense of the centuries *(emphatically)*, upon which people have often tragically built their lives and cultures.

It is not surprising then that you often feel insecure. The self <u>can</u> (underlined) be relied upon. That is the main message that you must get through your heads. Impulses are inner messages toward actions that are life-giving. When they appear otherwise, it is the result of habits and beliefs. Through all of history, one way or another, you have believed in the line of culture <u>leading to your own</u>—that impulses were disruptive, suspicious, and not to be trusted; ignoring the child's impulse to speak, and to walk and grow, to communicate. Those are the ideas you are combating—not simply Freudian or Darwinian concepts from your lifetimes, but the accumulated misinformation from that historic past. So tell Ruburt not to be so impatient with himself, to remind himself that he can indeed trust the self that he knows, <u>regardless</u> of what he had been taught to believe.

The same applies to you, and I expect both of you, in the last halves of your lives, to demonstrate the bursts of creativity and new wisdom that should ideally appear in each life. Have him let himself go. Encourage him to follow his impulses to be the self that he is.

I made recommendations, but they seem to take too much effort to follow *(quietly ironic)* as far as Ruburt is concerned. You have done well there, for the yard work is helping, and the change <u>will</u> naturally bring your creativity to flower if you leave yourself alone. But a change of hours now and then is excellent, as far as Ruburt is concerned in particular. The changes stand for mental flexibility.

You may do as you wish about Yale. It matters little where the papers are kept; and the very academic characteristics that invisibly but definitely add their aura to Yale's hallowed halls also means that the papers will be treated fairly, conservatively, and without any evangelical air.

(Louder, and in answer to our talk earlier:) I am quite willing to hold as many sessions a week as suits your fancies. A point: I told you that the sessions must be fun—that is, creative, exploratory, and as free as possible – and, I add, not only for you but for me as well. I would not be here if I did not most of the time find it thoroughly enjoyable. There are moments when I wish I could <u>jar</u> you both enough so that you could perceive clearly the intimate, immediate and also far-reaching effect of your beliefs upon your lives. When I wish I could somehow make you understand that reality springs from your thoughts, and not the other way around, and that any given thought is far more real in basic terms than the table upon which Ruburt rests his foot *(stamping upon the table with that foot)*. End of session. A fond and exuberant good evening.

("Thank you. Seth. Good night." 10:15 PM. And yes, I too wish Seth could jar us....)

SESSION 856 (DELETED PORTION)
MAY 24, 1979 8:23 PM THURSDAY

(I described Jane's very relaxed states today in the notes for the regular, 856th session, from which the material to follow is taken. During her periods of relaxation she gained a number of insights about herself, her challenges and physical condition. She became especially aware of her own impulses and fears of what would happen if she gave in to those impulses. They all added up to a steady barrage of self-criticism and fear of not writing, of perhaps doing the dishes instead, or cleaning the house, of

making more work for me, of time spent answering the mail—whatever it might be. I tried to encourage her to relax more often, by saying to hell with whatever bugged her at the moment, as she did with good success today.

(I added that the more spontaneous she was about doing what she wanted at any given time—in other words, following her natural impulses—the more writing and painting she'd find herself able to do. As Seth remarked in a recent session, the relaxed muscle is able to do far more than the tense one, or words to that effect.)

(9:10.) A private note: what you want to do, ideally speaking, is the best thing to do.

Ideally speaking, your impulses lead you in your own proper direction, knowing the shape of your life, and your abilities and your needs. One impulse may be in response to one need, one to another—but all in all, taken together, they will sustain and guide you to your most fulfilling situation if they are allowed to, and if they are trusted.

(Pause.) Ruburt let his guard down ever so slightly, stopped stewing ever so slightly. The impulse to have the session came through spontaneously, as it should. He writes because he loves to write. He has an almost steady impulse to write. He has an almost steady impulse toward psychic activity, toward creativity.

When he thinks that he must do such and such, must prove his worth by sitting at his desk, then he lays a heavy hand upon those same impulses. He is afraid of doing anything else. That might show he is not "working." His creative and psychic abilities emerge precisely when he is relaxed. So do his normal physical ones. You were of great help this morning, allowing him to talk out the situation at the time.

Do not try to back over backwards over the tax issue—hence your back problem *(today)*. That also involves your joint ideas of work. You feel guilty about taxes, because you _feel_ that you have not contributed enough financially—therefore doubly angry that the money must be taken from Ruburt, and so forth.

(Whispering, then much louder:) Now I bid you a hearty and fond good evening.

(End of this material at 9:19 PM.)

DELETED SESSION
MAY 28, 1979 10:15 PM MONDAY

(The session started late because Jane became so involved in a painting after

supper. It was one in which she was attempting to follow in a still-life some of the techniques I'd showed her a few days ago, when I repainted another still-life composition she'd started, and showed her how to get more opaque effects for variety; a demonstration, then, for she'd asked for "a lesson." Since then there have been some rather humorous episodes—I mean it kindly—as Jane tries to use those methods, with very mixed results. But interestingly, she ran into conflicts between her old method, in which she used mostly transparent color, and the new one, which, she complained in her frustration, was "muddy, and lacking vitality. And without the vitality, what good is it?"

(At 9:30 she told me Seth might go into my dream of May 27—yesterday— in which I drove an automobile down West Water St. at 90 miles per hour, without harm. I also mentioned my Boy Scout dream of May 22, in which I saw her walking normally, and my vivid dream impressions of my father, of May 15, in which I woke up crying. I've begun a small painting of this last subject. All dreams are on file in dream notebook #2.

(Our dream discussion before the session led me to voice a question about dreams that I don't think Seth has covered in just that way. Sue Watkins visited us last night, and related several recent dreams in which she saw Jane functioning normally physically. [I've also had others in which Jane was okay physically – walking well, and so forth.] "But what happens," I asked, as we waited for the session to begin, "after I have the dream about you, for example? Do you receive it? Do you accept it or reject it, or does it do you good on certain levels? How come, with all of these positive dreams, you aren't improving physically to any observable degree? If you get the messages we sent you, do they do any good at all?" The questions would apply in any dream exchange among people, of course.

(Jane was "just mad," though, as we waited for the session to start at 10:10. Mad about it all, she said. "What good does it do for Seth to go into me? None that I can tell...." She'd been upset about her painting too, of course. She's been trying to follow her impulses more spontaneously recently, in light of the recent session material, and I think has shown good improvement there. But she was blue earlier today, when various portions of her anatomy bothered her. Her legs have bothered a lot lately, and she's felt down at times.

(My own physical condition has improved considerably, so in some way I've managed to learn something. I suspect the better results may simply be the results of the body healing itself once I removed the pressures I'd been imposing upon that basically innocent structure. I've been painting a lot more lately.

(I'm making an extra carbon of this session for my own use with the dream material.

(Jane's delivery was good, interspersed with many pauses. and often fast and

emphatic.

(*Whispering:*) Good Evening.

("*Good evening, Seth.*")

Now: at one point or another, your private reality becomes to some extent a public one, to one degree or another, as it is viewed by and participated in by others.

You show a certain picture of yourself to the world. You stress certain characteristics, and show them to others. There are habitual patterns of behavior that operate, as you more or less stabilize your picture of yourself in relationship with families and friends. Sometimes that picture is a fairly faithful representation, and sometimes people make <u>artificial</u> portraits of themselves, and instead of speaking for themselves to others, they let their artificial portraits do it for them.

(*Pause.*) Sometimes to protect themselves because of their beliefs, people then form distorted portraits of themselves, and project these outward "to take life's arrows," so to speak. (*Pause.*) The real personality, however, is never satisfied with such a procedure, and seeks a much fuller, freer expression.

Many illnesses are physically experienced facades that are meant to alter the person's relationship with the world. They act often like barriers, or coats of armor, and according to the situation another person must first confront this condition or coat of armor, if he ever hopes to establish contact with the personality. I hope that is clear.

(*Pause.*) Now Ruburt has had such a condition, for many reasons often given. He is trying to free himself. To do so he must change his own reality, alter his feeling of relationship with himself, and between himself and others. His physical situation—the symptoms—are public to the extent that others know he has difficulties. New sentence: When attempts are made to change that reality, then the reality of family and friends is also changed to some extent. Your dreams and Sue's allow you, ever so subtly, to change your own views of Ruburt's behavior. You see him operating normally. So has Tam, incidentally. Such dream behavior helps to break the heavy-handed stress of "daily physical evidence." (*Pause.*) Exterior changes begin on the inside, and appear then physically—and not the other way around.

When <u>Ruburt</u> has such dreams, his muscles and joints react in sleep, mimicking normal actions—and he well might be sorer than usual upon awakening, because in sleep, <u>at such times</u>, now, without the weight of his body, standing and so forth, the muscles and joints will make motions of a releasing nature quite painlessly in the dream state. Sometimes waking consciousness will vaguely be aware of the motions, and because they are expected to bring discomfort, they do.

(This is a very important paragraph. Worth excerpting and keeping handy for daily reference.

(10:35.) Such dreams on Ruburt's part bring one vital message: that he <u>can</u> walk normally, and that this can be <u>easily</u> (underlined) brought about. In some of the dreams he is surprised that he can perform so well. In others he takes it for granted, as in your *(Boy Scout)* dream. In waking life, however, you have both been literally hypnotized by the idea that such a recovery is one of the hardest things in the world to achieve *(intently).* In the waking state Ruburt believes that he cannot walk properly. In the dream state he holds no such beliefs.

(Long pause.) Now he <u>wanted</u> to hold such beliefs because he felt he needed that quite painful facade to protect himself from his own spontaneity, and then to protect himself against the world because he felt he was too spontaneous. The answer was to cut down on physical spontaneity. Spontaneity is easy, so we will make it hard. We believe it is the most difficult thing in the world. I have given endless material on that. Privately and through your dreams and Sue's, Ruburt with your help in the dream state sees that motion can be and is easy. He responds telepathically to your dreams.

Let us look at his painting. He digs into it, this present one, concentrates. Forgets how much he loves to paint, and considers all the problems involved in a new technique. And considers how he can never be as good as you in that regard. He uses effort. He forgets his <u>ease</u>, and the same thing applies to "trying to get better."

Psychocybernetics (underlined) is a good handbook, very simplified, with some distortions, but its premise is quite correct: you <u>do</u> hypnotize yourself into such situations. I want to make a point that Ruburt <u>can</u> often interpret relaxation as depression, because the loss of tension can still be frightening. You have actually helped in that regard. The dreams show your activity in Framework 2 —and again, may I recommend on Ruburt's part some sense of creativity in his physical situation? Even suggestions should be given playfully, not heavy-handedly. For his point-of-power exercises have him just playfully for five minutes pretend—knowing that it is a game—that he feels perfectly normal and relaxed. Let him consider impulses also playfully, not looking at each one as if it were as important as the ending of the world.

Now: remember that while your dreams occur one night at a time, their logic is timeless. You may deal with several issues over several nights. Your hearing the voice of God dream *(this morning)*, and your fast car dream *(of the morning before)* were, then, related. The beginning of our sessions represents to you your own version of hearing the voice of God, in that you felt that it was the first time in your life that in whatever guise, some portion of the universe "had a message for you"—or that you were in contact with anything beyond the ordinary, that at least held hopes for a glimpse of any real knowledge beyond the known.

(Pause.) The trooper, elevated from the ground in the car dream, was another dream version carrying the theme further, though it actually occurred, I believe, before the God dream *(the morning before)*. Do you follow me?

("Yes.")

In this dream, you are given permission by a somewhat elevated authority to go faster than the other people along Water Street. You are told more or less that you can go faster without harm, yet the dream itself poses a question, for it does not seem that you actually cover the ground to the red light at Hoffman Street any faster. The question is why, of course; if you have been given permission to go faster, then why have you and Ruburt not covered the physical ground faster, or why do you still have problems? Since you have been given such permission, why have you not learned faster?

(10:58.) The answer of course is that the permission you were given to go "faster" applied to a completely different dimension of motion and activity. You actually interpreted it in more mundane terms than was meant, and <u>because</u> you so interpreted it, the end result was that you did not <u>seem</u> to cover the ground any faster than others.

The speed applied to the energy generated by Framework 2—energy that transforms the road or ground so that you do not have to travel the road in the same old fashion, that is, I am answering the dream's question *(all intently)*. The idea of the sessions, accepted on their own merits, applies easily. You cannot <u>make</u> them apply (underlined). You allow them to flow.

Your father dream. Your father represented your father, but he also stood for your version of the race [species] of man itself, of the nameless old men seemingly worn down by age, the lack of communication between nameless fathers and sons. Yet the old man does sleep in a gigantic shoe that is also like a cradle, from which he and all of civilization continue to emerge. Your question was why the lack of communication and compassion, the inarticulateness of love? And as you consoled your father, you tried to console humanity. And how? Through expression of the words, but also through your art, for you saw all art as an expression of love, a love in which the old man and civilization was ultimately held.

The withered foot *(of my father)* represented any and all deformities, and the great gap you felt existed between man's ideal, and his actualization of it.

(Heartily:) End of session, and a hearty good evening.

("Thank you. Good night, Seth."
(11:08 PM.)

SESSION 857 (DELETED PORTION)
MAY 30, 1979 9:28 PM WEDNESDAY

(The following material is from the 857th session.

(Jane has been following the material in recent private sessions about trusting her impulses and spontaneity, with good results.

(10:42.) A note: Ruburt is doing well. Continue to encourage his expression of impulses. You have been exceedingly helpful. For a while, have him look at some old suggestions! He knows what ones I mean. They emphasized the fact that he could indeed walk better.

("Can I ask a question?")

You may indeed.

("Do you want to say something about Jane's dream about her mother, on Monday—the one that upset him?")

Give us a moment....

He saw his mother, but the image was a projected one. It was a feared image of himself, wrapped too tightly in the bedding, which represented the restraints of old beliefs. He felt he could not <u>see</u> properly, meaning he could not see his way out of the situation. Yet when he asked his mother, "Can you see?" it was obvious that she could.

He tried to loosen the hampering bedding, and could not, but a doctor —a young man—came to his aid, loosened the bedding. The doctor represents newer beliefs, and the spontaneous nature of the self, which can act so much more effectively with those new beliefs.

The tabloid turns into a parade float, the contrast showing that the resolution can end in a parade, with rejoicing. The earlier portions of the dream did, however, represent fears that Ruburt was, say, dying of suffocation—not physical suffocation, but from being bound too tightly.

The last session, its private portions for Ruburt, should be reread, with its emphasis upon creativity and trust in unconscious processes.

End of session, and a hearty good evening.

("Thank you. Seth. Good night."

(10:54. Jane's delivery was strong and steady through the session—much more so than usual. She said that Seth didn't mention one part of the dream: that after it she became aware of herself saying "You'll have to say goodbye to your cats." She took

this to mean she was thinking of dying, and she didn't want to do this, or leave the cats. Jane has written her own account of the dream of May 28. As we talked about it Seth returned.)

(10:55.) Ruburt is too persistent to die young. The cats did not represent your physical cats *(Mitzi and Billy Two)*, but old comfortable beliefs about the nature of the spontaneous self connected with ideas he picked up from his mother, in which cats represented the worst aspects of human behavior and impulses: they fawned upon you, yet were evil, and could turn against you in a moment.

(Whispering:) End of session.

(10:56 PM.)

DELETED SESSION
JUNE 1, 1979　9:46 PM FRIDAY

(Yesterday afternoon we were visited by my brother Bill and his wife, Ida, from Ontario, NY. We all had a most enjoyable visit—I thought. We usually see them but once a year. But it developed that Jane had one of her most uncomfortable nights in years last night; she woke up often, very stiff, particularly in the dawn hours. She realized that she was reacting to what she'd taken to be all of the negative suggestions and circumstances surrounding Bill and Ida's lives and beliefs. Later we wished we'd had the presence of mind to get up at dawn, say, when Jane's more acute discomfort began.)

(As today passed Jane picked up from Seth—and herself—material on the events of yesterday afternoon, so that finally she had an idea at least of what Seth would discuss tonight. [I suggested she have this session, although the thought crossed her mind also.])

(Jane also through the day received from Seth some material in answer to my remarks at breakfast this morning about the jacket colors chosen for Volume 2 of "Unknown" Reality. The proof arrived in the mail while Dick and Ida were here; we looked at it without much reaction, but still thought about it on other levels a good deal. It lacks what I call good taste, as I'd feared it would, and is too cold and creepy. I for one have long reached the point where I expect little else from Prentice-Hall except shoddy work, and I think that by now Jane more or less agrees. She didn't like the jacket colors.)

(Just before the session began Jane started coughing quite a bit. Her voice became hoarse and dry. "It must be because of what I know Seth's going to talk about," she said between coughs. "Your brother and his family, and my reactions. I'll

try to have the session, but I don't know how far I'll get...."

(Yet, not long after Seth came through. Jane's voice cleared easily, and she delivered his material easily and rapidly for the most part.)

Now: by the standards your brother Richard once believed in, and by the standards that your sister-in-law once believed in, they are both relatively successful.

He is a senior executive. She is a woman with children grown, and they have a fine home in the country. They <u>are</u>, as Ruburt declared so emphatically, nice people, well-intended people.

Along the way, they discovered those original standards were wanting *(hoarsely).* They did what they thought they were supposed to do, but do not feel nearly the sense of accomplishment or pleasure with their lives that they once expected. Ruburt is fond of both of them, as you are, but he saw them in their actuality, as themselves and as representative of many people in general.

They actually represent the ways in which beliefs can dull native qualities of mind and heart alike, so that the intellect seems opaque, and emotional relationships are unduly tangled. Ruburt is working with the nature of impulses, and old ideas about impulses, spontaneity and discipline rose to mind, for the family situation of your brother and his wife almost typifies the kind of situation that Ruburt was determined to avoid. And he thought, what was the entire affair, really, for it seemed to lack any kind of discipline. It seemed to him, with the force of old beliefs, that Ida, Richard and the children were indeed driven willy-nilly by contradictory impulses, and that their lives lack any organizing inner purpose.

The boy *(David, who has quit school)* had an automobile accident. What was that but impulsiveness, unthinking behavior? <u>Ruburt had used all kinds of discipline</u>, you see, lest he fall back into the common ground from which it seemed most people came from.

He is in a period where he is trying to release impulses, but one look at that situation—momentarily, now—panicked him, so that he began to wonder if any discipline was not worthwhile to prevent what he considered that kind of intuitional and intellectual sloth.

He is loyal to your family. He tries to help them, and he tried to deal with his own responses. He tried to rouse William's intellect and intuitions, but to his utter amazement he found both more dormant than he had expected. Let me clear the issues. Generally speaking now, Dick and Ida seldom followed their own impulses; no matter for example how impulsive Dick might have seemed at times in the past. Both of them distrusted the self to a far greater degree than either of you ever did, so that the fine grains of originality were dulled in all areas of their lives.

They did what they believed was expected of them. For a time they rebelled, not in response to their own impulses, however, but in response to the demands of others. Your brother to some extent identified strongly with your father, seeing him as the intellectual, the inventor held in bonds, almost in thrall by the "emotional" demanding woman. He blamed your mother for all of their problems. In his own family he made sure that the male domain, the study, was separate from the family rooms, not to be shared. Books were not left around the house for women or children to misuse.

(Pause at 10:06.) He squashed what intuitive abilities he had, and finally considered, for example, poetry unmanly. His place of work became his male domain. He <u>wanted</u> children to be frightened of him, for this proved that he was indeed superior, and not given to emotional outbursts.

His behavior, however, led him of course to quite powerful emotional outbursts, which frightened him. Ida married him because she believed his educational status, and his Anglo-Saxon background, meant a step upward for herself and her children. She did as she was told, for many years.

(Pause.) You have always been a hero, and yet a mystery to your brother Dick, a source of pride and yet of embarrassment. He considers studying dreams feminine, and to paint <u>pictures</u> of them presents a second mystery *(intently)*. His own buried intuitional abilities, however, have always acted as a bridge between you, so that he feels a close affinity that he does not understand. He feels some affinity to Ruburt for the same reason, but Ruburt also upsets him, because he disapproves of women who think, and is very frightened because Ida in later years has started to criticize some of their joint beliefs.

But Ruburt thought: "This is what most people are like, and if I give in to my impulses, will the days slide by me like that?"

Dick finds pleasure in golf, because it represents an area in which he has hope of performing with some effectiveness, of acting with a spontaneity that knows its own order, and of experiencing his natural sense of power.

(A note: Yet Bill told me of his troubles with golf this season, lamenting how he has problems getting any distance in his drives, speaking of taking some lessons and practice in an effort to improve his game. We also discussed a major tournament that as it happened both of us had seen partially on TV last weekend.)

Ruburt wrote a poem yesterday morning *(Thursday)*, considering it afterward briefly, wondering whether it was really good enough to type as it was, throwing off in an odd moment a thought, a concept that would represent the highest revelation to Ida, <u>if she could understand</u> what it means.

Ida and Dick both believe to a far greater extent, again, than you two ever did, that the self is unsavory and dangerous. Ida was afraid to see the psychologist again, for fear that therapy would throw up evidence of this feared evil thing, and Dick is afraid of writing poetry again lest the intuitions upset his life. He used meditation as a tranquilizer to dull his senses and mind, and not for understanding himself. Ruburt's impulses gave birth to his poetry, to his writing, and to the freedom of his intellect and the heavy-handed discipline has always been impeding.

He felt partially helpless, realizing that neither Dick nor Ida read the books. He wanted to improve physically before their eyes, in a flash of a moment, to show them physically that it could be done. All of this caused muscular tensions, but he was appalled at what he considered Dick and Ida's laxness in so many areas, and it seemed that that was the natural human condition, so that you must exert great discipline to keep yourself aloft from it. It is not the natural condition of the species to begin with, and <u>naturally</u> (underlined) neither of you were that way. The truer you are to yourselves, and to your natural impulses, the less you will be that way *(intently again)*.

Ruburt has been doing well, with your help.

(10:25.) I want to emphasize that your brother and sister-in-law have their own purposes, and I am not putting down their realities. I want you to realize also, however, that like many others, they have no handle on the world, so to speak, no perspective outside of their experience, from which they can view their lives, and I want you to appreciate those dimensions in your own reality.

Do you have questions?

("Jane said she picked up from you this morning some things about Prentice-Hall—our troubles with them about cover designs, their attitudes, and so forth.")

I forget. That was to me implied, but it was not stated here.

Dick, again, uses golf in order to actualize to some extent his feeling toward an ideal. He does not have that in his work any longer.

The people at Prentice and generally speaking at any publishing house, live more or less at the level you saw yesterday. Each person senses an ideal, and has good intent, but those ideals and good intents are distorted by beliefs, and by the conditions accompanying them.

There are people who work in art departments as a living, gifted certainly more than most with an ability to visually portray an idea. They sense an ideal, but those ideals and abilities are everywhere distorted by millions of other considerations. What do they think of their art themselves? To what purpose do they use it? What does their wife or husband think? What does the boss think? Whose version is the final one for a cover? What does the artist think of the subject matter? What are the artist's standards of excellence?

The artist's standard of excellence is often the necessity of keeping his job, and he has to keep his job because he fears he is not after all a true artist, or he would be painting a great painting. And at work his art must be further distorted, it seems to him, by the ideas of salesmanship and advertising.

Your covers represent the attempt to express an ideal in the context that exists in the publishing field. The difference between your idea of an excellent cover and the actuality, and the difference between your kind of experience and your brother's, should help you become more aware even of the need for our joint work in the world.

I do not think you understand completely. I am not speaking of the fact that your brother has a family and children and you do not, and I am not forgetting you have problems. I am saying that the quality of your lives is far more satisfying in comparison to others' than you realize, and that the kind of experience you have chosen offers the most productive challenges. You always have something to look forward to, clearer insight, the closest approximation to truth that you might attain, where many others live in a maze, in which it seems *(pause)* that any hope of effecting change is literally impossible, privately.

Do you have questions?

("Nope.")

Your way is difficult, but it has unusual rewards. Those who have followed old beliefs do not have it easy either, and they do not know where to turn. Count your blessings.

Incidentally, Ruburt "should" get up at such times *(as when Jane woke up feeling so uncomfortable in the early morning).*

End of session, and a fond good evening.

("Okay. Thank you."

(10:43 PM. Jane laughed. "I noticed that my voice cleared up as soon as I started the session." Almost, at least, I said. Then Jane added: "I just got that he's going to devote part of another session, a private one, to beliefs people have about old age. Because of the meeting with Dick and Ida...."

(Note: See the opening notes for the 881st session.)

JANE'S DREAM
FRIDAY, JUNE 1

All I recall is final scene. No idea how or why, but a large multitude of people including myself have come to the ocean shore. The sky is sudsy, like soapy clouds, mixing with the water. Some people are in a huge bathtub filled with hot soapy water. Another person says something I've forgotten to the idea that… the ocean water or sky, … were dangerous or maybe that it was lightening, but I dismiss this, stand in the bathtub and the water is great, hot and soapy. Then a man begins to recite a poem as he walks up and down the shore. The poem isn't very good but I feel indulgent because his intentions are good.…

JANE'S DREAM
SATURDAY, JUNE 2

Recall brief last scene again. A man who looks somewhat Lou Grant (television star Ed Asner) writes me a note saying that I've touched him as no other woman ever has. I read this, and on the other side is a note by a woman that is disruptive in some way. The man is very nice, warm, dark haired, a little dumpy.

JANE'S DREAM
SUNDAY, JUNE 3, NAP.

Scene 1—At an art gallery supposed to be the Arnot. A woman is in trouble from taking drugs. I talk to her sympathetically, give a terrific dissertation on art, its therapeutic qualities, and use as a natural high. Lots of people around.

Scene 2—Office of large corporation. On phone a man makes appointment to take me to dinner to discuss giving me an excellent position but I can't hear him properly and got to another office to check time, etc. I'm in line for a great job… walk with other women thinking how amazed Rob will be if I take it or get it… and that it would be good for me to mix with people for a change. I haven't said anything about being a writer… they might figure I don't need the work… think that it's full-time though and briefly wonder how I could handle that with writing.

Scene 3—These same women, myself, and at least one man are hiding though I don't remember why. We're in a large storage building. Some men, maybe police, come in and we hide in the shadows; a door beside is going to open so we get down and drag ourselves on our bellies to another door at the end of the room to hide in the shadows. The man with us may have his hands in shackles or something; I have to help him climb over some walls. As we move toward door shadows, almost same, I see one woman carrying Rob's landscape (the one in our bedroom) pushing it ahead of her. When we almost have it made one woman says to hell with it, she can't take it another minute; she's just going to stand up and show herself no matter what. I'm furious at her. Rob wakens me.

SESSION 858 (DELETED PORTION)
JUNE 4, 1979 9:01 PM MONDAY

(The private material below is from the 858th session, but it came through first in the session instead of at the end, for a change.

(Before the session I asked Jane if she had any questions for Seth. She'd written poetry today, besides doing a little housework. Now we went over her recent dream activity, in the event Seth chose to offer material on that. Jane's dreams have been vivid and positive for the most part, concerning physical improvements, etc. Attached is her record of her dreams from June 1-3. Seth opened the session by discussing her June 3 dream. Jane had been much more relaxed than usual today.

(Whispering:) Good evening.

("Good evening, Seth.")

Ruburt's dreams will be part of this evening's discussion, as they apply directly to him and as they represent the beautiful, even exquisite imagery of the dreaming self in general. The art dream *(of June 3)*, as I call it, has its opening scene in an art gallery, which represents a conventionalized view of art. Ruburt used painting as an art in the dream rather than writing *(pause)*, because it symbolized your joint ideas of art—to some extent, now—and allowed him to have you in his mind as he viewed the dream events.

In the first scene in the gallery he is explaining with some eloquence the mental and physical benefits of art, and its action as providing "a natural high." The word "high" is important, for art, his art—writing, poetry—was his version of, say, the high mass of his childhood, where he and not the priest was in connection with the universe. By a kind of shorthand, the art gallery suggests the church, then, and his dedication to art, that is, to his art quickly replaced his dedication to the church. It became his vocation in quite religious terms.

The second scene takes place in a large office building that represents the world and its usual pursuits. Ruburt is offered a rather lucrative and fairly prestigious position. When his prospective employer sets a time for a meeting, however, by telephone, Ruburt cannot hear him clearly and so must double-check. This simply means that the voice of the world did not come through clearly as far as it offered other vocational opportunities. Ruburt knew he could gain sufficient-enough prestige by using his abilities in other directions; by being, say, a director of a gallery, or by accepting any of a number of positions, such as teaching, that had been offered him in the past.

And in the past, he toyed with some of those ideas and positions. When he tried teaching he began to get ill, for he was afraid that he would settle for the respectable-enough prestige it afforded, give in and stop his writing and other pursuits. He was in his late thirties, and sometimes tempted to do so.

Developing symptoms kept him at home, away from such temptations. This should be taken into consideration with other material, of course.

Timewise and symbolically, the third scene brings us to the point where Ruburt is determined to defend his art, his dedication, to such an extent that he hides from the world, and symbolically crawls on his belly, all the while seeking to escape the dilemma by finding an open door, or by hiding from pursuers in the shadows. These efforts fail. One portion of himself is a character, male, with bound hands, and Ruburt must help this person over barriers, of course because his hands are tied symbolically behind his back.

One woman, another follower, for Ruburt is the leader of this group, pushes a landscape of yours across the floor ahead of her—preserving, you see, your art as well as Ruburt's. Finally one of the women objects strenuously and decides to stand up and show herself. She is tired of crawling on her belly, for whatever reasons. That woman represents Ruburt's decision to be done with the symptoms, to stand up, to walk.

(9:20.) Ruburt, however, objects, and that Ruburt represents the portion of the personality who is still clinging to old beliefs, but losing its leadership. The group of beliefs are breaking up, and can no longer count upon such blind obedience. As Ruburt wakens, he realizes that nowhere in the dream did he have any reason to hide. No reason was given for the pursuit itself, for he was being pursued now and then at least, by several people.

He began to question as he awakened his motives for such frantic behavior. The dream gave him three scenes representing various areas of his life in terms of time—the institution of the gallery and his early ideas, the office representing the world, and his hiding place, which was a kind of storage barn. It stored old beliefs. From which he was seeking escape.

His other dreams, of the walking series *(pause)*, are giving him practical physical education, for the muscles remember their proper motions, and these dreams help counteract his waking belief that it is difficult to walk. Messages are also going out to other people, who are aware at dream levels of Ruburt's intent. They do add help and support. The dreams themselves have contributed to Ruburt's relative compliance with growing bodily relaxation, and with his growing trust in his own impulses.

The fact that you have been of such help shows how much you have learned, for in the past you did sometimes sabotage his efforts—not at all lately —because of your own distrust of impulses, and because the situation to some extent served you also.

Such behavior, of course, operates in any condition, from the overweight person to the alcoholic, for each individual forms his own reality, and yet does so unconsciously knowing the needs and beliefs of others.

(9.35. Now Seth gave another page of material on other matters, which is presented at the 858th session, and ended the session at 9:50 PM.)

JANE'S DREAMS
JUNE 11, MONDAY, NAP 1979

Dream 1—I was looking at some weird contraption, maybe mechanical, that my father had made, to leave me some money after his death; money was supposed to come out of it. A nice old man, sort of a kindly bum, came by and told me father had made it two hours before his death so that I'd have some inheritance; and the old man might have had a key that worked it; I'm not sure; but there was something about a key.... maybe also one missing. Anyhow a dribble of something, maybe coins, came out. I think the old man may have been helping himself, too, along the way. I told him that both of my parents were dead.

Dream 2—Don't recall the beginning but it was in a huge amphitheater and there was a picture in great color on a giant screen to the left. After though, Pat Norelli (I think it was her, though she didn't look like Pat particularly) myself and two young men were climbing along a high ledge toward the top of the gigantic theater. Down below were many people all watching a show or something. Pat went on along the ledge to where it met the front wall but I was frightened of falling and stayed where I was with the young man who was my companion, When Pat reached that point, the young man who was her companion did something.... and the front of the amphitheater moved so that a ledge lowered to meet her so she could make it safely to the stage. Laughing I sang out as a joke some religious line from a hymn.... that now I've forgotten because the stage looked somewhat like an altar, and she was saved from falling, and deposited on the stage, she stood in the center, wearing slacks and a blouse, arms out, waving at the people. I yelled "Pat;" meaning to wait, she responded, grinning. Then the man with me and I began to backtrack down the ledge the way we came. Rob awakened me here.

DELETED SESSION
JUNE 11, 1979 9:20 PM MONDAY

(As we sat for the session Jane gave me a copy [which is attached] of the dreams she had while taking a nap this afternoon. "I think I have the interpretations of them," she said, "but maybe Seth will talk about them too. In fact, I just got the last part of the second dream as I was sitting here...."

(She was again very relaxed today. She'd also been picking up from Seth through the day some quite amused comments on a variety of subjects we'd mentioned, ranging from "carpets and health" to the "nature of the law, the connection between the law and ideals and their actualization; the reactions of Tam Mossman to our feelings about Fate Magazine, *" etc.*

(Last Thursday night our guest was John Beahrs, a psychiatrist from the Seattle, Washington area. Now I'm in the process of writing a long letter to Larry Dowler, of the Yale University Library, and this activity showed up also in Seth's bleedthroughs and comments.)

Good evening.

("Good evening, Seth.")

"The importance of definition" is our heading for this evening—at least for a starter.

Ideals are vital, for they provide an impetus toward beneficial action, action that is meant to lead to some actualization of that ideal in fact. An ideal represents events that do not as yet exist in fact. They should serve as plans for concentrated action.

Many ideals, however, must remain by their nature somewhat generalized, a matter of inspiration, for example, that cannot perhaps so easily be put into words; or sometimes the ideal exists simply as a yearning for a better situation, though no immediate steps come to mind that offer any concerted plan for action.

The ideal may be specific, then, or ill-defined, and man's idea of "the good" varies considerably. The better you can define your idea of the ideal, the better off you are, for it—the definition—at least clears your own mind, and suggests lines of action too. "The best" idealist is a practical one—someone who realizes that most men like to work with specifics. Many might shy away from any philosophical discussions concerning the nature of "the good," but many would also understand and appreciate the meaning of the word "better," when applied to any situation.

Generally speaking, in those terms, the law is wise, for it forces you to make specifications, each one bringing about further definition, so that all parties at least understand (in parentheses <u>theoretically</u> *[louder]*) the meaning of the terms.

You may not achieve ideal solutions with the law, but it should allow practical specific actualization, at least in part, of an ideal situation. You are both quite lucky, in that in your main work you can deal directly with the ideal. In writing and in painting you tackle it. The creative artist is always involved in the expression of the ideal, and his work expresses that ideal as best he can.

In the matter of publishing, or selling paintings, others are involved—others who very rarely in their lives experience that important encounter between, say, the self as actualized and the idealized sensed self, between the painting or the poem as an ideal and the actualization of that ideal. You cannot give such people a general impression of what you want. If you are concerned with such matters as covers that do not live up to your ideals of what covers should be, then you must begin your definitions. Ruburt has primarily been concerned with the ideal that is behind all of his books, and with the practical matter of getting those out into the world. *(Pause.)* He was willing to put up with a good deal to do so, to overlook lacks of taste in presentation, say.

(9.39.) You feel sometimes a visual outrage, because your natural ideals tend to follow the design and integrity, the lines and flowing patterns that belong to the nature of the universe. Some part of you feels that when such blatant distortions occur, as sometimes occur in the packaging of the books, that far greater invisible lacks of integrity lie buried within. Now that is true and not true, as you know—for ideally, how marvelous it would be if each person could indeed understand those balances and artistic lacks of balances when they appear.

On the other hand, of course, the very individuality implied in art itself tells you that even the ideal must follow its own eccentric patterns, and that man must find his own way out of his l-a-c-k-s *(spelled)*. Ruburt, however, would rarely deal with such issues at all, though he was aware of them, so you felt you bore the brunt. You cannot expect Prentice to understand the nature of your own idealism, or Ruburt's, in such a way that Prentice as an entity can apply that idealism to its packaging. Not unless you define, you specify. You get together, the two of you, on each issue, as it happens, and make your decision together, and stick by it. You have not done this before because each of you would become irritated at the other's mode of behavior.

Ruburt felt that your idealism could threaten the practical distribution of the books, so that his idealistic purpose—to get those words out—could be held back. You felt that the lack of taste, and often of artistic integrity, was so blatant that it blighted the words themselves, marred the message. Both of you were concerned with the ideal. You felt Ruburt was being too "practical," and would put up with almost anything, and he felt that you were being too impractical at times.

Because neither of you <u>really</u> (underlined) defined and carried through on your definitions some black or white thinking resulted. It would seem to you that all of the books were marred, in that manner, now, or it would seem to Ruburt that nothing was wrong at all, in that manner. You would find it hard to express pleasure with a given cover, or you would forget, as with *Seven Two*, for its attributes would seem lost in your larger displeasure. Or Ruburt, feeling displeasure with Prentice on any occasion, would find it difficult to admit to you.

Do not think in terms of a generalized ideal situation, but in terms of better covers, better communication with Prentice in both friendly terms as per Ruburt's calls to Tam, and in the definitive terms of <u>clearly</u> stating specific requests. Otherwise neither of you will be satisfied. Other companies may have more money to spend. Prentice is not a great trade publisher. Yet you will still be dealing with the same kinds of people, and Ruburt has done well as far as publishers are concerned, in handling innovative books published by the firm. Some other companies might well have exerted even more pressure to keep Ruburt writing along certain proven lines. They were also innovative, <u>in their terms</u>, in the publishing of material before the current interest in unofficial events.

Are you ready for the dreams, or do you want a brief break?

("We can take a break."

(9:57. Jane laughed as she came out of trance. "I couldn't do it, but I have the feeling that he could go on all night. You know, tie it all together. The law, Prentice, health, the poor and nationalized medicine, our ideals—and start doing it from any point you wanted him to."

(Resume in the same rather fast manner at 10:02.)

Dream one is in answer to Ruburt's wondering whether or not it was a good idea to make out a will now, rather than to wait until a later date.

Ruburt's father always planned to make a new will before his death, and kept putting it off. In the dream Ruburt finds a strange mechanism made by his father that is supposed to dispense some money. A kindly old man appears, who says that Ruburt's father made this contraption two hours before his death, to ensure Ruburt some inheritance.

Ruburt suspects this man of helping himself in somewhat the same manner, in the meantime. In any case, the mechanism deposits a few coins or so. There is a missing key, and the old man also possesses one to the mechanism, which he finally gives to Ruburt, who then operates it. The odd mechanism represents the mechanics of the law, which his father used poorly, and in fact he died before he had time to make the contraption mentioned in the dream.

The coins represent the small amount of money Ruburt did receive. The old man also stands for Ruburt's father, as Ruburt thought of him bumming around, frittering away his time and energy, so he was stealing from the pot. There would be nothing left. Ruburt was not greedy, but curious. The missing key represented <u>Yale locks</u> *(with emphatic amusement).* The dream said "Do not wait too late to set up the legal mechanism," and affirmed that Yale was at least a good idea. *(Pause.)* The old man also stood for old man time in the dream, and reinstated the fact that an executor is important, for the old man also stood for —in the dream, now—Ruburt's father acting as his own executor—meaning that his nature led him to leave ends loose.

Dream two involves two couples, and they are both you and Ruburt.

(Pause.) You appeared as both young men. Ruburt appeared as himself, and as Pat Norelli. The amphitheatre stands both for the world, and for the dramatic action of your lives, in which your ideals and aspirations are actualized or played out to whatever extent. The couples show your own double faces. One couple is brave, daring, assured, headed for the center of the stage. The other couple, while headed in the same direction, are frightened of the high ledge that must be covered, and afraid that it can lead to a dead end.

Pat was chosen symbolically, yet stands for a definite situation, when you two visited Boston on tour. At that time, Ruburt saw Pat, who is a teacher, and was traveling through belief systems with the greatest of ease, converting to Judaism and then out of it, and so forth. I spoke on television, and you were both appalled at the gulf between what you saw as the idealized message of our work, and the ludicrous *(pause)* lack of integrity of the environment in which that ideal was expressed. I am referring to the other performer, et cetera—the circumstances which you know well.

While still devoted to the ideal, you were both quite appalled, simplistically speaking. The brave portions of your personalities went on helping each other, as per the dream, until Pat Norelli, as Ruburt, easily working through belief systems stands center stage, ready to speak to other frightened portions of yourselves still on a high ledge. They begin to realize that everything is all right; they can come down or join the other couple.

To do so, however, they must back down through previous limiting beliefs, and had you not wakened Ruburt, the four of you would have joined each other on the stage. Ruburt was correct in what he picked up from me today *(half laughing)*—concerning both your rugs and nationalized medicine, and some of its effects upon the poor if it were established.

At the very least, you should have your rugs cleaned, even if you are grumpy, both of you, for a day, since you are obviously spoiled now and afraid of cold bare floors.

Do you have questions?

("No.")

I try my best *(louder)* to define and redefine your ideas of the ideal, so that you can achieve greater practical benefits, and feel some satisfaction with the actualization of at least portions of the ideal in daily life.

End of session and a fond good evening.

("Thank you, Seth."

(10:28 PM. Jane's delivery had been good throughout the session, and once again she was relaxed now that it was over. Seth's reference to the poor and nationalized health care referred to material Jane had picked up from him during the day; The poor were actually better off as they are now, without such a national health-care plan, for as it is they're isolated from and immune to a number of ills they would start falling prey to if they could afford to pay for such treatment—that is, if the costs were paid for them. An interesting point of view.)

DELETED SESSION
JULY 12, 1979 9:19 PM THURSDAY

(No session was held last night, as scheduled. The night had been very warm, and Jane had been bothered by the heat and humidity. She'd also been quite relaxed at times through the day, so I didn't ask her for a session. It seems that we also got our signals crossed, for I learned today that she'd been ready for a session; but because I didn't come out of the writing room and ask her if she wanted one, she thought I didn't want one....

(But at about 9 PM this evening Jane surprised me by suggesting a brief session. It was just as warm tonight. All our doors and most windows were open because of the heat, yet when Jane went into trance her delivery was quite energetic, almost fast, and at times very emphatic. Without greetings, then:)

Now: particularly to Ruburt. The following sentence:

You do not have the responsibility to change the world for the better. That is, changing the world for the better is not your personal responsibility. You have a natural need to impress your world—to act through it, with it, and upon it, to illuminate it with your own vision, in which case you automatically change it for the better. The original prerogative is the creative one, from which all benefits automatically flow.

If you think that it is your personal responsibility alone to change the

world, then you are always bound to feel a burdening sense of failure. The world
is being changed through our work—but because that work is primarily a creative endeavor in the fullest, deepest meaning, now, of the word creative. When
you hold the attitude I have mentioned, however, you begin to insist upon
immediate creative results in the way that the shoemaker does, again—and
again, we are not making shoes.

The scientist's *(Truzzi's)* letter had some good results, in crystallizing your
attitudes in Ruburt's poetry, and in passages for his book. It also made him
think, however, that he was not changing the world in any way that mattered in
any important degree—that those in authority did not even read them, and that
even my latest work *(Mass Reality)* would make no inroads. He did not want
book dictation on the one hand, for that reason. On the other hand, of course,
he did. We will of course finish our book in our usual style.

*(I should have asked whether Seth was referring to last night's missed session,
or to this one.)*

I do want to emphasize, however, the existence of people like the young
man who came today. You are speaking to the younger generations strongly, and
they are the people who will make up the fabric of the so-called official establishments in the future, and they will come to those establishments with far different values than those people now ruling. Period.

*(Seth referred to Greg, a young man who arrived here yesterday afternoon in
a taxi. and carrying a box of a dozen long-stemmed carnations of four colors. The
taxi waited, since he could stay but a few minutes before taking a bus out of town.
Greg simply wanted to say thanks for the work Jane is doing, with my help. [He
knows Barb and Jack Ebright—now separated—of Colorado Springs, Colorado.])*

Remember to keep open-minded about individual scientists, also. It is
against the official views of science as a field that you hold great variance.

(I didn't catch Seth's last word. "Hold great—?")

(With emphatic humor:) Variance—disagreement—you pick the word.

It is fairly easy to recognize the ways in which organized religion discouraged vigorous intellectual speculation. It is more difficult, perhaps, to see that
science fears the unofficially directed intellect quite as much as it does the unofficially directed intuitions.

In schools, for example, there are courses in the criticism of literature. Art
criticism, and so forth. The arts are supposed to be "not real." It is quite safe,
therefore, to criticize them in that regard, to see how a story or a painting is constructed—or more importantly, to critically analyze the structure of ideas,
themes, or beliefs, that appear behind, say, the poem or the work of fiction.

When children are taught science, there is no criticism allowed. They are told "this is how things are." Science's reasons are given as the only true state-ments of reality, with which no student is expected to quarrel. Any strong intel-lectual explorations of counter-versions of reality have appeared in science fic-tion, for example. Here scientists, many being science-fiction buffs, can safely channel their own intellectual questioning into a safe form. They can say "This is after all merely imaginative, and not to be taken seriously."

(9:36.) This is the reason why some scientists who either write or read sci-ence fiction, are the most incensed over any suggestion that some such ideas rep-resent a quite valid alternate conception of reality. In a fashion, at least in your time, science has as much to fear from the free intellect as religion does, and (with irony) any strong combination of intellectual and intuitional abilities is not tailor-made to bring you great friends from either category.

Science has unfortunately bound up the minds of its own even most orig-inal thinkers, for they dare not stray from certain scientific principles. All ener-gy contains consciousness. That one sentence is basically (underlined) scientific heresy, and in many circles it is religious heresy as well. A recognition of that simple statement would indeed change your world.

(Pause.) Our books are read also more often that it seems, for they are bor-rowed from others, and from libraries, by people who would not buy them in a store—not for financial reasons necessarily. The letter in any case made him think in terms of responsibility again, but this session should set him right.

He is doing well physically. The relaxation episodes will continue again, when he realizes he does not have to be changing the world in each moment. Have him imagine shrugging his shoulders. Back leg muscles are indeed length-ening, as are the arms. Eye mobility is increasing. The relaxation periods aid in all respects. He does still need you to remind him of the safety of relaxation now and then.

(9.45.) Give us a moment.... With some sense of freedom and play, both of you can combine high qualities of intuitional and intellectual abilities so that they sometimes merge into a higher mind.

Some of this is difficult to explain, but as the world of appearances pre-sents its own evidence, on the level of sense, so your inner reality presents as strong evidence of its reality. But that evidence remains largely invisible, because you have not trained yourselves sufficiently to be alert to those manifestations. You do have a telepathic interplay between you of course, that escapes your notice. There are connections in the same manner between you and your ani-mals and the trees in your yard.

You can at least keep these facts in your minds. It is a matter of organiza-tion and of focus. When you think of Framework 2, do so playfully. Remember that its processes are creative.

I am not going to go into Ruburt's *[Johnny]* Carson dream, since he interpreted it properly himself. The star in the medical theater is the absent one, and that applied to his personal situation. *(Pause.)* The connection he did not get had to do with the television commercials on the Carson show; the pressure applied by the medical profession, telling you not to trust the body, and the man, Doc *[Severinsen]*, who is the master of ceremonies in a big show—signifying nothing as per your joint overall interpretation of the show in particular. Do you have other questions?

("I guess not. Last night I was going to ask how Volume 2 is doing in sales.")
Very well. I bid you a fond good evening.
("Thank you. Good night."
(9.55 PM. "I'm glad I did have the session, then." Jane said. "At least I got that straightened out, about the book sessions...." When I asked her what she meant, Jane said she'd been blue lately, wondering what good the work on Seth's books could do in the world.)

DELETED SESSION
JULY 16, 1979   9:20 PM MONDAY

(Jane had been very uncomfortable today, since it had been so hot and humid. A late afternoon shower had helped cool things down, although it didn't last long enough. Jane waited until the last moment before deciding to have a session, since she was still uncomfortable. "I feel about as much like having a session as a blue hornet," she said with unwitting humor as we sat waiting for Seth to come through. I replied that I didn't know any blue hornets with which to make comparisons.

(Jane's physical improvements continue to take place at a slow pace. Recently there have been noticeable changes for the better in both of her hands, although each one works differently. Earlier today I'd voiced the hope that Seth could give some material on Jane's eyes, which haven't progressed as much as we'd like. At the same time, Jane told me that there's been an improvement in her color perception, even with the double vision.

(In spite of the warm night, when Jane began to speak for Seth she did so quite emphatically and fast for the most part. I might add that I think the session contains some material re Framework 2 that's very good; well working with on a daily basis.)
Good evening.
("Good evening. Seth.")
Now; I will be simplifying somewhat, to make several points.

To some extent, creativity involves you *(pause)* in a contradiction with the evidence of reality within your world. It puts you in a peculiar state of being— or in a peculiar relationship with the accepted world of factual evidence. The state of creativity <u>can</u> (underlined) be discussed <u>as if it were</u> (underlined) a separate state, like waking or sleeping. It can, in fact, involve waking dreams. In the usual awake state, in the terms now of this discussion, you deal with the available physical evidence of the world as it appears to present perception, that is, or with what you can see or feel or touch, either immediately or through physical instruments.

In the dream state you deal with objects that may or may not have a physical reality. You mix times and places, and the dream itself is a kind of completed act. Creativity allows you, while awake, to ignore or even to contradict what seems to be the hard evidence of known reality, either in large or small terms. The creative act involves you in a process whereby you bring from a mental dimension new events into the world <u>that were not there before</u>.

Some of this is so obvious that it escapes you, but since I want to connect it with other matters I will discuss it rather thoroughly.

Ruburt may suddenly have an idea for a book. He wants to write it. In physical terms that book is not before his eyes. It has not been written, it has not been published. The evidence says physically that there is no such book. It is not a part of the world's physical evidence. The idea for the book may come from a dream, or in that state of creativity where dreams reach toward physical actualization. Now Ruburt could say "I cannot write that book, or wonder how many pages it might have," or think of the endless impediments that might prevent the book from being written. Instead, he simply ignores the physical evidence of the book's absence, and creatively begins to write.

To some degree, creativity always involves a <u>denial</u> of life's daily official evidence, for creativity deals with that which you are about to bring into being. You are quite aware of the absence which you intend to fill. Period. This applies obviously in the case of inventions. Creativity involves productive change.

(9:35.) In your painting, you are constantly involved with bringing some event into the world that was not there before. You fill the gap. You recognize the absence in the present of the physical painting you want to produce, and your creativity brings that painting into reality. With ideas, with our books, you deal, both of you, with such issues all the time. There is so much physical evidence in the world. It has been put together through the centuries, in your terms, in countless ways, bringing pictures of reality, each vivid, each contradicting the other to some extent. When man <u>believed</u> the world was flat, he used his thought processes in such a way that they had great difficulty in imagining

any other kind of world, and read the evidence so that it fit the flat-world picture.

The world's evidence, the objects, sensations, and so forth, should be respected and enjoyed. It should not be forgotten, however, that such evidence gives a composite picture—not only of patterns of perception, but of <u>habits</u> of perception.

It would therefore be highly limiting for me to deliver our material in such a way that I emphasized those matters in which science might agree with my material. In your society people have been taught in many areas that change can only lead to a deterioration, and this seems to have a scientific justification. Creativity thrives on change, however.

I want you both to look at Ruburt's physical condition in the light of what I have just said about creativity always contradicting the evidence to some degree. In your works, you both automatically have the courage, the daring, to allow creativity its way. To some extent, however, you are both still hypnotized by the evidence of Ruburt's condition—where instead it should be used as a jumping-off board, as a gap to be filled with reality *(emphatically)*. When you create you dream. Creativity, again, thrives on dreaming, and dreaming serves as a conduit for Framework 2's activity. You do not concentrate on what stands in your way. You do not imagine impediments.

Ruburt has done well, following impulses, and the altered sleep patterns have indeed been beneficial; for his body, to compensate for the lack of normal steady motion, wanted the extra activity. *(Pause.)* For another thing, this allows a breakup of certain mental and physical habits—a gentle shock to the mental and physical systems that allows for beneficial change. Some years ago, just before you took on the second apartment, Ruburt complained in his journal that it seems as if the day was gray, or that color had fled the world. His condition had bothered his eyes then, and they recuperated over a period of time.

The lack of motion, however, in the last episode, was more noticeable, the constriction in the neck muscles and head. The situation there is as I have given in the past, and again, the problem is that you find yourselves confronted by "the evidence." No one symptom exists by itself, but on an overall basis.

(Pause.) There is an exercise Ruburt read that will help here, where one imagines the eyes sinking backward into the head. It is in a book of his. If you really learned to trust Framework 2, you would set your goals there, and trust that they would be as creatively manifested as your books or paintings. *(Whispering:)* The same applies to the production, the physical production, of the physical books at Prentice, or to sales.

If you began to think in terms of beautifully produced books, without imagining impediments, then automatically the process would begin. You would be led to make proper suggestions, for example, ahead of time, or the creative process of someone in the art department would suddenly be stimulated to a new idea, or whatever. You would ignore any evidence to the contrary, except that you would recognize a gap to be creatively filled.

Do you have questions?

("I guess not.")

Listen to what I have said again: apply creativity to all levels of your lives. And I bid you a fond good evening.

("Thank you, Seth. Good night.")

(9:56. But within a minute Seth returned:)

I meant to remark that the very late evening or predawn hours are indeed excellent times for creativity. Particularly since the minds of men and women *(with humor)*—are not so focused upon the physical evidence of the world, so that in a strange fashion the "burden" of that evidence is less, and there is some built-in advantage.

It is as if, now, the mental atmosphere was clearer—and you would find ideas flowing into your mind in those hours also, particularly with that <u>playfully</u>, now, in mind. I am not saying that you should make the nighttime hours your own official ones, but they do provide creativity with an additional ease, along with the changes in official patterns. End of session.

("Thank you.")

(10:01 PM.)

SESSION 869 (DELETED PORTION)
JULY 30, 1979 9:05 PM MONDAY

(The following material is from the 869th session.

(The evening was very warm and humid. Jane had been so relaxed all day that she finally slept after supper. She's experienced many physical sensations and changes in her body—and I could tell that it was responding very well to her constantly improving attitudes. More than once she expressed the hope that these multitudinous changes were leading to lasting, obvious improvements in her physical condition.

(While she slept two women from Trumansburg visited, unannounced. I talked to them for an hour on the back porch. Jane got up at about 8:30 PM. The changes in her body continued. She said she'd try to have a session, but wasn't sure that she could manage it.

("Well, Seth's about ready," she laughed at 9:01, "but I don't know about

me...."

(*Whispering:*) Good evening.

(*"Good evening, Seth."*)

Now: Ruburt's body is reducing tensions. Those tensions were projected upon it by mental states of mind. In the last several days in particular, that tension level has been splendidly reduced.

In Ruburt's particular case, tense states of mind have been primarily responsible for his physical difficulty. Your behavior has been most helpful, and that behavior is the result of a new acknowledgment on your part of a belief system—a belief system that you have intellectually accepted for some time—one that you are now beginning to emotionally understand and accept.

(*Pause.*) People's actions, again, are primarily determined by their systems of belief, for those systems set up the patterns of behavior and define the potentials and limitations that are accepted usually as literal fact.

In your culture there are several built-in unfortunate circumstances in particular. The human personality is naturally a seeker of value fulfillment and creativity. It is not just, again, that man does not live by bread alone, but that his life is intimately bound up with his need for creative expression—his need to develop as an individual, and therefore to affect his world.

The various, numberless individual human abilities are part of your, say, gene pool as a species, so the drive to creatively use individual abilities is a spiritual and biological necessity. The Freudian, Darwinian dictates quite emphatically degrade man's capacity for "greatness," for heroic action in those terms, and greatly devalue the entire meaning connected with an individual self. Psychology's emphasis upon the average norm, as mentioned previously, made people think that one individual should almost be a carbon of any other individual. Idiosyncrasies were frowned upon, and signs of creative ability were suspect in direct proportion to the strength of those abilities.

(*9:18.*) People were put in a position of trying to use very important creative drives, believing that those drives were, in fact, unnatural, highly suspect, tied in with madness or insanity—or at the very least, that those abilities would lead to antisocial behavior.

In that system of belief many creative people have felt that safeguards were necessary, for they had been taught to fear their own abilities. In that framework of belief, Ruburt felt justified in using physical symptoms as protection on both levels. They gave some protection even from inner spontaneity, so that the inner abilities would be regulated, and they protected him also from any derogatory behavior on the part of his fellow men in the world.

That insidious mistrust of creative abilities is alarmingly dangerous to the society, and frightening to the individual. The person is taught to mistrust the most the abilities he or she instinctively trusts the most. This is bound to lead to division. Creative people are not self-destructive, but if they sometimes appear so in the western world, it is because of that division, that artificial barrier.

That vision means that such a person is taught to mistrust the very abilities that could most help bring about creative solutions. When you leave that framework of belief, such self-protecting defensive mechanisms are no longer necessary. Ruburt is beginning to get that through his head.

In the old system also, any physical problem is seen as naturally remaining or worsening. In our system of belief, you see, that is not the case. In the old system, you must almost fear personal improvement, lest you become self-deluded—another irony in that old system. Ruburt's body is responding because his main affiliation—main (underlined)—is changing, so that actions necessary in the old system do not any longer apply.

A note: our books do reach people in all walks of life. If you will forgive me, the excellent material means automatically, however, that many people with excellent intellects are naturally drawn to it, and some of the minds that will be important in following years are already acquainted with the material, or will be.

A small note *(etc.*

(9:28. This marks the end of the private material.)

SESSION 870 (DELETED PORTION)
AUGUST 1, 1979 9:21 PM WEDNESDAY

(The following material is from the 870th session. It came about because of a dream I had during my nap this afternoon. I found to my great concern that Jane had fallen from her chair in the doorway of the bathroom. The short dream was so vivid that I was jolted wide awake out of a deep sleep. See the account in my dream notebook.

(10:27.) Give us a moment.... Your dream merely reflected fears about Ruburt. He grunted and so forth in his sleep. You heard him, and wondered if he was perhaps in the bathroom and needed your help. The dream reflected your deep concern, and your fear that he might not make it, but get worse after all. And the worries were caused simply by an upcropping of old negative beliefs that came to your attention so that you could be aware of them.

Ruburt's improvement in a way triggered your hopes, and because of your beliefs of the past also triggered your deep fears.

Those conditions, physically now, responsible for the eye trouble, are being reduced. He still needs encouragement as far as relaxation is concerned, but he has turned the corner. Do not let the improvements rearouse old fears, but remind yourselves that improvement is natural and spontaneous, and easy in the new system of beliefs.

(10:31.)

SESSION 871 (DELETED PORTION)
AUGUST 6, 1979 9:40 PM MONDAY

(The following material is from the 871st session.

(At about 3:30 PM last Thursday, Jane participated in a startling experience —one that we hoped Seth would at least mention this evening. At that time Jane was sitting at the kitchen table, perhaps seven feet from the open porch door. The day had been hot and humid. A thunderstorm had been trying to develop for some little while; finally it began to rain and blow as I helped Jane prepare a dish to be baked for our evening meal.

(The wind increased in intensity, blowing across the valley from the south and racing up Holley Road. Sheets of rain raced before it. I went into the bedroom to close windows. As I did so, a terrific blast of wind struck. Dimly in the racket, as I watched the heavy rain, I heard Jane cry out. I thought she may have yelled at the cats—but in the kitchen I saw that she was sitting at the table with shards of glass littering the rug at her feet. For some reason that day I'd forgotten to stopper the storm door, and the sudden blast of wind had slammed it shut with enough force to shatter the bottom of the two glass panels.

(At first I couldn't believe my eyes. The broken glass had catapulted toward Jane, yet she sat unharmed by the razor-like edges. Underneath the table I found a large jagged piece of glass, close to a foot across, propped up against the inner table leg where I usually sit. In some strange quirk of speed and physics, this knife-edged piece had not only been blown into the kitchen, but had managed to turn nearly a right angle, missing Jane, in order to come to rest opposite her legs against the table's leg. It could have severely cut her.

(Almost at once the strong wind began to subside, although the rain continued. Just as quickly, as we realized that she was unhurt, we also realized that something unusual had indeed taken place. We felt that she had been spared injury, for whatever reasons. As I cleaned up the dozens of pieces of glass and put them in a heavy carton we talked about why she might have been protected, and decided to ask Seth to comment.

(Jane became so relaxed as session time approached that she told me several times that she'd have to put off the session until tomorrow night. At the same time, she had a lot of material in mind from Seth—on the glass experience; a dream I'd had on August 1, in which I'd found her lying on the floor in the bathroom doorway; and a fairly strong earthquake that had struck south of San Francisco, California, this afternoon. Seth, she said somewhat wonderingly, planned to tie all of these episodes together. They seemed to make up a most unlikely combination. Jane also sensed more information pertaining to my questions of a few sessions ago, on the relationship of disease with human beings.

("I guess I'm confused," Jane said as we sat there. "I'm so relaxed, yet I feel all that material there. I want it but I don't feel like doing it.... Oh, all right," she finally laughed as I worked on these notes. "I'll have the session. At least I'll try....")

Now; one thing at a time—and we hope to tie it all together.

When Ruburt allows his body to relax, it uses the opportunity while it has it, so that the relaxation seems exaggerated. It is most beneficial, however. If he really trusted it this evening, he would simply have had a change of plan, and held our session tomorrow. But then he worried that perhaps he might not get all of the material tomorrow, so it is a matter of learning to trust yourself *(with some gentle humor).*

He has been doing exceedingly well, for him, in that regard, following impulses to houseclean and so forth—trusting the entire shape of his nature. He simply then for a while bumped into some of the old beliefs again, worried that his impulses would not lead him to write sufficiently. That kind of temporary concern can be expected now and then. It is simply a matter of remembering the new framework of beliefs, and <u>trusting</u> that your impulses are leading in the proper direction.

He has been getting up in the night because his body wants to exert itself fairly regularly, <u>at this period</u> of time. His creative abilities have not deserted him, but it is that fear that they will if they are not consciously, persistently exerted that bothers him.

You do not need to force yourselves to be creative. In Ruburt's natural, quite periodic rhythm of creativity, he writes rather steadily, exuberantly, and inspired. That is how he operates naturally. In between, he needs variety, change, rest. He is regenerating, and those periods are also natural, and act to increase the creative "periods" of obvious daily production. The creative self is <u>always</u> creating, and it does its best when it is simply trusted. Then it surfaces with its productions. Period.

With Ruburt rising in the night, sometimes you vaguely worried whether or not he could navigate properly and sometimes when you are out of the house you also wonder: is he safe alone? Your dream brought your fears to the surface of your mind, and when those fears became conscious both of you determined to show yourselves that Ruburt was indeed safe and protected. Period.

(9:53.) Because of the changes in routine, you "forgot" to put the stopper at the door. You must remember that you have an inner knowledge of all weather conditions. So you were both at certain levels aware of the approaching storm.

(From here on Seth's material leads into more generalized information, so it's presented as the 871st session. Part of his discussion deals with the broken-glass episode. An extra carbon of the notes describing that event are presented with the 871st session.)

DELETED SESSION
AUGUST 12, 1979 11:10 PM SUNDAY

(At 10 PM I asked Jane if she felt like having a session. We'd been visited today by Loren, Betts and Doug, and Dick, Ida and David, and at times my left groin area had bothered me considerably. Now after everyone had gone—Dick and family stayed until about 8 PM—I felt poorly indeed. As I had last spring, I didn't know whether my symptoms of unease were physical or mental, and was very concerned. I thought of a hernia—and Loren had been operated on for a hernia this summer— yet I suspected the unease was basically mental. This had been the case last spring. And now, those feelings had returned. Try as I might, I couldn't find the proper adjective to describe the groin sensations; they weren't ones of pain—but what?

(In fact, I'd been bothered more and more in recent days—ever since, I thought, the family get-together had been suggested by Betts a couple of weeks ago. Yet all through the summer I didn't think I'd fully bounced back from last spring's rather drastic upsets. I'd taken to giving myself suggestions each morning upon arising, before calling Jane, and these had helped. Yet I knew the symptoms lingered beneath the surface, one might say.

(Today as the family members talked and took photographs and watched television and ate. and so forth, I felt the discomfort in the left groin sweep over me in waves. Twice I went off to use the pendulum. Each time it helped, temporarily. I thought of asking Jane for help, but disliked doing so because I could see that she was doing very well. I didn't want to introduce negative elements into the day, especially so since her performance was much better than it had been last year when everyone had gotten together. [After that gathering she's had strong upsets of her own.]

(When I mentioned a session to Jane finally she said she didn't really feel like it; she was getting relaxed, "really out of it," and I could tell she'd rather not do it. I

went for a walk, which helped. When I returned home the sensations did also. Then as I sat making notes, Jane called in to me that she felt better, that she'd try a session after all. So:)

Now—a repeat performance—an instant replay of material given in other ways before, with a new slant.

Think of the slides shown today *(by Loren)* of postcard Tunkhannock, Pennsylvania, USA, home of conventional, American, Protestant values. I <u>am</u> (underlined) generalizing here to make a point: a largely postcard land, in which social clichés pass for communication, in which social ceremonies take the place of private communications—a land in which beliefs must be like landmarks, unchanging, utterly dependable, always there to be used for touchstones lest the puritanical Protestant stray from worthy goals. A land in which things must be judged thus-and-so, a land in which people disappear as much as possible into established family and social roles, where the lines are clearly marked.

Now: generally again, such communities have teachers, judges, lawyers, dentists, some farmers on the outskirts of town, some factory workers, a sufficient number of ministers, and some car lots. Everyone knows in which social level each other person belongs. The wife's position is usually dependent upon the husband.

The few upstarts move away. The community fits together because certain beliefs are indeed shared. They are conventional and stereotyped. This does not mean they may not be of some service to those people.

(11:19.) Such communities have few poets, few artists, and fewer mediums. Tunkhannock is actually an idealized version of that kind of community. <u>In those terms</u> (underlined) it is for Loren a step up from, say, Sayre, whose history is richer even in "lower class" origins. Sayre, however, generally now, represented the poorer man's version of that American ideal, and it was from there that many of your beliefs and those of your brothers had <u>their</u> origins.

A man showed himself a man, say, by getting paid every Friday night, coming home after a stop at the pub with coins jingling in his pocket, to give his wife the house money for the week. I do not want to hurt your feelings— but your particular beliefs about a male and money are in their way quite parochial, and you <u>must</u> understand that as far as <u>money</u> is concerned, also, those beliefs have little moral value—<u>moral</u> value.

You may laugh with some disdain when I mention, for example, that in some other societies, both today and in the past *(pause)* a gentleman proved his moral worth and value by not working. Now that idea is no more ludicrous than the idea you have, for both attempt to prove personal merit through the manipulation of money and status.

It is as ridiculous to prove your worth by working in a conventional sense as it is to prove your worth by <u>not</u> working in a conventional sense. Americans have had a fine and often understandable disdain for what was thought of as the European gentleman, or even the literary gentleman, or the man who somehow or other did not have to "rub elbows with the masses."

Not to work at an ordinary job, or at a clearly defined occupation, has always had a tint of <u>European decadence</u> to Americans—and that is to some extent the result of the early Protestants' attitude toward the wealthy, robed gentlemen of the late medieval, Roman Catholic Church.

(Quietly amused:) Now, with that simple explanation, when you know your brothers will visit, you instantly leap to the old beliefs of childhood, when your mother wanted you to set an example—which meant be someone in society, in normal middle-class society, now. Use your art to make money. Otherwise it was a liability in her eyes. She expected a clearly defined role. Now, she being uniquely herself, is more than pleased with your situation: a good house in a fine neighborhood, and who cares where the money comes from *(with more than a little humor)*?

(11:34.) But you worry that you are a failure in the framework of that postcard American system, even though now you see quite clearly that the postcard system is not bright and glossy, but a facade, behind which lurks a great sadness.

You have, again and again *(with amusement)* an unconventional mind, unconventional abilities—abilities that straddle several fields of endeavor. You have an unconventional wife. <u>Because</u> you have both utilized your abilities and tried to bring some release to that postcard world, your works have automatically resulted in a comfortable living. Your endeavors cannot be labeled, nor can <u>your</u> *(to me)* contribution to <u>our</u> joint work be assessed. There is no one who can tell you how many dollars per hour you receive for your work, or what value it has.

You are afraid you will be thought of as a gentleman of leisure—at the worst a moral crime most certainly in light of the beliefs that originated at the time the Protestants first abandoned the Roman Catholic Church.

The man of letters is not understood either, and you feel that your brothers cannot understand <u>what</u> you do, since their minds seem relatively closed — relatively closed—to the books themselves, which would automatically offer an explanation.

Your body, on its own, is very happy to be so well provided for *(more humor)*. Ruburt said that he used to like his class money because it was tangible, and you understood. But you also told him that the money for books, that came in a check, was just as good, and that there was more of it.

You want to show some tangible means of support, however, in that same literal fashion, to your brothers, since you feel they cannot understand <u>what</u> (underlined) you do.

(Pause.) I do not want to give you a big head, but your wit and your abilities simply place you in another area of activity, for which you should be grateful. Do not be overly parochial or nationalistic in your views. There is a great history of masculinity that expressed itself through the development of thought, quiet meditation—and I do not necessarily mean of the mystical kind—of communion of the mind with nature.

There is nothing wrong with your body. The memories and associations bring old beliefs to mind, and you see in such family visits the culmination in your brothers of those old beliefs. You must say: "They are mine no longer. I appreciate my own unique worth." You must liberate yourself whenever such thoughts arise to mind—not by inhibiting them but by confronting them, recognizing their origins, and realizing that you have left them intellectually behind, resolving that you will emotionally free yourself from their effects.

I made a few comments about supply and demand recently, but there are far deeper issues. Unless negative beliefs stand in your way, then creative ideas that you contribute to the work will automatically take care of your needs, and it is truly idiotic to want to substitute that good fortune for such parochial concepts like the male as breadwinner, or the male performing in a given definable fashion.

(11:51.) You have had in the past to some extent a disdain, <u>because</u> of your beliefs about yourself, for people perhaps met on the streets during business or working hours, or for people who did not have jobs, or who did not punch a time clock or whatever, and it is by those attitudes that you judge yourself *(intently)*, and find yourself wanting in the eyes, say, of your brothers.

When your art was commercial you could say, again, <u>you were working</u>. When you paint, you feel you cannot justify your art, and in our books you wonder what percentage your notes and contributions might make in the overall royalties, say.

(Pause.) Most men's abilities are prosaic enough and conventional enough so that their value can be ascertained—or worked out by labor unions *(amused)*. If all a man can do to "prove his value" is to put a bolt in a car, or drive a truck, or even teach a class, then he is very careful that that contribution be noticed, and that a <u>definite value</u> be given it. You cannot estimate the value of ideas or of creativity in that fashion.

<u>In this probability</u> (underlined), the particular combination that resulted

in our work required both of you, and entails combinations of abilities on both of your parts, and is built upon your entire relationship with each other.

(Long pause.) You are afraid you look as if the money comes to you too easily, when in the old system of beliefs everyone knew <u>that you must work hard</u>.

I want to rid you of any lingering misconceptions, but you still have a lingering belief that your old ideas about money and the male have some kind of high moral value. *(Louder:)* The Protestants have always thought that artists were decadent, that contemplation was dangerous, and that leisure was a crime. *(With continuing amusement:)* To enjoy your work was suspect—and if you enjoy unconventionality of mind, some leisure in which to contemplate the world about you, then it is about time that you dismissed such parochial concepts, and realized <u>that there is no moral rectitude</u> given them.

Your body tries to enjoy those privileges that appear as the result of the creative abilities you are using. It enjoys good meals, a comfortable bed. It gets quite upset when a part of you thinks that it should be doing something else to make a livelihood. These ideas to some extent even inhibit natural plans rising in your mind, notes of your own that would automatically lead to a book of your own—because you pursue yourself.

You should do a book of your own <u>if</u> you want to, because you want to —not because of the money that might be involved. Some part of you still thinks there is something wrong with money unless you can show precisely where it came from—or people might think you a crook, or a gigolo living off your wife. You must learn to dismiss such ideas as the rubbish that they are. Your body is in the right place at the right time—and *(louder)* I can see that I was in the right place at the right time for our chat.

Do you have questions?

("No. I need some time to go over all of this.")

Then I bid you a fond good evening. I have stuck to the most important beliefs about money, and the male's status—but also such *(family)* gatherings also bring into focus beliefs about age and illness, and so forth.

You can use such situations, again, as springboards. In a large measure, those beliefs represent the evidence of the old world before it is set upon by the light of new creativity. Bounce against that world, into the more creative realm that you know in your heart is a far truer representation of reality,

Allow your body to relax, and <u>now</u> I bid you a fond good evening.

("Thank you. Seth. Good night."

(12:13 AM. I felt better already. "Boy," Jane said, "if you'd told me I could have had that session after they all left, I wouldn't have believed it. I was exhausted. I felt selfish, too. I just wanted to watch the television program [Upstairs,

Downstairs], but when that was done I felt better, and I knew you needed the help...." Her delivery had been animated and fast throughout the session, with many indications of wit and amusement.

("The only thing I might have asked," I said, after having had a few moments to think it over, "was why I would choose to pick on myself here." I pointed to my left groin. "I know that in those earlier sessions Seth said I equated the left side with the unconscious portions of the personality and the masculine role in society [see the deleted sessions for April 4 and 16, 1979], but—"

("He's still around," Jane said. Then:)

Now: beliefs—that is correct. I do not want to overemphasize this point, so do not overemphasize it yourself—but the idea is that you sometimes become angry at your own "unconscious creative abilities." I put that in quotes because you equate creative abilities as largely unconscious. You think, then, that if you were not so creative you could have a proper niche for yourself, and therefore you tense a portion of the body that seems to be connected to the unconscious side of the self, and chose the groin, which connects old beliefs about males to the beliefs about creativity.

Again—not to overemphasize this—at such times a part of you thinks — or you think partly—that if you were "a simple working man" life would be easier. Do you follow the connections clearly?

("Yes.")

Do you have questions?

("Not at this time. Thank you, it's very good."

(Jane paused, still in trance. I expected her to end the session, but as she sat there I saw that it was one of those times when she—or Seth—could say more. I was surprised, considering her feelings before the session. Then:)

There is a long history connected with such American Puritan beliefs about morality, having to do with the fact that medieval priests were sometimes licentious, and opulent. They did not work in the field (except for the poor monks), and the Protestants determined, for example, that <u>their ministers</u> would have families, work with the people, and be too busy for licentious leisure activities.

They scorned all decoration, and considered art sinful. Poverty was worthy, and proof of morality. In your country, this was coupled, however, with the growth of economic individualism, Darwinism, and so forth.

Though men could compete for a livelihood, wealth itself was and still is highly suspect. Even a wealthy man, in the light of those beliefs, dabbles in art —dabbles—justifying any <u>love</u> of art as a good investment.

(Long pause.) In the past eras of history, as you know, artists had patrons,

but your society has not learned to deal with its creative people. It underpays them, ignores them, or extravagantly overpays them. They never fit that Protestant work ethic, and the very idea of a creative mind has not fit in—so far, at least—with the overall patterns of the society in terms of religion or science.

Take all of this to heart. You have been given the very circumstances your life and creativity requires. It is sheer nonsense to look back for, or desire, such rigid frameworks of self-worth or merit. End of session.

("Thank you.")

A fond good evening.

("Yes."

(12:31 PM. Something had really turned Jane on after all. Seth was still around, she told me. "But now what I'll have is a little milk, a cookie, and a cigarette—and go to bed," she laughed. Her energy was still up. Even sitting in bed, she remarked that she was picking up more of that generalized material from Seth.

(Her mood or framework of reception even continued the next day. Here's a copy of the notes she wrote for me:

("I started to get some material from Seth right after breakfast. I felt as if it were being gently inserted into my mind and that for some reason I became aware of it. It's as if this often happens, material being inserted and then "stacked up" or stored there for, say, the next session. For a few minutes, five or more, I was aware of quite a bit of material on work, and the Protestant mainstream [as separate from, say, Emerson or James or Thoreau, even]. Thought I'd write it down and told Rob some of it. Now though, I just remember the subject matter more or less; now I'm not even sure of that [and it's only about ten minutes after I told Rob what I'd picked up].

("It's vague now: Americans not trusting creative thought unless it applies specifically to practical considerations.... nothing new there; I guess I've just forgotten it.... There <u>was</u> the idea that true creative work is the springboard for the more usual kind.... and something about vocations being distrusted in this country....

("Twenty minutes later I'm sitting at the front living room table, feeling relaxy and good about things, when I catch an odd brief but lovely experience; something happened momentarily; I felt as if I was seeing with all of me, instead of just with my eyes.... as if my molecules almost <u>saw</u> what I saw too in their own fashion. Physically my vision was the same, I think.... but there was a fuller visual appreciation or fullness difficult to verbalize...."

(One final note: At the beginning of this session I wrote that I had trouble describing the very uncomfortable sensation in my left groin—that it wasn't pain. but what? I felt much better by the end of the session; remarkably so, so Seth's material was on the mark. Then in the bathroom it came to me as we prepared to retire: the feeling in the groin was like a <u>knot</u>—and my realization had been triggered by

Seth's remark about tension I had created in that area. In a flash the understanding led me to a very obvious conclusion that, it seems I should have reached on my own earlier: the knotty feeling was very much like the muscle spasms I'd experienced in the back, years ago when we'd lived on West Water St. These had been so bad that I'd lost months of work; the sessions had begun as Jane tried to help me, as well as for her own needs, in 1963.

(This morning I felt much better after an excellent sleep. I concentrated upon suggestions that the groin muscles would be relaxed today, and function well, and so forth, as I tried to remember this session before typing it. At 9 PM the improvement holds.)

DELETED SESSION
AUGUST 13 1979 9:29 PM MONDAY

(Jane finished reading last night's deleted session at 9:00 PM—I'd worked most of today typing it from my notes. She thought it was great, and so did I. It had produced almost immediate relief for my symptoms, of that I was sure. I'd slept very well.

("But now where's all that stuff I was picking up from Seth today?" she demanded. "Here it's session time and I don't have an idea in my head...." So after all this time she still preferred to know in advance what was coming up in a session.

("I'm just waiting," she said. "That's what shits me—and here last night and this morning I was getting it all so clearly." Then a bit later: "What I'm getting now are just disconnected things." So something was there after all. "Come on, Seth," she said with unconscious humor, "for Christ's sake let's go. Now I'm getting something over there [to her left] that's entirely disconnected from what I was getting two minutes ago over here. You know what it's like when you test water with your finger to see if it's the right temperature before you jump in? Well, things have to come together in a certain way before I feel right...."

(It's difficult to describe, but Jane's voice in trance was pitched a bit lower than it usually is. and it was very clear and precise and quiet in a strange way. Her diction was easier to understand, her pace quite deliberate.)

Now—

("Good evening, Seth.")

—good evening.

I told you that dreams played an important part <u>in what you think of</u> (underlined) as evolution. In a way, this is an extension of last evening's session, but the art connection is important.

The dream state is (underlined) a statement of perception and communication. Men in one section of a continent dreamed of animals they had never physically seen, that inhabited other geographical areas. They dreamed of more fertile lands, perhaps hundreds or even thousands of miles in the distance. Their dreams incited them, then, toward physical exploration of their world.

Art was often used in the way you are using it now—at least to some extent in your case—as a method of defining such dream images, which were not necessarily to be found in the immediate environment at all. Some cave drawings are an example.

Art as painting or drawing was then an important element in what you think of as man's evolution. When several different persons of a given tribe, say, dreamed of and drew similar animal images, then the people began to look for the physical materialization. Men dreamed their own maps in the same fashion, one man dreaming perhaps a certain portion, and several dreamers contributing their versions, drawing in sand in the waking state, or upon cave walls.

Drawing and painting during such periods was considered both sacred and immensely useful at the same time. There is indeed a kind of communal dream life, then, in which each individual contributes—a dream life in which both living and dead play a part, in your terms.

At its very heart, creativity of that nature is indeed both sacred and highly useful, and from that dimension of activity all of the initial patterns (underlined) for your highly technological society have come. Your society has emphasized and exaggerated the objective characteristics of life to such an extent, however, that art seems to be an esthetic, fairly remote phenomenon, quite divorced from physical time. It might delight the eye as decoration, or cover a blank spot upon the wall.

(Pause.) The Roman Catholic Church seized upon art, inserted its own strong symbolism, provided art with a recognizable religious, social, and political value. (Pause.) It became, however, a supercharged symbol itself of churchly opulence, and this applies also, for example, in the past to architecture. What good were ornate cathedrals, replete with carved angels, saints, and gargoyles, gleaming with glazed colorful windows, when the people lived in hovels and labored in the fields? So the buildings in America were to be prim and proper, undecorated, when the country was established. Even clothes began to become less colorful, as for example in the Puritan's straight garb.

(9:48.) In those previous "decadent" European centuries, a man's or a woman's worth was indisputably settled by the circumstances of birth. Nothing from that point on could change the intrinsic value of the individual. There were endlessly complicated, multitudinous religious and cultural justifications for such a situation, so that the entire affair seemed, often, even to the most intelligent of men, self-evident.

The peasant was poor because he was basically brutish as a result of his parentage. The gentleman was accomplished because a certain refinement came into his blood because of his royal—or nearly—parentage. The ownership of land of itself provided not only built-in social status, but an entire built-in world of privileged beliefs. A man of property, whether he be a scoundrel or a fool, was first and foremost a man of worth.

God made the wealthy and the poor, the privileged and the non-privileged, and therefore it was obviously up to man to continue that status quo. If a man had wanted—I am sorry: if God had wanted all men to be rich, he would have them all born in castles. That was more or less the reasoning.

When all that was changed, as indeed it should have been *(pause)*, the world underwent great changes. It may not have been much, but a yeoman's son in the past would always be a yeoman's son. He would follow in his father's footsteps. He was not of equal value with a prince, either of church or state. His position was a poor one, yet its freedoms and limitations were known, and his value, whatever it was, was accepted as his station in life. He might be a good yeoman or a poor one, but a yeoman he was.

The world of art or literature, or music or learning, was closed to him. When your country began its own saga, each individual was to be considered equal, regardless of birth. Many of these same people had been denied advantages in Europe. They were upstarts. What they did was establish equal starting lines for an incredible race in which each began with an equal position and then tried to outdo the other, freed of the class distinctions that had previously hampered them. Because there were few ground rules, and because it takes time to develop a culture, this rambunctious group set out to tame the continent, to show Europe that Americans could do Europe one better, without a king and without pomp.

(Pause.) The founders of the country were still largely men of property, however, and of culture—the signers of your constitution, so they were also careful to provide leeway for the existence of slaves, who, not being considered fully human, need not be granted the rights of the constitution *(with irony)*. They left suitable loopholes there.

Now: in a fashion, <u>for the sake of this discussion</u> (underlined), the blacks as slaves partially represented the great creative, exuberant, unattached, unconscious powers that were to be restrained, at least for a while. Their belief in dreams, love of music and song, even a certain mystical feeling of connection with the land—these elements were allowed the Negroes only because they were not considered fully human. White men and women were not supposed to act like that.

A person's sense of worth became connected with the acquisition of land, though to a lesser extent, even as it had in Europe. Later the acquisition of technology's objects became an added embellishment. A man proved his worth as he moved through the new society's levels—an exhilarating experience after centuries of a stratified society.

(10:12.) If men were considered equal, however, the ideas of Darwin and Freud came along to alter the meaning of equality, for men were not equal in honor and integrity and creativity—or heroism: —they were equal in dishonor *(louder)*, selfishness, greed, and equally endowed with a killer instinct that now was seen to be a natural characteristic from man's biological past.

A man's purpose seemed to be no more than to put bolts together to make an automobile, to spend hours in a factory, working on an end product that he might never see—and because many such people felt that there was little <u>intrinsic value</u> to their lives, spent in such a fashion, they began to demand greater and greater compensation. They could then buy more and more products, purchase a house and show through their possessions that their statuses meant that they must be the men of worth that they wanted to be.

All people want meaningful work. All meaningful work means in the meaningful and productive relationship between oneself and the natural world, that contributes to both one's own survival and fulfillment, and to the survival and fulfillment of the natural world.

In such a way the individual, the society, and the natural world meet, merge, and contribute to each other's existence.

In many past societies, soothsayers, dream experts, poets and artists were the most revered members, for they constantly replenished man's creative abilities, allowed him to see his position within society and in the natural world with fresh eyes. He, or she, helped form the pattern for the society's future developments, for its growth, for its give-and-take with nature.

Now <u>that</u> is one of the most important kinds of work—and <u>that</u> is what you are involved in *(intently)*.

(Pause at 10:22.) Because many people do realize that important contribution, you are financially secure. In that larger framework of activity, your creativity is being rewarded *(still intently)*. Then what an outrage do you work against yourself when you try to justify your position in terms of money or worth according to the most parochial limits and social expectations of your time.

This attitude is twice as limiting since it robs you of the very enjoyable and natural sense of worth that your body and mind both inherently possess—that is, overall you realize the rightness of your position. You have a natural sense of inner balance and equilibrium that is only marred by such considerations.

They also rise partially whenever you think of yourself as a male first or primarily, and then as an individual. You are an individual first of all and a male secondarily. You could be an individual male or female, but *(louder)* you could be neither if you were not an individual first of all—and that individual, again, happens to have an unconventionality of mind and ability most needed in your time and space.

(10:30.) Give us a moment.... To some extent you felt you had to prove your worth as a conventional male, in—if you will forgive me—the narrowest of parochial terms, though you were possessed of abilities that were considered conventionally male only if they could be suitably laundered: art turned into commercial work, and other creative abilities, such as your writing, that at one time could have turned into several fields—the writing of Westerns, even. You felt the ordinary male accomplishments in terms of sports, which brought instant approval, yet you did not choose that road.

(Pause.) Ruburt tried to prove his worth while being possessed of a fine intellect not considered womanly. All of this applied to your family situations. The more you each developed your individual abilities, the less you fit the sexual stereotypes to which your family *(to me)* in particular believed in so firmly.

To be a good male in that family's eyes, it seemed you had to be the less an artist or the less a thinker. To appear as a good wife Ruburt had to appear less a thinker, less a writer, so that you each followed double standards for <u>yourselves</u>, each trying to appear to express completely different characteristics.

I do not know if I am expressing this clearly. Ruburt tried in the family to express independence, to show that he <u>was</u> (underlined) a writer, and at the same time he tried to express dependence, to show that he was a good wife, and this applied to many social relationships as well. If he succeeded as a writer, it seemed he was less the loyal wife, and sometimes in the past—the distant past— you felt the same when you tried to be "the male provider," and take a job to satisfy that narrow role.

The artist portion became outraged, so that the better husband you were, in that regard, the poorer it seemed the artist became—but *(louder)* at least you were seen to leave the house every day, as a good man should *(with sly amusement)*.

Now you can drop such nonsense, and realize that often both of you have fought paper dragons. The same applies to Ruburt's bouts with "work," sometimes directly opposed to his ideas of creativity. He has to be "working" all the time, so people will see he is not just a dumb housewife. *(I laughed.)*

Now: do you have questions?

("No, this will be fine for now.")

I bid you the fondest of good evenings—and I would enjoy it if you truly became, both of you, a trifle less provincial—

("Okay.")

—in your thoughts. Try to realize that even in your terms there have been multitudinous cultures upon the face of the earth, each one defining for all time, with great moral rectitude, the roles of men and women. There have been freer, more exuberant beliefs systems, and there have been more limiting ones, so look at those of your culture as they influence you as simply one of the ever-varying social fabrications by which a man colors his days.

Your eternal worth, and even your daily worth, is intrinsically far separated from such manufactured values. Live with a sweeter touch.

(Quietly:) End of session.

("Thank you, Seth.")

My viewpoint is, I admit, more cosmopolitan than yours, but your own inner knowledge is <u>also</u> far-reaching in those terms, and that knowledge can indeed be shaken loose from social confinement. You can often follow social mores quite easily, when you realize they are mores *(intently)*, and not moral pronouncements—and that is all. I think you are learning.

("Good night."

(10:48. "I had no idea if that was the stuff I was getting this morning or not," Jane said. *"I was pretty far out of it. It was fun—as if you were looking at another culture and seeing that that was how those people were living. Yet you didn't have to pay that much attention to it. I couldn't say what I got just now."*

(Jane was also surprised at the amount of time that had passed. She'd had no sense of time passing, whereas at other times she might have quite a definite sense of "the psychological distance," or time that had passed.

("I don't know why I get that directional thing." she said. "but before the session I was getting that Negro material over there [to her left] and the cave drawing stuff over there [to her right], and I had to wait for them to come together....")

DELETED SESSION
AUGUST 20, 1979 9:31 PM MONDAY

(Jane received about 50 letters, forwarded from Prentice-Hall today. Among them was one from a Dan Curtis production company, who wants to option her life

story for a possible movie for television. Their credits seem very good. Jane didn't want to feel that she <u>had</u> to get material tonight from Seth on such a project.

(While looking for a private session for Sue Watkins yesterday I came across the one dated April 12, 1971. A line in it stayed with me, so that I read it over this afternoon. I ended up discouraged, I'm afraid, for much in it about Jane's symptoms, and our joint reasons for allowing them to linger, still applied. Jane read it before the session. Some of it concerned her holding back on her own success for fear that my lack of success would be painful to me, compared to her achievements. I asked her if she thought such thinking could still play a part in her hassles. She didn't think so. I certainly hoped it didn't. The session contains an excellent opening line or two that I want to use in a note for Mass Events.

(I'm getting used to thinking about Mass Events *now, and am organized to start producing the notes for it—something like making myself a new nest within which I can feel comfortable for working on the new job.*

(Jane was getting more and more relaxed as we sat for the session. "But I didn't want to miss a session," she said sleepily. Then: "I feel him around now, at least— I guess I'll be ready in a second....")

Now.

(I smiled a greeting.)

Most of this has been said before. Ruburt's symptoms have always been a cautionary and protective measure. He believed such measures must be taken because of his erroneous concept about the spontaneous self and creativity.

He believed that his creativity was highly specifically oriented to its artistic expression only. He did not understand that the spontaneous <u>self knows its own order</u> *(gently)*, or that the spontaneous creative self had any notion of his conscious needs and desires. He <u>believed</u> that often creativity expressed itself <u>at the expense of</u> other portions of the self, and that if it were allowed to spill over the edges *(with gestures)* from artistic productivity into normal living, then it would lead to all kinds of disruptive activity. This is obviously not the case.

Specific creativity is but one important aspect of the psyche's vast, almost incomprehensible productivity, for it produces your lives. You had parents and brothers, a family. Ruburt has no one in that same manner. He had an unfortunate marriage behind him when you met. When he fell in love, it was wholeheartedly, and he was determined to merge his creativity and his marriage.

(Billy now meowed, and then jumped up on Jane's chair as she spoke in trance—something he seldom does. He settled down behind her.)

Because of his cultural beliefs, he was also determined that his "womanly nature" would not impede his progress as a writer, or yours as an artist. He considered it his duty to help you succeed as an artist, believing fervently that such was your primary desire.

Certainly he tried to see to it that his success did not put you down in the eyes of others. Again, this material has all been given. His physical problems to some extent—do not overemphasize this point—put him in the role of the dependent woman. At the same time he is not that, of course, since he cannot completely carry out the woman's role of housekeeping, and so forth—so in that (underlined) way, he also shows that he is a writer. Not confined to such lowly woman's ways.

You also give him much more attention than you used to before the emergence of the symptoms—attention that he believes he deserves. All of this, however, is connected with the misunderstanding concerning the nature of the creative self, and on both of your parts.

The apartment house was one thing, a mixture of various classes of people. When you came here *(to Pinnacle Road)*, to a more lucrative kind of middle-class America, Elmira-style, you wondered what people thought, that you were home all the time. To some extent (underlined), and again, only as part of the picture, the symptoms have been a social device that to varying degrees, now, suited your purposes, both of you. Beside that, the session given recently on the creative state, is vital, for you became hypnotized, of course, by the materialized situation. So reread that session with this one.

(Jane often rereads the private session for July 16, 1979.

(9:49.) Many other issues were involved, as stated often—but all were based upon the misunderstanding of the spontaneous self—its creativity. To some extent the symptoms provided you both with a cushion against too many distractions from outsiders. They became very handy devices for a multitude of reasons. They can only serve so far, of course, before the body's objections state most clearly its disagreement. Ruburt has been doing well and is heading in the proper directions, particularly with the ideas of effortlessness and informal self-hypnosis.

The session just referred to on the creative state has important hints that Ruburt has been using, but can use better. *(Pause.)* The symptoms have served, then, as a framework. Oftentimes body language is used in such cases, to state a situation, to communicate an attitude that is otherwise not clearly stated. Bringing such issues into the open does help, for the more consciously you become aware of what you are saying through a physical condition, the more adequately you can state it verbally, or in other ways. You do not need your body then to make such a statement for you.

Our books will become even better read. I do not want to overemphasize this either, but they will offer alternatives to more and more people who are caught between the growing fervor of fundamentalism, that comes about with the disenchantment with science.

Ruburt's work, as far as his symptoms are concerned, rests primarily in his mental attitudes, and they are indeed changing for the better. The state of creativity is one you both know intimately. In it there is a kind of mental or psychic plasticity, where the evidence of the normal world loses its hard edges, becomes less real, and yet is touched by the psyche's creativity so that it <u>can</u> (underlined) in a moment be literally transformed.

In such a state the channels to probabilities are open and receptive. Physical matter is seen out of the corners of mental eyes, so to speak. Matter actually pulsates at a different rate when you are in that kind of a creative state, so the body is then very amiable to healing. It all works together, you see.

The sessions, dream activity, Ruburt's writing of books, his poetry and his painting—these states by themselves contribute to his health. Worrying, future projections of unpleasant conditions, concern over a public image, or whatever, even overconcern about his work itself—these cause strain and tension. *(Pause.)* When you see yourselves as being <u>primarily</u> in direct opposition to the ideas of the world *(pause)*, then Ruburt feels the need also to overprotect himself from it. You should see yourselves as primarily in an excellent position to <u>help</u> the world, which brings about an entirely different set of feelings and beliefs.

(10:06.) You must each try to get the <u>feeling</u> (underlined) of creativity as you are acquainted with it, and then <u>let that</u> feeling splash over to other portions of your life, and particularly to the area of Ruburt's mobility.

He <u>has</u> been doing more housework by a good degree. This is important, not only because of the increased mobility it entails, but also because of the change of attitude.

(Pause.) Painting should be enough, you may think sometimes, but you <u>chose</u> to be the kind of person who wanted to explore the greater reaches of reality, from which art itself emerges. You were looking for some kind of vehicle, and you found it. Ruburt should understand that. <u>Consciously</u> (underlined), at the start of your marriage you would both have been delighted to work together doing comic strips, fulfilling male and female roles quite conventionally, with just an added flair. Your abilities led both of you far beyond, and it is time that you updated your ideas.

Talking the subject over again together will help, for it will clear up any lingering misunderstandings. I will speak about your movie inquiry later.

Do you have questions?

("Jane got her first letter from Germany today." I meant of course that it was her first from a reader of the German edition, of Seth Speaks. *It was written in English, and was amazingly typical of some she gets from this country.)*

The books will do well and there will be further translations. Taking probabilities into consideration, there are cultural movements involving the western world as it tried to form a new philosophical stance, and our books may well provide a highly valuable alternate position for people—again—between the passionate beliefs systems of religion in many countries, and the overly objective dictates of science.

The upsurge of fundamental religion in the Arab world *(meaning Iran)* has a certain correlation with the upsurges of fundamental Christianity in your country, and will indeed serve as a needed reminder around the world of the exaggerated nature that religion can take when it is allied with government. Science allied with the government has its own dogmas, however *(intently)*, so the civilized world will be looking for new alternatives.

(Long pause.) So far, there has been an overreliance upon, say, objectified science, and a repudiation of the intuitive portions of the self. This leads in some cases, then, to an exaggerated repudiation of objective reasoning, and to the alliance of a fundamental kind of religion with the intuitive portions of the self.

A civilization must avoid either extreme, as of course each individual should. So we will to some extent provide alternatives. Your letters show such alternatives are needed. *(Pause.)* If you are mentioned in an unfavorable light by people who are fanatics in one way or another, then it shows that you <u>are</u> (underlined) making inroads, and that our books <u>are</u> (underlined) being read enough by the followers of a particular doctrine to make the leaders of such doctrines uneasy.

(Seth probably refers here to a letter Jane received today from a fan in Ohio, who enclosed a copy of a letter he wrote defending her to Jacques Vallee, who evidently had mentioned Jane in one of his books. The letter is on file. Vallee had his facts wrong, it seems, ascribing Jane's work to automatic writing, etc.)

(Pause at 10:25.) You must again realize that you chose your situation, and because it is a valuable one you sought it out. If Ruburt understands that, then he will realize he does not have to protect himself privately or socially, for all of his characteristics are meant to help him deal successfully with the challenge he has chosen. The same applies to you.

(Pause.) You do not understand the nature of your own psychological extensions, or how your written words influence others. You said that Benny Hill *(the English comedian)* advertises his beliefs in his program, and in the same way your notes in our books advertise your own beliefs, and provide an exam-

ple of a creative and also reasonable framework in which to interpret psychic behavior.

End of session *(whispering)*. A fond good evening.

("Thank you. Seth. Good night.")

("You know, he was quite different in trance," Jane said. "I know there was something different going on. I know I did." But she didn't explain, or couldn't.)

("Like what?" I asked.)

("I don't know. I remember I was talking as Seth, and I looked over and Billy was giving me an entirely different look than he'd ever given me before. I just know it. He just looked at me like I was an entirely different person—either that, or I perceived him differently in trance.")

(For perhaps fifteen minutes after he'd jumped up in Jane's chair, Billy had descended from that spot and curled himself up against me as I sat taking notes on the couch. He'd remained in that position until the end of the session. This too was a little unusual for him to do.)

SESSION 874 (DELETED PORTION)
AUGUST 22, 1979 9:43 PM WEDNESDAY

(The following material is from the 874th session. I'll quote a few lines from the closing passages for that session in order to lead into what follows for Jane.

(10:37.) None of those sperm are as yet people. But all of them have the capacity to become people, according to the actions of probabilities. In a way, then, each thought bears the same relation to its materialization in fact as the sperm bears to *its* possible materialization as a person. The sperm has to find the egg. The thought has to find *its* physical nest. When you are in a creative state knowingly, you help form the nest that you want to collect the thoughts that you <u>want</u> to materialize. You are dealing with the undersides of reality.

Ruburt was in such a state during his experience last evening. It was indeed a healing one, when he was dealing with the plasticity of events, and bringing those he wanted into better focus, by consciously drawing upon his own larger creative abilities. He should do such exercises daily.

Do you have questions?

("During Monday's session I was going to ask about that dream he had—on Monday afternoon, I think. But now I don't remember it.")

Give us a moment.... Overall, that dream, and today's, both represented deep feelings that challenges could be met successfully, even in an adventurous fashion—that he was safe. Though the skies quaked or folded he would serve meals to many—meaning that he would offer them nourishment of another kind. That includes both dreams.

(See the copy of Jane's dreams attached. The session ended after this at 10:48 pm.)

JANE'S NAP DREAM
AUGUST 20, MONDAY

(I'm writing this down finally two days later and even right after the dream, much was confused. I'm sure of this much: a group of people were with me at a large round table. Right in front of us was the sky, which somehow came right down to the floor; the view was spectacular and the sky was doing something very strange; it was all made up of large sky-folds which blew and changed, huge folds coming down from inexpressible heights, past us, I think. Maybe the sky shuddered or something too? Or the earth did. No one was alarmed but when the sky stopped doing that I said something about always being very relieved each time it was over. Then I began to serve dinner to these people, started counting how many to be served, and got a bit confused because there were more people than I'd counted on....

(Either the end of above dream or the end of another. I'm dancing at a swank dance floor with a younger man with dark darting eyes that now remind me of Frank Longwell, Jr. I know I've seen him once before and that he's a thief. This is sort of like a TV movie, To Catch a Thief. *I tell him what I know about him and tell him he better split; something of value is going to be stolen and he'd get blamed with his record. I may have been a thief too....)*

JANE'S DREAM
AUGUST 21, TUESDAY

(Long involved adventure type dream, spy adventure I think; I climb cliffs, castle moats etc, seeking clues and am very effective.)

DELETED SESSION
AUGUST 29, 1979 9:23 PM WEDNESDAY

(This afternoon I brought Mitzi home from the vet. Doc Davidson spayed her yesterday instead of Monday, as planned. She is fine, and seemingly is as active as ever

—an amazing display considering that she was operated upon only about 24 hours ago. Every time she jumped up on a chair—or down—Jane and I winced, but Mitzi wasn't concerned at all. Some cat.

(Billy, of course, was highly intrigued by the change his nose told him had taken place in his sister. Indeed, our only problem was keeping him from constantly nosing after Mitzi, since she usually ran away from him each time he tried to investigate what must have been changed bodily odors of hers. For the session I put him in the cellar.

(The evening, dark, was a beautiful one. As we sat for the session in our "new" den we could hear through the open sliding glass door the mixed chorus of tree toads and various insects echoing through the woods in back of the house, and up and across Holley Road.

(This afternoon and evening, and somewhat to my surprise, Jane has been talking about discussing her physical symptoms in her new book, God of Jane. *I thought her changed attitude stemmed from her long phone conversation with Tristine Rainer, of Dan Curtis Associates, a television production company that wants to option her life story. [See the notes for the deleted session for August 20, 1979.] They wrote August 8. If her life story were ever to be filmed, the symptoms would have to be considered, we found ourselves thinking. They are obviously a strong part of the drama of the whole thing.)*

Good evening.

("Good evening, Seth.")

Now. *(Long pause.)* You are to some degree a sports-minded culture. Sports are regarded as an enviable field of endeavor. Sportslike abilities are encouraged from early childhood, particularly as far as the males are concerned.

Sportsmen and athletes are admired and well-rewarded. As you know, the running records have been broken in late years time and time again. The crowds acclaim the sense of competition, the excitement, the rewards, and the belief in performance have all been responsible for the breaking of previous records. On the other hand, psychic abilities have generally (underlined) been held in such poor reputation for centuries *(with gestures)*, so discouraged, that you might think it quite a wonder that they still show themselves.

Persons displaying such abilities have had to be strong personalities in order to hold up under a barrage of varying disreputable distortions thrown upon them by science, or religion, and particularly in the past, even by governments.

No mainline Western culture for centuries has granted the validity of psychic abilities. Yet those abilities arise in each generation, misinterpreted or no. They cannot disappear, because they are an important part of man's heritage.

They are invisible contributors to his knowledge. They are natural methods of perception that cannot be legislated away by governments, cannot be ripped out of people's make-ups by religions or by sciences.

Let us look—once again—back into the past. Your own psychic abilities, and Ruburt's, saved you *(as I remarked after supper)* at the time of your physical difficulties. I must insist once more that you take probabilities into consideration.

The psychic abilities <u>are</u> (underlined) the creative abilities—natural extensions of what you think of as the creative abilities. They do not just help you paint a picture, or write a poem, but they help you form the living picture of your lives. <u>In a way</u> (underlined), you were too contemplative *(pause)*, even perhaps too intellectually inclined, perhaps even too solitary, to be an artist alone.

(Pause.) You could not treat your paintings as products in the marketplace. Though you worked in the art department, you did not want to rub up against your fellows quite that closely *(with amusement)*. You were interested not only in a painting, and the painting's origin, but in your origin as an artist, and in all of those relationships that are involved between the perceiver and the object, that then is turned into the artist's model. You were looking for a larger framework of existence itself, from which to view the reality with which you were familiar.

At the time of your problems, you seemed to be facing a dead end, for very little in the world that you saw or experienced seemed either sane or rational. Within the framework of your beliefs, nothing seemed to make much sense. Even art itself seemed to provide but a momentary glimpse of some undefined perfection, toward which you <u>felt</u> intuitively. Each person must somehow be drawn, period.

You saw in your parents the first signs of illness and age as you thought of those things. You were into your 40's, and felt your own abilities still somehow <u>unchallenged</u>, not fully used. You fell ill. *(Pause.)* The two of you from your first meeting actually responded largely to portions of yourselves <u>unmanifest</u> then— to portions of yourselves that you are only now becoming. You sensed the shape of the probability that is now your life, that is now your life together *(intently)*. And from that probable future in your past, your creative abilities were accelerated.

(9:50.) The York Beach affair happened, Ruburt's *Idea Construction* experience, and the beginning of the sessions. Those events were necessary, or events very much like them, if, granting probabilities, the two of you were eager to have years of satisfying life and work. You were both growing very bitter, your idealism turning into a disillusionment that could most easily have turned into

despair.

You were well aware, intuitively, of Ruburt's strong abilities, though you had no labels for them. Ruburt was appalled at your situation, and moreover your moodiness at the time led him to fear that you might turn away from him. He sensed your abilities also, and psychically the two of you pooled your creative resources to reach beyond the reality that you know, to search for some other vaster framework that could help explain the events of your private reality and the events of the public world. For that world did indeed seem chaotic, particularly with your president's assassination and the situation in Cuba.

You bought your rifle and your food supplies in case you had to withstand a disaster of nuclear proportions. Some people died in those years because they did not want to live in that kind of world. They became ill because there seemed to be no reason to life.

Creative people were unfortunately particularly affected, because their very abilities require an exuberance, an energy, that can only be quelled by a sense of meaninglessness. (Pause.) Neither of you were taught to trust creative abilities, much less psychic ones. (Pause.) In a fashion (underlined), Ruburt thought of his abilities as fascinating but untrustworthy allies: give them an inch and they will take a yard.

Left alone, he never wrote conventional fiction. His abilities would not confine themselves to such a limited form, and he was always trying to bring them into line. He grew up at a time when it was considered somewhat dangerous to be different from others. In the home, the Catholic asylum, he was often punished for noncomformity. He tried to form a protective self to keep himself in line.

(Long pause.) His basic nature, again, has always insisted upon expressing its high exuberance, its natural abilities. He had problems to face, then, that resulted in his symptoms—but (louder) they are nothing like the problems he would have had to face had he not found this greater framework for himself and others.

There is a power of value fulfillment and growth within each individual that must be satisfied. It is the power that makes physical growth possible, the power that is behind the fetus. You know ahead of time the nature of the period into which you will be born. (Pause.) You were both born with certain abilities, and you knew ahead of time that you would have to enlarge the framework of conventional concepts if you were to have room to use those abilities. In a way, they gave you both a second life, for in the old framework there was no satisfying (underlined) or creative way to go.

(10:10.) Again, in a way (underlined), you have given a second life to many other people. *(Pause.)* Some of this is simplified, but it all basically applies. Ruburt's main problem was that he tried too hard to protect himself because he believed it was necessary. These ideas have been delivered to you in serial time. Some get through easier or quicker than others, and a belief in the need for protection has been the most stubborn lingering belief from Ruburt's past in this life.

The other is the lingering doubt *(pause)* about the self's good intent. These are the two most nagging issues in the society, of course. Ruburt combatted them to a strong degree, in order that the sessions could even emerge *(intently)*.

Stating his position will clear his psychic air, and relieve him of the strain of hiding his symptoms. Beyond that, however, it may help initiate important insights, and has the possibility of bringing about extremely important developments.

I spoke about this instead of your community of sperm this evening. But Ruburt was correct: There was nothing defective about the genes mentioned in your article *(in the* National Enquirer*)*, in which individuals were born girls, and turned into boys. The gene bank contains multitudinous—in fact, numberless —varieties of development, meant to insure against unimaginable catastrophes, changes or climate, or whatever.

These developments reoccur now and then in <u>trial runs</u>, so to speak, restating various genetic positions, though they often appear in your world as abnormalities. Instead, they provide genetic protection against possible eventualities.

End of session unless you have a question.

("Well. Jane's change of attitude, about discussing her physical hassles, came about because the movie company got in touch with her, right?" See the notes at the start of the session.)

It was the trigger that led to his decision to reveal himself more fully in his book *(God of Jane)*. End of answer.

("Okay.")

You have both used the material I have given you, and what you have learned on your own through that material very well—some of it so smoothly that you are not even aware of your accomplishments. In some areas you still cling to old beliefs, but there is no end to what you can do, still, with growing comprehension. That is, you can still accomplish as much, if not more, than you already have.

(Pause.) You must almost think of yourselves in important ways, as almost having been born in 1964. Think about that.

End of session *(heartily)*. A fond good evening, and I have not forgotten your sperm.

("Okay. Thank you.")

(10:25.) A note: the two of you—for you are both involved since 1964—have not only initiated a new framework from which <u>others</u>, as well as yourselves, can view the nature of reality more clearly, but you also had to start from scratch, so to speak, to get the material, learn to trust it, and then to apply it to your own lives—even while "the facts were not all in yet." At no point did you have all of the material to draw upon, as for example your readers do at any given point. So tell Ruburt not to judge himself too harshly, and *(whispering)* in all of this have him try to remember his sense of play, and to read often that July session on the creative state.

End of session.

("Thank you, Seth. Good night.")

(10:29 PM. "I vaguely know what he said about 1964," Jane said. "He put that in to make me feel better, about being reborn.")

(A copy of the article from the National Enquirer, *for September 4, 1979, was attached. Unfortunately, it's missing from this session's record 26 years later, in 2005....)*

SESSION 877 (DELETED)
SEPTEMBER 3, 1979 9:09 PM MONDAY

(This session has so much general application that I'm including it in the regular record. At the same time, an extra copy of it is inserted into the deleted notebooks so that Jane can refer to it along with the rest of the material Seth has given for her.

(Wade Alexander and his son Brian visited us for 3/4 of an hour at supper time. We discussed the Seth tapes Wade is keeping for us, and Yale University Library. The visit was very pleasant but it disrupted our schedule enough so that we ate an hour later than usual. This in turn left Jane feeling not quite ready for the session at the usual time. But we sat for it as usual, and eventually Jane began to feel Seth around.

(This reminded her that sometime this afternoon she'd picked up something from Seth about a topic for this evening's session. She'd forgotten what it was, though —"except that it wasn't about me."

(Earlier this afternoon Jane reread several deleted sessions dating from 1973. They left her feeling quite relaxed, so that she took her nap earlier than usual, and passed up her exercise period. The material in those sessions concerned her ideas of

work, spontaneity, and order, among other things. She'd thought that spontaneity didn't have any order.)

Good evening.

("Good evening, Seth.")

Now: Spontaneity knows its own order, and it is from spontaneous order that all secondary classifications of order emerge.

You could not have any of your arts, cultures, governments, religions or sciences without first being couched in nature's spontaneous order. That spontaneous order shows itself in time, but it is apart from time, in that its <u>origins</u> (underlined) are not physical.

(Pause.) What you think of usually as order is an aspect of the spontaneous order that is within and behind the "mechanics" of all physical actions. The usual idea of order is greatly concerned with serial time, but spontaneity's natural order, with its origins outside of time, has "all time to play with."

You think of the beginnings or endings of civilizations, for example, marking them with specific dates. At the level at which spontaneous order operates, however, perception would span those dates. There could actually be no beginning or end to any culture. The idea of discipline as you think of it comes into effect most generally when you try to impose a secondary kind of order over the primary one. I am not speaking here of discipline as punishment, but of discipline accepted by a person or a civilization in order to direct action along certain lines. Such disciplines usually exaggerate and intensify one kind of natural spontaneous order over another. This is done because the natural spontaneous nature of order is not understood.

People feel that they must push themselves or their civilizations along certain lines—that they must <u>impose</u> an order from without, since they do not trust the spontaneous order of nature.

(Pause.) In your terms man is of course still learning, and as he set up barriers between lands and formed separate nations, so he also set up divisions between aspects of his own consciousness and awareness, in his terms, so he could deal with them one at a time. He made distinctions that are largely arbitrary.

Spontaneity knows its own order. *(Pause.)* In a definite manner of speaking, spontaneity, being apart from time while operating <u>in</u> time, is aware of, say, private abilities before they show themselves in time.

The spontaneous self was never meant to appear as an alien to the conscious personality. The spontaneous self, of course, represents your closest private touch with the universe, with your origins, and with your relationship to All That Is. Your impulses, intuitions, and creative abilities have <u>always</u> innately provided open channels of communication through which man was guided toward those probable actions most beneficial to his private reality—and those actions would automatically, again, add to the best probable reality for the species as well.

(Long pause at 9:30.) The physical universe <u>had</u> to spring from a source that exists beyond life itself. The universe came alive through a divine spontaneity that knew its own order—a spontaneity whose creations would automatically fall into meaningful patterns. At what point did apelike mammals alter their own genetic message, in terms of evolution's tales? What sperm first knew itself different, knowing it would mature—if it did as a man instead of an ape? And what apelike female changed her genetic messages, knowing that her egg, if it matured, would literally give birth to an entirely new species, one that centuries later would read and write?

What agency in the environment brought about such stupendous changes? I tell you that no agency in the environment brought about that change *(intently)*, because, Ruburt's earlier romantic poetry to the contrary, that change did not occur.

There were some species of man <u>before</u> there were some species of ape.

(Long pause.) Consciousness makes its own patterns. Creativity is still the closest field of endeavor that can possibly teach you about the origin of the species, for your creativity mimics that higher creative spontaneity, out of which <u>all</u> (underlined) order emerges *(again intently)*.

<u>Basically</u> (underlined), any portion of the human body has the inherent capacity to reproduce itself—and further, to become a reproductive organ. Is that clear?

("Yes.")

Ruburt believed he must impose a secondary kind of order upon his creativity and spontaneity. Sometimes it seems that you are bothered by visitors when you do not want them, but those visitors are also a part of that spontaneous order, whether or not at any given time you recognize the purpose of such a visit, or its place in your lives.

I cannot explain adequately that basically childbirth <u>is</u> a joyful—one of the most joyful—creative activities. In a way the child is—<u>in a way</u> (underlined), the child is—the finalized version in your reality *(long pause)* of a vast number of sperm and eggs.

Now: the characteristics of the settled-upon sperm and egg predominate, but these are also related—in a manner most difficult to describe—to all the other sperm who did not make contact with that given egg, and also to the other eggs that might have formed instead of the one that did *(all intently)*.

There is a gestalt relationship between all the sperm, say, in a man's body at a given time, in which the sperm that do not connect still add their latent characteristics to the one that seemingly triumphs. <u>In a fashion</u> (underlined twice), they pool their resources, and climb aboard the one ship that makes it to the shore *(animated and restless).*

This verbal description must necessarily distort the true picture, because the true events completely escape your vocabulary, but the explanation is valid-enough to give you some idea of what I mean.

(9:49.) Those other characteristics, say, then, of the probable eggs and sperm, provide an infinite bed of personality characteristics and abilities <u>that can ride</u> to the surface if they are needed.

(Pause.) All creativity is basically joyful, it is play in the highest sense of that term, and it is always alive with motion. The sessions and our work can help bring about a new <u>mental</u> race of men and women. *(Whispering:)* Ideas change the chromosomes, but the sessions and Ruburt's books, and so forth, must first and foremost be joyful expressions of creativity, spontaneous expression that fall into their own order. So have him avoid undue feelings of responsibility and heavy-handed attitudes.

He should indeed reread those sessions that he read today, and you paint because you love to paint, and forget what an artist is supposed to be or not to be. Have Ruburt forget what a writer or a psychic is supposed to be or not to be. Ruburt's spontaneity let all of his creative abilities emerge. It is foolhardy to try and apply discipline, or secondary order, to a spontaneous creativity that automatically gives you the finest order that nature could ever provide.

(Pause.) Do you have questions?

("I guess you've gone into my main question, about the sperm: If practically all of them are never going to fulfill their primary purpose, what other roles do they have in life?")

I answered part of that question, and the discussion is still continuing.

("Okay.")

End of session, and a fond good evening.

("The same to you.")

I approve of your notes.

("Thank you. Good night.")

(9:59 PM. The notes Seth referred to are those I wrote this afternoon and tonight for the first session of the latest Seth book, Mass Events. *They're rough and too long yet, but Jane liked them. I've been leading up to the actual writing for a couple of weeks now, what with my making chronologies, and so forth, and will be happy to get really into it. At the moment I still feel that I'm searching for that one*

intense focus-approach to my work for Mass Reality *that will finally mean I'm under way on that project.)*

SESSION 878 (DELETED PORTION)
SEPTEMBER 10, 1979 9:07 PM MONDAY

(The following material is from the 878th session.

(10:05. "Were you uncomfortable?" Jane asked as soon as she came out of trance.

("Yes," I said, for I'd felt my stomach act up pretty strongly several times while Seth had been speaking. This had made me change my position while writing in order to compensate—futilely, I might note.

("Do you want to wait for a minute, and get something on it?" Jane asked.

("I don't know. I'm so disgusted I don't give a shit," I said. My stomach had begun bothering me quite a bit a few days ago. I'd felt much better since last June, and thought I'd learned enough since then so that I didn't need to bother the stomach any more—but evidently I hadn't after all.

("Well, taxes come up this week," Jane told me, "and every time they do your stomach starts up. You're sure the pendulum said there wasn't any connection?"

("Who knows? It told me once that this time taxes weren't involved. I didn't keep asking it. The best answer I got was when I laid Through My Eyes *aside to work on* Mass Events *I felt bad about doing that. Not that I resented working on* Mass Events. *I wanted to do both at the same time, and figured I couldn't manage that. So I felt guilty—I thought—about not concentrating on Seth's book. Painting wasn't involved either...."*

(Then at 10:09:) Now: Right now, self-disapproval is involved. You disapprove of yourself because you feel poorly—and because you do not approve of the basic feelings that are behind the difficulty.

The coming taxes are involved—but only because they serve as a springboard—as your family visit did—the springboard that rearouses feelings of disapproval.

(Brother Bill visited last June 1, and Jane reacted more strongly to that event than I did. See the deleted session for June 1. Then on August 12, Bill, Loren and families visited us. That time I reacted much more strongly, and Seth came through with an excellent session about it all. I've felt pretty good since then.)

You do not approve of yourself because you think you should be making money "on your own." You do not approve of yourself because you think you should be a better artist, or a better writer—but in any case, you do not let yourself appreciate the self that you are.

When you realize this, then you disapprove of yourself for not being wise enough to understand. Behind this is still the idea that self-disapproval is somehow valuable—it will somehow make you better.

Overall, you are too demanding of yourself. It is understandable enough, in your society, that you have certain feelings resulting from society's insistence that the male in any family must be the main, primary, and clear-cut breadwinner, no matter what the cost. If you understand that those feelings are par for the course, you can accept them—and <u>then</u> go on to see where their source lies. You can <u>understand</u> those feelings, come to terms with them, and they will automatically begin to vanish.

(Pause.) This self-disapproval does not hound you more than other men. It bothers you less than it does most people, for your own understanding has made inroads. Try to be more compassionate toward yourself and your feelings. Do not judge your feelings. The disapproval causes you to bury them. Out in the open, you can handle them easily.

Ideas have changed also since your boyhood, when those ideas were instilled in you. The feelings become exaggerated, and prevent you from accepting the quite valid feelings of your own worth. Approve of yourself as you are, now. Avoid thoughts of regret *(as I mentioned to Jane this morning)*. Doors of all kinds will open when you take away that restraining mental habit.

(Pause.) Peace.

("Thank you.")

End of session.

("Thank you, Seth."

(10:23. "Well, I hope that helps." Jane said.

("It's bound to," I snorted. "That means that four times a year, then, I feel lousy because of those damned taxes.... What a dumb position to put yourself into." Then Seth returned.)

Now: You would be better off saying to yourself: "Everyone has their foibles. Every time the taxes come up I feel poorly, but no one is perfect. To hell with it." That attitude would be better than disapproving of yourself because of the difficulty. Do you follow me?

("Yes.")

End of session.

("Thank you.")

Now: I had many dealings with taxes. I paid the piper, as the saying goes. On some occasions I wheeled and dealed, as you say. I was cynical on occasion *(pause)*, but I had the good sense to know when I was well off—and I did not make my poor belly pay in its corporal innocence. So free your body from distortions of disapproval.

("Okay, thank you.")

(10:27 PM. "There was more there," Jane said, "but he felt he'd better quit because you were so uncomfortable. Also—he wasn't justifying that he wheeled and dealed at that time....")

DELETED SESSION
SEPTEMBER 13, 1979 8:40 PM THURSDAY

(Jane was so relaxed yesterday and last night—as she has been often lately—that we held no session. At the same time she's been extremely creative, working on her God of Jane, *and the introduction to* Mass Events—*producing many pages of excellent material for those works. She's been quite inspired. Even though she was again very relaxed today, she was also active writing. In fact, after supper tonight she produced two more pages of notes that she'd picked up from Seth on his new book:* Dreams, "Evolution," and Value Fulfillment. *She laughed. "I keep trying to change that title, though." She'd picked up the title as long ago as July 30, 1979—see the 869th session note. A copy is attached of her notes having to do with the new book. I've been expecting Seth to begin it at any time.*

(Jane suggested having an earlier session, although I hadn't really expected her to have one at all. My only recent concern has been that she not let the sessions go on a regular basis just because I'm working on the notes for Mass Events.

("I think I'm about ready...." When she went in trance, Jane's delivery was very active and energetic—in marked contrast to her near bleary-eyed state before Seth came through. This is a transformation that I've seen happen more than once.

(With amusement:) Comments.

("Okay. Good evening, Seth.")

(Pause.) The two of you thought of yourselves specifically as a writer—or rather a poet—and an artist before our sessions began. I would like to clear up some important issues.

You identified primarily now, as a poet and an artist because those designations, up to that time, seemed most closely to fit your abilities and temperaments. Ruburt's writing set him apart. Your painting set you apart. These were recognizable, tangible proofs of creativity. You therefore identified with elements, characteristics, and traditions that seemed to suit you best.

To some extent you had your own niches, recognizable by society even if they were <u>relatively</u> (underlined) unusual. You did not know that there was a deeper, older, or richer tradition—a more ancient heritage, to which you belonged, because you found no hint of it in your society. It seemed at different times since our sessions began that there were disruptive conflicts, for example: was Ruburt a writer or was he a psychic? Were you an artist, or weren't you? What about the writing you did—both for our books, and the writing that you sometimes plan to do on your own?

Those kinds of conflicts can only exist in a society in which the entire concept of creativity is segmented, in which the creative processes are often seen as inner assembly lines leading to specific products: a society in which the very nature of creativity itself is largely ignored unless its "products" serve specific ends.

Ruburt was correct in his introductory notes today *(for* Mass Events*)*— about the poet's original, long-forgotten abilities, and his role. Ruburt has been a poet <u>all</u> of the time in the most profound meaning of that term. For the poet did not simply string words together, but sent out a syntax of consciousness, using rhythm and the voice, rhyme and refrain, as methods to form steps up which his own consciousness could rush.

(8:53.) Early artists hoped to understand the very nature of creativity itself as they tried to mimic earth's forms. Poetry and painting were both <u>functional</u> in ways that I will describe in our next book *(humorously, elaborately casual)*, and "esthetic." But poetry and painting have always involved primarily man's attempt to understand himself and his world. The original functions of art— meaning poetry and painting here specifically—have been largely forgotten. The true artist in those terms was always primarily—in your terms again—a psychic or a mystic. His specific art *(pause)* was both his method of understanding his own creativity, and a way of exploring the vast creativity of the universe—and also served as a container or showcase that displayed his knowledge as best he could.

That is the heritage that both of you follow, and have followed faithfully. It was an honored tradition. Also involved is, as Ruburt correctly picked up from me, a group of accomplishments that we will call the psychological arts. You are involved in those also.

(To me:) I want you to specifically understand that there is and can be no conflict, for example, between your writing and painting, for in the most basic of ways they represent different methods of exploring the meaning and the source of creativity itself.

The sessions I give you, in <u>usual</u> (underlined) terms, are a new extension of that creativity—but again, that extension has an ancient heritage. *(To me again:)* Your own writing, of course, is art. It is also a method of understanding and perceiving creativity. It is a method of learning that redoubles upon itself, and you are uniquely equipped *(pause)* to discover comprehensions from a standpoint that is most unusual, unique.

Explore, for example, your own feelings toward me; whether or not they have changed through the years. How much I seem to be myself, or part Jane; or part Ruburt, or part you, or part Joseph, or whatever. Realizing that you are in the position you wanted to be and realizing that your abilities are not in conflict with each other, nor you with them, will automatically fulfill and develop all of those abilities, in a new kind of overall creativity that is itself beyond specifics.

Now: When Ruburt begins to trust himself, as he has, the physical *(arthritic)* armor loosens. The creative abilities become even more available, hence his new creativity, and the new physical steps he has taken. They all go together.

He believed in the specific nature of the creative self, so that it could only be trusted in certain areas. He believed he needed strong mental barriers as well as physical ones, set up against his own spontaneity. He is beginning to understand that the spontaneous and creative aspects of personality are the life-giving ones. They can and must be trusted. He knows now he does not have to slow down, and that relaxation leads to motion.

(9:09.) He did indeed pick up from me a <u>partial</u> list of the subject matters to be covered in our new book—which will be called *Dreams, "Evolution,"* (in quotes) *and Value Fulfillment.*

(Pause.) The book will necessarily of course include much material on the true nature of creativity and its uses and misuses by civilizations. You do not have to fight to trust the thrust of your own life. That thrust is always meant to lead you toward your own best fulfillment, in a way that will benefit the species as well.

When you trust the thrust of your own life, you are always supported. Tell Ruburt that.

I want you both, then, to understand that in the greater light of creativity, understanding its true meaning, you have taken the right course, and therefore drop from your minds any lingering ideas of conflict and doubt. Such a stand will automatically clear up all problems involving things like taxes, sex roles, or whatever—on both of your parts.

You *(both)* are studying the nature of creativity as few others have done or can do—and that is bound to make possible new creative frameworks, and to offer new solutions to situations that cause difficulty only within smaller frameworks. Do you have questions?

("No. Jane's been doing great lately, and I'm very pleased to see that.")
He should—meaning predictive, he will. End of session.
("Thank you.")
A fond good evening.
("Good night, Seth.")
(9:16 PM. And right at the end of the session, Jane's head flopped down loose-ly, as she quickly returned to the very relaxed state she'd known before, while speak-ing for Seth.)

SESSION 881 (DELETED PORTION)
SEPTEMBER 25, 1979 8:50 PM TUESDAY

(The following material is from the 881st session. Before the session I'd expressed the hope that Seth would have something to say about Jane's frequently-very-relaxed state today.)

(9:47.) Today, Ruburt's body wanted to relax. He has been doing very well, and he tried to approve, but since he lost work time yesterday his approval barely went skin deep *(louder)*.

When you mentioned his ink sketches, he instantly wanted to play at painting again, but felt, guiltily, that he should not. He forgot, once again, that the creative self is aware of his entire life, and that his impulses have a creative purpose.

(Pause.) These sessions themselves involve the highest levels of creative productivity, at many, many levels, so he should refresh himself painting or doing whatever he likes, for that refreshment adds to his creativity, of course. He will finish his book *(God of Jane)*, and do beautifully with it. He should follow the rhythms of his own creativity without being overly concerned with the time. For a while, again, have him write three hours of free writing, and paint or what-ever. His book will be provided for. You can see how your own creativity is emerging in the notes for *Mass Events*. Granted, you need time to write physi-cally, but the basic creativity has its own time.

End of session and a fond good evening.
("Can I ask a question?")
You may.
("What was that feeling he had today in his chest, back and body, like an elec-tric pulsation?")
Because he did not approve of his own relaxation, he put brakes upon it.
("Okay.")

(This marked the end of the private material, and Seth ended the session short-ly at 9:56 PM.)

DELETED SESSION
OCTOBER 10, 1979 9:17 PM WEDNESDAY.

(Jane was so relaxed Monday evening that no session was held.

(Yesterday we received from Prentice-Hall the Dutch edition of Seth Speaks *[Seth Spreekt], published by Ankh-Hermes. We saw at once that the book had been rather drastically cut—not only my own notes, which contain excerpts from Seth material at times—but Seth's material itself. This is particularly obvious in the appendix, where only a few pages are left of all of that material. No greetings or responses are included except in isolated instances, nor any good-evenings and closing notes. Times are also left out, and no words are underlined. I suspect also that throughout the book, without my having checked yet, portions of the sessions have been cut whenever they were dependent upon notes that were cut. Some of the ses-sions, then, are only a page and a half, or two, long.*

(Our first reactions were ones of such stunned surprise that we didn't even get mad. It took a while for the extent of the revision—or condensation—to sink in, I guess, and I'm still understanding the cutting as I leaf through the book occasionally, before making a list of what I can be sure was cut.

(Jane immediately called Tam, to learn that, ironically, all of the bigwigs at Prentice-Hall are in Europe, attending the book fair at Frankfurt, Germany, I believe is where it is. It appears that we can do little until the 22nd of October, although I plan to start writing letters before that. I bitterly resent the cutting in the first place, and the time that will be spent away from Mass Events, *now, as I do all the work necessary to make our points. Jane finally agrees that we must take certain actions now in our professional lives, and we don't know what will happen. I can only think at this writing [on the 14th] that we must do all we can to stop such prac-tices by foreign publishers, or we'll surely regret it deeply in the years to come. We def-initely know we've been taken advantage of, but basically feel it is Prentice-Hall's fault for not checking the work in progress.*

(In my letters I intend to demand that we see the version in manuscript to be published by any foreign press, or the galleys, or whatever. We'll also want written into our contracts our right to be notified when any deals are made, the payments made, and our right to refuse the deal if we decide we don't like it. We'll also want to see a copy of the contract itself, and probably know the names of the foreign editors and publishers so we can contact them personally.

(Jane also discussed with Tam a number of points growing out of our last roy-
alty statements; some of these are quite legitimate gripes that we've kept quiet about
for some time. Her implications to Tam were clear enough—we hope: that for the
first time she was thinking of alternate courses of action to being published by
Prentice-Hall, perhaps trying other publishers, Eleanor Friede among them. I was all
for that, I told her. During the week after the Dutch edition arrived, we received
from Tam the contracts for God of Jane *and* Mass Events, *both of which contain*
phrases and clauses in an effort to get around Prentice-Hall's habit of withholding
percentages of earnings against returns. She told Tam she wouldn't sign them, nor do
I want her to. Prentice-Hall even wants to apply any losses for God of Jane *against*
Mass Events *after 18 months, in an effort to make one book pay for another! As it*
is, Prentice-Hall is now applying earnings from the paperback Politics *against the*
hardcover losses—a method Tam says is common in the trade, but which I think is
ethically dishonest, to say the least. They did the same thing with Adventures; *in this*
case, that action wiped the board clean for the hardcover Adventures, *and even*
showed a small profit from the paperback sales. But still, it costs us. I view such tac-
tics as the publisher's way of guaranteeing their publishing costs with no risk to them-
selves. Instead of charging hardcover losses against taxes as a business expense, say, they
charge the author for them; this means they do not have to pay the author any roy-
alties on paperback sales, for at least several years. I don't think Jane yet grasps the
implications here.

(In addition, I want to do what we can to get sales reports from Prentice-Hall
re Bantam sales [which we know aren't great], and from the Pocket Books/Fell fias-
co. I plan to write the editor-in-chief at Pocket Books as soon as I find out his name
and address, asking him for sales figures; we haven't had a royalty report from Fell in
a year. I want to ask Eleanor Friede for the name of a lawyer to see what can be done
to get information from Fell. [She offered to help us that way several years ago, I
think.] Perhaps Eleanor can advise us about Pocket Books names, also. Eleanor is also
in Europe, by the way.

(Day before yesterday we received from Tam a copy of his memo to J. Nelson,
P. Grenquist, and A. Freemyer; he's checked the Dutch contract for Seth Speaks, *and*
learned that it contained a clause prohibiting cutting. I'm using the memo as a basis
for the letter I intend to start writing Grenquist tomorrow. At the same time I'll be
checking what portions of Seth Speaks *were cut, and listing them.*

(The upshot of all of this at the moment is that Jane will not be signing any
contracts at this time, and that we'll be informing Prentice-Hall that we won't be
contracting for any work for them until our questions and assurances are amply
demonstrated. I see no other way to head off lots of trouble in the future. I'm person-
ally quite willing to let the chips fall where they may, to coin a phrase, but I'm not

at all sure that Jane will agree to go along. My thoughts are that she'd be so terrified to find herself without a publisher that she'd stand for a lot more than what has happened, bad as that is. But we'll see. I for one have to do or say something, or I'd spend my days thinking about what a fool and coward I was not to stand up for my rights. Our meek acceptance of the deal, I'm afraid, would only lead to more of the same. This would surely drive me out of publishing if I let that happen. As it is, my opinion of Prentice-Hall has sunk to a new low, and it was low enough to begin with.

(We didn't ask that Seth discuss the Prentice-Hall affair this evening, but....)

Now: Good evening.

("Good evening, Seth.")

This will be a fairly brief session, but we will begin with your dream about your parents *(on Wednesday morning, October 10).*

In the dream they both stood for completely different attitudes of your own, and here you see them objectified in your separate parents—for you do indeed identify those different tendencies with your parents to a strong extent.

You have, in the dream's meaning, your father who wants to be left alone, who likes to work in solitude, and who is quite uncomfortable with the expression of emotion. You have, in the dream's meaning, your mother given to explosive bursts of emotional expression, who it seems makes emotional demands. In the dream's meaning, she chased after him, and in that context you felt one portion of yourself making demands upon another portion that resented the emotional involvement, the emotional outbursts that <u>that</u> portion naturally expressed.

As yourself, you were the observer of the conflict, which took place at the table where Ruburt's conversations with you took place, and his conversations with Tam over the telephone. Obviously, you want to work in peace: you resent the intrusion of having to take the time to express anger or disappointment.

The dream of course involved your conflicts over *Seth Speaks* in the Dutch edition, and your feeling on the one hand that <u>you</u> must speak out to Prentice, while at the same time resenting the loss of your peace of mind.

My own position cannot be as immediate as your own. I respect your emotional reactions whatever they are, and your right to them. *(Loudly and amused:)* Seth, it seems, speaks a bit more briefly in Dutch than he does in English —but the material is there, and if the Dutch have cut it, or your notes, it is, in the most basic of terms, now, <u>their loss.</u>

(Pause at 9:28.) Agreements of a legal order should, however, always be honored, and each society has been built upon that precept, so you have of course every right to state your objections—but more, to take precautions so that the same kind of situation cannot reoccur.

I do not want to upset you, but if the Dutch may cut a bit here and there, you might find that any French or Spanish translation might add a <u>flourish</u> here or there.

Whenever a book is translated, it is almost impossible, of course, to say the same thing in the same way. Such a book will always be expressed through those invisible national characteristics that are so intimately involved with language—and obviously, were that not so; no book could be understood by someone of a foreign language.

There are bound to be distortions—but the distortions themselves are meaningful. You have, again, a definite right to state your objections, and to change your contract accordingly in the future. You have every right to state your clear objections to Prentice about whatever issue you feel unfair. Regardless of <u>all</u> of that, however, and taking <u>all</u> of that for granted, if you will forgive me *(whispering)*, I sometimes feel that you might perhaps both lack a certain trust *(loudly)* in the nature of your own intents, and in the activity of Framework 2 as far as it concerns you and that publishing house.

In Framework 2, for one thing, the probabilities concerning national economics are known, and your course is indeed being plotted, for your benefit, among multitudinous issues, of which you are not consciously aware. I tell you that such a mechanism does operate. Your characteristics, intents and purposes are taken into consideration, and constant readjustments are also made. You both wanted a year with lower taxes. That was indeed part of your intent, but then when this occurs we only hear cries of woe.

(But not from me, I told Jane the other night. I think that here Seth referred to Jane's and my upset over the small amount of her royalty check this fall, and the way Prentice-Hall has taken to withholding certain percentages of profits against returns.)

If you really <u>understood</u> your own intents and purposes, then you would see how faithfully they were met *(emphatically)*.

In a manner of speaking there is no Prentice, but a group of individuals in certain positions. The creator's feeling toward his creative product—or hers— largely determines its development, its progress, its distribution, and so forth.

(Is Seth saying here that Jane and I actually created, or wanted, the foul up with the Dutch edition? I should have asked, but Jane's delivery was rather fast; nor did I particularly think of it, let alone not being in the mood.)

I really do not want you to think that I am lecturing the both of you. I am only trying to show you how you form the events of your lives.

(Pause at 9:41.) If, hypothetically, either of you believe that Prentice is trying to "screw you up," and if you accept that statement, or belief, then invisibly

you set out to prove it. The evidence comes in. In your society writers need publishing houses. Most publishers are businessmen. They rarely pretend to be themselves creative—yet all publishers, and people who work for them, are also intrigued by the products of creativity, and at least to some degree, being well reimbursed, they do indeed use their quite different abilities to distribute the creative products that they could not themselves initiate. To date, and in the long run, and despite quite legitimate gripes, considering the nature of our books, and your own joint characteristics, Prentice has been a good choice.

They have been conservative in many ways—but neither have they exploited Ruburt's abilities, and neither have they made any attempt to tamper with the message, and some houses would have. They have not flooded the market, which in the long run could be quite detrimental, and in the main they have left you alone.

There are some reincarnational connections involving Tam, but the overall important point is that in its way, Prentice has attempted to maintain the books' integrity, and not made any effort to distort the message, to sensationalize it, as for example the Bantam covers, or to personally exploit Ruburt, yourself, or the situation.

They have not forced interviews upon you, and many houses certainly would try it. They have even, at times, kept the books in print that were selling poorly for a period, though this did not obviously apply to *Seven*.

When either of you say that your purposes and Prentice's merge, or your attitudes merge, you have a tendency to mean that this merging is somehow detrimental—that if you expected more (underlined), Prentice would do more: advertise, or whatever, and that is not the case.

You could stand some more advertising, but high-fired promotional jobs are something else entirely, and would not suit your best interests.

Of course, probabilities always operate, and I am speaking now of the situation as it stands. Prentice has also given Ruburt some considerable freedom, with the exception of *Emir*, to write a variety of different kinds of books—something that some larger corporations might well indeed not do.

If you trust in Framework 2, events will naturally lead to their best fulfillment in publishing, as in anything else. That faith in Framework 2 can indeed work wonders. If you could understand, that faith would be sufficient. The wrinkles in your relationship with Prentice would drop away, or that relationship would naturally and smoothly change into another, if that was the best solution.

(9:56.) A note: Ruburt has felt oddly, since his body has been creatively changing, both the head and eye areas, neck and knees. The knees are beginning

to work more properly, and slowly beginning to mimic and adopt a more natural walking posture. The steps he has taken without putting his full weight on
the table, for example, are highly important. He should look for that impulse
each time he walks with the table.

He will shortly find that some days he can walk fairly easily—perhaps 10
steps—in that manner, or maybe even twice in one day, while for a few days in
between he is not in good-enough balance. I would suggest walking three times
a day now, as he has been doing, but one more time.

The entire body is really being worked upon, with resulting looseness of
tensions that become more apparent at certain points. Both of you try—try
(whispering) to disconnect your creative work from the practical considerations
of contracts, and have Ruburt play with his own book. He will find the results
of such play excellent.

There is an abundance of energy available this evening for several reasons,
and I will help Ruburt's body utilize much of it. Ruburt mentioned your dream
contest. Start it up again. While we are working on our new book you may find
yourselves involved with some new types of dreams.

As for our books—I can only tell you that everything is working for your
favor, and regardless of any seeming conflicts. You might try taking that for
granted.

Do you have any questions?

("No, I guess not.")

I bid you a fond good evening—and everything is working in your favor.

("Okay.")

A fond good evening.

("Thank you, Seth.")

(10:04 PM.)

DELETED SESSION
NOVEMBER 6, 1979 8:56 PM TUESDAY

*(After supper I asked Jane if she'd hold a private session for me, since I felt so
bad. On Saturday, October 27, I'd evidently come down with a "bug" of some kind
—whether physical or psychological, and haven't felt good at all since. At first I'd
thought I was going into a beneficial relaxation episode like that I'd experienced on
April 23, 1979. We'd been working hard, and when I lay down for a nap Saturday
afternoon I felt relaxation effects. "Thank God for relaxation," I told myself again
and again as I fell asleep, hoping the effects would rejuvenate me. But I ended up*

with the cold chills, and for the next week was in often severe pain in the joints and muscles. We'd seen recent notices on TV of a local bug going around, but I didn't know if that was involved or not. The worst part of the whole thing was that I developed urinary difficulties during the malaise: urination became very painful indeed, and I had a strong sense of blockage and impairment at times. I always managed to "go," but it often took a while, and was very uncomfortable.

(We missed last week's sessions, of course, and last night's as well. even though Jane suggested one. My strength was coming back by now, but yet I was too down or disgusted with myself to accent help: that may be the most honest way to put it. The urinary problem still plagued me no end, and tonight the pressure was heavy; hence, I gave in and asked Jane for help.

(During last week Jane told me she'd picked up that my troubles had been set off by the death of Bill Crowder on October 2. Betts didn't write us about the death until we received her letter of the 25th on the 26th—which date being the day before I became ill. I hadn't paid more than normal attention to Bill's death, I thought, beyond feeling sympathy, and speculating with Jane about the money he must have left. Not that we wanted any of it. I hadn't thought his death could bother me that much, for certainly I hadn't dwelled upon it consciously at all.

(All during this time, October–November, we've also been involved in a series of hassles with the foreign publishers Ankh-Hermes and Ariston. We've learned to our sorrow and rage that both entities have cut their versions of Seth Speaks, without our permission or knowledge, and have struggled to exert what force we could in order to rectify the situation. I thought it much more likely that these sorts of challenges were much more likely to be behind my problems. We do feel let down on the issue of foreign rights by Prentice-Hall, and the overseas publishers as well. As I've said to Jane more than once, "I wonder what we ought to know that Tam _hasn't_ told us"—meaning of course that every time a hassle develops with Prentice-Hall we find out a new batch of information that Tam has known all along but never relayed to us. This makes for a series of ugly surprises along the way of our travels with Prentice-Hall, since they always seem to involve money in a negative way, or royalties being withheld, etc.

(We've lost the old sense of freedom we had with Prentice-Hall, where we can just do our work, ship it to them, and expect it to be well handled, with royalties paid every so often and a trust both felt and expressed between the two sides. Now we've become suspicious of everything they tell us. Jane still has on hand the contracts for Mass Events and God of Jane waiting for these to be straightened out: amended with Tam's promised "superamendment" that's supposed to protect us in the rights departments, paperback covers, and all the rest; jacket copy, etc. Prentice-Hall even wanted to have Jane sign contracts giving them the right to take money from Mass

Events *to pay for* God of Jane. *I sometimes have the feeling that we're little more than ciphers to them. I for one am in favor of taking a stand, as Jane well knows, but as I've told her, I don't expect her to go along. I think she'd be too terrified to be without a publisher, if it came to that, whereas my fighting blood is aroused and I'd be perfectly willing to let the chips fall where they may.*

(All of this material is on file in detail. Yesterday Jane confirmed with Tam by phone that we will take full control of foreign rights; not to try to make a lot of money, because we don't think it can be done, but simply to prevent our being taken advantage of by any more foreign publishers. In all probability taking control of foreign rights merely means that there won't be any. I've already written Ariston that we will sell them no more work after their dishonesty with Seth Speaks, *and plan to do the same thing soon with Ankh-Hermes. At the moment we're waiting to learn their reaction to correspondence from Prentice-Hall, demanding that the cut portions of the book be restored—a move I cannot see them complying with for economic reasons alone.*

(Yesterday we learned that P. Grenquist and others from Prentice-Hall met representatives, including the owners, of Ariston at the book fair in Frankfurt— another bit of information Jane and I wouldn't have been told without asking; my present suspicion is that eventually Jane and I will learn that those in charge at Prentice-Hall knew all along that both Ariston and Ankh-Hermes had made changes in Seth Speaks, *with their casual okay. and that we simply weren't informed for whatever reasons. I don't mean to be paranoid about this observation, merely that business is done that way and that the author, once he or she has produced the property to be played with, is relegated to a place much lower on the totem pole of importance.*

(I also think Prentice-Hall will go through the formality of protesting the cuts to the foreign publishers, without exacting much of any retribution, especially with all that money invested in plates. Jane and I will be left with the situation as it exists, then. Except that theoretically at least we'll be able to prevent it happening any more if we control foreign rights from now on. There doesn't appear to be any money worth mentioning involved, at least for us. I always thought the foreign sales were great for the foreign publishers, though, since they owe Prentice-Hall only 6%.

(I am merely making these observations here to get them on the record for possible later reference, and to give some background to my own personal problems of recent days. If I ever do any more extensive writing about the situation, then at least I'll have dated material on file.

(The little I've worked with the pendulum tells me my troubles are rooted in money attitudes, as well as the production time I've lost on Mass Events *for the last two weeks and more. I thought I was doing something by working hard on that book,*

to get it underway in an organized fashion, I told Jane as we sat for the session—so what happened? I added that I wouldn't put up with the kind of hassles involving Prentice-Hall beyond a certain point—that I'd take some kind of drastic action in order to rid myself of the problems connected with dealing with someone I no longer respect. This would involve holding the sessions, but letting Jane herself do any work about producing books for the market. I would go back to painting, try to sell some, and possibly end up with a part-time job for ready money—anything to break the vicious mental pattern of distrust I seem to keep creating. I believe that Jane at last understands that I'm quite capable of reacting that way, that I would refuse to indefinitely put up with our present kind of hassles with Prentice-Hall, or any other entity. I explained that I had such thoughts when we moved to Pinnacle Road, and could easily revive them and try a different kind of life.

(I might add that on the telephone with Tam the day before yesterday I really lit into Tam—rather to his surprise, I think. But I was determined that he understand our feelings—or mine, at least, in no uncertain terms, for as we talked I could feel him start using words to paper over our upset about foreign rights; I felt that his tactics would only make it possible for the whole thing to happen again with succeeding books, and that I was going to short-circuit at once. I believe my reactions, which were loud and clear, paid off, for Tam called Jane yesterday to find out, in his own way, whether I was mad at him personally. Jane said I wasn't, of course—but of course I was.

(So as I write this on Wednesday morning at 11:20 we expect to receive from Tam today a "care package," as he put it, of the latest correspondence involving our foreign hassles. I intend to finish this session today, and make preparations to resume painting each day. I think at the moment that I'll continue to rise early to get three hours in on Mass Events *in the mornings, paint and run errands in the afternoons, and have evenings for either sessions or more work on* Mass Events. *Let's hope things run smoothly enough. As I told Jane last night, there isn't much more we can do about foreign rights; let's hope that challenge has been met.)*

Now: good evening

("Good evening, Seth.")

The latest episode was indeed triggered by Bill Crowder's death—triggered.

Your mother looked up to him because he made money. She held his money up to your father, and in many ways let your father know that she did not think much of him. Overall, as a male or as a breadwinner. To her he fell from an initial high estate—meaning his early success, that offered her the possibilities of wealth and social status. All of this was in the back of your mind. Your early financial success also pleased your mother, and she felt that you had fallen from a high estate, not having lived long enough to see your financial gains.

As she was in life, she would not have understood in any case unless the money definitely came from a recognizable, socially accepted output on <u>your</u> part. <u>To some extent</u>, the affair of Crowder's death made you look at yourself through what you thought were your mother's eyes. You were judging yourself, and have, with some regularity, according to those standards. This is at an emotional level, of which of course you do not intellectually approve.

Crowder, you think, left a large moneyed estate—far more than either you or Ruburt possess. At the same time, you are more than a little contemptuous of what we may gently call the mental culture of Bill Crowder's life and mind. A part of you even thinks "Ma is <u>that</u> what you wanted me to be?"

Of course, you rebelled against such feelings and beliefs, but you did not rid yourself of them. You remembered being in Florida—the tempera episode —when you were supposed to be starting an enterprise with Crowder, and at that particular emotional level it seemed to you that you had made few inroads since —and again, you disapproved.

You have made rather sharp definitive divisions between the artistic world and the business world. Such divisions of course <u>do</u> exist. You have perhaps delineated them with a rather thorough determination, so that the contrasts are brilliantly apparent. I am trying to separate these strands, so bear with me.

In a fashion you see your father as inventive, creative, and highly vulnerable. These ideas merge with conventional beliefs about age, so that it seems you must take stock. But when you take stock with the feelings we are describing as the emotional yardsticks, <u>those</u> feelings consider valid only the beliefs that go along with them—a traditional male role: the accumulation of money through traditional means—and they discount as legitimate the accumulation of knowledge or wisdom as a pursuit of life. Your mother would say "posh."

And particularly they would declare as futile and nonsensical the concentration upon issues or work that does not immediately bring ordinarily recognizable prestige, or a sense of belonging.

(9:20.) Now you are in a position where you see the intersection point where art meets the practical world. That point is the publishing house. With painting it would be the gallery. You do not understand that your own abilities give you a far clearer picture of the "ideal," for example. You have understood that visually you see details that others do not—simply the world at large. In the same fashion, however, you see, say, book jackets, ideal situations, in a way that the people in the business world simply do not—and you do become literally outraged when their vision proves to be so inadequate.

Emotional shoddiness upsets you. When you become enraged at Prentice you are of course enraged against the larger defects of the world—but Prentice's defects are the ones that come of course to your own more immediate attention.

Your approach and Ruburt's are different. Ruburt knows the defects are there. In light of his desire for creativity he simply tries much harder to ignore them than you do, and his drive for communication with others through the books is strong enough, you see, so that like a battleship he drives on.

The issue of money has been important because of the conventional male values, and even with Prentice it seems you are not being a man unless you stand up to them. What you do is less important than what you think of what you are doing. Your painting is important. You should not abandon it—and that is also part of the problem.

(9:28.) Give us a moment.... The issue at Prentice, then, has been charged, not simply because of the errors made there, or abroad, but because of what those errors and stupidities represented to you—their symbolic content.

I am in no way putting the business world down. People in it have their own abilities and drives. As a rule, however, it is foolhardy to expect them to have a sense of the artist's values, whatever the art may be, and then to become upset when they do not live up to that picture.

Now, of course they think of books as products, so it seems to you that they should think in terms of the best products, in the same way that you might think of a best painting—but when you think that way, you are still projecting artistic characteristics where they do not fit.

Most businesses, including Prentice, do not have that kind of vision. Period. As you have said yourself, the people simply want to get through their day's job as quickly and as easily as possible. This does not mean they do not take some pride in their work, but that pride is in direct proportion to the poverty of their vision—so the vision must be yours and Ruburt's. You make such people feel put-upon, bewildered. They do not know what you mean, if you approach them in such a fashion.

There was no ill intent on the part of the Dutch publisher, or the German. They wanted the books to start with because they did indeed respond to the books' vision—but the versions they came out with represented the gap between what they understood and what they could not understand.

Give us a moment.... in a fashion Ruburt and Tam's seemingly emotional, fairly spontaneous relationship has represented good common business sense on Ruburt's part. Regardless of what better deals businesswise you may or may not have made in the past, both of you would have been highly discomfited by any frequent change of publishers. Part of your personal problem now is because you feel you have cut off the easy flow of creative energy into your painting and into *Mass Reality*, and even to some extent—on your part, now—because the contracts are unsigned, and the flow in that area momentarily is somewhat impeded.

Walking is, as you suspect, excellent.

Give us a moment.... Ruburt does not feel that you are amiss because you are not "making money on your own," but he feels deeply your own discontent in that area, and he feels bewildered—for years ago you said so often that it would be great if you could just paint or write without worrying about money. He feels that you are highly dissatisfied. He would do anything that you wanted. You would do far better, however, to think of painting rather than a simple job, which would certainly seem like cutting off your nose to spite your face.

Whenever you cut off your painting, you have difficulties—and that also involves this internal provincial concept of the male image, for you get upset about your painting because it does not bring in money, when a male's pursuit should. At the same time, because of matters discussed before, you will not deal with the galleries. You go back to writing notes for my book because you do think you make some contribution despite yourself, and because you then feel you are financially contributing.

(9:47.) The idea of a simple job attracts you because it separates your ideas of art from money—but in order to content you it could not involve money at all, for even commercial art brings you to the matter of the artistic ideal and its practical presentation.

The male as breadwinner and the male as artist, or the title of the saga is "Bill Crowder may have been stupid, but he fit in with the crowd."

It would be nice if you learned to appreciate your own abilities both as an artist and as a writer *(louder)*. It would be nice if you learned to appreciate your comparative financial freedom, instead of arguing with yourself as to whether or not you deserve it, or whether or not you are a good male if you accept it.

A good artist, of course, who was free of such nonsense, would accept it gladly without a qualm.

Give us a moment.... You must realize that I make considerable effort to understand your social mores, and your reactions to them even while I try to clear your minds of them. Much of this, then, is crystal clear to me, but do not put yourselves down because of their effects upon you, I do not have them to contend with.

First of all, you understand my message in theoretical terms, but then of course all of that must dribble down into your lives until it becomes more and more practical.

(Long pause at 9:55.) I do not want to define for you an ideal picture to which you can never live up. That is, I do not want your practical experience of life to seem inferior as you are in the process of learning how to live in a new fashion. The patterns of give-and-take between you and others are actually very simple to describe and delicate at a certain level of activity. There is some material of course that I have not given, though I will, because it would seem to you initially that in the light of what is possible, you were doing poorly—where instead in the light of your reality at this time, you are doing well. You must realize that you are judging your behavior by standards that are very high indeed, and that you are in a situation in which, say, all of the facts are not yet in. You have been geared to disapprove of yourselves, you have been taught to judge your performance in a very shallow fashion, according to social mores and sexual affiliation, and when you are breaking out of those patterns, you may indeed feel betwixt and between.

Divide your time between *Mass Reality* if you want to and your painting. It does not matter which of you handles the business end, as long as you have as much peace of mind as possible, and as long as you judge events as clearly as possible, according to their actual proportion as apart from their emotionally charged symbolic content.

I would actually of course never tell you to get a job or not—nor would I be perturbed at any decisions you might make. Personally, however, if I might be so bold, I would think that any such time might better be put to use in painting, if I were a painter.

I would give some thought then to my self-image, and to the image of an individual who is highly gifted as a painter, as a writer, as a thinker, and I would endeavor to loosen myself from any bonds that prevented me from using those abilities—in particular any sexual ones that defined my identity in terms of money alone.

I would try to be content with the self that I am, and rejoice in my uniqueness, and tell myself that my energy could flow freely in all areas of my life, and the physical problem will then easily clear itself.

Being a male does not cause problems. Limited concepts about maleness do.

Do you have questions?

("No, not unless you want to say something about Jane.")

Ruburt has done fairly well throughout all of this—fairly well. He found he could do much more than both of you thought when he had to, and you can encourage him to tell you about more, for sometimes he feels in your way.

His understanding is growing by leaps and bounds, but it is highly important that you both get back to what you think of as important—your work, which should also be your play, and also to your love-making. And in that area, you should also forget any idea of sex roles in conventional terms.

That area has also suffered because of your joint ideas of what artists should be like, and what men and women who happen to be artists should be like. Think that one over. That <u>emotional</u> flow is important.

Now I bid you a fond good evening.

("Thank you, Seth.")

(With a smile:) Do not take life so hard, either of you.

("Good night.")

(10:10 PM.)

DELETED SESSION
NOVEMBER 12, 1979 8:49 PM MONDAY

(I felt somewhat better this evening, although I still haven't recovered fully from the "illness" I began experiencing on October 27. The last session, for November 6, has helped me considerably, and I reread it each morning. I've also resumed painting on a daily basis. I planned to resume work on Mass Events *this week, but haven't done so yet. At the moment I paint in the mornings, with an absolute trust growing out of the last session plus what I know and feel about Framework 2, and that's it. I trust the rest will come. In the meantime I rake leaves in the early afternoon, write letters, and so forth. Right now I feel as far away from* Mass Events *as I did from painting when I wasn't doing that.*

(As I said to Jane yesterday, now that I'm back painting it seems incredible that I ever left it—even though when I chose to concentrate upon Mass Events *this summer I thought that was a good decision also. I still don't see anything wrong with the decision, but evidently my body—my psyche—rather violently disagreed, considering the beliefs I must carry around with me.*

(Jane said that she'd felt like having a session several times recently, but that obviously I didn't since I'd fall asleep on the couch, and so forth. But tonight, when we wanted to have one to get back on the ball, she said she didn't have any feeling for a session at all.

(Yet finally, as she talked about it, Seth came through—and earlier than usual:)

Now: the man who wrote *Alice in Wonderland* was, I believe, a mathematician of note in his time.

(Lewis Carroll [pseudonym of Charles Lutwidge Dodgson] 1832-98; English

writer and mathematician; author of Alice's Adventures in Wonderland.

(Pause.) He considered himself to be excellent at his work. It gave him a professional respectability, a feeling of worth and merit. He found it—his occupation—to be a responsible one, befitting an adult. The occupation filled many of his needs and expressed some of his abilities. In his spare time, however, for a lark, simply because he wanted to, he wrote his *Alice in Wonderland*—a book that is a masterpiece at many levels. What a shock when he discovered that the world was ignoring what he thought to be his important contribution to mathematics. He believed (underlined) that he should devote all of his time to his work, and could hardly forgive himself for his regrettable lapses into writing—and he was writing, after all, not even for adults, and not for young males either.

He was, in a fashion only, sexually ambiguous, his mathematics expressing what he thought of as an acceptable male aspect while the artistic levels in his mind, now, he related to his feminine aspects. So he was to some extent a divided man. His creativity showed itself, however, when he allowed himself to play, when he forgot what he thought he should do, and did what he wanted to do.

(Pause.) Because of his beliefs he considered himself somewhat of a failure, and the rich, evocative nature of his own stories did not meet with the approval of his academically attuned mind. Despite himself, however, he was stretching the dimensions of his own consciousness, exercising his consciousness in different directions, expanding the scope of his abilities—and in so doing contributing a small masterpiece to the world.

(9:00.) I want here to stress the basic playful exercising aspects of creativity. When a child indulges in physical play, it exercises its muscles and its entire body. No one has to tell a child to play, for playing comes naturally. Playful games in childhood, not dictated by teachers or parents, often give clear indications of a child's abilities and leanings. You can sense by watching a child's play the future shape that his or her life can most productively take. The child does not consciously exercise his or her legs so that they will be strong, but simply joyfully follows the inner impulse to do so.

All children exercise, though relatively few end up, say, as specialists in sports, so the end result of such physical play is the future development of a healthy, strong body. The end result, then, is not a product, but a more completed kind of being.

Now: creativity is basically a mental proposition, a mental or psychic activity. It is also, like physical exercise, an energizing phenomena, one that expands and extends the mental and psychic properties as surely as physical exercise develops the body's being. *(Pause.)* What you are dealing with, then, in creativity is a continuing kind of psychic play, an activity that probes into the nature of inner reality and explores it with as much sheer vitality as that with which the child explores physical reality. The child runs, falls down, skips, spins, climbs, swings, tries out its body in as many ways as possible, and naturally explores the body's relationship with its environment. Then the child explores the environment itself.

Beside this, the child, almost from its first moment of clear awareness, begins to play with its own consciousness, and in the same fashion. What can its thoughts do? Where can its thoughts go? Where do its thoughts go? How long can it hold a thought? And later—can a thought be held mentally as an object can be physically? Long before a child learns to place one playblock on top of another, it has already learned to mentally stack one thought upon another, so to speak.

(9:15.) It learns that in a fashion sounds are "stacked" inside the mind before, say, words are spoken. (Pause.) That kind of mental and psychic expansion in one way or another constantly occurs. In conventional art you end up with a product on many such occasions—a book or painting or whatever—as you attempt to define in physical terms the reality of an inner existence with which you have always been familiar, and to leave in physical reality some evidence, however slight, of inner visions that flicker within all consciousness.

(Pause.) The creative product is a remnant, then, a glowing fragment of a larger sensed whole.

(Long pause.) As a child, with no preconceived ideas in normal terms, you drew and wrote stories. Ruburt wrote stories or poems, and drew. The natural impulses were allowed their free play. Later you believed that artists should be artists. The concentration in painting should be so intense—should be—that there would be no thought of any other occupation. The concerns of the world, its progress or lack of it, the nature of existence—none of those issues would interfere with such an artistic vision.

As in the case of Cézanne, masterpieces would justify all else. Even relationships would make no difference—and Ruburt in his way made the same judgments about the "writer."

Cézanne, as you know, was not a happy man. He could have been a far better artist still, for if his vision was intense, my dear friend, it was cramped, and it moved within itself in an agony to find a creative release that could never be found in the creative product alone, but in the psyche from which that product emerges.

(Jane spoke very intently in trance. Seth's material on Cézanne was excellent.)
You are aware of the nonsense connected with artists and poets and so

forth—that they are too sensitive for the world, that great talent brings spiritual <u>desolation</u>, and that a man's genius more often destroys him than fulfills him. Add to that list the belief that the great artist or writer concentrates upon his or her art so intensely and single-mindedly, and single-heartedly, that the focus itself forces the artist or poet to use those abilities to their utmost, or that great genius demands one-sided vision and a denial of the world.

An artist or writer, believing such selective nonsense, will of course find all of his or her other creative abilities a distraction, a bother, a temptation that is bound to detract from the main genius, rather than add to it, deepen its application, and add an orchestration to its subjective moods that would otherwise be quite lacking *(all intently)*.

Leonardo da Vinci and Michelangelo, for example, would have gone out of their minds, acting as it seems people sometimes believe that an artist should act. Their stories have been greatly romanticized to fit the picture, if you will forgive the pun.

They often worked by choice with a multitude of workmen, apprentices, students, hangers-on and whatever. For all of Michelangelo's ranting, he found great zest in the political tumult of his time, in which he was of course quite intimately involved. He played church and state against each other, made an ass of the Pope whenever he could, and was deeply involved in the social, political, and religious fervor of those days.

That applies even more of course to Da Vinci, who was a social dilettante besides, but a man of incredible vision—a psychic if you prefer, who invented in his mind gadgets that would not physically come into your world for centuries.

Those sketches of his, it seems, do not stand up as creative products as a great sculpture might, but they stand for a truly creative originality in which a consciousness played with internal material, and projected outward many of the material properties that then simply did not exist. Much of his art in those terms did not show, but the art of his consciousness expanded beyond Michelangelo's.

None of your abilities contradict each other, or oppose each other, or minimize each other, or in any way negate any of your probable accomplishments. They are meant to be creatively stacked, not just to be combined for example in conventional terms, but the abilities naturally <u>are</u> psychically merged. They mean that your own consciousness, as you think of it, has a slant, a potential, a rich combination a peculiar savored blend that is meant to be its own creative brew *(very intently)*.

The creative products are important. They are physical landmarks of psychic and artistic inner journeys, but what you do with your consciousness, how you extend it, is even more important, for as physical play is meant to lead to a future physical body that is mature and fulfilled, so the creative nature of that kind of inner play leads to future extended consciousness, an inner being that is the mature version of an earlier self.

You get what you concentrate upon.

(9:44.) Are you tired?

("No.")

The inner creative man knows, as the child did, that the way will be cleared. There was Miss Bowman, there was art school and so forth—so I want you to remember that inner man. Social beliefs, beliefs from childhood or whatever <u>are</u> (underlined) overlays. They <u>are</u> superficial. They have unfortunate effects only when you do not trust the inner self.

When you do, your behavior is actually self-correcting, and if you understand that you will see that some behavior that <u>appears</u> contradictory is instead quite simply creative corrective activity. When you do not understand that, then you can become bewildered, thinking "Why did such-and-such work last week and not this week?"

Sometimes the advice I give you at any given time is meant to take the place of natural creative corrective behavior that ideally you would have taken on your own, but did not.

As long as you feel, for example, that there is a conflict between your writing and your painting, <u>then</u> (underlined) you must somehow or other give each an equal-enough play, or you become upset. After your bout *(of illness)* I therefore suggested you go back to painting—which is important to you, and it is quite true that when you do not paint for a while you feel uneasy, and psychically out of balance. The feeling of competition between the two abilities operates in the other fashion, of course, so that if you have not been writing you feel the same unease.

(Long pause.) You cannot separate the elements of a psyche, approving of some abilities and not others, putting some in competition with others, without experiencing difficulties. The very nature of your painting <u>is</u>, and must be, determined by the quality of your mind, which is inquiring, which refuses to be cramped, which piles questions upon questions, while you think that the artist should ideally ask no questions at all.

If you would try to see your own creative unity, then both your painting and your writing would give greater satisfaction, and become richer—your prose inspired by your imagery, and your painting by your ideas, so that both are sparked, producing not only products but a creative vision that sees reality through an extension that would be the natural art of consciousness, meant to blossom from those abilities.

(9:59.) Think of yourself as a creative consciousness, capable of both a detailed and an extended, both a visual and a thoughtful, merged focus.

When you are writing your mind is also playing with images. When you are painting your mind is also building ideas. Forget the old idea of exclusive expression.

Now: Ruburt's list is an excellent idea, and so is the note on the refrigerator. Remind him to walk at least twice daily, and to add to that when possible. Have him forget his ideas of the exclusive expression of creativity, mental or physical. His body is responding, and very well. Encourage his reception of relaxation. He is also being creative when he is relaxed.

This session should be of excellent use, really, to both of you—and remembering the playful nature of creativity will help Ruburt get back to his book. He does that by forgetting the book, and playing with the ideas that it contains.

You "were" right, then, when you worked on the book before your bout, and during that time you trusted yourself—but then your ideas of the comparative nature of your ideas intruded, triggered at that time by *(news of)* Crowder's death, and the ensuing beliefs about the male role in society, and as that applied to your own talents. Left alone, ideally, you might have taken a week of joyful painting, during which time your mind refreshed itself, and new ideas about your notes accumulated. Telling you—or rather suggesting—that you paint simply put you on that course. Do you follow me?

("Yes.")

But the conflicts can dissolve in a synthesis of understanding, in which case the problems do indeed vanish. End of session. You are free, then, to do as you prefer, if you realize that. I bid you a fond and hearty good evening.

("Thank you very much, Seth. Good night.")

(10:11 PM. Jane hadn't felt like having the session, but had done excellently. I doubt if I've ever heard Seth do better. I think that already the material has helped. "I'm so glad," she said. "I didn't have a thing in my head.")

DELETED SESSION
NOVEMBER 21, 1979 8:59 PM WEDNESDAY

(This is the first session held since the deleted one for November 12. I am feeling quite a bit better; I've been painting in the mornings and working in the yard

afternoons, doing errands, etc. The only thing that's suffered has been work on Mass Events, *but now I'm gradually moving back into that endeavor also.*

(Last Monday evening Jane had been so relaxed that she'd passed up the session. I thought she'd felt somewhat the same way today, and was rather surprised when she told me at 8:30 PM that she'd have the session....

(Whispering:) Good evening.

("Good evening, Seth.")

Now: a discourse on Frameworks 1 and 2, bank accounts, and psychic collateral.

Today you changed a bank account over from an ordinary savings account to what you might call a super-account, where the very same amount of money will give you approximately twice as much interest.

All that was involved, as you told Ruburt, was a shuffling of paper from here to there, and a promise to keep the money in the account and not withdraw it for a specific amount of time. Definitely in your circumstances, the second account is far preferable to the first.

(Again Seth surprised me. I hadn't expected him to use our bank accounts as analogies, but saw at once what he was up to. He referred to my changing my own account last Monday and Jane's today, to the purchase of six-month treasury certificates.

(Pause.) In the first place, however, even the ordinary account is to some extent different from the savings accounts of many other people. The money did not come by computing the number of hours worked on a project, for example, or the number of hours worked at a job, but instead accumulated because of the quality of creative work and the inquisitiveness of the creative mind. To some extent that money came because you trusted that it would.

It was, however, in a normal savings account, where it drew regular but rather small amounts of interest. Now with today's adventure, and a brief previous one, all of a sudden it seems the picture has vastly improved. Again, the interest on the same amount of money nearly doubles. You cannot draw it out, however, until a specified date.

Now we will call the ordinary savings account the usual rewards of Framework 1, for an analogy, of course. I must remind you again, however, that in the overall your activities are not all confined to that framework because of your creative interests and your personalities. Otherwise you would be drawing salaries.

In Framework 1 you receive certain rewards for ordinary endeavors. Most people can count upon what these are, if they are lucky: steady jobs—though these may be boring and have other disadvantages—a conventional social life, a family and so forth.

You share Framework 1 activity with others, for that world largely surrounds you, but remember, I am speaking in analogies to make certain points, for every person's life has its Framework-2 orientations. Your creative endeavors have brought you good rewards *(long pause)* in more areas than you realize, but part of your account was in an ordinary savings structure so that you were, in those areas, somewhat restricted—and restricted by Framework 1's largely trial-and-error framework.

(9:15.) The changing-over of your accounts physically means that you, Joseph, in particular came to an important constructive change of mind. You were changing from old attitudes to ones that would allow you to enjoy financial abundance, without feeling guilty on the one hand, or resentful on the other; to a concentration upon abundance rather that what money the government might take away from you.

Now: How do you get what you want out of Framework 2? You do it by changing over your accounts in whatever areas you are concerned, from the old savings account to the super-account with its nearly double rewards for the same effort. You do not watch for results. You give yourselves, say, six months, and you promise not to withdraw the issue from Framework 2's account in the meantime. You withdraw the account by worrying about it. You withdraw the account by trying to exert more effort in Framework 1, instead of letting the account take care of itself.

Now: You still have some money in a regular savings account, and that is handy for simple day-to-day expenses, so of course you always have some effort to expend in Framework 1, and some experience with its normal trial-and-error tactics. You would think that it was rather fruitless, now that you have changed over your accounts, to spend any time worrying about all the money in the past still in the old savings account that did not get the superlative interest that these new accounts will enjoy.

You were not secure enough then to make the step, and the old accounts certainly did serve their purposes. Besides having money left over and saved, you did (underlined) get some extra rewards, if not those that your accounts now receive.

So, when you change one *(smiling)* certain area of your lives into Framework 2's account, you do not spend any time worrying about the relatively little interest you received before. It is all a matter of changing your focus in certain areas.

(9:26.) Now Ruburt is healthy. He is not as healthy as he would like to be, because his physical mobility is impaired. He does enjoy many of the most nec-

essary elements of health, but he would like a higher interest, greater rewards in terms of health. He does this by mentally changing over his account *(emphatically)* from Framework 1, where he is indeed improving through effort, trial and error and determination—but improving at a far slower rate than he would like.

He changes his health account to Framework 2, where he need expend no more effort than he is now, but the results, or the interest, will be far <u>more</u> than doubled. He gives himself a time period during which he will not check the account. He will not worry in the meantime about how the results are to be accumulated. He will trust the account.

He will not worry, either, about the comparatively lesser interest or regards he received in the past. He will feel that the account is changed over.

Now: *(Louder:)* The same applies to your dealings with Prentice.

Those feelings must be changed, for they will otherwise apply even if you changed publishers. You must change over that account now. You do this in the same manner that I have just given for Ruburt's condition. You mentally change your account with Prentice from Framework 1 trial-and-error, a framework which has brought you some good rewards, but not as good interest as you would like. You do not concentrate upon the old, comparatively lesser returns, but you consider the account turned over, where for the same amount of effort your rewards will be far more than doubled.

When either of you concentrates upon your dissatisfactions with Prentice, or number its particular failings, or picture covers you did not like, or whatever, it is like Ruburt concentrating upon his symptoms. It holds you back.

You do not know what exact financial manipulations will happen to give you your greater interest in your new bank accounts. You simply know the interest will come—because you trust the banking establishment and the country's intrinsic worth, so you need not wonder or worry about what artistic or editorial or legal or economic facts might be involved to bring about the higher interest that you want from Prentice, because you trust the higher establishment of Framework 2—which holds <u>all</u> accounts.

Ruburt is doing well. The book of love poetry is an excellent idea. You should still help him to trust relaxation, but I want both of you to take this session to heart, so that it can help you accelerate your growing understanding, and bring you more beneficial practical results.

Do you have questions?

("No, I guess not."

(Actually, I took a moment or two to toy with the idea of asking Seth to comment upon the affair in Iran with the 49 American hostages being held at the American embassy. The whole thing seems to me to be a symbolic turning point in

world history, full of danger in the terms of Framework 1. To me, all the parties involved in the dispute seem helpless and frightened; it echoes similar conscious-mind threats that I think the species has created for itself throughout recorded history.)

<u>Trust</u> your impulses, and underscore that line three times, for again they represent your close connection to Framework 2's activity. End of session.

("Okay. Thank you.")

Visualize, the both of you, changing over those accounts.

(9:42 PM. At first thought I didn't know what to make of the session, which I suppose merely reflects my own indecisive state of mind about the hassle with foreign publishers, Prentice-Hall, money, art, writing, and so forth. All the details about the foreign rights fiasco are on file, so there's no need to recount them here, except to say that Tam, serving as liaison for us with Ariston and Ankh-Hermes, has failed, as far as we know at this writing, to elicit any response from anyone at either place. Just what I expected, I told Jane, and added that it looked like we would end up stuck with mangled work distributed in Europe.

(As far as changing our mental accounts re Prentice, I don't know whether I can bring myself to do that or not, especially after the foreign mess. Tam visits next week, so we may learn more, but at the moment I don't expect any miraculous results. Seth's analogy with the bank accounts and Frameworks 1 and 2 is an excellent one, of course, and in theory at least I agree with it completely.

(I haven't had a chance to talk it over with Jane yet—not until I get this session typed—but I'd like Seth to talk about the part <u>others</u> play when we, for example, do change over our accounts. That is, I need information on how <u>our</u> changeovers will affect others, perhaps leading them to alter habitual patterns of thought and operation so that <u>we</u> get what <u>we</u> want. But what about what <u>they</u> want or are used to? I want to know about resistances that may operate, and refusals to cooperate, even on subconscious levels. I don't see simply Jane's and my wishes having the power to change the behavior of other groups of people to that degree, I guess—unless our change of thought shifts all else into another probability.)

DELETED SESSION
NOVEMBER 26, 1979 8:55 PM MONDAY

(Once again Jane was quite relaxed, but she wanted to have the session anyhow. "Bleary as usual," she said. "I've been so out of it the past week...."

(I was feeling somewhat better, but wasn't clear as I wanted to be yet. I had a few questions I wanted to ask Seth if I got the chance, but hadn't talked them over with Jane before the session. We'd celebrated Thanksgiving last Thursday with our first turkey in two years.

(For the moment I'd forgotten the notes I wrote concluding the last session, deleted for November 12, having to do with Seth suggesting we throw our hassles with Prentice and foreign publishers into Framework 2; I'd written that I didn't know whether or not I was capable of doing that at this time. But the questions I'd posed in those notes furnished the background for tonight's session, somewhat to my surprise.

(Softly:) Good evening.

("Good evening, Seth.")

Now. *(Pause.)* Your questions about the operation of Framework 2 seem certainly to be simple, straight-forward questions, answerable in three or four or five pithy paragraphs *(with humor)*—and of course I will try to give you a straight-forward reply.

Behind your questions, however, there lies a vast area of unasked questions that we have barely touched upon. In dealing with Frameworks 1 and 2 alone, I have been simplifying, and those frameworks in a way <u>represent</u> (underlined) dimensions of events. How events happen is perhaps one of the greatest "mysteries" that you will encounter in physical life. Often I do need analogies, for to me that simultaneous, creative, cooperative nature of events exists with a sublime simplicity—a simplicity I am afraid that of necessity becomes complex as I try to describe it in terms that will make sense in your space-time framework.

(Pause.) All of our analogies taken together, you see, only hint at the true picture, but if I cannot describe clearly to you in your terms the interaction between Framework 1 and 2, then we will have difficulty with other later material. So we will try again this way.

Begin with the idea of a book. That idea alone instantly mobilizes, say, Ruburt's abilities, and the same applies to any writer. There is only one person involved. The same applies to an artist, so for simplicity's sake we will start with a single creative event—the idea the writer or artist has already geared himself, through training and practice, through intent and expectation, to receive to begin with.

Without consciously knowing how his body performs such manipulations, he trusts it—the hands to hold the brush, the fingers to type or whatever, and the idea becomes reality. The idea comes from Framework 2, and Framework 2's activity fuels the body's actions.

Now: We want to publish the book—and I will here continue, for our purposes, dealing with a book's production rather than a painting's. Still, however, we will keep the idea of a painting for a different reason. Now think of the book's production and everything connected with it as being part of the same kind of creative activity, but in an arena where events as you think of them become the medium. It is as if—forgive the crossing analogies—the production of the book *(pause)* is transferred to another level. A living peoplescape in which each person who plays a part in that book's production now joins the creative act at this secondary level as far as you are concerned.

This is <u>their</u> primary level, however, for it is when they enter the picture. Certain things at this point are already set, say: you already have a publishing house, and particular people are involved whether or not you know them. Again, I am fitting the discussion to your specifications *(with an amused whisper)*.

Your reality, and the reality of those people, exists primarily in Framework 2. Already in Framework 2 decisions <u>beyond</u> number have occurred, computations beyond number have been made, resulting in this particular reference frame of probabilities existing at the time. In one way or another, there are connections uniting everyone involved in such processes. There are reasons beyond business that make the people at Prentice involved with books rather than, say, toy manufacturing, or other even more profitable ventures.

(9:19.) The artistic acts always directly involve strong direct interactions with Framework 2. In the production of our book we want, say, people we may not even know to come together in certain fashions to make certain decisions that will be in direct agreement with our own creative intent. They each have their own lives and their own interests and intents, their own problems. We cannot move them around like toy people on a game board. When you continue to think of events—and publishing is one—as multidimensional creativity, involving many people instead of one, then you have some leverage to help you understand. In Framework 2 each person is connected to each other person. I have given you a good deal of material explaining how information is communicated both on a cellular basis and on a mental one—how it is communicated through the dream state, and I have explained the importance of impulses as direct nudges from Framework 2.

(Pause.) This is still very difficult to verbalize. *(Pause.)* The main, driving, clear, emotional intent in such a project is the author's. The book is his baby. Remember, we are dealing with emotional intensities—and it is because of emotional intensities that our books are in so many homes. That intensity has its own force and vitality.

(A note: I think Seth inserted his remark about the books being in so many

homes because our mail has rather strikingly reminded us lately of that fact; we've been talking about it.)

Ideally that force is to a large extent self-protecting. It is also perceived to whatever degree possible (underlined) by all those at Prentice who are involved. At Framework-2 levels those people want to produce an excellent book. Their desire is not as vigorous as yours. It is watered down by far more Framework 1 activity. There is much "static" at that level.

Now: When you concentrate mainly (underlined) in Framework 1 and its communications with Prentice, then while overall you do achieve results of a beneficial nature—the publication and distribution of the books in a largely adequate form—there are glaring discrepancies also: entanglements that you do not like because you have taken your intent from Framework 2, where the creative event began, and placed it into Framework 1's communication system almost entirely. Obviously you need Framework 1, with its letters, telephone calls, and so forth—but Framework 1's communication system, while physically handy, also is somewhat like a very poor telephone connection, with static at both ends.

You reach each person you want separately. You must make your message clear regardless of the other person's needs or circumstances, intents of the moment, and so forth. The more harassed you become, the more the static increases at both ends.

Now: Framework 2's communications system is set into motion as a primary rather than as a backup system of communications. When you learn to cut through the static—if you trust the system of communication—this is how it works.

(9:38.) First of all, you clear your wires by trying to clear your mind, and simply by trying to understand how Framework 2 works. You think of, say, any event in a book's production, distribution, translation or whatever, as the kind of multidimensional creative effort and event I have tried to explain. All of those other people are connected to that event in Framework 2 on a nonphysical level, as they are connected on a physical level. Framework 2's communication system is at once simpler and more complex that Framework 1's. Just as, say, your intent to paint a picture automatically has your fingers all moving in the proper directions, and your body manipulating properly, so that the desired painting results, so in a larger fashion your clear intent is communicated to each of the people involved—at a level without static—yours or theirs.

They do not then move as faithfully as your fingers, following your own intent, not theirs, but everyone involved cooperatively agrees to aid that creative venture—not only because you want it, you see, but because for their own reasons they are involved in book publishing and want to play a part in that kind of activity.

You set a far more favorable group of probabilities into motion, a group that aids you and them as well, for they are also seeking creativity from their separate viewpoints. They are also fighting their own static. You do not have to contact them one by one in Framework 2. The book itself is like a magnet—any book. The same kinds of reactions, however, are involved in all activities, and it is sometimes frustrating for me that you cannot perceive the fascinating facets of any event. All group interactions of course are involved here. *(Pause.)* You still —and I do not simply mean you two alone—do not feel the unsurpassable force that thoughts have. You do not understand that they do form events, that to change events you must first change thoughts. You get what you concentrate upon. To brood or worry, or become resentful, is as regrettable as it would be if you, say, painted a big X over one of your paintings because you were dissatisfied with a detail or two. Over a period of time, resentments X out large areas of otherwise productive experience.

(9:50.) Give us a moment.... When you have fearful thoughts about a book—or worse, about a future book—then you feed other people's static. You increase to some extent their doubts as well as your own. Your thoughts have reality, but behind that statement is the apparently unrecognizable truth that your physical world is the exteriorization of your thoughts.

Mankind's most majestic experiences, and his most unfortunate, still come from that same great creative force. I have been very careful in my use of the word love, because it is so bandied about and distorted—but all creativity, and any work of art, and any life, springs from love—a love that automatically brings all things into their own kinds of order. The artist paints because he loves to. His brain and fingers are able to produce a painting because they are themselves formed of love.

I am not speaking of some cold, idealized love, but of infinite, intimate expressions of it that help compose any physical form. That is the basis of existence.

I have one other point to mention, apropos: our session regarding the two men *(see the deleted session, for me, of April 18, 1979)*. You get in trouble only when you identify too strongly with the socially inoculated man, so that you can say "With <u>my</u> beliefs, I do not think I can learn to put Prentice in Framework 2." *(See my closing notes for the last deleted session.)* The "my" there, in that sentence, refers to the socially inoculated man. The other man has no difficulties at all in that regard, and that man is you, too. You could at least ask his opinion.

("Well, I reread that session often." Nearly every day, I might have added.)

That is why I add this to that material.

I want you both to remember that you are learning a new kind of orientation, and ideas directly opposed to those with which you were "inoculated"—so do not blame yourselves for inadequacies. Do not disapprove of yourselves. Do not compare yourselves to what you <u>think</u> you should do or be.

("I was going to ask about why I had those problems with the urinary tract when I got sick earlier this month. They're better now, but they're not cleared up completely yet."

(Earlier in the month I'd grown so disgusted with the whole business that I'd resolved not to bother asking Seth for help—then before tonight's session I'd spontaneously had the idea that I <u>would</u> ask if I got the chance. I reread daily many of the private sessions he's given for us in the last year or two—especially those in Book 20. A number of those deal with my challenges involving the side, groin, taxes, and so forth. I seem to be a slow learner; either that or my accumulated resentments seem to be so deeply ingrained that I should work much harder at eradicating old beliefs.)

In a capsule: Self-disapproval.

(Pause.) In a capsule, comparing yourself to what you think you should be, and largely because of troubles with communication. You wanted to communicate love of our work, and instead you felt that you could only communicate resentment at what you felt had been done to it. You felt like a victim.

The session should help you understand that you are not a victim. There is much more, however, about the interactions of people in such events. I hope to make it all as clear as I can, because I want you to understand the nature of events, and your participation in them, and that of others.

If you want, make a list of questions that you want to ask. Remember, however, to <u>concentrate</u> now upon, say, Prentice's failings are an exercise in negative meditation, in negative suggestion, so try, each of you, to avoid that. This session can help, particularly if you make comparisons yourselves along these lines between the private creative event and the mass one. Do you have questions?

("Well, I guess I'll wait.")

And in all cases, your main concentration should always be upon your daily accomplishments, joys, the domestic meal, the hour of dawn or twilight or whatever. That is highly important, for concentration upon negative experiences helped make you ill.

("I was wondering why I picked on the urinary tract.")

I have given some material on that before, and it all applies, as given, to contradictions in your own beliefs between the male as breadwinner and the male as artist. There are, I believe, several sessions dealing with that.

("I reread them too." In book 20.)

In this case there was also the belief that there was a lack in the flow of communication, a blockage in the flow of creativity, so tell yourself that your creative ventures can flow through you easily and well. When you are upset, ask the creative man what he thinks. End of session and a fond good evening.

(*"Thank you, Seth. Good night."*

(*10:10. "I had a funny feeling before the session," Jane said. "That it was one of those times when he had to dribble the material down to me word by word. It made me feel real impatient—not on his part but my own. I also had the feeling that there are about five frameworks out there, but that everything has to come down to us through Framework 1 before we can understand it."*

(*We've been talking about Frameworks 1 through 4 in recent days because of my notes for* Mass Events. *I felt somewhat relieved after the session. Seth had confirmed my own opinions, yet I fully acknowledge that I had been worrying about physical hassles for some time, and sometimes wondered whether I was right or should seek medical help.*)

SESSION 886 (DELETED PORTION)
DECEMBER 3, 1979   9:20 PM MONDAY

(*Last April 18 Seth gave a private session for me that for the past several months I've been rereading almost daily. It contains some excellent material, and it seems that just recently, especially with all the fuss about foreign publishers, I've just begin to really put it to fruitful use. In the session Seth postulates two men, both portions of myself, who represents the conflicting sets of beliefs I've carried for years. The first man is my primary self, who discovers that he must bear the burdens of the second man imposed upon him through cultural beliefs involving taxes, success, the male breadwinner role, and so forth.*

(*With all of the recent hassles involving family visits, publishers, and so forth, I've begun keeping that session in mind often. Now whenever I sense a conflict arising, I do as I'd figured out—and as Seth himself suggested recently: I ask the advice of the first man; what would he do in these situations? Usually the answer, in the vernacular, is short and sweet, as they say: The hell with it. This means that I sidetrack —but not try to repress—those cultural and learned beliefs I've let rule my life in large measure, instead of following the natural, creative dictates of my first, or primary man. I should give him a name.*

(*Anyhow, as I've explained to Jane lately, the method seems to be working fairly well, and I expect more success with it once I become accustomed to dealing with it. The idea, of course, is only to integrate the two often opposing points of view,*

instead of having them in conflict with each other, since, as Seth says, we always have
some practical need of Framework 1 activity. But now I'm turning more and more
toward Framework 2, making a try at placing my faith and need for solutions there
where they can generate their own, seemingly without effort. The result of this activ-
ity is that I find myself focusing on a few things I think really important: Writing,
painting, my love for Jane, the sessions, the house, the cats, etc. Even large portions of
these activities I now try to relegate to Framework 2's tender ministrations. It appears
to be working well. It's an amazingly simple luxury to consider a problem or chal-
lenge, then say the hell with it and throw it into Framework 2. It is, of course, rem-
iniscent of our behavior right after we first learned about the frameworks, and as I
remember it worked very well. I hope to revive those early successes, and to make
much more practical use of them this time.

(My own activities, then, have aroused in Jane the urge to try the same
approach, and I've suggested she think of her own women numbers 1 and 2. It seems
that she confronts the same basic challenges I do, I told her, so she could delineate the
two opposing portions of her personality well enough to understand that many of her
cultural beliefs have been imposed upon her natural, spontaneous, free, creative self,
and to such an extent that the acquired beliefs have turned into detriments rather
than aids, that she envisioned as helping her obtain what she wants in life. She want-
ed some material on the whole business tonight from Seth. She's also told me that just
this weekend has she realized that she really didn't want to walk, as "long as it did-
n't hurt too much not to." An important insight that she can use to help free herself....

(The following material is from the 886th session.
(10:13.) End of dictation. Give us a moment.

Personal, now: both of you know all that—that is, the material I have just
delivered.

In one way or another, your creative abilities have always sustained you, at
least with subconscious knowledge, and with a sense of the greater creative
capacities always present within you. *(Long pause.)* You have always sensed more
than you knew, both of you, so in that area Framework 2 has represented a natural affiliation with your conscious selves. You were creatively filled out by it.

You knew you were an artist, whether you sold or not, or whatever you
did. You knew you were an artist. Your impulses led you to paint. They led you
to write, also. They led you to fill out your creative self, to open new doors.

Ruburt in his way felt in the same fashion. You both felt sure of yourselves,
in that regard. In that regard. After that, Ruburt felt that he must protect his
ability, guarding it against the world, and even against any other tendencies that
he felt might run counter to his ability.

He wanted to protect himself against the "artistic temperament" as it is conventionally understood. He thought that body and mind were two different things, that the body must be controlled for the sake of the mind, that his consciousness existed apart—in his head, say—with its own abilities, while his body had its own pursuits as apart from his own.

His creative spontaneous self created the body to begin with, and all of its physical desires were precisely those that his creative abilities needed—a quickness of body and mind working together, a quick perception mentally and physically, a <u>natural</u> exhilaration that is <u>supported by</u> (underlined) the power, of his own nature.

(10:20.) He overspecialized his ideas of creativity, for everything that comes to his attention is grist for the mill. As I said before, he must realize that it is safe and natural and good to express his being freely—not just a certain decided-upon portion of it.

I will have more to say about this on Wednesday evening. And in the meantime, make a habit yourself of asking, as you did this evening, about walking after dinner. If you understand what I am saying, then you will realize that basically your impulses will never betray you, but always add to your natural fulfillment, and that of your abilities; so have him, again, try to be more permissive in that regard. He is still afraid that his impulses will lead him away from "work" —where instead they provide the greater context from which the greater existence springs.

His impulses provide him with inspiration also. There may be days when his impulses lead him to do housework, or—zounds!—to want to walk more, but that freer inner motion will also release him for the kind of inspiration he wants.

Now I have in the meantime some recommendations, which should not just be piled away, tell him: 1. Follow his impulses. 2. Write at least several paragraphs about his feelings each day. 3. Concentrate upon psychological, psychic, and physical motion.

End of session, my fine letter-writer, and a fond good evening to you both. *("Thank you, Seth."*

(10:32. "I had no idea he was going to do that,"" Jane said, meaning work on the new book. "I'm so glad we got back on the book. And whatever he said about me, just give it to me and I'll follow it to a T.")

SESSION 887 (DELETED PORTION)
DECEMBER 5, 1979 9:17 PM WEDNESDAY

(This noon Jane and I signed our wills, with, naturally, Bill Danaher and his

wife as witnesses. While they were here, we received a call from Tam's secretary, Nancy, who told us that she'd just mailed special delivery Tam's corrected version of the letter to Ariston that I'd sent him on Monday. It's Thursday night as I type these notes, and the letter hasn't arrived yet. I hope to be through with the Ariston affair over the coming weekend, then.

(We were also visited at 11:30 AM by George Rhoads, who left shortly after the Danahers arrived.)

(Jane has been somewhat depressed the last few days because her legs have bothered her, even though evidently they're in the process of loosening up in back of the knees. I've reminded her about walking twice each day. She's been rereading Seth's material for her on Framework 2, the necessity for trust in herself, etc. Both of us have been making pronounced efforts—although that's not the right word for it—to trust that our challenges will be taken care of in Framework 2. I think I've had some good success there.

(And trusting her impulses, Jane slept for a couple of hours this afternoon—yet wasn't happy with herself for doing so when she awoke. She was quieter than usual through supper and up until session time; although she said she wanted to hold the session. I suggested that we could go back to the old session routine of having a break halfway through, thus dividing book material from personal stuff that way, but she didn't seem to think much of the idea, nor did it develop this evening.

(Even when the session was held, Jane's delivery as Seth was for the most part rather quiet, comparatively subdued.

(The material that follows is from the 887th session.

(9:48.) Give us a moment.... End of dictation.

For our friend. *(Long pause.)* The backs of his legs are stretching. This will allow for much greater manipulation of his feet. It is unfortunate that he does not know how to distinguish between, say, symptoms of disorder and symptoms of healing.

(A very important point. We must ask Seth what can be done about that lack of distinction.)

Now. The stretching muscles <u>are</u> sore, but this will quickly vanish— but <u>that</u> soreness is a healthy sign, representing greater leg action. I never want to overemphasize any of your attitudes, but Ruburt has become so used to not trusting the body that even such signs of healing can upset him.

When the two of you work with Framework 2 then, say, Jane one and Rob one can help each other help Jane two and Rob two also, so that you add to your benefits. In Framework 2 both of your intents and natures are known. That is the source of your physical existence—the source of your impulses to begin with, and the more you learn to trust Framework 2 the easier it is for your natural selves to express themselves. It is the trust that makes all the difference.

You can request before you sleep that you rest mainly in Framework 2. Ruburt's body has been trying to relax all day. His legs stretched further during his nap.

("Does he want them to stretch?")

He does, indeed, and he wants to walk, by the way—but he does not want to waste his time. Not being fully mobile has given him a built-in excuse to avoid distractions. You both thought of anything not work as distraction. In a fashion the symptoms are a result of overorganization—the distrust of impulses not specifically related to writing time. His writing itself is impulsive, and encouraging impulses of <u>any</u> kind will automatically lead to his impulses to write, and the quick, clear nature of his inspiration. The two do go hand in hand.

(10:01.) He did think women had to try harder, as I have discussed many times. When Rob two and Jane two are overemphasized, then you both add to each others difficulties. When the two natural people are largely in operation, then you are able to help each other in an easier and more spontaneous fashion. Your ideas jointly about time, for example, add to both of your difficulties. If they are aired and their source recognized, you can deal with them.

If either of you "lose" an hour, often you project that one lost hour into fifty future ones, but you are learning.

Do have Ruburt ask the natural Jane (Jane one) what to do when there are difficulties, so that the natural self at least gets a chance to give an opinion.

Give us a moment.... You have vast reservoirs of energy in particular, both of you, that have been blocked simply because the natural person was simply ignored, and beliefs of the social person taken as the <u>indisputable</u> ones.

The natural person uses creative abilities spontaneously, and those abilities, as I have said often, will show themselves both in the area of Prentice and in the area of Ruburt's physical condition when you allow them play and leeway.

The natural person (number one) looks at the world and tries to see how his or her abilities can best be utilized and fulfilled. That person <u>grows</u> through its knowledge and experience with the world, as long as there is no attempt to make the natural self <u>over</u> to fit the world. When you make that kind of attempt, it seems you are always between selves, and always disapprove of the self that you are.

The natural self approves of itself as an animal does.

Now: We may end up with a spontaneous session now and then, but I am going to close this one—and I do want you to remember creativity, for it can allow you to spontaneously change areas of your life so easily that you wonder it had not been done before.

(Heartily:) I want our friend to relax—<u>but with an easy heart</u>.

I bid you a fond good evening.

("Thank you, Seth. Good night."

(10:13 PM.)

SESSION 888 (DELETED PORTION)
DECEMBER 10, 1979 9:04 PM MONDAY

(The following material is from the 888th Session.

(10:01.) To our friend. Ruburt's natural person is highly spontaneous, creative, imaginative, with an excellent intellect, natural habits of working with a spontaneous rhythm—a rhythm that follows its own internal, logical and intuitive order.

That is the self he should refer himself to. He does not need discipline as he thinks of it. He likes a change of pace, alterations in schedule—changing his hours, for example—two or three times a year, works well for him when he allows it.

Your advice, simply to stop worrying, is excellent. He forgets his natural contours of mind and spirit when he hassles himself about time or hours, for his particular kind of creativity works in a different fashion. I want him, again, to try and sense the natural rhythms within him, of work and play, to continue his notes, to write for now four hours a day, with one hour for poetry, to think of the ideas of his book instead of thinking about the contracts, or of a book as a book, or as work as work; and tune into the library.

("Yesterday we were talking about works like James *and* Cézanne. *Are you referring to things like that?")*

That is why I suggested the library. You cannot concentrate upon worries and expect psychic baubles to fall into your lap. His body felt active the last few nights. It would have hurt nothing for him to get up, and he would have done some creative work besides.

("Okay.")

End of session. My heartiest regards to both of you –

("Thank you, Seth.")

—And a fond good evening.

("Good night, Seth."

(10:10 PM. Jane was still bothered by her legs today, as well as other portions of her body. I suggested that if she didn't sleep well tonight she call me, and I'd help her get up. As it developed, she slept through, and felt somewhat better when morning came.)

SESSION 889 (DELETED PORTION)
DECEMBER 17, 1979 8:45 PM MONDAY

(The following material is from the 889th session.)
(10:08.) A small note. Ruburt is doing well lately, and so are you.

When you cease worrying, you allow certain events to take place. It is as if (underlined) you forget particleized boundaries for a while, and allow the greater capacities of your being to take over. They can perform in a flash activities that would take much time at another level. You bring into action, physically speaking, those greater powers of your being, and trust certain chores to be taken care of at that vast unconscious level, instead of, as mentioned this evening *(in the session proper)* working at a trial-and-error basis,

SESSION 890 (DELETED PORTION)
DECEMBER 19, 1979 9:17 PM WEDNESDAY

(The following material is from the 890th session.)
(10:29.) A small note.

Ruburt is doing more physically, and so now and then he comes up against his conflicts with time, of course, but with your help he is handling that well.

The Framework-2 activity is having results, and will have more, particularly with Ruburt's condition—and I bid you a fond good evening.

(Seth then closed out the session at 10:31 PM.)

SESSION 891 (DELETED PORTION)
DECEMBER 26, 1979 9:07 WEDNESDAY

(The following material is from the 891st session.)
(9:37.) Ruburt needs your help once again to reassure him that relaxation

is safe, that it is safe to let go, that he will not fall into darkness, that his muscles will actually become stronger as they relax, and that his creativity rises to the surface when his body and mind are more relaxed.

Inspiration comes when he is relaxed. His thoughts of late are good. His abilities need stimulation, a richer diet of activities. He can understand that the best way to use his abilities to their fullest is to relax his body and his mind, to allow both greater freedom, and to exert both.

SESSION 893 (DELETED PORTION)
JANUARY 7, 1980 8:43 PM MONDAY

(The following material is from the 893rd cession.

(9:34.) Now: it is easy to live—so easy that although you live, rest, create, respond, feel, touch, see, sleep and wake, you do not really have to try to do any of those things. From your viewpoint they are done for you.

They are done for you in Framework 2, and further discussions of Framework 2, incidentally, will be interwound throughout our present book. *(Dreams, Evolution and Value Fulfillment.)* Your beliefs often tell you that life is hard, however, that living is difficult, that the universe, again, is unsafe, and that you must use all of your resources—not to meet the world with <u>anything like</u> joyful abandon, of course, but to protect yourself against its implied threats; threats that you have been taught to expect.

But your beliefs do not stop there; because of both scientific and religious ones you believe in western civilization that there are threats from within also. As a result you forget your natural selves, and become involved in a secondary, largely imaginary culture: battles that are projected negatively into the future, individually and en masse. People respond with illnesses of one kind or another, or through exaggerated behavior.

Living is <u>easy</u> (underlined). It is safe and reliable because it is easy. This is for Ruburt's benefit…. He is on the right track. Tell him to give himself the following suggestions:

1. Life in general can become easier and easier.
2. I can walk easier and easier, and with perfect safety.
3. My body's natural safety is the result of its <u>built-in agility</u>, its ability to relax, to let go, to move and respond. It is safe and easy to move.

He learned something important, working with his attitudes this weekend in the bathroom, when he realized that he held back his weight when he put his feet on the floor. The difficulty in walking this month, with the added <u>seeing</u> problem of late, has indeed been a therapeutic adjustment.

Generally speaking, the process began when he had the impulses to walk unaided this autumn, and rightly followed through. Those notions, and that attempt, signaled that he wanted more activity, and the body began new work in that direction. Hips, knees, legs and feet are all involved, and to a lesser extent the upper portions of his body. Muscles and ligaments and joints loosened, but this could not be accomplished without certain bodily sensations, without certain imbalances, as the body tried to bring about another adjustment and alignment.

Because he has not built up the good trust of his body, however, any new discomfort, regardless of origin, alarms him—an alarm that causes him to tense his muscles, withhold his weight, become hesitant—actions that of course themselves bring about stress, and prolong what should be a fairly minor adjustment. It is true that a fine, exuberant leap of belief would make even those adjustments unnecessary, and at times Ruburt almost approaches such points. Remember, he did not have your background of physical trust in the body. Whenever you can, again, honestly comment upon an improvement, now upon his appearance, or on a physical accomplishment, do so, for he needs the reinforcement there.

He obtained a good sense of physical accomplishment this weekend, in the face of quite negative attitudes that he managed to encounter and deal with well. There is no reason why he cannot build up further accomplishments of the same kind. He knows when he has poor habits in that regard, but have him work with one, say, just one a week, rather than take on several at a time.

I am willing to have longer sessions for as long as you put up with me. I will work on one book one night and another one the next, if you prefer, or discuss private material or other questions of a general nature, or work twice a week on our present material—whatever suits your fine fancies *(with much humor)*.

("Yes.")

It is <u>easy</u> for Ruburt to recover—it really is. A fine Frenchman said that if you had to do a thing, think of it as easy, and it would become so. Ruburt has the quote, and the statement is true.

I gave you the same material when we discussed Framework 2, so Ruburt must begin to minimize impediments in his mind. In a way, singling out particular attitudes or habits can at times be helpful, for it gives him particular issues to deal with. He can begin to change the focus from which he usually views his reality, in whatever way possible, and in the point of power as I suggested.

That is enough for this evening. I bid you my warmest greeting and fond good night.

("Thank you very much, Seth.")

(9:58 PM. "Well, for someone who wasn't with it too much, I did okay," Jane said. She seemed rejuvenated to a degree. "If it weren't for the mail I'd try three sessions a week, but you can't type any more."

("I can type," I said. "I'd just make the time." I didn't remember her volunteering three private, or book sessions a week except when I'd occasionally ask her for material for one of us. When she had class, on the other hand, she held three sessions a week often.)

DELETED SESSION
JANUARY 23, 1980 9:23 PM WEDNESDAY

(Ann Kraky visited us at supper time last night. She brought with her a batch of papers Leonard Yaudes had saved for us; naturally our talk revolved around Leonard's recent heart bypass operation—see the opening notes for sessions 894-97, for example, and my own reactions to Leonard's situation.

(After her visit I began to feel a resurgence of the same uneasy, even panicky, chest symptoms that I'd experienced on occasion before while Leonard has been sick. These sensations persisted through the evening; they certainly felt physical in origin, even while I tried to tell myself to forget the whole thing. I was mad at myself. I felt badly as I took out the garbage, went for a walk, etc, and when I went to bed I nearly had to get up again because the feelings intensified. But I soon fell asleep all right. However, in the morning the symptoms returned as soon as I woke up, and have lasted at various pitches of intensity through the day. By session time they were somewhat diminished, but were very inhibiting during the day, making me hesitate to do the things I'd ordinarily do without a second thought, such as drive to the post office to mail Jane's intro for Sue's book Conversations With Seth.

(Jane was so relaxed by session time, so "out of it," that she didn't think she could manage a session. I told her to do as she pleased; I hadn't asked her to have Seth say anything about me. She decided to try for the session. As I sat on the couch Billy, who is much improved now, curled himself up half in my lap, so that writing as Seth spoke was more than a little difficult. Yet when Jane went into trance her delivery as Seth was fast and steady:)

Now: Good evening.

("Good evening, Seth.")

We will be making an analogy here, so understand it as such.

Your body consciousness is like the consciousness of <u>any</u> animal—alert, above all optimistic, focused in the present, as you understand it, glorifying in motion and in rest, in excitement and in quietude. The body seeks to use itself. The body consciousness enjoys its own expression.

Mitzi, running up and down the stairs *(as she was doing even now, chasing her wadded-up paper ball)*, is an example of the love of excitement and activity with which both man and animals are innately endowed. Animals enjoy being petted, stroked, loved. They react in their own ways to suggestion to the tone of your voice, to your expectations of their behavior, to your treatment of them— and in that regard your body consciousness responds to your <u>conscious treatment</u> of it. For this analogy alone, <u>meant</u> to further develop your joint understanding of the relationship between your conscious mind and your body, we will make further points. Think of your body, for the purpose of this discussion, as a healthy animal. Think of the human animal, only let the word "animal" carry all of those beneficial colorations that you hold when you think of other species.

If you treated your body as well as you treated your animals—your pets —there would be little difficulty, relatively speaking. There is no need here to again outline the barrage of negative cultural beliefs with which indeed your civilization has an overabundance.

There is certainly no point either in belaboring the fact that you are still, individually and jointly, affected by some of them. Animals and your own body consciousness <u>have little concept of age</u>. *(Pause.)* In a fashion almost impossible to describe, their consciousnesses—the body's and the animals'—are "young" in each moment of their existences. I must perhaps here clear up a point: I am taking it for granted that you understand that I am referring to the "mental attitude" of animals and of the body consciousness, for they both do possess their own mental attitudes—psychological colorations—and above all, emotional states.

(Mitzi was still playing on the stairs.)

You can learn much about your own body consciousness, and therefore to some extent about the natural man, by observing the behavior of your pets or other animals, and you can to some extent learn from their behavior, and therefore to some extent counteract any susceptibility to negative beliefs. I have given some material like this in the past—but on such occasions try to return to the moment, to the present. Perceive it as clearly as you can from the standpoint of the stimuli present before you. Mentally say "This is my present experience now." Then, if you find yourself exaggerating any unpleasantness within that moment, and projecting it into the future, you stop and say "That is not a part of this present moment. In the terms of my bodily reality, those dire imaginings, whatever they are, are not real. My body can only respond to the present. I will not overload that present by borrowing trouble <u>that in this moment</u> has no reality" *(all very emphatically)*. Such imaginings frighten the body consciousness, as you might frighten an animal.

(9:43.) Worrying begets worry, of course—and though it may not <u>appear</u> so, worry provides a certain kind of <u>invented excitement</u> that prevents you from seeking a more constructive excitement the longer it is indulged in.

Every animal wants to know what is going on in the area of its perception. That is a normal reaction. People are the same way. That is why they chase fire trucks, so to speak—not necessarily because they are looking for tragedies, but because of life's great curiosity, and also because life enjoys variety and the unusual. It is quite natural then, for example, to want to watch the news on television, and in the same way and for the same reason.

In news watching—which does satisfy a natural need—you also run into a barrage of cultural beliefs and attitudes that are secondary. They are secondary in that they are <u>interpretations</u> placed upon events. The events come first. The <u>body consciousness</u>, watching the news, would think—if it thought as you do— "What activity, what commotion, what excitement *(almost laughing)*, what a conglomeration of smells and sights, what a congregation of my fellows, running and chasing, rising and falling, even living and dying. What a sensual barrage of activity—and how <u>juicy</u> it all is, since, <u>relatively speaking</u> (underlined), I sit here in my cozy cave, gnawing my supper bone, peacefully, with a rug at my feet. My belly full and my bed nearby." *(All with gusto and emphasis.)*

In any case, the body consciousness innately makes that distinction. It knows that it is related to those events, but it is also <u>impeccably realistic</u> in animal terms. If the skirmish is not at the front door or in the neighborhood, the animal consciousness simply watches all with a wary or amused mental attitude.

That is animal sense. The conscious mind, however, with its cultural beliefs and fears, usually cut off to a large degree from the animal wisdom, feels as if it is in the midst of a battle. It instantly exaggerates any dire circumstances, because it has been told that to exaggerate a problem and worrying about it is sane adult behavior.

The same applies if a friend becomes ill—the beliefs behind it say that you are vulnerable creatures, the victims of bodily distress that operates regardless of your wishes, and each instance of another's illness can then be seen as proof of one's own vulnerability.

Any normal process or feeling of the body can then be magnified or dwelled upon until it seems to provide only further proof of the same fears—which are then projected into the future. Some few people in your world expect to work productively through their 90's at hard work, and do so. Not because hard work keeps them alive and healthy, but because their beliefs do. They are kind to their bodies. They give their bodies *(pause)* credit for having an animal's good sense, vitality and endurance. They do not think their bodies are out to get them.

(Pause at 9:59. Seth probably used his 90's analogy because the other evening on TV Jane and I saw a program about Eubie Blake, the jazz pianist, who is still performing on stage in his late 90's, and doing very well at it to. His fingers seemed to be as flexible as a child's. Incidentally, he talked about taking care of his hands. He played one of his own songs on camera. He's black, by the way.)

There is also something else you can do at such times—and try all of these suggestions of mine, for one or another may be particularly effective, while another simply does not suit you as well: one way or another, imagine a kind of neutral platform, a subjective platform. Imagine yourself standing upon it, and see it as being a certain distance away from the platform of your usual beliefs.

Self-disapproval is always detrimental, so it does not help, as you know, to become angry at yourself. These negative beliefs are the ones we are trying to combat in our own work. They are the beliefs <u>you</u> are trying to combat as well. Therefore, do not be angry with yourself, when you fall susceptible to beliefs that are so paramount in your world. Be thankful that you can recognize them.

Do you have questions?

("No, I guess not. It's very good.")

Remember the natural man. Remember his animal characteristics. Ask him what is wrong when you are bothered with symptoms, and he will most certainly tell you that you are frightening him by dire imaginings that do not exist in his world.

He understands the nature of death, <u>as in their way</u> all animals do, but he does not understand frightening pictures of imagined illnesses that do not exist in his present, or worries about death that is not as yet to be encountered. Again, he is like all animals, filled himself with unbounded, natural biological optimism, and when that biological support is allowed its freedom, you have people performing into the very latest of years, with vitality, agility, and an elegance that only age can provide.

Now Ruburt has managed to find a platform, lately, that has allowed him a good deal of freedom from his usual worries. This has allowed more body relaxation, and agility. In exercises his legs are indeed more flexible, his knees more agile, and relaxation of mind is the key, for it allows the body to express its <u>own</u> animal wisdom.

(Heartily:) We will return to our book at our next session. You are in good health, <u>structurally</u>, meaning there is nothing wrong with your heart. Now I bid you a fond good evening, and I hope a peaceful one.

("Thank you, Seth, very much."

(10:12 PM. Jane came out of trance quickly, but before I could even tell her how good I thought the session was, she now told me that lately she's been picking up from Seth that animal consciousness is turned inward to form the civilization of nature, and that ours is turned outward into our physical civilizations—but that ours have to be built upon that civilization of nature.

(She thought the information would be part of this book. Another idea—"It's no big deal"—was that for centuries man thought the universe was created for man, and everything else revolved around man.

(By now, speaking, Jane had fallen into a mode of dictating to me as I wrote; this was different than her simply telling me something in ordinary terms. It wasn't Seth speaking, but her own delivery was quite precise and unhesitating, and she paused just as Seth did to give me time to write down her words. So from here on I'll put her material in quotes:

("Man was created by God, so that nature only had meaning in relationship to man—man was dominant. Then science threw out the entire thesis: Man wasn't at the center of the universe anymore. The universe wasn't created by God, and man and nature alike had no meaning, so that thematically man went from being the center of the universe, a special creature, created by God, to a meaningless conglomeration of atoms and molecules, and a meaningless universe, and that philosophical drop was shattering to man. So he's now actually in the process of forming a new model of the universe between those two extremes—one that recognizes that each portion of the universe has meaning in relationship to all of its other parts, but that the meaning can't necessarily be deduced by an examination of exterior appearances, but only in so far as man examines the nature of his own consciousness in its relationship to other species—to nature itself, to the objective universe, and begins to understand the vital nature of interrelatedness, within which the process of divinity is actualized."

("Man's own subjective reality, in all of its manifestations [pause] is the only one real "tool" that will give him any indication of his own greater existence, and therefore of his own origins and that of the universe. The patterns for all of man's work appear first in the mind, and the fragments of man's individual and joint dreams fall together faultlessly to form the mosaic of individual and mass events."

("I guess that's it," Jane laughed as she paused. "I don't know what it was. I guess it's Seth—one of those in-between things...."

(10:24. "It's weird when I do that. It's fascinating, but it's really weird...." Then: "It's almost like a dream. I could go right on." Then with another laugh:

("Each individual mind is a storehouse of knowledge from which each person can draw, but you have been taught that all knowledge comes from the exterior world, and from the stimuli that arises from it. But all knowledge is originally direct knowing—a kind of molecular mentality, in which the atoms and the molecules give their own kind of intuitive translation of knowledge possessed by all units of consciousness —for all of the knowledge of the universe is inherently contained within even the smallest, most microscopic of its parts."

("Otherwise, all things upon the face of the planet could not grow in proper relationship to all other things, nor could the earth maintain its proper balance or stability...."

(10:29 PM. "I know that's from Seth," Jane said. "I'm sure it's from a line of his that I got in the john the other day, but why does it come through that way? Well," she said, pleased, as she moved over to the couch, "that's one of life's little surprises. Maybe next time we can ask Seth how come I got it that way."

(Billy was still curled up against my side. And even now, on Friday night, he's curled up on my lap as I type these notes.

(As we went to bed Wednesday night, I told Jane that I thought the material on the body consciousness was excellent—the kind of thing we'd never heard before. It reminded me also of a comment Seth had made months—years—ago, to the effect that he had reams of material, untouched, on the body consciousness. I'd always been interested in asking him about that, had we the time.)

DELETED SESSION
JANUARY 24, 1980 1:21 PM THURSDAY

(A note: While taking my usual walk on Crestwood Avenue at about 10 PM last night, I saw a herd of eight deer cross the street; they moved into a small patch of woods that I judged to be just below Stamps' house on Pinnacle; if they continued on that course they might have ended up crossing Pinnacle right by our own house. I spotted the deer, moving across the lighted street like gray-brown ghosts, just as I turned onto Crestwood from Greenaway. For some reason they didn't hear or see me, or if they did they didn't care much. There was a very light dusting of snow, typical of our winter this year. There were several young animals in the group. I don't recall seeing any antlers on the mature animals, but could have missed them. The first several deer, crossing the street perhaps fifty feet ahead of me, surprised me so that I stopped in my tracks, unbelieving, seeking to understand what I was seeing. I think

that most, if not all of the houses on Crestwood had lights on, so the neighborhood was hardly deserted.

(Jane called Leonard Yaudes this morning while I was painting [I thought she was talking to Peg G.], and said later that she was picking up from Seth a good deal of excellent material on the body consciousness, our social mores re illness, and my own recent panicky hassles after Leonard's operation a couple of weeks ago. At noon she said she could either describe what she'd been getting from Seth, or try to have a session after lunch. We chose to go for the session so the material could be recorded. This is our first daylight session in some time.

(With a smile:) Good <u>afternoon</u>.

("Good afternoon, Seth.")

First of all, it is because Ruburt was relaxed and open to his impulses that you have today's information.

The situation is basically as I described it to you *(last night)*, caused by frightening beliefs and suggestion. That fear, however, also helped bring about a kind of switchover in communications that I will try as best I can to explain.

I have told you that the very cells of the body are aware of the conditions in the environment, of other cells, and of course of the creatures within the environment. That information is very rarely made conscious. If circumstances warrant it, however, such information may be switched over to other channels of communication, so that it appears in the form of, say, an impulse to do a certain thing, to call a certain person, or whatever. Then you think of the information as telepathic.

You tried hard not to think of your friend Leonard because his situation so upset you. At the same time you were concerned for him, of course. His illness brought up a million questions about the nature of illness and death, age, and so forth, backed up by your society's negative beliefs, so you tried harder not to think of your friend Leonard, and of course you couldn't relax.

Your body cells knew at the same time that your friend was in some difficulty, and wanted help. The cells in Leonard's body—<u>in a manner of speaking</u>—sent out a message for help *(pause)*, "radiated" outward for a receiver.

Now: Had you been following your natural impulses, your body cells would have picked up that message easily. You received them in any case, because of your connections with your friend, your affection for him, and the years of association in the old apartment house. Had you been relaxed, following your impulses, and <u>unhampered</u> by the fearful beliefs that your friend's condition also aroused, then those cellular messages would have been smoothly translated into an impulse to call Leonard, or to have Ruburt call. Your fears got in the way. Whenever you thought of Leonard, you told yourself to forget it.

Your affection for Leonard is strong. Your desire to be in contact with him was greater than your fear. What happened was that the communications were forced to take another route. You experienced chest discomfort. Now that chest discomfort immediately reminded you of your friend, and was meant, again, to tell you that he was in some difficulty. By the time we had our session last night, the difficulty was largely over. Your own feelings, however, exaggerated the signals to begin with, and to some extent prolonged them.

Ruburt actually followed through for you—not realizing this consciously, by finally calling Leonard this morning, when he discovered that Leonard had been feeling poorly, off and on during the same time that you had your difficulties, and that Leonard was looking for someone to do an errand *(buy a thermometer)*.

Actually, Ruburt had thought of calling before, but also did not for fear of aggravating your own situation. He was even tempted to not tell you the entire situation for the same reason—and that entire process is a conscious version of what you did at other levels. You would not tell yourself that Leonard could stand some help, because your fear made you misinterpret the message.

(1:38.) In this case you had a kind of sympathetic drama that was symbolically and literally meant to remind you of Leonard. The cellular signals were sent out, but you could have reacted to them in any given number of ways once you received them. You wanted to receive them, or you would not have. Again, they could have been simply translated into a thought like: "Maybe I should call Leonard. He might want some help." But the fears you had set about the situation prevented that easy translation.

In a way, Ruburt's call resolved the drama, even though the message is late. Leonard is doing well, and it was indeed his own exaggerated fears about his condition that led to the rather frenzied message to begin with. Therefore, in a way, your body was subjected to stress <u>that it did not need</u>, as the message was translated into physical terms of discomfort.

This does not mean that people pick up the symptoms of another willy-nilly, without their permission. It means that the cells send out messages of exaltation and happiness as well as distress, and that you react to these in various fashions at different times, according to the conditions.

The similar nature of your complaint to Leonard's, however, should have instantly reminded you of such a situation.

Now to a lesser degree, and in a different fashion, your cat *(Billy)* also reacted. The overall emotional coloration and vitality of all of the creatures, say, within any given arbitrary environment is highly complicated, so that there is of course a psychological climate to which you react, as there is a physical one. If it rains you can stay inside, run naked between the raindrops, wear galoshes and carry an umbrella, take a cab, or be so involved in your own activities that you are not even aware that it is raining at all, and the same applies to inclement psychological climates.

It is as if seeing a raindrop, you are terrified of a thunderstorm, so you closed your eyes so as not to see the rain, until finally to your surprise your feet became soaking wet, and the message got through. That is a simplified version, certainly, of the psychological actions that occurred.

Do you have any questions?

("I had a few from last night's session, but this clears them up. ")

This should clear the air considerably—and I bid you a fine and hearty good afternoon.

("Thank you.")

(1:52 PM. Jane's delivery had been quite fast. She said that Seth had carried the material further than that she'd received from him this morning. She was pleased.

(According to this material, I told her, if one paid attention to this sort of thing, good evidence for telepathy could be achieved. But one would have to train oneself to meet *such situations and take action upon them, rather than hiding from them, as I tried to do. "It never occurred to me," I said, to actually* call *Leonard and check up on him."*

(In the call this morning, Jane learned that Leonard had overdone his physical activities at the house, and suffered some discomfort as a result. His doctor told him to take it easy, as did his sister-in-law. The errand he needed doing involved purchasing a thermometer. He told Jane it hadn't occurred to him to ask me to get it for him; instead he'd called another friend. So did Leonard pick up my own fears about his situation, and avoid calling me because of them?

(Billy, by the way, is better today, although still not fully recovered.)

DELETED SESSION
JANUARY 28, 1980   9:17 PM MONDAY

(This morning I quit painting at 11 AM to go to the bank and the stationery store. When I got home at 11:45 I washed several windows at Jane's request; they certainly needed it. As I finished the job I felt the onset of another "attack" of chest discomfort; it lasted throughout the afternoon, and was most uncomfortable. The same old panicky feelings. I was very upset and angry with myself. The pendulum told me my situation was related to the fact that I stopped painting early, the windows, my worries about Jane, my age—the whole bit, in other words, so that I ended up think-

ing I'd accomplished precious little over the years. Certainly my learning was defi-
cient, I thought. I simply wanted to help Jane, live quietly, and paint with some kind
of passion I'd always envisioned but never achieved. So why all the other hash in life,
I wondered? All of those other things seemed to get in the way of the few things I real-
ly wanted to do, including writing. With the writing I sought to make sense of every-
thing at least intellectually, but for the moment at least, I thought, this left untouched
what seemed to be the more powerful emotional tangle of beliefs.

(Jane said she'd have a session for me after supper. I replied that it didn't seem
to matter. I was still uncomfortable at session time, still wondering whether my feel-
ings were physical or emotionally based, though somewhat better too. At nap time I'd
had a very vivid dream in which I was driving a new blue pickup truck down a hill.
I had an accident of some sort that left the truck half hanging off the road over a
steep drop to the valley below; I had a view of this from below. No one else was
involved in the accident, though, and the truck did stay on the road. As it happened
I woke up with a start, feeling at first what I thought was a spasm in my chest, but
quickly realized it was a part of my dream reaction. Mixed in here somehow were
thoughts I'd been entertaining today about glazing the underpainting for a head I'd
done in green a couple of weeks ago. I'd wanted to work on it this morning but had
postponed doing so until tomorrow, so I could quit painting early this morning.
Strangely, the spasm episode in the dream involved the color effects I knew I'd get
when I glazed the painting: I was vividly aware of the <u>texture</u> *of the underpainting*
as the green color was altered into flesh color by the overlay of warm flesh colors in
oil.

(Jane was once more very relaxed as session time approached. "You'll be lucky
to get a session out of me," she laughed, but at the same time she felt Seth around.
Then whispering:)

Good evening.

("Good evening, Seth.")

Now: The body consciousness reacts to exterior stimuli, of course, and to inner stimuli as well. Its "deductions" about any given event are also necessarily colored by judgments that lie outside of its province.

The body consciousness must react to <u>your</u> (underlined) interpretation of an exterior stimulus as well. The body consciousness, for example, will react quite differently to, say, two slaps of exactly the same pressure—one an energetic love slap, and the other one delivered in ridicule or anger. The physical stimulus itself, however, would be precisely the same, but the body would react to your understanding of that stimulus.

The slap could bring pleasure or pain. In its moment-to-moment reactions, the body consciousness is, you might say, "literal-minded." It reacts literally, say, in that regard, to symbols. The symbols are the realm in which interpretations are made, but the body must always react moment by moment at that level of activity, irregardless of a vast knowledge of probabilities.

Ideas of course are highly important, for they are a part of your interpretation of the world, of personal events, and they are a part of the symbolizing process. The body consciousness is geared for action, vitality, growth, curiosity, excitement, whether it be mental or physical. If there is a large body of beliefs, however, that dampen those bodily purposes, that encourage timidity rather than courage, promote fear rather than faith, then you run into difficulty—particularly if the grounds for those beliefs are not present in any given moment.

I simply want you to understand those processes. That alone, you see, would be of great benefit. Again, remember what I have told you when people expect a hearty longevity, then that is their reality—and do not forget then that your difficulties lie also in the realm of cultural beliefs. That is, the body does know better.

With that in mind, Leonard's problem upset you not only because he was and is a friend. You did not get that upset over Bill Gallagher. Leonard lives alone, however, and though he has brothers and sisters, you thought of him as alone. The situation triggered many fears, about you and Ruburt being alone, your age, the age of your brothers, who would come to your aid, or Ruburt's. If necessary, Leonard at least had a knowledge of the medical world, while you and Ruburt do not. The connection between Leonard working at the school, and Loren—all that was in the background. One event or another would serve to connect all of those issues. This noon, for example, after going downtown, leaving your painting, you found that Ruburt wanted a few more windows done, and the innocent window became a symbol, combining the idea of chores with your fear: if anything happened to you, who would do the chores for Ruburt?

(9:35.) A few such thoughts were semiconscious. The idea of activity, of the body wearing down—all of those issues contributed. The body consciousness reacted with stress, for your fears tell it that there is immediate danger. It experiences your <u>projected</u> negative pictures as present, for your fear is immediate. Yet none of its own sources of information show any cause for alarm: you are both obviously in the house together. Ruburt is safe.

There is a period of almost animal bewilderment. The body consciousness is in a state of dilemma, which it signals through the feeling of panic. That is, you interpret that feeling as panic while the body consciousness, through physical sensation, is actually asking nervously: "What is wrong? Please clarify the situation."

With your cultural training and background, however, the feeling itself further alarms you, so that you become highly anxious, and it is that anxiety itself that is the real symptom, say; it is the anxiety you should question.

Almost all such instances (underlined) involve thoughts nearly conscious, conscious, or just below consciousness, in which you have projected imagined unfortunate situations into the future. The body senses your fear, looks for the source in the immediate environment of the moment so that it can suitably react to protect you—but it senses no immediate difficulty. Naturally it becomes anxious.

I do not want you to bury such negative thoughts. On the other hand, when you have them, make a point to recognize that they are the result of cultural beliefs, beliefs that often run counter to the body's natural knowledge of optimism (pause) and saving inner balance. That knowledge will take the brunt off the negative thoughts.

Also ask the natural man is he feels the same way you do. Ask him if he has anything to say. I do want to emphasize that in many, many civilizations men were expected to improve almost all of their abilities with age, as per for example Bill Gallagher's story of the old Indian who taught the young boys how to track animals in the forest.

Men have always grown old—and women too (amused)—but they often displayed far greater wisdom, health, and even vitality in old age because it was expected of them, and because they expected it of themselves. It is a matter of understanding the process—not of blaming yourself for reactions you do not approve of.

(Pause.) In a strange fashion in your life to date, you managed to think of yourself apart from your age. You did not think of yourself as an adolescent when you were one, for example, so follow that fine good sense now. It simply will help you sidestep issues that arise only in that context.

(Very perceptive on Seth's part. I'd say that I've also managed to think of myself as an artist independently of my age, also, though of course not entirely.)

I am not talking about imagining that you are younger than you are, but of being the self that you are, as you always have been despite whatever age you were. There were a few good points here thrown in (humorously) of general interest, regarding the interpretation of suffering. I hope you noticed.

("Yes," I said, smiling.)

Ruburt has been doing very well. Despite the circumstances of the last week or so, because he is trying to relate to the moment as it exists. The two of you can do that. It is a matter, again, of understanding the process. Otherwise, you are using suggestion in a very poor way. The whole idea of the body's wearing down, as that is understood in your society, is based upon the idea of the body's mechanistic model: energy is given at birth, and gradually wears down.

Many appearances make those statements look evidential but they are only evidential in that they show the power of beliefs and suggestion. <u>Understanding</u> that, you see, can really give you greater leeway, for while you might still recognize such beliefs in yourself at times, you will also be able to recognize their source—and by doing so automatically confound them.

Your dream also was a picture of your fears. Returning yourself to the present moment, and responding <u>only</u> to what is within your present environment, returns your body to a state of stability, where it is not crowded by imaginary fears of the future.

Do you have questions?

("No, Seth.")

Then I bid you a fond good evening.

("Thank you."

(10:00 PM. Jane's pace had been fast and steady. I think she's done a remarkable job of keeping her own equilibrium during my own troubles with the "Leonard affair." She agreed. I was still upset with myself, however. The business involving Leonard is the only major event that's penetrated my own attempts to concentrate in the moment, since I embarked upon that endeavor some weeks ago. I'd thought I was doing fairly well there, but evidently Leonard represents a host of old fears that rose up en masse when triggered, and caught me unprepared. But my learning seems terribly slow and ineffectual.)

ROB'S DREAM
WEDNESDAY MORNING, JANUARY 30, 1980.

(In color as usual: An odd dream that I want to note, even though I can't recall much of it. I dreamed that I was a woman of indeterminate age, perhaps around 50, and that in some way I was trying to improve, or wanted others to improve with me. Something also about improving one's station in life. My father was in the dream with me as I knew him in "real" life, and oddly enough he was about the same age as I was in the dream. Sayre was the location, I knew. Anyhow, he used a phrase that I remembered when I woke up: "I live in a brown-paper-bag part of town," meaning a lower middle-class neighborhood; he implied that that was his station in life, and that he had no idea of trying to change it, or felt that he couldn't. In the dream I wore a brown faded coat and perhaps a small matching hat. I had straight brownish hair and was rather slim. My shoes seemed to be low-heeled, at least in memory of the dream. I can't describe my father's clothes.

SESSION 898 (DELETED PORTION)
JANUARY 30, 1980 9:28 PM WEDNESDAY

(The following material is from the 898th session. Before the session I'd men-tioned to Jane that I'd like something from Seth about my dream of early this morn-ing. A copy is attached, and a copy of this part of the session is attached to the dream in my dream notebook.)

(10:10.) Now: this is not dictation.

In dreams you can recognize yourself even though the usual space and time references may be quite different than the ones with which you are famil-iar in the waking state.

You might find yourself in a completely different body, or in a differ-ent time, or of course in a different perspective of relationships—but you are your own reference point. That sense of identity follows you in any and all realities. All particles will try to combine with each other in as many dif-ferent probable ways as possible. You can call that a scientific law if you prefer.

The same applies to all "psychological" particles, to units of consciousness, and to their affiliations within personality. If you were your father's son, you were somewhere your father's daughter, and it was at that point of reference that you encountered the dream situation.

(Pause.) Your father's sentence—the paper-bag reference—was one he actually made in his own mind, in the life that you actually knew him in, and he considered that sons rather than daughters represented his one physical tri-umph —that is, he believed sons preferable, and they alone compensated for a working man's life—a life he felt did not befit him.

A daughter, however, would have given him a beneficial relationship, someone with whom he could discuss such feelings, as he did with you in the dream. With sons, he felt that he should not show emotions of defeat, and he felt that communication itself had the feminine overtones of an unfortunate nature.

The dream was simply a small scenario. *(Long pause.)* Such probable cur-rents ride beneath all relationships. If your father did have daughters, rather than sons in the life that you know, he actually would have fared better in the phys-ical world, because he would have felt it his duty to protect them financially: he would have considered them fairly helpless, and in need of his abilities. As his sons grew out of boyhood he felt that they dwarfed him. He was in a fashion frightened of the ideas of masculinity he grew up with—ideas he felt he did not embody, and he projected those upon his sons so that in a fashion they overawed him, or put him to shame.

Each son became the man he could not be. In the dream, however, you are a woman to whom he is able to express his feelings, and he therefore shows a side of himself to you with the paper-bag image.

Now: You are coming along again. The instance you mentioned, about the bare ground, became a learning experience, because you are beginning to understand the processes involved. Gradually you can change events that once led to "negative behavior" so that they then stand for small graduation exercises, and you are in the process of doing so.

Do you have questions?

("Just one, about the dream. In it, my father and I were about the same age.")

I referred to that, I thought, in my preliminary statement about time references—that you recognize yourself in a dream even if the other references do not agree with known reality. There is no contradiction in a dream if you and your father are approximately the same age, for example. From my understanding of it, there was no other significance to the age orientation, except that the two of you were adults, and thus would have had a long shared background behind you.

("Okay." I'd wanted Seth to say something more specific about my being the same age [as a woman] as my father in the dream.)

End of session—

("Thank you, Seth.")

—and a fond good evening.

("Thank you. The same to you."

(10:30 PM. Jane didn't remember the dream material. I thought it excellent, I told her. I was pleased to have tuned in to a probable reality, even if so briefly. More and more I appreciate the fantastic reality of dreams—the tremendous knowledge and variety, literally unending, that's embodied within them. "Just think of the number of people who have dreams like that," I said, "but who either don't remember them, or pay any attention to them if they do. Look what they're missing...." Later I thought that I should have asked Seth what kind of interpretation of the dream a conventional psychologist would have given.

(The bare ground episode concerned a small experience I had as I walked into the kitchen before taking my nap. I glanced out the window and saw the ground bare of snow, and thought that I wouldn't have to shovel snow. Immediately I began to feel light sensations of anxiety in my chest. Next I began to remind myself of Seth's material in the last three private sessions—to live in the present and stop projecting into the future, that my body didn't deserve to be treated that way, and didn't understand such musings. The sensations went

away, and I napped peacefully.)

SESSION 899 (DELETED PORTION)
FEBRUARY 6, 1980 8:51 PM WEDNESDAY

(The following material is from the 899th session.

(9:58) A note: Ruburt is making some important connections, as he is involved with his book now (*The God of Jane*). And you can both realize that as far as <u>any</u> of your problems are concerned, you have been fighting paper dragons.

The problems arise in response to ideas that you once accepted as facts of life —ideas that have indeed exerted great sway—ideas that are responsible for much of the world's woe. *(Pause.)* Our version of reality had to emerge in the midst of that environment. For a while it had to be tested in the world of beliefs that you knew, even while the evidence <u>seemed</u> to be on the side of official pronouncements.

You made brave breakthroughs, for the sessions never would have begun or continued—but to maintain your peace of mind you still had to keep your mental footing in the world of those old beliefs. It might have seemed sometimes that our ideas were fanciful projections, hoped-for but unreal hypotheses that had their own important intrinsic creative value, but did not necessarily stand for any real statements of fact about the physical universe.

They might have seemed like even brilliant *(amused)* theoretical statements, my own pronouncements, but little by little you accepted them intellectually while still being emotionally bound through habit, so that indeed, as Ruburt wrote, you almost became programmed, your questions about reality based upon the erroneous facts of Darwinism, Freudianism, or religion.

In the same way, however, you almost programmed yourselves to react in certain physical fashions, and for the same reasons. Our ideas are as close to fact as you can get, granting the necessary translations, and as you build your lives on those frameworks you will no longer be programmed, reacting to erroneous "facts" as if they had a basis in reality.

The more you liberate yourselves from such ideas, the freer you will become, the stronger your natural bodies, the more alive your natural selves. Remember Framework 2, for its vast creative nature can help provide the impetus to help break through such limiting beliefs.

It is very possible that Ruburt is setting himself up for significant breakthroughs, and that you are also. Ask your natural persons to express their vitality and exuberance, and refuse to dampen their experience by frightening them with paper dragons.

End of session *(louder)*, and a natural good evening.

(10:13 PM. "I can't remember the session now, but I think I covered everything I got from him yesterday and today," Jane said. Her delivery had been good, often forceful and somewhat stronger than usual.

(I hadn't felt especially good at various times today, and hadn't been very communicative about it with Jane. Traces of my chest discomfort, re Leonard, had also come upon me at times. Perhaps some of Seth's private material here had come about because of my own unease.)

SESSION 901 (DELETED PORTION)
FEBRUARY 18, 1980 9:20 PM MONDAY

(The following material is from the 901st session.

(First, though: Last week I received from our eye doctor, Jim Adams, the usual card telling me that it had been two years since my eyes had been examined and new glasses prescribed. At first I put it out of my mind, but soon began to be bothered by a mild feeling of strain, especially when painting—without glasses, by the way. I thought suggestion was operating, that I was telling myself I needed new glasses, whereas before receiving the notice I'd felt okay.

(After spending several rather uncomfortable days, I gave in over the weekend and decided to call for an appointment this morning. I hoped for a quick one—and got it for this afternoon through a cancellation. When JA examined me I got a very pleasant surprise, for he told me that my eyes had <u>improved</u> over last time, and that they were now bothering me because my present glasses were getting to be too strong. I'd thought it was the opposite, of course. JA also seemed surprised, and double-checked his data to make sure he was correct. Moreover, when the new lenses were assembled in his machine for me to check my vision, I was able to read 15-20 [or 20-15?], another improvement over the normal 20-20.

(Moreover, when JA tested me for glaucoma, my eye pressures checked out at 17 for the left and 16 for the right—a point or so better than last time, and midway in the normal range which ends at 25. "I'll take that," JA exclaimed. "Nice and low." I left his office feeling surprised and pleased. I'd also ordered an extra pair of glasses to experiment with for painting and writing—not bifocals.

("I must be doing something right," I said to Jane when I returned to the house, and explained the situation to her. I should add that as I was backing the car out of the driveway to keep the appointment, Leonard Yaudes pulled in, for the first

MV-619 (10/79)

State of New York - Department of Motor Vehicles

VISUAL ACUITY REPORT

This form should be used only for those patients who are able to achieve a minimu Snellen Test score of 20/40 with one or both eyes without use of telescopic lenses.

For patients who wear telescopic lenses, complete and submit Form MV-80 L.

For patients whose best corrected vision is less than 20/40 but not less than 20/7 complete and submit Form MV-80L.2.

INSTRUCTIONS

1. Visual Acuity Examinations may only be conducted by a licensed Physician, Ophthalmologist, Optometrist, Optician or Registered Nurse.

2. PRINT in ink or TYPE all information in Boxes 1 - 8 and 10 - 12.

3. Be sure to enter the patient's name exactly as it appears on his driver license.

4. Have patient sign full name in Box Number 9.

5. Sign your name in full and give your professional license number on Line Number 13.

6. Give this report to the patient. Do not mail this report to the Department of Motor Vehicles.

7. This report is not valid unless test is given within six months of license application.

1. Patient's Name Last	First	M.I.	2. Date of Birth			3. Sex
Botts	Robert	F.	6 Mo.	20 Day	19 Yr.	M

4. Patient's Address No. and Street	City	State		ZIP Code
1730 Pinnacle Rd.				14905

5. Best Vision Test Score (Snellen) with or without corrective lenses.			6. Date of Examinatio		
Right	Left	Both	5 Mo.	13 Day	83 Yr
20/30	20/40	20/30			

7. Did the patient wear corrective lenses to achieve a Snellen Test score of 20/40 with one or both eyes?	☐ YES ☒ NO

8. If answer to Question 7 is Yes, check applicable Box.

☐ No change in Prescription   ☐ Revised Prescription   ☐ Patient's First Prescription

9. Patient's Signature

Robert F. Botts Jr.

The patient described above has been examined by me and this report has been completed by me and is correct.

10. Name and Title of Examiner.	SEYMOUR A. KORNFELD, O. D.
	JAMES G. ADAMS, O. D.
11. Number and Street	418 WEST CHURCH STREET
	ELMIRA, NEW YORK 14901

12. City	State	ZIP Code

13. Examiner's Signature	Professional License Number
James G. Adams - O.D.	2709

(My vision is still good, 22 years after Jim's report.)

time since he'd had his bypass heart surgery. It had been Leonard's illness that had triggered a set of symptoms of my own, which Seth has been treating in these recent deleted sessions. Indeed, today was the first day in some time—at least a number of days—when I hadn't noticed some sort of chest symptoms of some degree, light or stronger. It took me a while to realize that Leonard's arrival was hardly a coincidence, although I had trouble being specific mentally about just what I meant by that understanding. Seth also comments.

(*10:19.*) Give us a moment....

Separate: You wanted some affirmation of your body's vitality, of its resilience and recuperative energies. You also wanted some reassurance that you could operate as an artist as long as you chose in this life. You used the incident of the optometrist's notice to give yourself a very fine lesson, for in the back of your mind you did indeed worry and wonder that your eyes were becoming tired. Under usual circumstances, those "symptoms" would be interpreted as signs of difficulty. You discovered instead that the so-called symptoms are signs that your glasses have become too strong because your eyesight has not simply held its own, but most remarkably improved, and in a way that is medically demonstrable.

They have improved because you are indeed learning to relax about yourself more, and the improvement occurs first of all in that area of your main interest —your work—but it represents what is an overall time of regeneration. Your eyes do not exist alone in your head.

(*Pause.*) Your dreams involving worries about sexuality actually represented, of course, worries about your worth as a contributing person, your sex and work being thus equated. Knowing that, had the eye affair been a dream, it could also be interpreted as a sexual regeneration. It is a physical answer in fact to the worries initiated by your friend Leonard's difficulties, and therefore it was no coincidence that he was here today.

Do you have a question?

(*"How's Jane doing?"*)

Give us a moment.... Well, with his attitude.

He became very alarmed over your own symptoms, though he did well enough in maintaining his own there. His work on his own book now is helping to put certain matters in perspective, and his eyesight is also improving in certain areas. Again, your lovemaking represents an excellent way of increasing your individual and joint vitalities, and of helping to stimulate Ruburt's own physical spontaneity.

End of session.

(*"Thank you, Seth."*)

A fond good evening.

("The same to you, good night.")

(10:30 PM. Jane felt much better than she had before the session. Naturally, Seth's material about a physical regeneration makes me think about other parts of the body regenerating itself—and Jane's too. When we got up this morning I told Jane that I'd had a dream that we'd been participating in group sex at a party, but that I couldn't recall anything more than that. No one we know was in the dream, and actually I recalled only the preliminary stages of the affair, not any actual sexual activity.

(I must admit the next day, as I type these notes, that regeneration or no, I had a "relapse" into the old chest difficulty this afternoon after washing the bedroom windows at Jane's request. The physical labor involved was minimal and took only a few minutes, coming after Jane had almost tearfully asked—even demanded—this noon that I try to keep the windows cleaner. The symptoms, rather strong at times, bothered me through the afternoon, and prevented me from napping comfortably. I finally ended up rereading a couple of the private sessions on the chest difficulty, and the trouble seemed to largely abate itself by the time we were eating supper.

(Jane, of course, was very upset by my chest difficulty, telling me after her nap that she was very worried, bothered of course by the fact that she'd asked me to wash windows. It will be remembered that one of my stronger reactions last month had come about after I washed windows, too. I told her that I agreed the situation was somewhat discouraging, since it seemed I hadn't learned much from all of this upset of the last couple of months. I'd felt good yesterday for the first time in a long while, again, and told Jane that even though I'd quite forgotten the problems yesterday, today's events showed that they hadn't been solved, but merely temporarily forgotten until triggered again.

(Note: I certainly do want to function as an artist into advanced old age....)

DELETED SESSION
APRIL 9, 1980 9:01 PM WEDNESDAY

(This is the first session we've had since March 6. I think Jane held it only because I haven't been feeling well for several weeks. She's only now really recovering from the cold she picked up from RW early last month; and somehow she also got off the track of the sessions.

(My own hassles with my side, groin and scrotum are the usual ones I've had at times before—especially last year at this time. My painting hasn't been going well lately, and I've been concerned about that. Actually I'm trying a number of different

painting approaches, and think I got sidetracked into too much experimentation, so as I told Jane I'm sure painting is involved in my upsets. However, at various times the pendulum has given me all kinds of other reasons for my physical ills: taxes, money, Jane's symptoms, success and failure—the works, one might say. I was pretty disgusted and out of sorts by this evening. Still, through it all I've been sleeping well and eating okay also. I don't suppose this description adequately describes the depth of my feelings, since I've really been bothered for some time, to the extent that I no longer feel free physically, and once again have contemplated seeking medical help as a last resort.

(For the past week we've been trying a "new" treatment for Jane's symptoms — one we read about recently, and which involves the application of cold packs to her knees and hands for starters. She's had some encouraging results, and we plan to give the idea a good try. It's the opposite of the usual treatment—heat—given for her kind of difficulties.

(Yesterday evening we were visited by Dr. John Beahrs and his bride, Claudette. The visit was quite enjoyable, and it marked the first time in days that I'd forgotten my aches and pains, as I realized when it was all over. I slept well— and the discomfort returned full force when I got up this morning. I was so bothered, in fact, that I had great difficulty concentrating on painting.

(A hard, refreshing spring rain, with thunder and lightning, was drumming against the house as we sat for the session. Very invigorating, to coin a phrase. It was warm. As I've told Jane several times lately, the renewing rain reminded me once again of the wonders of nature, and I thought once again of living a natural life out-doors in the environment of woods and elements, summer and winter. Maybe I did this in one life or another. But I often feel such stirrings on my late night walks on the hilly, shadowed streets neighboring our own Pinnacle Road.

(Jane was quite nervous before the session, as she usually is after a layoff.)
Good evening.
("Good evening, Seth.")
Now: The spider spins his web, and the spider's web is a combination of art, craft, esthetics, and utility.

The web is a work of art, the spider's home, and the source of his food as well. Although it may seem to your consciousness that one spider web is like any other, this is not true, of course, in the world of spiders. All creatures of whatever degree have their own appreciation of <u>esthetics</u>. They possess the capacity to enjoy esthetic behavior.

Many such creatures merge their arts so perfectly into their lives that it is impossible to separate the two: The bee's nest, for example, the beaver's dam— and there are endless other examples. This is not "blind instinctive behavior" at all, but the result of well-ordered spontaneous artistry. It is foolish to say that the spider's web is less a work of art because the web can be formed in no other way by a spider, since for one thing the differences in the individual webs are not obvious to you, only to the spiders.

The variations are indeed so artistically contrived, and so minutely constructed, as to escape your perception. I will have more to say in that regard, and also about your question concerning the gull, but for now I want to make certain specific connections.

Art is not a specifically human endeavor, though man likes to believe that this is so, and no scientist is going to grant a spider or a bee any sense of esthetic appreciation, certainly, so what you have is art in its human manifestations, and art is above all a natural characteristic.

I try to straddle your definitions—but flowers, for example, in a fashion see themselves as their own artistic creations *(emphatically)*. They have an esthetic appreciation of their own colors—a different kind, of course, than your perception of color. But nature seeks to outdo itself in terms that are most basically artistic, even while those terms may also include quite utilitarian purposes.

The natural man, then, is a natural artist. Children draw, play with images, with language, with the sounds of their voices creatively and artistically. The natural man, the natural person, knows that art provides its own sense of creative power. In a fashion it makes no difference how many other children have drawn circles or triangles with great curious glee, quite astonished at their own power to do so. They may have seen circles or triangles countless times, but the first drawn circle is always original to the drawer, and always brings a sense of power.

In a sense, painting is man's <u>natural</u> attempt to create an original but coherent, mental yet physical interpretation of his own reality—and by extension to create a new version of reality for his species. It is as natural for man to paint as for the spider to spin his web. The spider has its own kind of confidence, however, and a different organization in which he operates. The spider does not wonder "Is my web as beautiful as my neighbor's, as meaningful? Is it the best web I can construct?" He certainly does not sit brooding and <u>webless</u> as he contemplates the errors he might make.

Instead he focuses his abilities into the matter at hand—easy enough, you might certainly say, for the spider, yet not so easy for the man. The fact is, of course, that in the most basic manner, now, the man—the natural man—possesses that fine, keen spontaneity and inner confidence.

(9:23.) <u>In a way</u>, now, the artist's hand <u>can</u> be wiser than his questioning mind, certainly, if that mind learns to use its intellect in too obtrusive a fashion.

We will return to this shortly, and skip to a conversation of last evening.

If you listened to your own conversations now and then with—if you will forgive me—an objective ear, you could both often cut some of your troubles short, or nip them in the bud. *(To me:)* You were speaking to your guest John with some evidence of dissatisfaction in your voice, some self-accusation, some irritation, wondering why as a young man you did not make greater break-throughs in your art. You wondered why at your age you had not come further in your painting, and literally why you did not know what you know now some 20 or even 30 years ago.

Those ideas have been in your mind for some time, and they automati-cally throw a damper on your creative spontaneity. There are all different kinds of artistic development, of course, some more than others directly concerned with the play of life itself upon the artistic capacity, so that generally speaking, now, there are certain kinds of developments that in your world require the per-sonality's encounter with years of experience. That experience becomes art's sometimes invisible ingredient.

Developments of that nature do not come to the young. Other kinds of artistic expression do, of course. Creative people do have more than most an inner sense of their life's direction, even if they are taught to ignore it. *(With amusement:)* There is someone I know who tells Ruburt to trust his abilities. Very good advice—but that someone does not always trust his own abilities *(louder)*.

Your artistic abilities know what they are doing. You are not taught to understand creativity, of course. You are not taught how to live with it. If you study mathematics, there is a prescribed course. There are certain specified "facts" for you to learn. A good mathematician can still be a good mathemati-cian while being quite closed off from many of life's greater values. The artist takes the very qualities of living itself and transforms them into a kind of rar-efied esthetic reality.

Each such vision is unique, so there are no real guidebooks, and each artist chooses the ways in which life and art will interrelate, so to speak. The process is natural, and it happens spontaneously when you allow it to.

While some art does indeed require a good amount of experience in time, the source of that art is itself timeless. You cannot put specifications upon it, say-ing "By the age of so-and-so my art should be thus-and-so," for there is not that kind of correlation. When there seems to be, many other factors are also at work.

Picasso, for example, had a supreme confidence in his ability. He was also quite content to remain a child at heart. I am not making value judgments, for each individual has his own purposes, and his unique abilities are so intimately connected with his own characteristics that it makes no sense to make that kind of comparison—but Picasso, for example, was an alien to profound thought.

When you hassle your abilities, when you compare what you think of as your drive unfavorably with what you think of as the superior drive of others, you are denying the integrity of your own natural individuality, and robbing your abilities of your own blessings.

Take a brief break.

(9:45. "Oh. I'm so glad I'm back on the sessions," Jane said. "I get nervous as shit when I'm away from them—more than a week or so, I mean. But I just didn't feel good...." I told her the session was excellent indeed. Resume at 9:50.)

You are still learning. Your work is still developing. How truly unfortunate you would be *(louder)* if that were not the case. There is always a kind of artistic dissatisfaction that any artist feels, any true artist, with work that is completed—for the true artist is always aware of the difference between the sensed ideal and its created actualization—but that is the dimension in which the artist has his being *(intently)*. That is the atmosphere in which his mental and physical work is done, for he always feels the tug and pull, and the tension, between the sensed ideal and its manifestation.

If you have a mathematical problem in, say, geometry, you solve it in a certain specific fashion. You add QED at the end, and you work by prescribed steps along the way. But the creative problem is never entirely even stated: it is felt or sensed. It is psychologically experienced as a state of tension. I refer to a creative tension, but one that is of course to some extent also a state of stress, creative stress.

So in a certain fashion the artist is "looking for a creative solution to a sensed but never clearly stated problem or challenge, and that involves him in artistic adventure. It is an adventure that is literally unending—and it must be one that has no clearly stated destination, in usual terms *(intently)*. In the most basic of ways, the artist cannot say where he is going, for if he knows ahead of time he is not creating but copying, or following a series of prescribed steps like a mathematician.

Now the mathematician may possibly expect a better-paying job. If he is brilliant he may receive the acclaim of his fellows, but the artist, whether or not he finds acclaim, must still always be face to face with that creative challenge. And if he is acclaimed for work that he knows is beneath his abilities, he will find no pleasure in the acclaim.

The true artist is involved with the inner workings of himself with the universe—a choice, I remind you, that he or she has made, and so often the artist does indeed forsake the recognized roads of recognition, and more, seeing that, he often does not know how to assess his own progress, since his journey has no recognizable creative destination.

When you think "I should be thus-and-so along the way," and so forth, or when you look back into the past and think that those abilities you had then should have matured far earlier in your life, you are doing so of course from a structure of your present. You are looking at a person that exists now in your imagination. Certain portions of that person, as you know, would have been satisfied with drawing comics, or doing certain kinds of commercial work. That person was committed to a love of drawing but not to a life of art. That mind had potential, but potential at that time quite undeveloped, waiting to blossom if it were allowed to. There are many painters who are quite satisfied with themselves—fairly content. Their work is quite mediocre, but they are satisfied. They have lost the tension between the ideal and its manifestation. It has become slack.

(10:05.) The natural man has a body. When you assail yourself for how you think you have handled or not handled your natural artistic abilities, then you are assailing the natural man. When you assail yourself you are assailing the natural man. You are disapproving of your natural characteristics, as if an animal took a dislike or dissatisfaction to its own color. You become annoyed by the spontaneous, natural tension that is a part of your artistic being—and that tension becomes physically translated in the body.

We are back to self-disapproval, of course, but I want you to understand that while self-disapproval is a problem for most people in your society, it is a problem for the artist particularly, because it is the artist who must trust himself or herself most of all, and it is the artist who must often have no other approval to count upon.

Now Ruburt is doing the same thing, of course, and it is often easier for one of you to see when the other is involved in such behavior, than to see when you are yourself. It will be of help, then, if you each reinforce the other's sense of self-approval, particularly in regard to your artistic and psychic abilities.

You always fall into more difficulties otherwise. By its nature art basically is meant to put each artist of whatever kind into harmony with the universe for the artist draws upon the same creative energy from which birth emerges. When you trust your abilities you allow them, through their expression, to find their own creative reconciliation, for the creative product is indeed a reconciliation between the sensed ideal and the world's actuality.

It is very important, then, that the two of you maintain good emotional contact with each other, and when you are each feeling such dissatisfactions to voice them. They are then out in the open, and can be handled far more easily.

Do you have questions?

(I smiled at Seth as he stared at me, then shook my head. I had quite enough to think about for the evening. "No.")

Then I bid you a most fond good evening.

("Thank you very much.")

Try to remember—and Ruburt too—a sense of freedom in your creativity. Have Ruburt play with his ideas and with the ideas in my book, and not overstress this idea of responsibility, particularly as far as my books are concerned. The book sessions should indeed be fun, even as children have fun with their creativity.

A note: Beside your dream images, and so forth, which are indeed an excellent idea, you have advantages here that the young man of some 20 or 30 years ago would have envied: he would have been delighted with the screened-in porches. Perfect, he would have thought, at least one of them, for a summer studio. To have a house with screened-in porches amid trees—what an advantage! He would have found a way to use them in the summertime. There would have been an interplay then between dream activity and the physical images of a unique nature.

Simply a suggestion, since you have been so concerned at times with that young man's abilities. End of session.

("Okay. Thank you very much.")

(10:20 PM. "Okay, Bob, I'm making a statement of intentions," Jane said as soon as she was out of trance. "I'm back to the sessions. I was nervous before this one, and I'll ready the last book session before next Monday...."

(It's Friday evening as I finish typing this session. Yesterday I felt better—with the session half typed—than I have for some time. I also painted better. Today I felt almost as good, but reminded of the session content, which always helped. I also began finishing a painting with a new and free determination, working much more easily than I had been doing. I think the results may be good, and certainly they point the way toward what I want to accomplish with my "portraits." I feel quite good about the painting endeavor now, and will try to keep things in balance.

(I think the session is brilliant. Jane needn't have worried.)

SESSION 917 (DELETED PORTION)
MAY 21, 1980 8:49 PM WEDNESDAY

(The following material is from the 917th session.)

We will call this a letter to Frank, though hopefully it can be of use to some other people I know *(amused)*.

When you first learned to write in school, you had to be taught how to form the letters. You made many mistakes. Finally, however, you could form the letters quite easily. You felt triumphant. You forgot the mistakes you had made in the past. You had accomplished something.

Then you were told that you had to put those letters together to make words. Again you made many mistakes, and forgot them as with delight you now wrote separate words. Then you were told to put the words into sentences, and you followed the same procedure. You forgot your mistakes. Were you stupid or dumb—or an asshole—when you could only form simple letters? Obviously not. Your aspirations and your curiosity kept leading you toward a more complete development, until you could finally read and write whole paragraphs.

You could not only copy sentences, but—important development—you could form your own sentences, and express your own thoughts in that form.

These were all stages of development, then, and the same applies to your life. Your so-called mistakes exist as mistakes only in the light of your aspirations to perform better, to express more fully developed experiences, rather than to write better sentences.

It is self-defeating, therefore, to blame yourself for mistakes, so-called, simply because in the light of your present development they are seen as less-developed acts than those to which you now aspire. Whenever you catch yourself disapproving of yourself for past mistakes, read these passages. Do not check on yourself all the time. Trust that you will learn what you want to learn as automatically as you once learned to read or speak, or as automatically as you think.

In your realm of reality, mistakes are a part of the learning process. They do not even seem to be mistakes until you are "at the next level" of development, or a step higher in your understanding—as when, say, in the sixth grade you looked back and saw a page of your own childish lettering done at the age of five.

I realize it is difficult to understand at times, but even your so-called mistakes have many far-reaching beneficial results that do not show in any isolated fashion. They may add to your understanding of yourself and others. They may be applied beneficially in entirely different areas of your life—so stop disapproving of yourself, of your "mistakes." Try to set your goals and to trust that the proper impulses will come to you to bring them about and that others will be disposed in your direction, for their own reasons. In the meantime, try to live in the present as much as possible.

Do not undervalue or overvalue yourself. And know that in your own uniqueness such judgments have no place.

SESSIONS 921 & 922 (DELETED PORTIONS)
OCTOBER 8 & 13, 1980

(Here is the private material Seth has given for Jane in the last two sessions:
(From Session 921 for October 8:) Tell Ruburt to relax, and to encourage and trust his body when it is undergoing so many changes, for the changes are all for the better.
(From Session 922 for October 13:) Tell Ruburt to change his pillows more frequently.

SESSION 926 (DELETED PORTION)
NOVEMBER 3, 1980 9:27 PM MONDAY

(The following material is from the 926th session.
(10:20.) End of session and a fond good evening.
("Can I ask a question?")
You may.
("How's Ruburt doing?")
Ruburt did not want you to ask the question.

It is as I have said before, and the session is to help you and Ruburt trust his own processes, since consciously he cannot know all of the body's multitudinous happenings.

Lately, when he lies down, and the pressure is off, his hips, hip joints, and hamstrings have begun new adjustments that are at a certain level uncomfortable—but because that frightens him the discomfort is more than it would be otherwise. He tenses, for example.

He has noticed, however, that almost immediately afterward his arms are freer, and that he has taken some of the steps there *(pointing to the couch)* with his weight better distributed, though he is bent way over, and so he has made good efforts to understand. He still needs, however, to remind himself more often to trust the body's processes, and your help is invaluable in that regard.

Work is being done on the knees, also, so actually the initial good results are showing in the knees and feet and arms. He should indeed read sessions from the last group, however—one or two daily.

If you <u>hear</u> him uncomfortable in the night, a word of comfort does make him feel less isolated. Changing the position of one of his tables or some such can also give some practical help, simply because this breaks up posture patterns, which is advisable in the situation.

End of session.

("Thank you.")

A fond good evening.

("Good night."

(10:28 PM. "I know you asked." Jane said. "You don't have to put this down, but I sort of get mad at Seth when I don't feel good. I figure why doesn't he say something to help me out?—I'm not going to have Bob ask." She laughed. "Something like that.")

SESSION 927 (DELETED PORTION)
NOVEMBER 10, 1980 9:05 PM MONDAY

(The following material is from the 927th session.

(Jane is still being bothered considerably in her arms, legs, knees, back, etc., especially at night when she tries to sleep. She's been very uncomfortable much of the time. I've been letting her sleep in the mornings, which seems to be the most peaceful resting times for her. Sometimes at night I wake up when she's sitting up, and rub her, which seems to help, but her ill feelings often return.

(These overall bodily changes have been going on for over a month now, and she realizes that they are positive things; I told her this evening that her arms are definitely straighter, for instance. And this afternoon, "off and on for almost an hour," her eyesight improved remarkably as she sat working at her desk: "The type began getting bigger and bigger and bigger." She's missed walking with her typing table often lately, yet her walking from her chair to the couch has been much improved —steadier and better balanced, although she's still bent way over. I suggested tonight's session be about her. "He'll just say the same things," she said. Nevertheless....

(10:13.) Now, Ruburt's body is trying to right itself. When he lies down, it is trying to straighten out. Nerve patterns are being reactivated, circulation patterns reinforced, muscles contracting and expanding in their own exercises, right now, in a concentrated, rather intensified bodily commotion. *(Pause.)* You are used to thinking of any bodily commotion as disruptive, and put it in the worst possible light, because your backgrounds have given you little experience in such situations—you, Ruburt, or anyone else, largely in

your culture.

Afterward, however, Ruburt does sense certain releases. His steps by the couch are (underlined) firmer. His back begins to arch more naturally. It is very important that he understand and trust such occurrences. He does feel isolated and frightened sometimes under those conditions. You can be of help in just talking to him, or massaging. He can help himself by remembering what I am saying, by exercising gently at such times, and by remembering the miraculous processes within the body that are indeed supporting him.

He is also onto some excellent ideas on his own.

End of session, a fond good evening.

("Thank you. Good night, Seth.")

(10:20 PM. "Jesus, I ought to go in trance more often," Jane laughed. "I wasn't aware of how I was sitting or anything. I was the most comfortable I've been all day.... Actually, though, I did good this morning, though....")

SESSION 928 (DELETED PORTION)
NOVEMBER 12, 1980 9:19 PM WEDNESDAY

(The following material is from the 928th session.)

(10:13.) Now: Ruburt's condition is as I gave it last time, and it is highly important that you both keep this in mind: The bodily commotion is most beneficial. It is evidence of the healing process's acceleration.

End of session. My heartiest regards and a fond good evening.

("Thank you, Seth. Good night.")

(10:15 PM.)

DELETED SESSION
NOVEMBER 19, 1980 9:19 PM WEDNESDAY

(Jane held no session last Monday night because she was so relaxed and out of it, as she has been so often lately, what with the numerous changes still taking place in her body. Indeed, she felt the same way tonight, but decided to try for a session when I suggested she ask for something about herself. "But I can't stand anything that's all charged up about me," she said several times.

(Notes: Today Jane called Tam about the continuing hassles over the disclaimer for Mass Events, and learned several important things—among them that the legal department is now "drafting" a letter to us, explaining their position in the

matter. Discussed also were the memos the legal department has been sending to the board of directors at Prentice-Hall. Many of these have been derogatory; we now plan to ask Tam for the names of the individual board members, and we want to learn how to write to them to be sure they personally receive our messages. We would like to eventually tell our side of the story, and resent being treated like children in the interim. According to Tam, we're not supposed to know anything about much of what he's been telling us of the fuss over the disclaimer.

(All of this began when at break this morning I asked Jane is she knew her true feelings about the Mass Events affair. We had a long discussion—which helped, finally, clarify many things for us. I started it because of a couple of questions I had about our relationship with Prentice-Hall. Both of us are in conflict between getting the Seth books out, not caring about any disclaimer, and on the other hand saying no to the disclaimer and letting the chips fall where they may, to coin a phrase. Of course, we don't want to get sued, as the legal department fears we might. I personally resent a great deal the poor connotations that now have attached themselves to Mass Events; if the material has any validity, this has happened, and would be picked up by readers, even if counterbalanced by other good feelings. The fact that such ideas do not occur to entities like the legal—or even the editorial—departments at Prentice-Hall shows, I think, the great gap that exists between our own views of life and theirs. It's wider than I thought.

(I suppose we don't know what our response to the legal department missive will be. My best guess at the moment is that the disclaimer matters not at all, but the idea of it doesn't bode well for the future, I'm afraid, and there may be the real rub. Jane has God of Jane *and her book of poetry well in the works now, and both involve* Mass Events, *or material in it. We want those books published. A cutoff point is reached after these three books have been taken care of; then we would be free to try something else if we choose to.*

([November 16, 1980—Jane gives up walking with typing table. See Private Session June 2, 1981. Also see Private Session December 1, 1981—Jane hasn't walked in thirteen *months.]*

(Coupled with all of these things is the three-part article we're reading in The New Yorker *on the travails of publishing these days; the large sums involved, books being treated as "products," etc. According to that information, we're so far out of it in any meaningful way that we're left feeling quite inadequate. On the other hand, we haven't forgotten Seth's recent material about our being protected—and I for one really think that's true. It does take an effort to keep it in mind at times, though. It's also made it quite difficult for me to whip up any enthusiasm about getting back to work on the notes for Seth's* Dreams. *I'd just gotten nicely into that project when the disclaimer business started over* Mass Events—*it seems like months ago; actually, this*

may be the third month following the interruption, an incredible gap in creativity, for which I blame Prentice, no doubt about it.

(On top of all of this, we received from Prentice-Hall on Monday the revised movie contracts for Oversoul Seven, *and now must see Bill Danaher again about new notarization, etc.*

(Whispering:) Now—

("Good evening.")

—a few remarks.

(Pause.) The body is composed of organs, physical parts, living matter— but the body is also composed of processes, relationships that exist on all levels between various portions of the body and between the body and its environment.

All processes in nature are intelligent. They may involve a different kind of consciousness and intelligence than your own. But there are no <u>un</u>intelligent processes. *(Pause.)* There are no <u>closed</u> processes. There is no process that is not in one way or another related to others. In a fashion, any one natural process carries within it the implied existence of all others. The body is in that regard a highly energized gestalt of intelligent processes.

These include emotional processes, of course, mental ones, emotional ones, and constant transformation of energy from one form into another. Your stomach cannot read. What you read, however, is in one way or another translated into other terms, so that for example your stomach reacts in its way to your reading matter, as the visual information is translated into other terms.

There are whole patterns of interrelated energetic activities that determine the flow of energy overall, say, through the body, and many other relationships that remain, say, medically unsuspected.

In a fashion, as I have said before, you are highly uneducated about the activity of your own bodies, and taught to suspect your own bodily sensations. Patterns and pathways of energy are being reopened and reactivated in Ruburt's body. This applies throughout the body, and is also responsible for the sensations in the legs and hips.

(10:00.) He is correct in thinking that these sensations begin about 20 minutes after he lies down, as a rule, as the muscles gradually begin to relax. They relax further than his usual chair position allows, begin to stretch, call for added circulation, which they receive. Joints become more lubricated. At the same time, from his standpoint this is a fairly sudden intensification of sensation. The relationship of knees and hips begins to change, requiring also greater activity from the spine and back areas, so that he feels at times pulled in several directions at once.

Add to this the fact that he is <u>learning</u> to trust his body *(pause)*, but is still at times besieged by doubts, and his difficulty is explained. I must remind you both to emphasize, again, the flexibilities that <u>are</u> occurring, and that are for that matter sometimes apparent almost immediately after such episodes—for your trust builds as <u>you</u> allow yourselves to concentrate upon what is new evidence.

The same applies to Ruburt's steps over there *(to the couch from the chair)*. There is, in fact—though in a bent-over position—some considerable improvement and coordination in walking, as far as legs and arms are concerned. This does not show up yet when he is trying to walk in a taller position—but the improvement in the arm span will also help him there. The main thing, again, is that Ruburt's personal trust in the body be reinforced by himself through such reminders, and by your own reassurance. A large amount of energy is involved. That energy means action, of course.

(Pause.) In ways really difficult to describe, your bodily processes, and what you think of as, say, cultural or national events, are highly connected and a part of each other. Events are indeed also processes, partially physical and partially not physical.

(Long pause.) It is as if bits and pieces of any and all probable events exist in a jigsaw-like fashion throughout the minds of men, throughout the consciousnesses of plants and all natural things, wanting to be put together—and each individual consciousness has its part to play in directing which of those events occur or do not occur—but the processes involved in the formation of those events are hidden from the conscious mind.

(10:17.) There are certain interior physical events that can happen within Ruburt's body to help him move more naturally, but he cannot possibly consciously comprehend each change that must occur, and when viewed in that light the entire exercise seems so complicated as to be almost impossible. To the body, however, this is the kind of natural action it is always involved in, as it constantly rebuilds itself, maintains life, and it involves the body in work that it is indeed highly equipped to perform.

In that light, there is no reason to be overawed by the body's knowledge, either. It is a portion of your natural heritage. If you begin to concentrate upon the importance of the nature of thought, to become <u>overly</u> concerned with the processes involved with thinking or reasoning, then your very conscious concern would make those processes seem all the more complicated, while instead it is easy to see that those processes are quite naturally equipped to handle their own tasks with remarkable ease. Ruburt's body is also so equipped to perform its healing functions.

(Long pause.) You have been given no guidelines, however, that allow you

to trust those healing capacities, from your society, so you are still in the position of dropping negative habits, fears of the body, and so forth, piled up through years of misunderstanding. We will probably have more to say about processes in our next book dictation.

You are protected. When you know that you are, you can save yourselves considerable periods of stress and strain, because you realize that you are not at the mercy of other people or of their actions. When you think that you <u>are</u> in such a position, you react in threatened fashions, of course, and give them power that they do not naturally possess. I am certain that you know in what areas of your lives this material might be useful. End of session, a fond good evening.

("The same to you. Good night")

(10:29 PM. Once again after a session, Jane laughed: "I ought to do this more often. I wasn't aware of anything—my legs, my hips, my knees....")

DELETED SESSION
DECEMBER 1, 1980 8:49 PM MONDAY

(We're still in the process of checking the copyedited manuscript for God of Jane, *although we're nearing the end of that job. Today Jane told me that she thought Seth would go into the famous—or infamous—disclaimer that Prentice-Hall wants to attach to* Mass Events. *We'd received a formal letter about that from the legal department of Prentice-Hall last Friday; today Jane had been "picking up" on it. I didn't ask her what she'd learned; I thought it better to get the material in a session, if possible. Just before the session, Jane said that she thought Seth was "rather cavalier" in his attitude, and that my own wasn't very good. She was only half joking.*

(At 8:52: "I sort of feel him around, but I don't think it will be very long." Jane had been tempted to pass up the session and continue work on God of Jane, *but I reminded her that I could use Seth's information on the disclaimer in our reply to the legal department at Prentice-Hall. We knew by now that we were resigned to having the disclaimer inserted into* Mass Events, *but we wanted to have our say— partially out of anger and partially out of self-protection, since we didn't believe all the legal department had told us; we wanted them to know we understood the subterfuges involved.*

(Jane didn't feel too well before the session, what with all her bodily changes still taking place, but she did well once she began the session.)

Now.

("Good evening, Seth.")

Ruburt wondered the other day what my own attitude might be toward the famous disclaimer, and I began to tell him.

I had intended to mention the affair, again, in any case—but once more I am reminded that many facts are self-evident to me, while at your end they are highly questionable—and so your attitudes are bound to be <u>covered</u> in ways that mine are not.

(*Softly:*) Your existence is protected, your works are protected. Those statements are self-evident to me, while you of course are still in the process of thinking them over, and trying to fit them into the context of life as you know it. To that extent, then, of course our attitudes would be different. In any case, when you were first working with Frameworks 1 and 2, you saw many examples of Framework 2's activities, as they impinged into your reality, and you were quite pleased. Your living experiences often gave you clues one way or another that added to the <u>thematic</u> material.

Now: any disclaimer would not insult me. The entire idea of the disclaimer is a living example of the book's thematic material. It shows the elements of the society that we have criticized in action. It becomes almost an exterior <u>extension</u> of the book itself. Certainly it shows why the ideas in the book <u>are</u> so important at this time. I consider such a disclaimer as a mildly amusing case in point: a living example—almost as if indeed you had requested one—a proof of the pudding.

(*9:05.*) There is more involved. Our work has achieved <u>enough</u> notice so that it is indeed considered to have some effects upon your society. (*Pause.*) Otherwise, no disclaimer would be considered. That means that we have made inroads, that we are reaching people, and that even the Prentice legal department is aware of our readership.

In other words, the books are considered to have some social life. (*Pause.*) You are, or we are, certainly criticizing many of the aspects of your society. In that particular book (*Mass Events*)—rather powerful honored aspects, and criticism <u>will</u> (underlined) meet criticism. At the same time, as the book's criticism has a good import, so is the disclaimer in its fashion a creative example, again, of the book's premise, and also would serve for that matter in a way that may not have been anticipated: with the disclaimer the book may well sell more copies by far than it would otherwise (*humorously*), for people will be curious about what such a volume might contain that will be dangerous to the public good.

When you realize that you are indeed protected, such issues are <u>absorbed</u> along the way. They are actually changed in character, so that they work for your benefit rather than against it. It is extremely difficult for me, however, to make you understand quite clearly the role that your own attitudes play—for when issues hit close to home you have both the old tendency to blame the other party or parties for what is involved.

(In our defenses here, I'll digress a bit to note that although we may do that on occasion, Jane and I certainly do not blame others anything like we used to, or the way we still see others do. Our incidence is cut way down, in other words. Even when we do catch ourselves indulging, one might say, always in the backs of our minds lies the knowledge that, really, each of us creates our own reality, and are therefore par-ticipators in whatever events we may find ourselves enmeshed in—even those we dis-like. This background knowledge has had profound effects upon us, of course.)

That means that you read the involvement in a certain fashion that only seems to prove your point.

(Long pause.) Because the book met criticism at Prentice does not mean that you or it were not protected. *(Pause.)* The word "protection" in this context is interesting, of course, since the disclaimer is supposed to protect Prentice from any court action. It is in its fashion an attempt at protection at that level. The level is one where every bit of preventative protection is needed in a world where people constantly need insurance, preventative medicine, and so forth – again, all issues dealt with in the book.

(Long pause.) The disclaimer is also Prentice's way of allowing itself some freedom thematically, without getting its feet wet in any possible court actions. The company, as stated, is in its fashion a capsule of your society and its present climate. *(Long pause.)* The disclaimer in no way lessens the power of impact of the book. It only manages to stress many of the pertinent issues, and in its way it would point out the situation quite clearly. No one is seriously concerned about the possibility of a person dying of a disease because they followed any of the advice given in the book. They are afraid to some extent of being sued for such a purpose because they themselves dwell in a mental situation in which threats are everywhere, in which all precautions must be taken.

(9:26.) Lawyers deal in a world of limited, fairly well-established facts. Those facts may be imaginatively assembled at times, but they are very slow to accept the inclusion of any new data, and they must be backers of the estab-lishment from which, of course, they obtain their position.

I am making no recommendations, but hopefully adding to the informa-tion that you have at hand, and offering another framework from which you can view the situation. Your feelings about it are as important as your actions. You have every right to call them on any points you desire, of course. *(Long pause.)* In the overall cultural picture *(long pause)*, "psychic matters" are no longer as easy to dismiss as they used to be. People's curiosity has been aroused, and the established methods of gaining knowledge have been found less than satisfactory—so in a fashion the idea of the disclaimer is a kind of backhanded recognition. You and your works are protected. Your lives are aware as they are meant to be. You have made no great errors in your lives. You are doing what is right for you. If you accept those statements as true, then you will begin to feel an emotional sense of rightness with yourselves. You will drop habits of self-disapproval. You can even take it for granted that intellectually you may not know all of the reasons (underlined) for your own actions.

This does not mean that you do not know the reasons. They might not ever appear intellectually to you. They might very well be felt and understood emotionally, however, or intuitively, once you cease habits of disapproval and constant intellectual questioning about such seemingly hidden motives for your actions.

(*Pause at 9:39.*) Briefly: Again, help reassure Ruburt that his body does (underlined) know what it is doing. He does need that reassurance now. The legs and entire lower portions of the body have been in a constantly changing state of late (*for weeks*), as the legs and knees do begin to gain more motion. This causes all kinds of alterations of muscles and joints and so forth. The vibrator under this area (*underneath the thighs*) will be beneficial.

(*"Can I ask a question?"*)

You may.

(*"Has he been reacting physically to this disclaimer business?"*)

To the extent that he questions his own natural protection. Give us a moment.... You are dealing with two issues also. The natural person—the creator, the artist—in Ruburt, wants the book out without any interruptions, and cares little about other issues. The socially knowledgeable person does not want to be taken for a fool, be insulted, and wants to be treated with respect. To some extent that is a simplification, of course. Nothing is that simple, but the explanation does serve to clarify contradictory issues. Certainly the entire affair is to be used creatively. Art, including writing, of course—creativity itself—is bound to be, as per the Cézanne passage (*I'd called to Jane's attention a couple of weeks ago*) sometimes disruptive. It brings into being that which was not there before. It rearranges some aspects of the world, and it is in its fashion as brilliant as a child's clear eye. It sees truth clearly. Because it does, art can often make disclosures that offend the pious, the well-mannered.

Ruburt's own passages (*in God of Jane*) about the television preacher are a case in point. They upset him to some extent—not for himself, but because he did not want to hurt other people who so believed in the dogma that he was disclosing to the world. It is very important, then, that you learn to trust your own creativity and your own vision, and allow it its expression, for it will always lead to a more fulfilling vision. End of session. Unless you have another question.

("Nope.")

Then I bid you a fond good evening.

("The same to you, Seth. Thank you very much. Good night." 9:54 PM.)

DELETED SESSION
DECEMBER 8, 1980 9:35 PM MONDAY

(After last Monday night's deleted session [on December 1], I told Jane that I wished I'd asked Seth a second question when he'd given me the chance: I'm very curious as to why I'm so fascinated by those hilltop towns in central southern Italy, inland from Naples. I've read now that over 170 of these settlements, some of them dating from Norman times, have been devastated by the great earthquake of November 23. This event made me physically aware of that area in a fresh way—especially the isolation, and what I take to be my symbolic interpretation of a simpler way of life. As I wrote in the closing notes for the 929th session, I've been reminded once again of my feelings reincarnationally concerning those towns and villages. Fantasy must be involved also.

("I'm taking it for granted that I can have a session," Jane said as we sat waiting for Seth to come through at 9:13 PM, "but I sure know that I'm awfully uncomfortable." She referred to her hips and legs—the same areas that have bothered her a great deal now for a number of weeks. She especially has trouble leaning forward in her chair. She continues to have much trouble sleeping and getting up, alternated with blue periods, etc.

(She's also developed a strange hearing problem in recent weeks. In recent days I've finally realized that she often doesn't hear me speak in an average voice—especially so when she isn't looking at me. At first I thought the dry air in the house during the winter was responsible, since for a while I thought I was having trouble hearing her—but this doesn't seem to really apply. A couple of days ago we narrowed the cause down to the fact that since her hips and legs began to act up so, she's been taking ten arthritis-strength Bufferin a day; this has been going on for a month or so, and is far more than she usually took. Jane cut out much of her dosage—and all of the Bufferin—and her hearing cleared up within a day or so. And for some reason, I can hear her better, too.

(Yet Jane is in the midst of great discomfort, whether this represents healing changes taking place within her body or not, as Seth tells us it does. Her arms are noticeably longer. Twice today we had rather short discussions about our ideas of why the symptoms linger after all these years: nothing new, I'm afraid, although she said

she felt better afterward—before getting blue again. Personally, I think we have learned little—or have much still to learn. Our talks reminded Jane of a group of private sessions Seth gave in 1973, so she looked those over before I came out to see if she wanted a session tonight. That old material concerned the work ethic, she said, and our attitudes about it.

(Today I mailed to those in command at Prentice-Hall eight copies of our letter to the legal department, in response to their letter of November 24 explaining the disclaimer they want to use in Mass Events. *I felt considerable relief in doing so. Then this afternoon Jack Joyce visited to help determine our estimated NY State tax payment for this year. I felt additional relief at having that taken care of.*

(Jane vacillated several times between having and not having a session, before finally announcing that she felt Seth around. I told her that I thought she needed material about her own condition, that's all I cared about.)

Good evening.

("Good evening, Seth.")

Now: Underline five times: <u>Whenever there are difficulties, do not concentrate upon the problem</u>.

Though the following advice runs counter to all accepted ideas of common sense, at such times look for what is <u>right</u> in your lives, rather than becoming <u>overly concerned</u> (underlined) with what is wrong. Otherwise, the intense desire for a solution can lead you to concentrate upon what is wrong, so that it becomes the entire issue.

The sessions that Ruburt read this evening—that group—contain excellent material that was, at the time, used to bring about considerable understanding and improvement in Ruburt's condition. You would both do well to reread and discuss the information simply so that it is out in the open again. You can see what still applies, or what issues you think you have cleared up.

The material on work ideas connected with Ruburt still does have application. Many years ago his experience with different editors, in his short-story publishing days, led him to see that a story that hit one editor might not hit another, that his work would be much more easily accepted by some editors than others, and that some, it seemed, regardless of long enthusiastic letters, would not buy a thing.

Therefore his relationship with Tam Mossman was quite valuable to him, for it took a good deal of the unpredictable nature out of free-lance writing; particularly where projects like books were concerned rather than short stories, and particularly in an area that was itself controversial. All in all, he felt that to be a fairly reliable and adequate framework, whether or not he might get better terms someplace else financially, or in other ways. He long ago settled upon you and his writing, however.

(Pause.) This material should be read in conjunction with the sessions just mentioned, dealing with his ideas about work and creativity. He felt threatened over the disagreements last year about contracts, about Tam's frequent mention that he might leave. The matter of Yale led him in his own way to think of his work as if it were to be an institution, every word recorded, so that you only wrote down what you wanted other people to know—and therefore somewhat discouraged spontaneity of expression.

I am not agreeing here, necessarily, but stating his reaction. On the other hand, such an alliance seemed to bring some kind of prestige. He felt also that my ideas in *Mass Events*, and his ideas in *God of Jane*, were almost bound to bring about some controversy from the beginning—for reasons he largely worked out for himself—and they are related in his book.

The latest disclaimer issue simply falls into the same pattern, and therefore was added to it, but all of those issues involve his feelings and beliefs about work and creativity. Any issues with you also involved work and creativity, along with the expectations that you had of each other—not just in your married roles but as partners and colleagues in your artistic endeavors.

(9:55.) Overall, being is its own reward—not that there are not others, but that being obviously makes all of your experiences possible, so you cannot tie being up in a package of work only, regardless of the nature of the work. All of this goes back to ideas that existence must be justified, and Ruburt's early ideas that writing would justify his life—but writing should express life, and is an expression of being, an expression of spontaneity, an expression of emotion, of body as well as mind *(all intently)*.

His early writing, and his best later writing, spring alike from that realization, when he forgets ideas of our work's responsibility, or how respectable he should appear, and simply does it because it is a natural expression of his being —one expression among others.

Painting and poetry, cleaning the house, seeing the tax man, doing chores —these are all expressions of being. They add to its quality, to its texture. They are part of life's art. They are the raw stuff from which art comes, whether or not in any given case you can see the connections.

Now Ruburt's hips are definitely changing their positions. Certain joints that worked very poorly are releasing, allowing portions of the body to move in new directions. His body is thrusting itself upward. Much work is done when he is in bed. It can be uncomfortable, but far less so with understanding and a bit of patience. He becomes frightened, for the reasons given in late sessions, and again, he can use as much reassurance as you can give him—as much understanding. And the better the communication between you, the better the entire situation.

You must both try to have a larger perspective. You go through periods, of course, where you utilize Framework 2 more proficiently than you do at other times, but reminding yourselves in conversation of Framework 2's existence and importance can be an invaluable assistance.

In the next few days, have Ruburt read over that group of sessions. Enjoy the intimate behavior of life, the compensations that are available, and your own relationship, which provides more creative solutions than you realize. You should both be more spontaneous *(whispering)* with loving touches and conversations, and see even your difficulties existing in rich environments of being, in which you are not isolated. You are in the stream of life because you are alive.

This will be a short session, but as always it can help you considerably if you do more than just read it, and take it to heart as well. You both have purposes in life. You are coming to grips with issues that you were bound to grapple with, and you are dealing with the challenges that are involved. Therefore, trust that despite your difficulties you are doing what you set out to do, and remember that the difficulties are not absolute, and avoid thinking of them in absolute terms. End of session. A fond good evening, and do not give up on yourselves.

(10:14 PM.)

DELETED SESSION
DECEMBER 10, 1980 9:31 PM WEDNESDAY

(After supper this evening I read over some of those 1973 private sessions that Seth referred to in last Monday night's deleted session. Jane had marked three of them —running from September 10 to September 24, as being particularly good. They are. But I found that I thought an earlier one, for June 30, 1973, to be even better, more basic perhaps.

(This afternoon Jane told me that she'd been picking up from Seth about the poor Italian villages that had been destroyed in the great earthquake of November 23. As noted, I'm quite interested in that area, though not only in our present time frame.

(Once again it was obvious that Jane didn't feel well before the session began, although her delivery turned out to be quite steady and sometimes forceful. She moved about in her chair often while speaking for Seth.)

Now—some remarks generally, having to do with the kinds of villages in Italy that so took your interest. There were many such villages in the mountains in the overall times of Nebene and your Roman soldier, and they were much in character like the villages recently destroyed in the earthquake. They dealt with a different <u>framework</u> of consciousness—one that is somewhat now out of character with your kind. I mentioned that modern psychology actually shortchanged you, trying to fit itself into Darwinian beliefs. Those Italian villages exemplified really a kind of consciousness, or an orientation of consciousness, that existed before modern psychology and Darwinian belief: a framework of consciousness and experience that was overall similar in the recent past and in the time of the Romans—one, in other words, that existed up into the present.

It is not just that the people related more to the land—though they did—but that they had a different kind of psychological extension, not only with nature, but in and with time itself. If they were isolated in <u>spatial</u> terms, they extended their imaginations and to some extent their lives and emotions both backward into the past and ahead into the future in ways that modern psychology has made most difficult.

Even though those village people lived in your era, however, they were largely untouched by modern technology, and so kept to their own ways. They and the land seemed one, sharing the present seasons, the daily work—but more than that, their fathers and their forefathers and usually many past generations of given families came from the same area. People lived in houses shared by their elders that had earlier been shared by <u>their</u> elders backward through family lines, so that daily experience and family incident was not nearly as restrained to the present in your terms.

Ancestors had worked the same fields, walked the same paths, and to that extent the past was open-ended rather than closed. The people believed that those ancestors still existed in the Christian heaven—or, earlier, in the Roman equivalent and they also believed that such a dimension awaited them to give them a further extension of existence after their own deaths.

This provided them with a different kind of time framework psychologically—one that any peasant could relate to. The ordinary person, for example, in the western world cannot relate to a Darwinian past in that same fashion, and psychology robs him of any personal extension in the future <u>after</u> death, so in practical life most modern people have freedom of extension in space but less in time. The peasants of course worked closely with the land and seasons, with earth's natural timing, and even though such work seemed to make time go faster, in the overall the sense of present time included a rich dimension from both present and past, so that in your terms it would seem longer by contrast

—richer—when people went to bed earlier, lacking the night's electricity.

(9:51.) These were unlettered people. In a fashion *(long pause)* in this latest disaster, they took their land with them in their deaths. The land that is the environment, and the consciousness in your terms of the people, were part of each other in such a strong fashion that their energies merged *(pause)* to bring about the earthquake conditions.

You had a mass burial—land and people together, a folding-in of consciousness upon itself, of energies upon energies, as those people realized that their kind of existence could no longer be maintained. Those who survived reacted in the old fashion, sweating to build again, refusing better shelter, but the times had indeed changed. The balances of nature, culture, communication, transportation, had altered to such a degree that a real poverty had resulted, not simply simple basic but adequate living conditions. The people compared themselves to the rest of the world at times, and many of the young were beginning to leave, but those villages were, again, very like those in the times of Nebene and the Roman soldier. They had been plundered at times by wandering Roman soldiers of Rome's empire. Some of the soldiers themselves had been recruited from such areas, leaving their families behind, and the old men to do the work.

They were not in a way quite as isolated then, however, for horses and carts and so forth could travel on mountain passes, and were abundant in the entire area—while today, for example, the roads are poor and sometimes not passable for automobiles.

The towns represent to you that different kind of orientation, however. It was one that Nebene knew of and respected, where the Roman soldier scoffed at what even then he considered the old ways. A lifetime, of whatever length, seemed longer then than it does now, for it was psychologically lengthened by that rich extension into both the future and the past. People just before the earthquake even related imaginatively not only to their own ancestors, but to their children's children after their own deaths, as those children lived their lives in the same locations, in the same land area.

(10:09.) The entire structure was beginning to topple, however, and the poverty was overtaking the damned. There are many reasons, but mainly the relationship between the village people and the rest of the world had strained too far, stretched too far. *(Pause.)* The Roman soldier had been in several skirmishes in such a village, stealing livestock for his companions. Nebene had hidden out in one such village from the Romans. The farmers protected him. So there are different emotional connections along those lines.

It goes without saying that such people were not innovators. They had little use for book learning. People who were unusually intelligent were suspect, and did not fit in. They were usually forced to leave one way or another—sometimes simply because they felt so isolated in their own surroundings. Change was frowned upon. In the old days they paid what tribute they had to to the government, but otherwise kept to their own ways, and the same applies to the villages that were destroyed.

I do not want you to think that I am idealizing them, for their ways were not particularly gentle, but their experience with time was a rich vein of experience that is now most unusual—one that you were at least aware of in your own reincarnational episodes.

You feel now, by contrast, that you must get all of your living in between birth and death, that you must hurry to get everything done, so that time itself is indeed shortened. Your life seems to have no past behind it or future ahead of it, so identity itself seems foreshortened.

Now that particular feeling is relatively new in history as you understand it, for almost all cultures in the past have had their built-in extensions of identity that included a dimension of actuality of one kind or another, from which each individual emerged, and to which you would return. Such a framework may have been filled with potential problems, but there were usually ways in life to get around those ways that were specified according to religion or culture.

Hellfire, for example, hardly presents any desirable extension, but there was before hell always the hope that the sinner would repent, and even if hell became the feared future existence, it still preserved the nature of the human consciousness involved. Psychology and evolution thematically simply cut off man's existence with death.

(Long pause at 10:25.) Nebene had a scholar's distaste for the peasants, but he also possessed a solid respect for the overall <u>framework</u> of their existence. He had a tendency on the one hand to idealize them for their love of nature, and on the other hand he somewhat scorned their lack of intellectual breadth. The Roman soldier understood them far better, for he was originally of their stock.

(Long pause.) I mention these ideas of time also now because they fit in so well with your joint personal preoccupation with time—how to use it, and so forth. *(Long pause.)* Nebene could also give you more on such issues if you ever find the time *(amused).*

Do you have a question?

("I reread some of those sessions from 1973.")

You can both put them to use now, as you did then. Do not think of them as information in the past that in "all of this time" you should have used better —for time as you see does not behave in that fashion. *(Long pause.)* There are rhythms in your experience, so that some information comes freshly newly in life in your experience that in certain ways you overlooked before. But in all of this you must understand that whatever course you took in the meantime was in its way a proper course—not, say, a wrong one.

This difference in attitude is highly important.

In the overall structure, all seeming errors are indeed redeemed, forming syntheses of creativity of their own kind, leading to understandings and future developments that, say, outshine whatever problems you might have encountered. You will both benefit, however, by reading and then discussing together those sessions.

Now I bid you a fond good evening.

("Good night, Seth."

(10:38 PM. All very well, I suppose—I agreed with Seth's closing remarks about new creativity arising out of our experiences, yet this truth hadn't seemed to do much to relieve the depths of feeling I'd experienced while rereading those 1973 sessions.

(Interesting, that we're not supposed to focus now on the problem, but yet are to study and discuss the old material.... As I understand the present dilemma, over the long run, the more successful Jane becomes as a writer the more she feels she needs the symptoms to keep her chained to her desk, to cut out all distractions. In the short run, our troubles with Prentice-Hall lately, especially those revolving around Tam's decision to leave Prentice full time, have touched off Jane's latest poor reactions re her hips and legs. At the same time, her body tries desperately to reassert itself, while she feels threatened by the events stemming from Prentice, and so wants to keep clamping down.

(While I was Christmas shopping this afternoon Jane called Tam; he'd just received our disclaimer letter. It appears the argument over the medical disclaimer for Mass Events *may be on the way to a solution. Tam liked the letter.)*

THE SETH AUDIO COLLECTION

RARE RECORDINGS OF SETH SPEAKING through Jane Roberts are now available on audiocassette and CD. These Seth sessions were recorded by Jane's student, Rick Stack, during Jane's classes in Elmira, New York, in the 1970's. The majority of these selections have never been published in any form. Volume I, described below, is a collection of some of the best of Seth's comments gleaned from over 120 Seth Sessions. Additional selections from The Seth Audio Collection are also available. For information ask for our free catalogue.

Volume I of The Seth Audio Collection consists of six (1-hour) cassettes plus a 34-page booklet of Seth transcripts. Topics covered in Volume I include:

- Creating your own reality – How to free yourself from limiting beliefs and create the life you want.
- Dreams and out-of-body experiences.
- Reincarnation and Simultaneous Time.
- Connecting with your inner self.
- Spontaneity–Letting yourself go with the flow of your being.
- Creating abundance in every area of your life.
- Parallel (probable) universes and exploring other dimensions of reality.
- Spiritual healing, how to handle emotions, overcoming depression and much more.

FOR A FREE CATALOGUE of Seth related products including a detailed description of The Seth Audio Collection, please send your request to the address below.

ORDER INFORMATION:
If you would like to order a copy of The Seth Audio Collection Volume I, please send your name and address, with a check or money order payable to New Awareness Network, Inc. for $60 (Tapes), or $70 (CD's) plus shipping charges. United States residents in New York State must add sales tax.

Shipping charges: U.S.—$6.50, Canada—$8, Europe—$20, Australia/Asia—$22
Rates are UPS for U.S. & Airmail for International—Allow 2 weeks for delivery
Alternate Shipping—Surface—$9.00 to anywhere in the world—Allow 5-8 weeks

Mail to: **NEW AWARENESS NETWORK INC.**
P.O. BOX 192,
Manhasset, New York 11030
(516) 869-9108 between 9:00-5:00 p.m. Monday-Friday EST
Visit us on the Internet—www.sethcenter.com

Books by Jane Roberts from Amber-Allen Publishing

Seth Speaks: The Eternal Validity of the Soul. This essential guide to conscious living clearly and powerfully articulates the furthest reaches of human potential, and the concept that each of us creates our own reality.

The Nature of Personal Reality: Specific, Practical Techniques for Solving Everyday Problems and Enriching the Life You Know.. In this perennial bestseller, Seth challenges our assumptions about the nature of reality and stresses the individual's capacity for conscious action.

The Individual and the Nature of Mass Events. Seth explores the connection between personal beliefs and world events, how our realities merge and combine "to form mass reactions such as the overthrow of governments, the birth of a new religion, wars, epidemics, earthquakes, and new periods of art, architecture, and technology."

The Magical Approach: Seth Speaks About the Art of Creative Living. Seth reveals the true, magical nature of our deepest levels of being, and explains how to live our lives spontaneously, creatively, and according to our own natural rhythms.

The Oversoul Seven Trilogy (The Education of Oversoul Seven, The Further Education of Oversoul Seven, Oversoul Seven and the Museum of Time). Inspired by Jane's own experiences with the Seth Material, the adventures of Oversoul Seven are an intriguing fantasy, a mind-altering exploration of our inner being, and a vibrant celebration of life.

The Nature of the Psyche. Seth reveals a startling new concept of self, answering questions about the inner reality that exists apart from time, the origins and powers of dreams, human sexuality, and how we choose our physical death.

The "Unknown" Reality, Volumes One and Two. Seth reveals the multidimensional nature of the human soul, the dazzling labyrinths of unseen probabilities involved in any decision, and how probable realities combine to create the waking life we know.

Dreams, "Evolution," and Value Fulfillment, Volumes One and Two. Seth discusses the material world as an ongoing self-creation—the product of a conscious, self-aware and thoroughly animate universe, where virtually every possibility not only exists, but is constantly encouraged to achieve its highest potential.

The Way Toward Health. Woven through the poignant story of Jane Roberts' final days are Seth's teachings about self-healing and the mind's effect upon physical health.

Available in bookstores everywhere.